Indigenous Peoples' Land Rights under International Law

Indigenous Peoples' Land Rights under International Law

From Victims to Actors

SECOND REVISED EDITION

By

Jérémie Gilbert

BRILL
NIJHOFF

LEIDEN | BOSTON

Library of Congress Cataloging-in-Publication Data

Names: Gilbert, Jérémie, author.
Title: Indigenous peoples' land rights under international law : from victims to actors / by Jérémie Gilbert.
Description: Second revised edition. | Leiden : Brill Nijhoff, 2016. | Includes bibliographical references and index.
Identifiers: LCCN 2016021031 (print) | LCCN 2016021093 (ebook) | ISBN 9789004323247 (pbk. : alk. paper) | ISBN 9789004323254 (E-book)
Subjects: LCSH: Indigenous peoples--Land tenure. | Indigenous peoples--Legal status, laws, etc.
Classification: LCC K738 .G55 2016 (print) | LCC K738 (ebook) | DDC 346.04/32--dc23
LC record available at https://lccn.loc.gov/2016021031

Typeface for the Latin, Greek, and Cyrillic scripts: "Brill." See and download: brill.com/brill-typeface.

ISBN 978-90-04-32324-7 (paperback)
ISBN 978-90-04-32325-4 (e-book)

This book is dedicated to the memory of Jacques Debray (1957–2015) who passed away too early. Thank you for your inspiration in fighting for social justice.

Contents

PART 1
Indigenous Peoples as Victims: Theories of Dispossession

PART 2
Indigenous Peoples as Subjects: Theories of Protection

PART 3
Indigenous Peoples as Actors: Negotiating Land Rights

Preface to the New Edition

The first edition of this book was published in 2006, at the time the negotiations for the adoption of the United Nations Declaration on the Rights of Indigenous Peoples (UNDRIP) were still underway. The adoption of the Declaration in 2007 by the General Assembly of the United Nations (UN) marks an important moment not only in terms of lawmaking but also represents the achievement of long decades of lobbying and advocacy from indigenous peoples' representatives. This new edition reflects on the 10 years which have followed the adoption of the UNDRIP to examine to what extent this has had an impact regarding indigenous peoples' land rights. The aim of the new edition is not only to reflect on the importance of the UNDRIP in terms of international standards, but also to reflect on the 'maturing' of international law when it comes to indigenous peoples' land rights. Indeed over the last 10 years the rights of indigenous peoples have reached a new level of visibly and a voluminous new jurisprudence and doctrine has been developed. The adoption of the Declaration is not the only important legal document that has emerged in the last 10 years, as it is also representative of the significant legal developments that took place during that period, which arguably saw the development of a very large body of international law dedicated to the rights of indigenous peoples. Since then there have been positive and negative developments.

On the positive side, there is no doubt that indigenous peoples' rights have gained visibility and maturity. This is reflected both in terms of lawmaking and within the ever-expanding jurisprudence emerging from international and regional institutions. Probably, the most significant development relates to the significant jurisprudence on indigenous peoples' land rights emerging from international and regional institutions. Regional human rights institutions play a very important role regarding indigenous peoples' land rights. In some instances the international legal framework is even lagging behind regional institutions which have been much more proactive in receiving claims from indigenous peoples. This includes an important volume of rulings from the Inter-American Court of Human Rights regarding indigenous peoples' land rights. It also includes the very positive developments that took place under the guidance of the African Commission on Human and Peoples' Rights regarding indigenous peoples' land rights in Africa. The evolution of the jurisprudence goes beyond the traditional human rights forum, with for example the adoption of a decision by the Caribbean Court of Justice regarding indigenous peoples' land rights in Belize.[1] Indigenous peoples' rights, and their right to land, have become much more global. There have been some significant legal developments at the national levels both in terms of new legislations but also in terms of jurisprudence. There has been some important decisions taken by national courts, and in these decisions international law has played a significant role.[2] This new edition of the book reflects on these evolutions and examines their impact regarding the international legal theories on land rights.

There are also been some very significant positive developments regarding the institutional space occupied by indigenous peoples at the international level. The UN declared the decade 1994–2004 as the first 'World Decade on the Rights of Indigenous Peoples' and 2005–2015 as the second decade. The main objective was the strengthening of international cooperation for the solution of problems faced by indigenous people in such areas as human rights, the environment, education and health. This has notably been translated by more visibility within the mandate of international organisations. The rights of indigenous peoples assume a more prominent place within the mandate of several international institutions. In recent years, specialized institutions such as the Food and Agricultural Organization (FAO), UNESCO, UNICEF, and WIPO have started to focus some of their work on the rights of indigenous peoples.

On a less positive note, when it comes to land rights for indigenous peoples, despite some significant legal developments at the international and regional levels, at the national and local levels the story is still predominately grey. While certainly some indigenous communities have managed to get an increased recognition of their rights to land and natural resources, in general most indigenous communities still do not hold official rights over their lands; and most communities are still experiencing dispossession or reductions to the access to their ancestral territories. Over the last decades there have been some serious and violent acts of repression against indigenous peoples who are protecting their lands from both States and private actors. These attacks and violent repression have often resulted in violence and leading to physical injuries, social

1 Caribbean Court of Justice—Appellate Jurisdiction- The Maya Leader Alliance v. The Attorney General of Belize—CCJ Appeal No BZCV2014/002, BZ Civil Appeal No. 27 of 2010—[2015] CCJ 15 (AJ).

2 See for examples: Constitutional Court of Indonesia, Constitutional Court Decision 35/PUU-X/2012, reviewing Law 41 of 1999 on Forestry, issued 20 March 2013 (Traditional Forest Community case (2012)); Supreme Court of Belize, *Maya Land Rights case,* Consolidated Claims Nos. 171 & 172 (2007); Matsipane Mosetlhanyane, Gakenyatsiwe Matsipane and Others v. The Attorney General of Botswana (2010) H3 BLR 372 HC—High Court of Botswana (2010); Jagpal Singh & Ors. Vs. State of Punjab & Ors.—Supreme Court of India (2011).

disruption, and in some cases, death. The current global phenomenon of 'land grabbing' and the increased pressure to extract and exploit natural resources have added another layer of pressure on indigenous peoples rights to lands. Investors and private actors have increasingly been encroaching on indigenous territories. From that perspective, this updated version of the book includes a much more comprehensive focus on the relationship between international legal standards on indigenous peoples' land rights and private actors such as corporations and investors.

The structure of the book has not been drastically changed, as the argument of the book is still that indigenous peoples have been the victims of international legal theories supporting the colonisation of their territories (Part 1), and that they have become subjects of protection under the main human rights treaties (Part 2), to finally become more active and direct actors to the development of their own rights (Part 3). But to add to such argument the new edition has been revised to put even more emphasis on the fact that indigenous peoples play a much more direct and participatory role into the development of international law.

Jérémie Gilbert
London and Inishowen, March 2016

Table of Cases and Decisions

Privy Council

St Catherine's Milling and Lumber Co. v. The Queen, [1887] 13 S.C.R. 577
St Catherine's Milling and Lumber Co. v. The Queen, 14 App. Cas. 46 (1888)
Nireaha Tamaki v. Baker, [1901] A.C. 561
Secretary of State for India v. Kamachee Bai Rajbai, 42 Ind. App. 229 (1915)
In re Southern Rhodesia, [1919] A.C. 211
Amodu Tijani v. Secretary, Southern Nigeria, 2 A.C. 399 (1921)
Vajesingji Joravarisingji v. Secretary of State for India, 51 Ind. App. 357 (1924)
Hoani Te Heuheu Tukino v. Aotea District Maori Land Board, 2 All E.R. 93 (1941)

International Arbitral Decisions

Cayuga Indians (Great Britain) v. United States, 6 R.I.A.A. 173 (1926)
Island of Palmas (Neth. V. U.S.) 2 R.I.A.A. 831 (1928)
Clipperton Island Arbitration (Fr. v. Mex.) 2 R.I.A.A. 1105 (1931)

Permanent Court of International Justice

Certain Questions Relating to Settlers of German Origin in the Territory Ceded by Germany to Poland, 1923 P.C.I.J. (ser. B) No. 6
Legal Status of Eastern Greenland (Den. v. Nor.), 1933 P.C.I.J. (ser A/B) No. 53
Minority Schools in Albania (Advisory Opinion), 1935 P.C.I.J. (ser A/B) No. 64

International Court of Justice

Reparations for Injuries Suffered in the Service of the United Nations, Advisory Opinion, 1949 I.C.J. 174
Western Sahara (Request for Advisory Opinion), 1975 I.C.J. 12 (Oct. 16)
Frontier Dispute (Burkina Faso v. Mali), 1986 I.C.J. 554
Land, Island and Maritime Frontier Dispute (El Salvador/Honduras: Nicaragua intervening), Judgment of Sept. 11, 1992, 1992 I.C.J. paras. 95–96
Territorial Dispute (Libya v. Chad), 1994 I.C.J. 6 (Feb. 3)

East Timor (Portugal v. Australia) (1991–1995), 1995 I.C.J. 90
Legal Consequences of the Construction of the Wall in the Occupied Palestinian Territory (General List No. 131, Advisory Opinion, July 9, 2004)

European Court of Human Rights

Lithgow and Others v. the United Kingdom, App. No. 2/1984/74/112-118 (July 8, 1986)
Buckley v. the United Kingdom, App. No. 20348/92, 1996-IV Eur. Ct. H.R. 1271 (Sept. 25)
Carol and Steven Smith v. the United Kingdom, App. No. 22902/9 (Jan. 21, 1997)
Chapman v. the United Kingdom, App. No. 00027238/95
Jane Smith v. the United Kingdom, App. No. 25154/94
Lee v. the United Kingdom, App. No. 25289/94
Coster v. the United Kingdom, App. No. 24876/94
Bear v. the United Kingdom, App. No. 24882/94

European Commission of Human Rights

Könkämä and 38 other Saami Villages v. Sweden (App. No. 27033/95)

Inter-American Commission on Human Rights

Aché Indian in Paraguay, Case No. 1802 (Paraguay), Annual Report 1977, OAS Doc. OEA/Ser.L/V/II.43 Doc.21 (1978)
Yanamomi Decision, Res. No. 12/85, Case No. 7615, Annual Report of the Inter-American Commission of Human Rights 1984–85, OEA/Serv.L/II.62, doc. 10, rev. 1 (1985)
Plan de Sánchez Massacre, Guatemala (Case 11.763), Report No. 31/99 (Mar. 11, 1999)
Enxet-Lamenxay and Kayleyphapopyet (Riachito) Indigenous Communities Paraguay, Report No. 90/99, Case No. 11.713, Sept. 29, 1999
Maya Indigenous Communities v. Belize, Case No. 12.053, Report No. 78/00, OEA/Ser.L/V/II.111 Doc. 20 rev., at 129 (2000).
Mary and Carrie Dann v. United States, Case No. 11.140, Report No. 75/02, Inter-Am. C.H.R., Doc. 5 rev. 1, at 860 (2002).

Inter-American Court of Human Rights

Velasquez Rodriguez Case, Judgment of July 29, 1988, Inter-Am. Ct. H.R. (ser. C) No. 4 (1988)

Aloeboetoe et al. Case. Reparations (Art. 63(1) of the American Convention on Human Rights) Judgment, Sept. 10, 1993

The Mayagna (Sumo) Awas Tingni Community v. Nicaragua, Inter-Am. Ct. H.R., (ser. C) No. 79 (Aug. 31, 2001)

Moiwana Village v. Suriname, Inter-Am. Ct. HR (ser. C) No. 124 (June 15, 2005).

Yakye Axa Indigenous Community v. Paraguay Inter-Am. Ct. HR (ser. C) No. 125 (June 17, 2005)

Sawhoyamaxa Indigenous Community v Paraguay, 29 March 2006

Case of the Saramaka People v. Suriname. Preliminary Objections, Merits, Reparations and Costs. Judgment of November 28, 2007. Series C No. 172

Xákmok Kásek Indigenous Community v Paraguay Merits and reparations. Judgment of August 24, 2010. Series C No. 214

Kichwa People of Sarayaku v Ecuador Merits and reparations Judgment of June 27, 2012. Series C No. 245 at para 149.

Case of the Kuna Indigenous People of Madungandí and the Emberá Indigenous People of Bayano and their Members v. Panama. Preliminary objections, merits, reparations and costs. Judgment of October 14, 2014. Series C No. 284.

Case of the Kaliña and Lokono Peoples v. Suriname, Judgment of November 25, 2015 (Merits, Reparations and Costs),

African Commission on Human and Peoples' Rights

Katangese Peoples' Congress v. Zaire (Communication 75/92)

The Social and Economic Rights Action Center and the Center for Economic and Social Rights v. Nigeria (Communication 155/96)

The Bakweri Land Claims Committee (BLCC) v. The Republic of Cameroon (Communication 260/2002)

Centre for Minority Rights Development (Kenya) and Minority Rights Group International on behalf of Endorois Welfare Council v Kenya, Communication 276/2003 (2010).

Human Rights Committee

MikMaq Tribal v Canada (Communication No. 78/1980), 39th Sess., Supp. No. 40, 200, U.N. Doc. A/39/40 (1984)

Sandra Lovelace v. Canada (Communication No. 24/1977), U.N. Doc. CCPR/C/OP/1, at 10 (Aug. 14, 1984)

Ivan Kitok v. Sweden (Communication No. 197/1985), Report of the Human Rights Committee, GAOR, 43th Sess., Supp. 40 (A/43/40)

Marshall v. Canada (Communication No. 205/1986), U.N. Doc. CPR/C/43/D/205/1986 (1991)

I. Länsman et al. v. Finland (Communication No. 511/1992), U.N. Doc. CCPR/C/57/1

J. Länsman et al. v. Finland (Communication No. 671/1995), U.N. Doc. CCPR/C/58/D/671/1995

Lubicon Lake Band v. Canada (Communication No. 167/1984), U.N. Doc. Supp. No.40 (A/45/40), at 1 (Mar. 26, 1990)

Simunek, Hastings, Tuzilova and Prochazka v. The Czech Republic (Communication No. 516/1992), U.N. Doc. CCPR/C/54/D/516/1992 (1995)

Hopu and Bessert v. France, (Communication No.549/1993), U.N. Doc. CPR/C/60/D/549/1993/Rev.1 (Dec. 29, 1997)

J G A Diergaardt (late Captain of the Rehoboth Baster Community) et al. v. Namibia (Communication No. 760/1997), 10.3, U.N. Doc. CCPR/C/69/D/760/1997 (2000)

Apirana Mahuika et al. v. New Zealand (Communication No. 547/1993), U.N. Doc. CCPR/C/70/D/547/1993 (2000).

Anni Äärelä and Jouni Näkkäläjärvi v. Finland (Communication No. 779/1997), Views adopted 24 October 2001, Report of the Human Rights Committee, Vol. II, U.N. Doc. A/57/40 (Vol. II), at 117–30.

ILO Committee of Experts Representations

Report of the Committee set up to examine the representation alleging non-observance by Denmark of the Indigenous and Tribal Convention, 1989 (No. 169), made under article 24 of the ILO Constitution by the Radical Trade Union of Metal and Associated Workers, Docs.GB.273/15/6, GB.276/16/3.

Report of the Committee set up to examine the representation alleging non-observance by Denmark of the Indigenous and Tribal Convention, 1989 (No. 169), made under article 24 of the ILO Constitution by the Sulinermik. Inuussutissarsiuteqartut Kattuffiat (SIK), Docs. GB.277/18/3, GB.280/18/5, submitted 1999.

Report of the Committee set up to examine the representation alleging non-observance by Ecuador of the Indigenous and Tribal Convention, 1989 (No. 169), made under article 24 of the ILO Constitution by the Confederación Ecuatoriana de Organizaciones Sindicales Libres (CEOSL), Docs. GB.277/18/4, GB.282/14/2, submitted 2000.

Report of the Committee set up to examine the representation alleging non-observance by Mexico of the Indigenous and Tribal Peoples Convention, 1989 (No. 169), made under article 24 of the ILO Constitution by the Trade Union Delegation, D-III-57, section XI of the National Trade Union of Education Workers (SNTE), Radio Education. Doc. GB 270/16/3; GB 272/7/2 (1998).

Report of the Committee set up to examine the representation alleging non-observance by Mexico of the Indigenous and Tribal Peoples Convention, 1989 (No. 169), made under article 24 of the ILO Constitution by the Authentic Workers' Front (FAT), Doc. GB.282/14/2 (Mar. 19, 2004).

Selected National Cases

Australia

Cooper v. Stuart (1889) 14 App. Cas. 286
R. v. Murell and Bummaree 1976 N.S.W.L.R. 581
Milirrpum v. Nabalco Pty. (1971) 17 F.L.R. 141
NSW v. the Commonwealth (1975) 135 C.L.R. 388
Koowarta v. Bjelke Petersen (1982) 153 C.L.R. 168
Gerhardy v. Brown (1985) 57 A.L.R. 472
Mabo & Ors. v. State of Queensland (1988) 83 A.L.R. 14
Mabo v. Queensland [No 2] (1992) 175 C.L.R. 1, 107 A.L.R. 1
Aboriginal Legal Rights Movement v. South Australia (July 26, 1995)
Aboriginal Legal Rights v. South Australia [No 1] (1995) 64 S.A.S.R. 551
Aboriginal Legal Rights v. South Australia [No 2] (1995) 64 S.A.S.R. 558
Aboriginal Legal Rights v. South Australia [No 3] (1995) 64 S.A.S.R. 566
North Ganalanja Aboriginal Corporation v. Queensland (1996) 185 C.L.R. 595
Wilson v. Minister for Aboriginal and Torres Strait Islander Affairs (1996) 189 C.L.R. 1
Fourmile v. Selpam Pty Ltd. (1998) 80 F.C.R. 151
Wik Peoples v. Queensland (1996) 141 A.L.R. 129
Ward v. State of Western Australia (1998) 159 A.L.R. 483
Fejo v. Northern Territory (1998) 195 C.L.R. 96
Kartinyeri v. The Commonwealth (1998) H.C.A. 22
Nulyarimma v. Thompson and Buzzacott v. Minister for the Environment (1999) F.C.A. 1192, 165 A.L.R. 621
Yanner v. Eaton (1999) 201 C.L.R. 351
Ward v. Western Australia (2000) 170 A.L.R. 159
Western Australia v. Ward, Attorney General (NT) v. Ward, Ningamara v. Northern Territory, Ward v. Crosswalk Pty Ltd. (2002) H.C.A. 28
Members of the Yorta Yorta Aboriginal Community v. Victoria (2002) H.C.A. 58

Belize

Supreme Court, SATIIM (Sarstoon Temash Institute for Indigenous Management) v Attorney General of Belize (2014)

Brazil

State of Roraima Federal Court, (Yanomami Lands) Process No. 92,0001615-4 (July 16, 2001)

Botswana

Matsipane Mosetlhanyane, Gakenyatsiwe Matsipane and Others v. The Attorney General of Botswana (2010) H3 BLR 372 HC—High Court of Botswana (2010)

Ranyane Community v. Ghanzi Land Board, District Council and District Commissioner—High Court of Botswana (2013)

Bangladesh

Ain O Salish Kendro (ASK) & Ors v. Government of Bangladesh & Ors, No. 3034, 2 C.H.R.L.D. 393 (1999)

Canada

Calder v. Attorney-General of British Columbia, [1973] 1 S.C.R. 313

Hamlet of Baker Lake v. Minister of Indian Affairs and Others, [1979] 107 D.L.R.(3d) 513

Guerin v. The Queen, [1985] 13 D.L.R.(4th) 321

R. v. Horseman, [1990] 1 S.C.R. 901, 108 N.R. 1

R. v. Sparrow, [1990] 1 S.C.R. 1075

Attorney-General of Québec v. Sioui et al., [1990] 1 S.C.R. 1025

R. v. Van der Peet, [1996] 2 S.C.R. 507

R. v. Adams, [1996] 138 D.L.R.(4th) 657

R. v. Badger, [1996] 1 S.C.R. 771

Delgamuukw v. British Columbia, [1997] 3 S.C.R. 1010

Reference re Secession of Québec, [1998] 2 S.C.R. 217

Daishowa v. Friends of the Lubicon, [1998] 39 O.R.(3d) 620 (Ont. Ct. (Gen. Div.))

R. v. Marshall, [1999] 3 S.C.R. 533, 179 D.L.R.(4th) 193

Campbell v. British Columbia (Attorney General), [2000] 189 D.L.R.(4th) 333

Haida Nation v. B.C. and Weyerhaeuser, Feb. 27, 2002 (B.C. Court of Appeal)

India

Edwingson v. The State of Assam, A.I.R. (1966) S.C. 1220

State of Assam v. K.B. Kurkalang, A.I.R. (1972) S.C. 223

District Council of U.K. & J.H. v. Sitimon, A.I.R. (1972) SC 787

Samatha v. State of Andhra Pradesh (1997) 8 S.C.C. 191
Madhu Kishwar v. State of Bihar (1992) 1 Supreme Court Cases 102 Petition
Jagpal Singh & Ors. Vs. State of Punjab & Ors.—Supreme Court of India (2011)

Indonesia

Constitutional Court Decision 55/PUU-VIII/2010, reviewing Law 18 of 2004 on Plantations, issued 6 September 2011 (Plantation Law case (2011)).
Constitutional Court Decision 3/PUU-VII/2010, reviewing Law 27 of 2007 on the Management of Coastal Areas and Small Islands, issued 16 June 2011 (Coastal and Remote Areas Law case (2011)).
The Indigenous Peoples'Alliance of the Archipelago (AMAN) v Government of Indonesia- Constitutional Court, 2013

Japan

Kayano et al. v. Hokkaido Expropriation Committee, Sapporo Dist. Ct., Mar. 27, 1997, *reprinted in* 38 I.L.M. 397 (1999).

Malaysia

Adong bin Kuwau v. Kerajaan Negeri Johor, [1997] 1 M.L.J. 418, [1998] 2 M.L.J. 158
Kerajaan Negeri Johor & Anor v. Adong bin Kuwau & Ors, [1998] 2 M.L.J. 158, 2 C.H.R.L.D. 281 (Feb. 24, 1998)
Nor Anak Nyawai et al. v. Borneo Pulp Plantation Sdn Bhd, [2001] 2 Current L.J. 769
Numpang Suntai et al. v. Quality Concrete Holdings Berhad et al.—High Court in Sabah and Sarawak at Kuching (2012)
Superintendent of Lands and Surveys Kuching Division & State Government of Sarawak v. Mohamad Rambli Bin Kawi, Court of Appeal, Malaysia Putrajaya (July 2014)

New Zealand

Wi Parata v. Bishop of Wellington [1877] 3 N.Z. Jur. (N.S.) S.C. 72
R v. Symonds [1847] N.Z.P.C.C. 387 (S.C.)
Te Weehi v. Regional Fisheries Officier [1986] 1 N.Z.L.R. 680

Philippines

La Bugal-B'laan Tribal Association, Inc., et al. Vs. Victor O. Ramos, et al G.R. No. 127882 January 27, 2004

South Africa

Du Plessis and Others v. De Klerk and Another, 1996 (3) S.A. 850, 1996 (5) B.C.L.R. 658 (C.C.)
Makuleke Community v Pafuri Area of the Kruger National Park and environs Soutpansberg District Northern Province, 1998 J.O.L. 4264 (L.C.C.)
Ritchersveld Community and Others v. Alexkor Ltd. and Another, 2001 (3) S.A. 1293 (L.C.C.)
Ritchersveld Community and Others v. Alexkor Ltd. and Another, 2001 J.O.L. 8621 (L.C.C.)
The Ritchersveld Community and Others and Alexkor Limited and the Government of South Africa, Case No. 488/2001 (Mar. 24, 2003)
Alexkor Limited and the Government of South Africa v. The Ritchersveld Community and Others, Case No. CCT 19/03 (Oct. 14, 2003)
Richtersveld Community v. Alexkor Ltd. and Another, LCC151/98 (Judgment date: Apr. 29, 2004)

Tanzania

Lekengere Faru Parutu Kamunyu & Ors v. Minister of Tourism, Natural Resources and Environment & Ors, 46 I.C.H.R.L. 46 (Mar. 29, 1999)

United States

Fletcher v. Peck 10 U.S. 87 (1810)
Johnson and Braham's Lessee v. M'Intosh, 21 U.S. (8 Wheat.) 543 (1823)
Cherokee Nation v. Georgia, 30 U.S. (5 Pet.) 1 (1830)
Worcester v. Georgia, 31 U.S. (6 Pet.) 515 (1832)
United States v. Percheman, 32 U.S. (7 Pet.) 51 (1833)
Mitchel and Others v. United States, 34 U.S. (9 Pet.) 711 (1835)
United States v. Santa Fe Pacific Railroad, 314 U.S. 339 (1941)
Osage Nation of Indians v. United States, 1 Ind. C1. Comm. 54 (1948), *rev'd on other grounds*, 119 Ct. C1. 592, *cert denied*, 342 U.S. 89 (1951)
Tee-Hit-Ton Indians v. United States, 348 U.S. at 285 (1955)
Shoshone Tribe v. United States, 11 I.C.C. 387 (1962)
United States v. Dann (Dann I), 572 F.2d 222 (9th Cir. 1978)
United States v. Sioux Nation of Indians et al., 448 U.S. 371 (1980)
United States v. Dann, 706 F.2d 919 (9th Cir. 1983)
United States v. Dann, 470 U.S. 36 (1985)
Lyng v. Northwest Indian Cemetery Protective Association, 485 U.S. 439 (1988)

Table of Treaties and Instruments

Convention on the Prevention and Punishment of the Crime of Genocide, 78 U.N.T.S. 277 (1948, entered into force 1951)

Universal Declaration of Human Rights, (1948), G.A. Res. 217A(III), U.N. Doc. A/810 (1948)

European Convention for the Protection of Human Rights and Fundamental Freedoms, 213 U.N.T.S. 221, E.T.S. 5 (1950)

Protocol No. 1 to the European Convention for the Protection of Human Rights and Fundamental Freedoms, E.T.S. 9 (1954)

Convention Concerning the Protection and Integration of Indigenous and other Tribal and Semi-tribal Populations in Independent Countries (ILO No. 107), 328 U.N.T.S. 247 (1957)

International Convention on the Elimination of All Forms of Racial Discrimination, 660 U.N.T.S. 195 (1965), *reprinted in* 5 I.L.M. 352 (1966) (entered into force 1969)

International Covenant on Civil and Political Rights (1966), G.A. Res. 2200A (XXI), U.N. Doc. A/6316 (1966), 999 U.N.T.S. 171, *reprinted in* 6 I.L.M. 368 (1967) (entered into force 1976)

International Covenant on Economic, Social and Cultural Rights (1966), G.A. Res. 2200A(XXI), U.N. Doc. A/6316 (1966), 999 U.N.T.S. 171, *reprinted in* 6 I.L.M. 368 (1967) (entered into force 1976)

American Convention on Human Rights (1969), O.A.S. Treaty Series No. 36, 1144 U.N.T.S. 123 (entered into force 1978)

Vienna Convention on the Law of Treaties, U.N. Doc. A/CONF. 39/26 (1969), *reprinted in* 8 I.L.M. 679 (entered into force 1980)

Declaration on the Granting of Independence to Colonial Countries and Peoples, G.A. Res. 1514(XV), 15 U.N. GAOR, Supp. (No. 16), U.N. Doc. A/4684, (1970)

Declaration on Principles of International Law concerning Friendly Relations and Co-operation among States in accordance with the Charter of the United Nations, G.A. Res. 2625(XXV), 25 U.N. GAOR, Supp. (No. 28), U.N. Doc. A/8028 (1970) *reprinted in* 9 I.L.M. 1291 (1970)

African Charter on Human and Peoples' Rights, O.U.A. Doc. CAB/LEG/67/3, *reprinted in* I.L.M. 58 (1982)

American Declaration of the Rights and Duties of Man, OEA/Serv.L./V/11.71, (1948)

Convention Concerning Indigenous and Tribal Peoples in Independent Countries (ILO No. 169), 72 ILO Official Bull. 59, *reprinted in* 28 I.L.M. 1382 (1989)

Convention on the Rights of the Child, G.A. Res. 44/25, U.N. GAOR, Supp. (No. 49), U.N. Doc. A/44/49, *reprinted in* 28 I.L.M. 1448 (1989) (entered into force 1990)

Convention on Biological Diversity, *reprinted in* 31 I.L.M. 818 (1992)

Rome Statute of the International Criminal Court, U.N. Doc. A/CONF.138/9 (1998, entered into force 2002)

United Nations Declaration on the Rights of Indigenous Peoples, General Assembly, A/RES/61/295, Adopted on 13 September 2007.

List of Abbreviations

ACHPR	African Charter on Human and Peoples' Rights
ACoHPR	African Commission on Human and Peoples' Rights
ACHR	American Convention on Human Rights
ATSIC	Aboriginal and Torres Strait Islander Commission
CECAR	ILO Committee of Experts on the Application of Conventions and Recommendations
CERD	Committee on the Elimination of Racial Discrimination
CESCR	Committee on Economic Social and Cultural Rights
DoCip	Centre de Documentation, de Recherche et d'Information des Peuples Autochtones
ECHR	European Convention for the Protection of Human Rights and Fundamental Freedoms
ECoHR	European Court of Human Rights
EMRIP	Expert Mechanism on Indigenous Issues
FPIC	Free, Prior and Informed Consent
HRC	Human Rights Committee
IACHR	Inter-American Commission on Human Rights
IACtHR	Inter-American Court of Human Rights
ICCPR	International Covenant on Civil and Political Rights
ICERD	International Convention on the Elimination of All Forms of Racial Discrimination
ICESCR	International Covenant on Economic, Social and Cultural Rights
ICJ	International Court of Justice
ICMM	International Council on Mining and Metals
ILCCR	ILO Conference Committee on the Applications of Standards
ILO	International Labor Organization
IWGIA	International Work Group for Indigenous Affairs
NCP	OECD National Contact Points
OAS	Organization of American States
OAU	Organization of African Unity
OECD	Organization for Economic Cooperation and Development
PFII	Permanent Forum on Indigenous Issues
UDHR	Universal Declaration of Human Rights
UNESCO	United Nations Educational, Scientific and Cultural Organization
UNDRIP	United Nations Declaration on the Rights of Indigenous Peoples
WGDD	Working Group on the draft declaration on the Rights of Indigenous Peoples
WGIP	Working Group on Indigenous Population

Territoriality: The Thread of Indigenous Cultures

> We have to find the strength to make a place for ourselves in this world. Otherwise there will soon be no more of us. We will all be gone. And so will our memories.
>
> MAHONGO, Southern Africa[1]

Over the centuries, indigenous peoples have developed a profound relationship with their lands and territories. Despite this long-term attachment to their traditional lands, indigenous peoples are often facing forced displacement and loss of access to their ancestral territories. From the time of colonization to the contemporary appetite for the natural wealth located on their territories, indigenous peoples have been dispossessed of their lands. Historically, indigenous peoples' relationship to their lands have been disregarded by other more powerful actors, and international law has played an important role in this history of territorial dispossession. On many occasions indigenous peoples' representatives have approached the international stage in search for effective formulas of mutual co-existence,[2] though it is only in more recent years that they have been able to successfully assert their rights under international law. One of the crucial calls from indigenous peoples at the international level is for international recognition of their right to live on their lands—lands that they have thrived on since time immemorial. While all forms of human societies relate to a specific territory, one of the fundamental features of indigenous peoples is the centrality of the connection to their territories.[3] Land has to be accepted as a vital element of indigenous culture. As Malezer, an Aboriginal leader from Australia affirmed: "Our claim to a global identity is based upon our ancient cultures and viable relationships with our territories, in contrast to the modern

1 Mario Mahongo is a leader of the !Xu Traditional Council and chairman of the !Xu and Khwe Communal Property Association, *quoted in* Anthony Swift & Ann Perry, Nomadic People Speak: Vanishing Footprints 134 (2001).

2 See: Douglas Sanders, *The Legacy of Deskadeh: Indigenous Peoples as International Actors. in* The Human Rights of Indigenous Peoples 87 (Cynthia Price Cohen ed., 1998); Franke Wilmer. The Indigenous Voice in World Politics Since Time Immemorial (1993); Ronald Niezen, the Origins of Indigenism: Human Rights and the Politics Of Identity (2003).

3 *Indigenous Peoples and their Relationship to Land*, Final Working Paper Prepared by the Special Rapporteur, E-I Daes, UN Doc E/CN.4/Sub.2/2001/21.

 | DOI 10.1163/9789004323254_002

political identities of nation states and consumer cultures."[4] For indigenous peoples, a territorial attachment is often the keystone of their social, spiritual and cultural view of the world. In most indigenous peoples' societies, territory provides for social identification, but the territory also provides spiritual and cultural distinctiveness. Hence, the recognition of indigenous peoples' land rights has to be seen as one of the most pressing issues for indigenous peoples.

In result, one outstanding convergence in indigenous peoples' claims under international law is their claim for the recognition of their to lands and territories. Even though indigenous peoples reflect the tremendous diversity of the world, living in some of the most remote parts of the globe, it is striking to realize how they all share the same attachment to their lands, which plays a central cultural, social and economic role within indigenous societies globally. Coming from the four corners of the globe to the United Nations (U.N.) headquarters in Geneva or in New York, indigenous peoples' representatives have all insisted on this essential factor. As Stavenhagen, a former U.N. Special Rapporteur on the Rights of Indigenous Peoples puts it: "[T]he thread that weaves these factors together is the indigenous peoples' attachment to land and territory."[5] Although indigenous peoples' relationship with their lands is based on the need to find resources, the precise characteristic of the relationship is deeper and not restricted to the physical element. Most indigenous communities have stressed that lands and territories are not only the basis of economic livelihood but are also the source of spiritual, cultural and social identity. As noted by the United Nations Permanent Forum on Indigenous Issues (PFII): "Land is the foundation of the lives and cultures of Indigenous peoples all over the world. (...) Without access to and respect for their rights over their lands, territories and natural resources, the survival of Indigenous peoples' particular distinct culture is threatened."[6] In return, it is imperative that international law acknowledges the special relationship between indigenous peoples and their territories as crucial to their existence and to all their cultures, customs, beliefs and traditions. Land rights have to be viewed as an expression of indigenous

4 Les Malezer, *Permanent Forum on Indigenous Issues: 'Welcome to the Family of the UN,' in* Indigenous Peoples and Human Rights 67 (Joshua Castellino & Niamh Walsh eds., 2005).

5 Report of the Special Rapporteur on the Situation of Human Rights and Fundamental Freedoms of Indigenous People, Mr. Rodolfo Stavenhagen, *Mission to the Philippines*, U.N. Doc. E/CN.4/2003/90/Add.3, para. 6.

6 Permanent Forum on Indigenous Issues, Report on the sixth session (14–25 May 2007) Economic and Social Council Official Records Supplement No. 23 UN Doc. E/2007/43, E/C.19/2007/12, at 2.

peoples' identity and heritage, and thus their recognition is essential to ensure indigenous peoples' rights.[7]

The centrality of land rights for indigenous peoples is also reflected in the definition of being "indigenous." The etymology of the word tells us that "indigenous" means "originating in the region or country where found; native."[8] The word comes from the Latin *indigena*, a contraction of *indu* (in, within) and *gen* (root).[9] In French the equivalent term *autochtone* is defined as "he who comes from the land where he lives and who did not come as a result of immigration."[10] This term comes from the ancient Greek *khthôn,* which meant land.[11] In general terms, 'indigenous' refers to anyone having an historical attachment to a specific land, including anyone who is not a recent migrant. However in recent years the term 'indigenous peoples' has gained another signification under international legal theories. Whilst there is a general agreement at the international level that a strict legal definition of indigenous peoples might not be necessary; and there is no agreed binding legal definition adopted, several attempts at defining indigenous peoples exist.[12] The definition proposed by Cobo in his Study of the Discrimination against Indigenous Populations is usually accepted as authoritative.[13] The definition proposed is a mix between objective criteria, such as "historical continuity,"

7 Article 13 of the ILO Convention 169 states: "In applying the provisions of this Part of the Convention governments shall respect the special importance for the cultures and spiritual values of the peoples concerned of their relationship with the lands or territories, or both as applicable, which they occupy or otherwise use, and in particular the collective aspects of this relationship." Convention Concerning Indigenous and Tribal Peoples in Independent Countries, (ILO No. 169), 72 ILO Official Bull. 59 (1989), *reprinted in* 28 I.L.M. 1382 (1989).

8 Dictionary of Etymology 521 (Robert K. Barnhart ed., 2003).

9 *Id.*; the word was apparently integrated in the English language in 1646. Note that in Spanish, the term *indigena* comes from the same etymology.

10 Le Petit Robert, Dictionnaire alphabétique de la langue française (1991).

11 Lexis, Dictionnaire de la langue française (1975).

12 See notably Eide & Daes, "Working paper on the relationship and distinction between the rights of persons belonging to minorities and those of indigenous peoples," UN Doc. E/CN.4/Sub.2/2000/10 2000; *see also* Benedict Kingsbury, *Indigenous Peoples' in International Law: A Constructivist Approach to the Asian Controversy*, 92 Am. J. Int'l L. 414 (1998).

13 See: U.N. Doc. E/CN.4/Sub.2/1983/21/Add.8. The former Sub-Commission called it "a reference work of definitive usefulness" and invited the working group to rely on it. *See* Sub-Commission Res. 1985/22, §4(a). *See also* the definition proposed by Daes, U.N. Doc. E/CN.4/Sub.2/AC.4/1996/2.

and subjective factors, including self-definition. The definition proposed by Cobo states:

> Indigenous communities, peoples and nations are those which, having a historical continuity with pre-invasion and pre-colonial societies that *developed on their territories,* consider themselves distinct from other sectors of the societies now prevailing in those *territories, or parts of them.* They form at present non-dominant sectors of society and are determined to preserve, develop and transmit to future generations *their ancestral territories*, and their ethnic identity, as the basis of their continued existence as peoples, in accordance with their own cultural patterns, social institutions and legal systems.[14]

In the definition, one of the central factors is the territorial connection of indigenous peoples to their territories. There are three temporal levels to this territorial attachment:

(1) *Past:* indigenous peoples have a historical continuity with "pre-invasion" and "pre-colonial societies" that developed on their territories.
(2) *Present:* indigenous peoples live on these territories (or part of them).[15]
(3) *Future:* indigenous peoples are determined to transmit to future generations their ancestral territories.

Hence, indigenous peoples are peoples who used to live, continue to live and wish to perpetuate their specific attachment to a defined territory. The other definitions that are often used under international law also put a great emphasis on the centrality of the territorial basis of indigenous peoples' cultures. Article 1 of the International Labor Organization (ILO) Convention No. 169 Concerning Indigenous and Tribal Peoples in Independent Countries (ILO 169) states that indigenous peoples are peoples "regarded as indigenous on account of their descent from the populations which inhabited the country, or a geographical region to which the country belongs, at the time of conquest or colonisation or the establishment of present State boundaries."[16] Likewise, on the issue of the definition of indigenous peoples in Africa, the African Commission's Working Group of Experts on Indigenous Populations/Communities concluded that "a key characteristic for most of them is that survival of their

---

14 U.N. Doc. E/CN.4/Sub.2/1983/21/Add.8 (emphasis added).

15 U.N. Doc. E/CN.4/Sub.2/1986/Add.4.

16 ILO 169, art. 1.1(b), *supra* note 11.

particular way of life depends on access and rights to their traditional land and the natural resources thereon."[17] The World Bank Operational Directive 4.10 refers to groups possessing a "collective attachment to geographically distinct habitats or ancestral territories in the project area and to the natural resources in these habitats and territories."[18] On the whole, regarding the definition of indigenous peoples under international law, the centrality of a distinctive attachment to a particular land has to be regarded as one of the fundamental elements to "indigenousness," as territoriality is to be seen as one of the crucial identifiers of indigenous peoples. As a result, this special relationship to a land has to be seen as a crucial issue of concern in the protection of indigenous peoples under international law.[19] As noted by the Inter-American Court of Human Rights (IACtHR), the recognition of juridical personality of indigenous peoples is an essential element to ensure that their rights to lands and natural resources are recognised at the national level.[20]

Land rights remain an arena of great conflict. As Shipton notes: "[N]othing evokes deeper passions or gives rise to more bloodshed than do disagreements about territory, boundaries, or access to land resources."[21] Access to land rights and security of tenure constitute the basis for access to food, livelihoods, housing and development for most indigenous peoples. In most countries, access and rights over lands are frequently stratified on a hierarchical and segregated system where indigenous peoples do not hold security of land tenure. Control over the allocation of rights to land has historically been an instrument of oppression and colonisation. In a more contemporary approach, demands and competition for access to land are growing as individuals, communities, the private sector, States and foreign investors seek to use and benefit from these

17 *Report of the African Commission's Working Group of Experts on Indigenous Populations/Communities submitted in accordance with 'Resolution on the Rights of Indigenous Populations/Communities in Africa adopted by the African Commission on Human and Peoples' Rights at its 28th ordinary session*, at 89 (IWGIA 2005).

18 World Bank, OP 4.10—Indigenous Peoples, paragraph 4 (amended 2013); note that at the time of writing the Wold Bank is engaged in a process of revision of its procedure regarding indigenous peoples, for further information, see: http://www.worldbank.org/en/topic/indigenouspeoples.

19 *See Working Paper on the Relationship & Distinction between the Rights of Persons Belonging to Minorities & Those of Indigenous Peoples*, U.N. Doc. E/CN.4/Sub.2/2000/10.

20 See: I/A Court H.R., *Case of the Saramaka People v. Suriname*. Preliminary Objections, Merits, Reparations and Costs. Judgment of November 28, 2007. Series C No. 172, para. 168 and ss.

21 Parker Shipton, *Land and Culture in Tropical Africa: Soils, Symbols, and Metaphysics of the Mundane*, 23(1) Ann. Rev. Anthropology 347 (1994).

resources for different, often opposing, purposes. Arable lands are becoming increasingly valuable due to greater investors' interests, changes in agricultural production systems, population growth, migration, and environmental change. All these factors usually have a negative effect on indigenous peoples, whose rights to land and natural resources are not recognised. In recent decades indigenous peoples have been put under increasing pressure from private actors such as multinational corporations (MNCs) or investors that are increasingly encroaching on indigenous peoples' territories to exploit natural resources.[22] The exploitation of the natural resources found on indigenous peoples' territories is one of the primary areas of conflict between indigenous peoples and other interests. Despite the fact that indigenous peoples' territories usually represents some of the wealthiest places on earth in term of natural resources, indigenous peoples remain at the fringe of economic development. The recognition of indigenous peoples' land rights also ensures indigenous peoples a right to pursue their own economic and social development. In this regard, the recognition of indigenous peoples' land rights also carries indigenous peoples' economic aspirations. Thus, overall, indigenous peoples' attachment to territory is multifaceted; it includes social, spiritual, cultural, and economic aspects of indigenous peoples' lives.

Scope of the Book

This book analyses the right of indigenous peoples under international law to live, own, and use their traditional territories. Its main aspiration is to provide a comprehensive understanding of the international legal approach to indigenous peoples' land rights. To be able to offer such comprehensive analysis, the book adopts an historical analysis of land rights under international law. While the book aims at focusing on the contemporary situation faced by indigenous peoples, an important aspect of such analysis has to integrate an historical analysis of international law. The contemporary rights to land that indigenous peoples have under international law can only be fully appreciated when viewed in its historical context as having emerged from the systematic denial of indigenous peoples' rights. The main aim of the book is to analyse and evaluate the international legal response to the dispossession of indigenous peoples. This includes a presentation of both the theoretical debates and

22 *See* Extractive industries and Indigenous Peoples, Report of the Special Rapporteur on the rights of indigenous peoples, James Anaya, Report to the Human Rights Council UN Doc. A/HRC/24/41 (2013)—and discussion in Chapter 6.

the jurisprudence of international bodies on indigenous peoples' land rights, and an evaluation on how international law has sought to address the different economic, social and cultural aspects of indigenous peoples' relationship with their lands. Land rights concerns have rarely been addressed from an international legal perspective, for traditionally land law remains within the competence of States' national jurisdiction with little interaction with international law.[23] However, the past decades have witnessed an increased focus on the relationship between land rights and international law from the particular perspective of indigenous peoples' rights. This has predominately been developed under the banner of international human rights law, which has increasingly developed a very specific jurisprudence on indigenous peoples' land rights.

International law addresses indigenous peoples' land rights from two main angles: first, by way of its general discourse on human rights and second, in terms of specific indigenous peoples' rights. In terms of instruments, the book analyses both the general application of human rights instruments and their impact on indigenous peoples' land rights as well as specific instruments dedicated to the rights of indigenous peoples. This includes the International Labor Organization Conventions No. 107—the Convention Concerning the Protection and Integration of Indigenous and other Tribal and Semi-tribal Populations in Independent Countries (ILO 107)[24]—and No. 169—Convention Concerning Indigenous and Tribal Peoples in Independent Countries (ILO 169).[25] Great attention is also given to United Nations Declaration on the Rights of Indigenous Peoples (UNDRIP) which was adopted in 2007 by the UN General Assembly after more than twenty years of negotiations. The adoption of the Declaration marks an important moment as it universally proclaims and consolidates the specific international legal corpus of rights dedicated to indigenous peoples. In terms of its legal value, it is a declaration adopted by the General Assembly of the UN, in that sense it is not strictly binding as it represents a statement

23 On the issue of human rights approaches to land rights, *see* Roger Plant, *Land Rights in Human Rights and Development, Introducing a New ICJ Initiative*, 51 Int'l Comm. Jurists Rev. 17 (1993); Jérémie Gilbert, *Land Rights as Human Rights: The Case for a Specific Right to Land*, SUR Journal on Human Rights, Vol. 18 (2014); *see also* the U.S. contention that land title is not human rights issues in *Mary and Carrie Dann v. United States*, Report No. 113/01, Case No. 11.140, at 124 (Oct. 15, 2001)—IACHR.

24 Convention Concerning the Protection and Integration of Indigenous and other Tribal and Semi-tribal Populations in Independent Countries (ILO Convention No. 107), 328 U.N.T.S. 247 (1957).

25 Convention Concerning Indigenous and Tribal Peoples in Independent Countries, (ILO No. 169), 72 ILO Official Bull. 59 (1989), *reprinted in* 28 I.L.M. 1382 (1989). [hereinafter ILO 169].

of intent from the international community. However as highlighted by many authors, based on its content which reflects the evolution of many binding customary norms, the UNDRIP offers a comprehensive legal framework regarding indigenous peoples' rights under international law.[26] Moreover, the Declaration does not create new sets of rights; instead, as noted by Anaya: "the rights affirmed [by the UN Declaration] are simply derived from human rights principles that are deemed of universal application."[27] Hence it has been argued that the Declaration is based on customary principle of international law and other legally binding rights protected under other treaties.[28] Furthermore, due to the prolong negotiations between States and indigenous representatives that led to its adoption, the UNDRIP also contains a valuable tool to reflect the state of the law as accepted by all actors. In that sense, the UNDRIP is examined in details in the book as the most developed, accurate and up to date statement on international law regarding indigenous peoples. The book also includes references to the current drat text of the Proposed OAS Declaration on the Rights of Indigenous Peoples in the Americas. Whilst the final text is still opened to negotiations and changes, several articles have been adopted by consensus by members of the OAS.[29] As such the text provides a good indication on the evolution of indigenous peoples' land rights in the context of the American continent.

The other approach offered by international law to indigenous peoples' land rights comes under the universal international human rights system. Neither the Universal Declaration of Human Rights (UDHR), the International Covenant on Civil and Political Rights (ICCPR), the International Covenant on Economic, Social and Cultural Rights (ICESCR), the International Convention on the Elimination of All Forms of Racial Discrimination (ICERD), nor the regional European, African and American human rights conventions refer specifically to indigenous peoples. Nonetheless, as the book explores, through the general human rights discourse on civil and political rights, economic, social and cultural rights, non-discrimination and peoples' and minority rights,

---

26 See: Making the Declaration Work: The United Nations Declaration on the Rights of Indigenous Peoples (Claire Chartres and Rodolfo Stavenhagen, eds., 2009).

27 James Anaya, *Why there should have to be a Declaration on the Rights of Indigenous Peoples* in James Anaya, Ed., International Human Rights and Indigenous Peoples (2011) p. 59.

28 For references and analysis, see: Mauro Barelli, Seeking Justice in International Law: The Significance and Implications of the UN Declaration on the Rights of Indigenous Peoples (2016—forthcoming).

29 See: Working Group to Prepare the Draft American Declaration on the Rights of Indigenous Peoples, Draft American Declaration on the Rights of Indigenous Peoples, OEA/Ser.K/XVI, GT/DADIN/doc.334/08 rev. 11 corr. 1 (2015).

human rights law addresses indigenous peoples' land claims. In analysing the jurisprudence and the doctrine emerging from the interpretation of these general instruments, the book examines whether such general discourse adequately accommodates indigenous peoples' specific land claims. Accordingly, the book examines whether there is a need for a more specific legal framework to address indigenous peoples' land claims or whether the existing human rights instruments properly address the issue.[30] When addressing indigenous peoples' rights under international law, one of the issues ultimately to be examined is whether the current human rights instruments adequately address indigenous peoples' land rights or whether, because of the unique nature of their claim, there is a need to further develop the existing system in order to properly address it. In terms of the debates surrounding indigenous peoples' rights, one of the main contentions is focused around the question of whether a specific regime is necessary for the protection of indigenous rights or whether their claims can be subsumed under general human rights law. By focusing on the specific issue of land rights, the book intends to go to the heart of this debate and to determine ultimately if international human rights law can successfully accommodate indigenous peoples' land claims.

In addressing this question, the book wishes to consider three important theoretical issues in the development of indigenous peoples' land rights. First, that land rights are often understood as collective rights, and that States are usually reluctant to recognize collective rights.[31] This area of tension between indigenous claims for collective land ownership and States' reluctance to recognize collective rights is examined in some details throughout the book. Second, as Plant points out, "land rights do not fit easily into the typological distinctions usually drawn between civil and political rights on the one hand, and economic, social and cultural rights on the other."[32] Consequently, the book proposes an approach based on the indivisibility and interdependence of human rights by exploring how human rights law offers different avenues for indigenous peoples' claims under the various categories of rights (civil, political, economic, social and cultural rights). Because indigenous peoples'

---

30 *See* Jeff J. Corntassel & Tomas Hopkins Primeau, *Indigenous 'Sovereignty' and International Law: Revised Strategies for Pursuing 'Self-Determination.'* 17 Hum. Rts. Q. 342 (1995); Patrick Thornberry, Indigenous Peoples and Human Rights (2002).

31 Douglas Sanders, *Collective Rights*, 13 Hum. Rts. Q. 368 (1991); Cindy L. Holder & Jeff J. Corntassel, *Indigenous Peoples and Multicultural Citizenship: Bridging Collective and Individual Rights*, 24(1) Hum. Rts. Q. 126 (2002).

32 Roger Plant, *Land Rights in Human Rights and Development. Introducing a New ICJ Initiative*, 51 Int'l Comm. Jurists Rev. 17 (1993).

attachment to their traditional lands affects all aspects of their lives, indigenous peoples' claims to land rights illustrate the indivisibility and interdependence of all human rights. In addition, it also tests the capacity of human rights law to accommodate indigenous peoples' land claims that do not fit neatly within its seemingly watertight compartments. From this perspective, the book explores very different areas of human rights law, from political rights to cultural rights but also focuses on other fields of international law that have added to the discourse on human rights law, such as international criminal law and international environmental law. Third, indigenous peoples' land claims are one of the areas of tension that potentially threaten the sovereignty of States. Land rights touch upon the issue of territoriality, and State territorial sovereignty is certainly an area that States are most reluctant to allow any encroachment upon.[33] In many ways, international law has been established to protect States' territorial sovereignty; indigenous peoples' land rights pose some crucial questions for the relationship between States' territorial integrity and fundamental human rights. This potential conflict between States' territorial integrity and land ownership for indigenous peoples is central to the discussion throughout the book, as it remains the most contentious issue in the development of indigenous peoples' land rights. Territorial rights also concern what Kymlicka has labelled "self-government rights," as ultimately indigenous peoples demand some form of territorial jurisdiction, "so as to ensure the full and free development of their cultures and the best interest of their people."[34] The book intends to examine these issues, which create tension with States sovereignty and the role of international human rights law in resolving such a conflict.

Finally, in terms of methodology, while the book is focusing on the analysis of international law, a limited amount of national legislations and jurisprudence are also included since indigenous peoples' land rights are one of those areas of international law in which the relationship between international law and national laws is deeply interlinked. Indeed when it comes to land rights, as it will be examined throughout the book, there is often a great interplay of domestic and international standards which deserves to be explored to be able to fully comprehend the international legal regime on land rights for indigenous peoples. The book does not hinge on any particular case study or situation, as the domestic case studies are selected either for their potential contribution to international legal theory or as examples of situations where international law

33 On the notion of territorial sovereignty, *see* 1 Robert Jennings & Arthur Watts. Oppenheim's International Law (9th ed. 1996).

34 Will Kymlicka, Multicultural Citizenship, A Liberal Theory of Minority Rights 27 (1995).

has served as a positive force for domestic development of indigenous peoples' land rights.[35] Thus, the choice of case studies throughout the book is based on situations where national laws, or case law, have been greatly influenced by international law, or where national laws and case law present a potential model for the development of international law.

Structure of the Book

The label "indigenous peoples' land rights" is a recent one, but, since its beginning, international law has had a direct impact on indigenous rights of territorial ownership. Even though the purpose of the book is to explore the present situation faced by indigenous peoples, the shadow of the past will always be present, as the current situation of indigenous peoples cannot be dissociated from their past history. The question of land rights is often an issue of restoring lands that were taken under a past discriminatory enterprise, an issue often linked to an on-going denial of indigenous peoples' land rights. Thus, in many ways, indigenous peoples' land rights is an issue of restoring previously denied rights rather than granting or creating new rights. For this reason, the book reflects the historical nature of indigenous peoples' land rights. The book is based on the assumption that there has been an evolution in the relationship between indigenous peoples and international law, and will explore indigenous peoples' land rights in this context. There have been many phases in the development of international law, but one of the main findings and assumptions of the book is that the approach of international law to indigenous peoples' land rights can be broken up in three different periods. From the indigenous peoples' perspective these three different eras are defined by their status under international law as 'victims' (Part 1), 'subjects' (Part 2) and 'actors' (Part 3). Thus, the general structure of the book is based on such an evolution of the status of indigenous peoples regarding their right to land.

The first part of the book explores the application of the rule governing title to territory in the context of indigenous peoples' rights. This part explores an area that seldom receives attention, as traditionally under international law the principles of title to territory come within the strict purview of the mandate of the sovereign State without taking into account its impact on indigenous peoples. In doing so the book proposes to adopt a new reading of the rule governing title to territory from an indigenous peoples' perspective, given that

35 For in depth analysis of land rights cases at national levels see: Land, Indigenous Peoples and Conflict (Alan C. Tidwell, Barry Scott Zellen, eds. 2016).

they were victims of a system aimed at acquiring their lands. This part of the book focuses on the theories of dispossession and their politicised interpretation under which indigenous peoples became victims of legal theories framed with a view towards acquisition and control of their territories.

Adopting a more positive view on international law, and notably based on the development of international human rights law, the second part of the book examines how indigenous peoples have become 'subject' of protection. There have been a lot of doctrinal debates highlighting how gradually indigenous peoples have become 'object' of protection under international law. Rather than 'object' of protection, this second part of the book analysis how under the human rights agenda, indigenous peoples have gradually become 'subject' of protection. This notably comes under the expansion and positive interpretation of property rights and cultural rights under human rights law, which has allowed indigenous peoples to become 'subject' of protection.

The third part of the book scrutinizes the latest development in the negotiations between indigenous peoples and States on territorial issues, and the role of human rights law within these negotiations. The book further examines the human rights led development of the discourse as regards indigenous peoples' land claims, which is based on the notion of consent and dialogue. This part argues that under recent developments, indigenous peoples have gained access to international law as 'actors,' with some control over their own future given that the development of contemporary human rights law is based on the notion of consent between States and indigenous peoples. This part elaborates on how the human rights discourse is supporting the development of a new phase in the relationship between States and indigenous peoples in which the latter will finally be recognized as actors.

PART 1

Indigenous Peoples as Victims: Theories of Dispossession

The rights of indigenous peoples in international law have evolved greatly, especially since the establishment of the U.N. system. However, to understand the actual challenges in building the current system, it is crucial to go back to the history of international law's impact on indigenous peoples' land rights. Even though indigenous peoples' land rights have only been addressed recently in international law, it is an issue that is deeply embedded within the history of colonial dispossession. The primary impact of international law on indigenous peoples came through the rules governing title to territory. These rules, which were a central focus in the development of international law, did not address indigenous peoples' rights but addressed the rights of colonial powers to acquire indigenous territories; in this regard, one of the first effects of international law on indigenous rights was through the legacy of their dispossession. This first part of the book offers an analysis of what Daes designed as the "doctrines of dispossession."[1] Under such a label, the former Chairperson/Rapporteur of the former U.N. Working Group on Indigenous Populations (WGIP) made reference to rules, such as "discovery," "*terra nullius*" and "conquest," that legally sanctioned the colonisation and subjugation of indigenous territories.

Regarding the rules governing title to territory, two separate legacies have been developed under international law: the laws regarding territorial disputes between so-called "civilized" States and the rules regarding the acquisition of "non-civilized" territories.[2] Based on such dichotomy, colonial powers engaged international law, making two major assumptions regarding indigenous peoples' land rights: indigenous peoples do not legally exist—thus their lands can be acquired; or indigenous peoples exist but are inferior—thus their right to occupy their homelands can be extinguished. Under the first approach, indigenous peoples were regarded as "savages," and consequently non-existent under international law—thus their territories were open to acquisition—whereas the second approach implied that indigenous peoples have once legally existed and exercised territorial ownership, but this territorial control has been extinguished with the arrival of other actors in their lands. Based on such distinction, the dispossession of indigenous peoples was based on two different means: the means of acquisition and the means of extinguishment. Accordingly, one of the arguments developed in this first part of the book is that two major and different approaches have been undertaken by States to dispossess

---

1 Final Working Paper prepared by the Special Rapporteur Mrs. Erica-Irene A. Daes, *Human Rights of Indigenous Peoples, Indigenous Peoples and their Relationship to Land*, U.N. Doc. E/CN.4/Sub.2/2000/25 (June 30, 2000).

2 See Mark. F. Lindley, The Acquisition and Government of Backward Territory in International Law 11–12 (1926 *reprinted in* 1969).

 | DOI 10.1163/9789004323254_003

indigenous peoples of their territories. First, States have had recourse to "classical" theories of territorial acquisition, such as conquest and territorial occupation, to colonize indigenous territories: this will be examined in Chapter 1, dealing with the "means of acquisition." Second, States have considered that indigenous ownership disappeared with colonisation as indigenous rights were "extinguished" by the arrival of colonisers. The latter can be regrouped as "means of extinguishment," meaning that indigenous peoples' existence was acknowledged by the colonial powers but their territorial rights were abolished. This approach will be analysed in Chapter 2.

The laws of acquisition and extinguishment are waves of the same movement that was aimed at imposing the superiority of one system over another; either by conquering it or by extinguishing it. In this sense, the two notions were often used alternatively and complementarily, since ultimately the issue was to define to what extent the superiority of the colonisers allowed them to "legally" ignore, conquer or extinguish indigenous rights to live on their territories. However, regarding the legal theories behind these two movements, it is worth analysing how, in one case, indigenous peoples' dispossession was based on the right of acquisitions, while the other views indigenous peoples as having some rights but these are extinguishable. This distinction has some important consequences regarding the shape of the contemporary legal regime on indigenous peoples' land rights that this part of the book will explore. From this perspective, it is important to explore the different rules that have had, and still have, direct impact on the alienation of indigenous territories. It is essential to go back to the history of international law regarding acquisition of territory, as most indigenous peoples in their claim for the recognition of their right to land, will have to deal with such legacy of colonisation. The purpose of the present part is not only to give a traditional historical overview before engaging the subject, but to show that this history itself is at the core of indigenous peoples' land claims. The contemporary situation faced by indigenous peoples is the clear result of a system that was drafted in the last five centuries, and, in some parts, international law regarding possession and territory has not changed much since then.

CHAPTER 1

Means of Acquisition

> The inflow of the white race cannot be stopped where there is land to cultivate, ore to be mined, commerce to be developed, sport to enjoy, curiosity to be satisfied. (…) Accordingly, international law has to treat such natives as uncivilized.
>
> JOHN WESTLAKE, 1864[1]

Traditionally, international law recognizes five different forms of territorial acquisition: occupation, prescription, cession, accretion and conquest.[2] To different extents, these forms of territorial acquisition have largely contributed to indigenous dispossession. Although it is not the purpose of the following chapter to explore the different ways of "legal" acquisition of territory,[3] it is nevertheless crucial to discuss their impact on the dispossession of indigenous peoples' rights to land. Regarding the theories of acquisition of indigenous territories, two main categories emerged: first the acquisition by conquest and second the acquisition of so-called legally "empty" territories. Under the first approach the rationale was that indigenous peoples exist but are "savages"; thus, imperial colonial powers are superior, which is legally translated by the right of conquest. Under the second approach, indigenous peoples did not legally exist; thus their territories were open to colonisation. Building on this assumption, the first section of this chapter examines the rules that guided the conquest of indigenous territories, while the second section focuses on theories that advocate the non-existence of indigenous peoples' territorial rights.

A The Conquest of Indigenous Territories

One of the fundamental issues that gave birth to international law was the issue of the so-called "savages" and their incorporation within the "family of the

1 John Westlake, Chapters on the Principles of International Law 136 (1894 *reprinted* 2000).

2 Robert Y. Jennings, The Acquisition of Territory in International Law (1963) *see also* Seokwoo Lee, *Continuing Relevance of Traditional Modes of Territorial Acquisition in International Law and a Modest Proposal*, 16 Conn. J. Int'l L. 1 (2000).

3 On this issue, *see* Joshua Castellino & Steven Allen, Title to Territory in International Law (2003) [hereinafter Castellino & Allen].

 | DOI 10.1163/9789004323254_004

nations." One of the founders of international law theory, Vitoria, is recognized for his theories relating to the so-called "Indians."[4] Later in the history of international law, Grotius, the "father" of international law, defined the fundamental rules of territorial sovereignty influencing attitudes towards indigenous peoples' territorial entitlements. To some extent, most of the influential early theorists of international law have dealt with the issue of indigenous peoples' rights to territory. Some of these theories justified the establishment of a legacy that automatically viewed indigenous territories as open to conquest, as one of the first mandates of the laws of colonisation was to legitimise the superiority of the coloniser's claims over the indigenous presence; and in this they provided the moral and legal theory to justify conquest.

1 *Justifications of Conquest: Commerce, Christianity and Civilization*

> Savages are dangerous neighbours and unprofitable customers.
>
> House of Commons, Select Committee on Aboriginal Tribes, 1837.

Some of the most fundamental doctrinal theories of international law were drawn with the conquest of the "new world," as European imperial powers sought to establish rules for organising such conquests. In this sense, early international law has been used as an instrument of violent conquests by the European empires. Of course, colonisation was not only a European fashion—other non-European imperial powers have conquered indigenous territories since time immemorial.[5] For example, the Japanese started the colonisation of the Ainu lands as early as 1604.[6] However, the European colonisers were adept at using the law as a tool to legitimize and justify their actions. It is relatively undeniable that most of the debates that gave birth to the laws relating to territory and possession took place within the boundaries of Europe.[7]

4 Vitoria is frequently cited as one of the founders of the modern discipline of international law. *See* James Brown Scott, The Spanish Origins of Modern International Law (1932); Arthur Nussbaum, A Concise History of the Law of Nations (1947) [hereinafter Nussbaum]; and discussion on Vitoria's theory at Section A.1.b.

5 For a history of colonisation seen not only from a European perspective, *see* Marc Ferro, Histoire des Colonisations (1994).

6 *Id.* at 74.

7 However, the Arabic Empire used the precepts of Islam as a legal justification for its expansion between the seventh and tenth centuries, but those laws are not reflected in the contents of international law. *See* Majid Khadduri, The Islamic Law of Nations, Shaybani's Siyar (1966).

To properly understand the rules that governed the colonisation of indigenous territories, it is crucial to understand the context in which these rules of conquest were established. International law is the superstructure reflecting the socio-economic factors of a defined period;[8] thus, even though the colonial powers had different approaches regarding colonisation,[9] these different approaches gave rise to a specific branch of international law regarding conquest. The formula of the "three C's," Christianity, commerce, civilization, expresses perfectly the basis on which the first laws of conquest were written.[10] Early international law is the legalistic translation, or justification via law and doctrine, of those three concepts. When the first explorers arrived in the "new world" it was mostly in the name of "God for gold."[11] Hence, it is necessary to read the laws of conquest through the prism of the Christian doctrines of those times.[12]

In the Name of the Pope: The Holy Conquest

One of the first international "legal rights" of conquest came from the Pope as part of the papal "universal territorial jurisdiction."[13] In 1452, Pope Nicholas V issued a papal bull declaring "a war" against all non-Christians throughout the world. This papal bull was the first in a long series in which the Vatican granted a title and trading monopoly to Portugal in Africa.[14] This papal bull granted the king of Portugal the right to "invade, conquer, storm, attack and subjugate and reduce into perpetual servitude the Saracens, pagans and other enemies of Christ." In 1455, the *Romanus Pontifex* that was addressed to King Alfonso V of Portugal contained the promotion of the conquest, colonisation and exploitation of the non-Christians and their territories. At the request of the Spanish Crown, in 1493 Pope Alexander VI gave his blessing to the Spanish

8 Alain Pellet, *Le "Bon Droit" et l'Ivraie—Plaidoyer pour l'Ivraie, in* Melanges Offerts a Charles Chaumont, Le Droit des peuples a disposer d'eux meme 465 (1984).

9 *See* Anthony Pagden, Lords of All the World: Ideologies of Empire in Spain, Britain and France c.1500–c.1800 (1995).

10 For general reading, *see* Imperialism (Philip Curtin ed., 1971).

11 *See* Immanuel Wallenstein, The Modern World System: Capitalist Agriculture and the Origins of the European World Economy in the Sixteenth Century (1974).

12 It is also important to go back to the Catholic doctrine that justified the crusades during the 11th and 12th centuries, as the arguments used and developed by the popes were reused for the colonisation of the new world. *See* Carl Erdmann, The Origins of the Idea of Crusade (1977).

13 *See* Robert A. Williams, The American Indians in Western Legal Though: The Discourses of Conquest 80–81 (1990).

14 Any other Christian monarch that interfered with the papal bull would have been excommunicated, *id.*

Crown to spread the catholic faith across the world in lands "undiscovered by others." Therefore, like Portugal several years before, the Spanish Crown held a spiritual entitlement to own all the lands of the so-called "new world," meaning the parts of the world that were not under Christian rules.[15] Since Portugal contested the broad reading of the papal bull, the Pope issued another bull that established the famous north to south papal line of demarcation for the entire Western Hemisphere.[16] Following these two papal bulls, the Treaty of Tordesillas of 1494 finally divided the "new world" between the Spanish and the Portuguese Crowns.[17]

Following their arrival in South America, the colonisers put in place a system aimed at the distribution of the two principal economic resources: labour force and lands. The first pillar of the Spanish colonisation was the *encomienda*.[18] The *encomienda* was a 'grant' of Indian workers within a geographic region, which were given to an *encomendero*, a Spaniard who received a grant of a land and 'Indians' to work it.[19] The second pillar was the system of *repartimiento* (distribution) aimed at the allotment of a parcel of land to the *conquistadores* (the colonisers). Originally, this system did not grant the *conquistadores* land tenure; however the colonisers (and his descendants for two or three generations) did often own a parcel of land and the right to the labour of the "Indians" living on it. Such a system of enslavement implied a *de facto* spoliation of the indigenous rights to own their lands. The Royal Act of 1503 put this system on a legislative footing, but this act was reorganized in 1512–1513 with the laws of

15 The Spanish Crown frequently defended its rights over the New World by reference to the papal grant of title. *See* Robert A. Williams, *Colombus's Legacy: Law as an Instrument of Racial Discrimination Against Indigenous Peoples' Rights of Self-Determination*, 8 Ariz. J. Int'l & Comp. L. 51 (1991).

16 The papal bulls have never been formally revoked (though the 1537 Bull *Sublimis Deus* had the effect of revoking it), although indigenous peoples' representatives have asked the Vatican to do so. On this issue, *see Chroniques d'une Conquête* 14 Ethnies 7 (1993). See also formal apologies made by Pope Francis for Catholic crimes against indigenous peoples during the colonisation of the Americas, June 2015.

17 This treaty between Spain and Portugal received the papal blessing in 1506. Parallel to this division, the King of England granted John Cabot a "Charter of Conquest" in 1497. For general references, *see* Leslie C. Green & Olive Dickason, The Law of Nations and the New World (1989).

18 The *encomienda* was a system of tributary labour used as a means of securing cheap labour. This system was first used over the conquered Moors of Spain. Robert Himmerich Y. Valencia, The Encomenderos of New Spain (1991).

19 Robert Chamberlain, *Pre-Conquest Labor Practices, in* Indian Labor in the Spanish Indies (Robert Chamberlain ed., 1966).

Burgos and Valladolid.[20] The laws of Burgos were the "first comprehensive legislative code dealing with Indian affairs in the new world."[21] The laws of Burgos organized and justified the *encomienda* system, affirming that such a system was "in agreement with divine and human law" but also infused a spirit of total assimilation of the Indians. One of the rules imposed upon the *encomendero* (the coloniser) was an obligation to build a church and to give a parcel of land to the "Indians" for the purposes of agriculture, but they did not provide the "Indians" with a right of ownership. The Indians merely held a right to use the land while ownership remained in the hands of the coloniser. In sum, the system was based on a deal between the Spanish Crown, the Church and the colonisers, the deal being that the Crown provided the settlers with native lands, and in exchange, the settler agreed to convert the indigenous to Christianity, to treat them "humanely" and to care for their physical well-being.[22] Even though there were some attempts to reform and abolish this system, in many instances it remained in place until the end of the 17th century.[23] In addition, the *requerimiento*[24] provided the Spanish Crown with a justification for entering into war with the indigenous and the subsequent conquest of their lands. The *requerimiento* stated that the Indians should not refuse or resist the Spanish powers, as they were representing the Church by virtue of papal donation. If they "resisted," the *requerimiento* threatened the Indians:

> But if you do not do this or if you maliciously delay in doing it, I certify to you that with the help of God we shall make war against you ... and

20 These laws came as an answer to "the friar's account of the genocidal fury of the Spanish colonists and conquistadors" that were reported especially by Antonio de Montesinos. *See* Robert A. Williams, *The Medieval and Renaissance Origins of the Status of the American Indians in Western Legal Though*, 57 S. Cal. L Rev. 1 (1983) [hereinafter Williams].

21 *Id.*

22 At this stage it is worth remembering that during the colonisation of the Americas, the entire population decreased by 95 percent in the century and a half following the first encounter. *See* Rodolfo Stavenhagen, The Status and Rights of the Indigenous Peoples of America (1991); and Bartolomé de Las Casas, A Short Account of the Destruction of the Indies (1542 *reprinted* 1992).

23 In 1542 Emperor Charles V of Spain abolished the *encomienda* system to replace it by a system of new laws. However, following a huge violent protest in Peru and Spain, the *encomienda* system was reintroduced in 1545. *See* Lewis Hanke, The Spanish Struggle for Justice in the Conquest of America (1949).

24 The *Requerimiento* was a statement read to indigenous populations before military action requesting they surrender and accept authority of the Spanish Crown and Christianity, used as a justification for aggression against these populations. *See* Matthew C. Mirow, *Latin American Legal History: Some Essential Spanish Terms*, 12 La Raza L.J. 43 (2001).

> shall subject you to the yoke and obedience of the Church and of their highnesses, we shall take you and your wives and your children and shall make slaves of them, and as such shall sell and dispose of them as their highness may command; and we shall take away your goods and shall do to you all the damage that we can, as to vassals who do not obey and refuse to receive their lord and resist and contradict him; and we protest that the deaths and losses which shall accrue from this are your fault, and not that of your highnesses, or ours, or of these soldiers who come with us.[25]

This quotation illustrates how the Crown used the Catholic faith as the principal justification of its conquest. The papal donation provided the Spanish colonisers with a *"justa causa"* being a "holy war of conquest." As captured by Wight: "[I]n the notion of Holy War, the premise is that the true believers are right, and that infidels are to be converted or exterminated. (...) It is a religious conception, of war as the instrument of God's will, or of history."[26] In 1537, the Pope issued another bull "which had the effect of revoking *Inter Caetera* insofar as it purported to give the Spanish monarchy title to the Indians' land, although Spain continued to have the duty to convert the Indians to the Christian faith."[27] This notion of Holy War was not a Spanish and Portuguese legacy only, as all the other European imperial colonial powers based their conquest on Christian foundations, as is evidenced by the English 1608 *Calvin* case in which Chief Justice Coke stated: "if a Christian King should conquer a kingdom of an infidel ... there ipso facto the laws of the infidel are abrogated, for ... they be against ... the law of God and nature."[28] Likewise, the letters patent granted by the Kings of France and England during the 15th and 16th centuries all spoke about the duty of bringing the "savages" to the Christian faith.[29] The French and English granted their respective trade companies a right of conquest on the basis of bringing faith to the pagans and conquering their territories in the name of "the Christian Prince or peoples."[30] Later, such Christian references to a right of conquest were to be found in the notion of "manifest destiny" used

25 *Quoted in* Williams, *supra* note 22.

26 Martin Wight, Systems of States 34–35 (1977).

27 James Falkowski, Indian Law Race Law: A Five Hundred Year History 25 (1992).

28 [1608] 7 Coke's Rep. 1a, 77 Eng. Rep. 377, 398.

29 *See* Mark. F. Lindley, The Acquisition and Government of Backward Territory in International Law 24 (1926 *reprinted* 1969) [hereinafter Lindley].

30 For examples of such grants, *see* especially the first Charter of Virginia (1606), the French grants of 1635 and 1642 to the Compagnie des Isles de l'Amérique and the Hudson Bay Company grants (1670); Lindley, *supra* note 30, at 25–26.

in the conquest of the west of the North American continent. The notion of "manifest destiny" suggested that a country could claim land destined by God to be its territory. According to this view, God's will is reflected in the superior economy, political system and culture of the conquering country.[31] While this Christian foundation for the annexation of indigenous territories by the European colonial powers was widely accepted, there were notable critics of the policy who began gradually to emerge. At the beginning of the 16th century a few voices started to criticize the exclusively papal foundations of the annexation of indigenous territories by the Spanish Crown. Those debates gave birth to a new doctrine based on a more "humanist" theory. This theory was shaped by to the idea that all men have the common element of human reason and have certain rights flowing from "natural law."[32] Based on such an approach, the voices of a number of eminent publicists started to criticize the exclusively Christian justification of the conquest and defended the idea that the so-called savages might have a natural right to live on their lands.

The Naturalist Theory: A Conquest for "Civilization"

Among the new humanist writers, Francisco de Vitoria was certainly one of the most influential in rejecting the legacy of the papal donation to the Spanish Crown.[33] In his revolutionary *De Indis et de ivre belli relectiones*, he affirmed that the Indians owned the land in America, and that "discovery" was not a proper legal means of acquiring title to territory. Vitoria explained that discovery could not transfer title to the land "anymore than if it had been they who had discovered us."[34] The central argument of the author was based on the notion "that certain basic rights inhere in men as men, not by reason of their race, creed, or color, but by reason of their humanity."[35] This position reflects the revolutionary idea that the naturalist framework endorsed—the notion of equality between all human beings.[36] Relating to land rights, based

31 On this issue, *see* Steven Paul McSloy, *Because the Bible Tells Me So: Manifest Destiny and American Indians*, 9 St. Thomas L. Rev. 37 (1996).

32 Frederick Pollock, *The History of the Law of Nature: A Preliminary Study*, 1 Colum. L. Rev. 11 (1901).

33 *See* Felix S. Cohen, *Original Indian Title*, 32 Minn. L. Rev. 28 (1947); Nussbaum, *supra* note 6.

34 Francisco de Vitoria, De Indis et de ivre belli relectiones 139 (1532 *translated* 1917) [hereinafter Vitoria].

35 *Quoted in* Felix S. Cohen, *The Spanish Origin of Indian Rights in the Law of the United States*, 31 Geo. L.J. (1942).

36 On the relationship between natural law positive law, and *jus gentium* in Vitoria's theory, *see* David Kennedy, *Primitive Legal Scholarship*, 27 Harv. Int'l L.J. 1 (1986).

on this notion of equality, the "Indians" should had have a right of ownership "just like Christians." Vitoria's theory was based on the idea that the "Indians" had a certain right to property unless the conqueror had a "just cause" to take the land. Thus, in his secular vision, Vitoria also brought another central element to the legacy of the colonisation of indigenous land by referring to the concept of "just cause," a concept that was first framed in Roman law as part of *jus gentium*.[37] Following this principle, the "Indians" had inherent obligations as defined by *jus gentium*. Regarding access to their territories, Vitoria defined four major duties that the Indians had to respect:

(1) leave a free passage into their lands for the colonisers;
(2) allow the colonisers to trade among them;
(3) share the wealth of their lands;
(4) permit the propagation of Christianity.[38]

If the "Indians" refused, or interfered with the "rights" of the colonisers, then the colonisers had a right to enter into a "just war" against the "rebel" Indians. A just war would provide the colonisers with a "legal" title to territory as part of a legal conquest. Taking the four duties imposed on the Indians, Williams pointed out that: "Vitoria anticipated liberal arguments of the seventeenth and eighteenth centuries on the legitimate exercise of state power."[39] The four rights of the colonisers are based on the fundamental rights and duties of the colonial powers to impose and develop "commerce, Christianity and civilization." In this sense, despite Vitoria's progressive recognition of Indians' territorial rights, he clearly endorsed the equation "Commerce plus Christianity equals Civilization." Vitoria's theory reflected what was to be the justification for any acquisition of territory by colonisers in the following centuries. Therefore, notwithstanding the rejection of the theory of discovery and the recognition of indigenous right of ownership, Vitoria supported the development of a legal framework for the conquest of indigenous territories. The colonisers were entitled to enter into a "just war" against the "Indians" and to colonise their lands if they refused a free passage into their territory, prevented the Spanish from making profit from the wealth of their land that they were obliged to share and, finally, if they opposed in any way the propagation of Christianity.

37 On this issue, *see* Nussbaum *supra* note 6.

38 There are usually seven or eight legitimate titles; three of them are also linked with the propagation of Christianity and the others are based on voluntary choice. *See* J.S. Davidson, *The Rights of Indigenous Peoples in Early International Law*, 5 Canterbury L. Rev. 391 (1994).

39 Williams, *supra* note 22.

Thus, the "Indians" had the choice between contemplating the Spanish taking gradual control of their resources and imposing their own culture, or opposing them and then offering the coloniser a right of conquest based on a just war. Even though Vitoria did not deny a right of territorial ownership for the Indians, his theory left them no choice but to accept their colonisation or attempt resistance in a "just war." In this sense, the concept of "just cause" became a tool at the service of imperial interests. As captured by Williams: "[T]he duality in Vitoria's attitudes toward Indian political and cultural autonomy on the one hand led him to deny the legitimacy of papal hierarchical domination, while on the other hand permitted him to legitimate a functionally equivalent Spanish hierarchical subordination of the Indian."[40] This duality is explained by Vitoria's idea that for the benefit of the Indians, the Spanish should undertake the control of the "new territories." Vitoria wrote:

> Although the aborigines in question are ... not wholly unintelligent, yet they are little short of that condition, and so are unfit to found or administer a lawful State up to the standard required by human and civil claims. Accordingly they have no proper laws nor magistrates, and are not even capable of controlling their family affairs; they are without any literature or arts, not only the liberal arts, but the mechanical arts also; they have no careful agriculture and no artisans... It might, therefore, be maintained that in their own interests the sovereigns of Spain might undertake the administration of their country, providing them with prefects and governors for their towns, and might even give them new lords, so long as this was clearly for their benefit.[41]

Clearly that was one of the first secular references to a theory that prevailed until recently in international law, i.e. that indigenous peoples were not "able" to properly own and use their lands, even though they have a theoretical natural right of ownership. This theory was the clear expression of the *mission civilisatrice* that was perceived as the moral responsibility of the European colonisers. In this sense, Vitoria is one of the fathers of what later became known as the "trusteeship theory."[42]

40 *Id.*

41 Vitoria, *supra* note 35, at 161.

42 *See*, for example, Judge Tanaka, "The idea that it belongs to the noble obligation of conquering powers to treat indigenous peoples of conquered territory and to promote their wellbeing has existed for many hundreds of years, at least since the era of Vitoria," South West Africa Cases, 1966 I.C.J. 6, 66 Am. J. Int'l L. 116, at 265 (1967).

A contemporary of Vitoria was Bartolomé de las Casas, a Dominican clerk, who was one of the first theorists to criticise the *encomienda* system, and also the first theorist who actually went to the "new world."[43] Las Casas, who is often considered as the first defender of the "Indians," was opposed to Ginès de Sepulveda in the famous controversy of Valladolid in 1550–51. The issue was to determine if the "Indians" had enough "soul" and reason to be considered as human beings.[44] During the debates, the issue was not focused on the lawfulness of conquest but concentrated more on the solely Christian justification for this conquest. Las Casas did not argue that the Pope had no right to confer upon the Spanish Crown the right to evangelise the "savages" but that those "savages," having a human soul, should voluntarily accept such Christianisation, and that the colonisers should respect their social institutions. In his treatise, Las Casas rejected the argument developed by the colonisers (and Sepulveda) that indigenous inhabitants of the new world were so primitive and barbaric that their lands were open to colonisation.[45] On the issue of just war, contrary to Vitoria, Las Casas rejected the idea that the indigenous nations had a duty to leave a free passage into their lands to the colonisers to allow trading. One of the major contributions of Las Casas is to be found in his *Historia de Las Indies:* as based on the concept of *restitutio in integrum* he affirmed that the lands that were stolen from the Indians by violence should be restored to them.

Vitoria and Las Casas, who are often designated as the fathers of the Spanish School, have been extremely influential on the development of the theory of international law through the repercussion of their theories on other recognized publicists.[46] Most of the theoreticians of the 16th and 17th centuries, such as Suárez or Gentili, reaffirmed the principles of just war and developed the notion that the heathen beliefs of the so-called "savages" were not a satisfactory justification for taking their property.[47] At the beginning of the 17th century, Grotius affirmed the rejection of discovery as a legal title of ownership, "even though the occupant may be wicked, may hold wrong views about

43 On the importance of Las Casas in the framing of universal rights, *see* Paolo G. Carozza, *From Conquest to Constitutions: Retrieving a Latin American Tradition of the Idea of Human Rights*, 25 Hum. Rts. Q. 281 (2003).

44 On the Valladolid controversy, *see* Lewis Hanke, All Mankind Is One (1974).

45 Bartolomé de Las Casas, The Defence of the Most Reverend Lord, Don Fray Bartolomé de Las Casas of the Order of the Preachers, Late Bishop of Chiapa, Against the Persecutors and Slanderers of the Peoples of the New World Discovered Across the Seas (1552 *translation* 1974).

46 Greg C. Marks, *Indigenous Peoples in International Law: The Significance of Francisco de Vitoria and Bartolome de las Casas*, 13, 37 Australian Y.B. Int'l L. 1 (1992).

47 On this issue, *see* Michel Morin, L'Ursupation de la Souveraineté Autochtone 32–40 (1997).

God, or may be dull of wit. For discovery applies to those things which belong to no-one."[48] Thus, Grotius strengthened the secularity of the international legal discourse and affirmed that, based on natural rights, all peoples can enter into a treaty including "strangers to the true religion." In his treatise *Mare Librerum*, Grotius argued that Portugal had no title to the East Indies on the basis that the inhabitants of the East Indies had "perfect public and private ownership" of their possessions and could not be dispossessed without just cause.[49] Grotius described the seizure of property on religious ground as theft. He re-endorsed the concept of just cause to enter into a just war and defined it precisely by identifying three causes for just war, "defense, recovery of property, and punishment."[50] Besides restating the just causes for entering into a just war, Grotius also reaffirmed the idea that the indigenous populations had a duty to leave a free passage into their lands for the purpose of commerce. Thus, he supported most of the just causes defined by Vitoria, apart from the obligation to allow for the propagation of Christianisation. This theoretical view is reflected in the transfer of power that took place from the European monarchs to the trade companies. Furthermore, even though the notion of Christianisation was rejected, Grotius introduced a more secular view by introducing natural moral obligations such as the prohibition of anthropophagy, human sacrifices, homosexuality and inbreeding. The violations of such natural rules gave a right to enter into a just war against the "barbarous." In sum, Grotius's concepts of just cause are quite similar to those developed two centuries before by Vitoria, except that Grotius brought a more secular position to international law. Instead of a right of conquest based on the propagation of Christianity, conquest was aimed at enforcing natural "civilised" laws that prohibited acts supposedly committed by the "savages."

Most of the early theorists of international law provided the fundamental justifications for the conquest of indigenous territories.[51] As highlighted earlier, one of the central arguments developed by these authors was the fact that conquest was justified by the spread of commerce, Christianity and civilization. From the 15th century to the 19th century, the "three Cs" provided the

48 Hugo Grotius, The Rights of War and Peace (De Jure belli ac pacis) 550 (1625 *translation* 1925).

49 Hugo Grotius, Mare Liberum 13 (1609 *translation* 1916).

50 Hugo Grotius, The Rights of War and Peace (De Jure belli ac pacis) 171 (1625 *translation* 1925); *see also* Hugo Grotius and International Relations (Hedley Bull, Benedict Kingsbury & Adam Roberts eds., 1990).

51 However, for another view, *see* Samuel Pufendorf, De Jure Naturae et Gentium Libri Octo (1688 *translation* 1989).

conqueror with a "just cause," providing the colonisers with the right to enter a just war and ultimately giving them a legal title to territory. This notion of justification or "just cause" is central when dealing with the right of conquest. Until recently, international law had recognized conquest as a valid mode of acquiring territory, as long as it was morally justified. As noted by Lindley: "a Conquest, however, which could not be justified, for example, on the ground that it represented just retribution for wrong committed, or that it was in gain to humanity, would tend to bring upon its perpetrator the censure of public opinion."[52] To provide a good legal title to territory, a conquest must be justified. In this sense the "fathers" of international law provided the legal justifications for conquest, but one must not forget that these authors also highlighted that, based on the notion of natural law, indigenous peoples had a right to own their lands. This natural right of ownership could be lost as a consequence of conquest. In this regard the justification of conquest developed by the theorists of international law would serve as a basis for the conquest of indigenous territories.

2 *Discriminatory Rules of Conquest*

International law is often regarded as the law of peace, or at least as a body of laws that aims at maintaining peace and security between nations and States. If this view is correct in a contemporary perspective, it is only rather recent. International law used to be the "law of conquest." Conquest "constitutes an act of force by which, in time of war, a belligerent occupies a part or the whole of the territory of the enemy State with the intention of extending its own national sovereignty over that territory."[53] Until recently, international law recognised the right of the victorious party to a conflict to acquire the territory of the defeated party, thus recognising conquest as providing legal title.[54] As noted by Oppenheim in 1905: "[A]s long as a Law of Nations has been in existence, the states as well as the vast majority of writers have recognized subjugation as a mode of acquiring territory."[55] In 1928, in the *Island of Palmas* case, Huber reaffirmed conquest as providing a good title to territory.[56] Hyde, in an editorial note in 1936, also referred to the way in which States still considered conquest as a legitimate rule of international law despite the promises

52 Lindley, *supra* note 30, at 160.

53 Erich Kussbach, *Conquest, in* Encyclopedia of Public International Law 119 (1982).

54 Sharon Korman, The Right of Conquest (1996) [hereinafter Korman]; *see also* Hedley Bull, The Anarchical Society: A Study of Order in World Politics (1977).

55 Lassa Oppenheim, International Law 288 (1st ed. 1905–06).

56 Island of Palmas Case (Neth. v. U.S.) (1928), 2 R.I.A.A. 829 (1949).

contained in the Covenant of the League of Nations.[57] He concluded: "[I]n a word, the Covenant, despite the hopes of some who were responsible for it, became an instrument that in effect registered respect for conquest and deference for the successes of the victor."[58] Even during the debates that led to the development of the Briand-Kellogg Pact, some States affirmed that conquest should be regarded as a central rule of international law.[59] It was only in 1974 that the U.N. General Assembly adopted Resolution 3314(XXIX) stating that "no territorial acquisition or special advantage resulting from aggression is or shall be recognized as lawful."[60] In concordance with the rules of intertemporal law, in 1970, the U.N. General Assembly declared that the modern prohibition against the acquisition of territory by conquest should not be constructed as affecting titles to territory created "prior to the Charter *régime* and valid under international law."[61] Thus, even though it could be argued that, in principle, contemporary international law prohibits the acquisition of territory by conquest,[62] it is crucial to recognise the importance of the rules that governed the acquisition of territory by force in past centuries, since those rules, even though illegal by contemporary standards, provide the legal basis for many titles to territory. Thus, whether conquest is a valid way of acquiring territory is not an issue, for the question here is more to appreciate how the right of conquest has been specially used to conquer indigenous territories. What has not been emphasised is that the right of conquest has been used in a discriminatory way towards indigenous nations.

First, in many situations conquest was wrongly recognised outside pure war situations. In most cases there was no genuine war between the indigenous nations and the colonisers;[63] thus, there was no right of conquest, as conquest presupposes a war situation. The Permanent Court of International Justice has

57 Charles Cheney Hyde, *Conquest Today*, 30(3) Am. J. Int'l L. 471 (1936).

58 *Id.* at 472.

59 For example, *see* Edwin Borchard, The Multilateral Pact—'Renunciation of War' (1928); *see* M. Cherif Bassiouni, International Criminal Law 316–17 (2d ed. 1999); *see also* Francis A. Boyle, Foundations of World Order: The Legalist Approach to International Relations, 1898–1922 (1999).

60 G.A. Res. 3314(XXIX), Definition of Aggression (Dec. 14, 1974) art. 5(3); *see also* Robert Langer, Seizure of Territory, The Stimson Doctrine and Related Principles in Legal Theory and Diplomatic Practice (1947).

61 G.A. Res. 2625(XXV) (Oct. 24, 1970).

62 However for a discussion on this point, *see* Korman, *supra* note 54.

63 For a discussion on this issue from an anthropological perspective, *see* R. Brian Ferguson & Neil Whitehead, War in the Tribal Zone, Expanding States and Indigenous Warfare (1992).

insisted that: "[C]onquest only operated as a cause of loss of sovereignty when there is a war between two States and by reason of the defeat of one of them sovereignty over territory passes from the loser to the victor."[64] In the case of the so-called conquest of North America, Churchill pointed out that officially the United States "waged fewer than fifty 'Indian Wars' in the course of its expansion. That leaves well over 400 now-subordinated peoples with whom the U.S. never exchanged a blow."[65] Despite this situation, the U.S. courts often refer to conquest to justify the U.S. jurisdiction over native territories.[66] Evidence of this "non-war situation" is that many colonial powers refused to recognise the application of the laws and customs of war in their conquest of indigenous peoples' territories. With the development of the rules of international law regarding the conduct of hostilities at the end of the 19th century, some voices started to ask for the application of such rules in conflict situations between colonisers and indigenous populations.[67] One of the first calls to the international community for the protection of indigenous peoples came from the *Comité de Protection de défense des indigenes*, which called upon the International Congress to apply the Hague Regulations to indigenous populations, including the prohibition to seize the enemies properties.[68] In 1907, the International Congress on Subject Races organized by the Subject Races Joint Committee passed a resolution that invited States to respect the Hague Regulation, which read:

> That in territories over which control is acquired from their native occupants by any of the Powers signatory to the Hague Convention: (...) there shall be no forcible appropriation of land and its produce by the newcomers, and any amicable division of land between the two communities the native shall be left permanently in possession of ample and suitable areas for their sole use, with full liberty to maintain their institutions, political, social, and religious, subject only to their

64 Legal Status of Eastern Greenland (Den. v. Nor.), 1933 P.C.I.J. (ser. A/B), No. 53, at 47.

65 Ward Churchill, Perversion of Justice, Indigenous Peoples and Anglo-American Law 35 (2003).

66 *See* Robert A. Williams, *Colombus's Legacy: Law as an Instrument of Racial Discrimination Against Indigenous Peoples' Rights of Self-Determination*, 8 Ariz. J. Int'l & Comp. L. 51 (1991).

67 *See*, for example, H. Pratt & J.F. Green, A Permanent International Commission for Africa (1896) (United Nations Library, Archives).

68 Comité de Protection de défense des Indigènes, 13 Juin 1907 (United Nations Library, Archives).

> observances of engagements voluntarily entered into the advantages of both communities.[69]

This was recommended to the International Peace Conference but there was no follow-up, and usually the conquest of indigenous peoples' territories in North America, Asia and Africa were not regarded as falling under the category of the emerging laws of war. It was only during the 16th International Congress for Peace that specific mention of the obligation for States to apply minimum standards of warfare regarding "minor" populations was made.[70] However, whether on purpose (in order to disregard the minimum standards of the law of war) or as a *de facto* situation, in most of the situations there was usually no formal war situation as such between colonisers and indigenous peoples. Therefore, legally, in many cases, what was designated as acquisition of territory by conquest in reality did not meet the first criteria—the existence of a war. In this regard, the rules governing acquisition of territory in time of conquest were disregarded in relation to indigenous peoples.

The second discriminatory aspect of the application of the rules of conquest regarding indigenous peoples concerns the rules governing title to territory once a conquest is made. In most of the cases involving the seizure of indigenous territories, conquest alone was recognized as providing the conquered powers with full title to the indigenous territory. In his classification of the modes of acquisition of territory Oppenheim has rightly used the term "subjugation" in place of "conquest." Oppenheim's argument was that conquest, i.e. "the taking of possession of enemy territory through military force" is not sufficient to confer title to territory. The conquest should be followed by a formal act of annexation;[71] generally, these acts of formal annexation were not made in the case of conquest of indigenous territories. This non-respect of the rules governing conquest was pointed out during the 11th Peace Congress in 1902 by the Aborigines Protection Society in a document relating to punitive expeditions in Africa. The Aborigines Protection Society highlighted that colonial powers used punitive expeditions as ways to ensure the "effective occupation" of their colonies, as a means to show their authority over vast tracts of lands

---

69 International Congress on Subject Races, Subject Races Joint Committee, The Hague 8th and 9th August 1907 (United Nations Library, Archives).

70 Résolution du XVIème Congrès Universel de la Paix, Munich 9–14 Septembre 1914, at C.8. The resolution recognized the need to apply laws and customs of war to "minor" populations (United Nations Library, Archives).

71 Hersch Lauterpracht, Oppenheim's International Law 495–528 (7th ed. 1948).

that were part of their sphere of influence.[72] Such document proves that the rule of effective occupation of the conquered territory was not respected when dealing with indigenous populations. More recently, in the U.S. Supreme Court ruling of 1954 in the case of *Tee-Hit-Ton Indians*, Justice Reed stated: "the very presence of whites in North America had affected a conquest over all the continent's indigenous peoples."[73] The judges justified State territorial possession based on conquest even though the Tee-Hit-Ton Tlingits of Alaska had never raised arms against the colonisers, and the United States had never formally annexed their territories. These cases are only examples of a widespread practice in situations of conquest of indigenous peoples' territories. Thus, despite the rather clear rules of international law that conquest would be recognised if the conquering power would have effective control of the territory, in the case of indigenous peoples, these rules were not considered relevant.

Third, in a time of conquest it has been recognized that the victorious party has to respect the doctrine of "acquired rights." The significance of this doctrine is that a change of sovereignty over a territory does not affect the acquired property rights of the inhabitants.[74] As noted by the U.S. Supreme Court in the 1833 case of *United States v. Percheman*, when there is a change of sovereignty: "the people change their allegiance; their relation to their ancient sovereign is dissolved; but their relations to each other, and their right to property, remain undisturbed."[75] The rule is that mere change in sovereignty, i.e. conquest, does not affect property rights.[76] Under British colonial laws, when a conquest was made, there were two approaches to the effect of the acquisition of territory on the customary land rights of the inhabitants. The first approach was based on the doctrine of continuity, which favoured the continuation of pre-existing customary land rights, the idea being that conquest did not adversely affect these rights unless there is an express legislative intent to do so.[77] The second approach was based on the doctrine of recognition. This doctrine affirmed

72 H.R. Fox Bourne, *Expéditions de Représailles en Afrique* (Onzième Congrès universel de la Paix, Monaco, Avril 1902) (United Nations Library, Archives).

73 Tee-Hit-Ton Indians v. United States 348 U.S. 272 (1955).

74 *See* L. Benjamin Ederington, *Property as a Natural Institution: The Separation of Property from Sovereignty in International Law*, 13 Am. U. Int'l L. Rev. 263 (1997).

75 United States v. Percheman, 32 U.S. (7 Pet.) 51, 87 (1833); *see also* Certain Questions Relating to Settlers of German Origin in the Territory Ceded by Germany to Poland, 1923 P.C.I.J. (ser. B) No. 6 (Sept. 10).

76 Relating to indigenous peoples, the difficulty is that, in many cases of conquest, there was no transfer of sovereignty as the indigenous' nations were not legally regarded as sovereign. This point is discussed under the notion of extinguishments in Chapter 2.

77 This approach gave rise to the notion of native/aboriginal title; *see* Chapter 2.

that rights to land had to be given a formal recognition by the new power, as annexation resulted in the abolition of all pre-existing rights.[78] In the case of indigenous peoples, neither the doctrine of continuity nor the doctrine of recognition was applied. For example, in South Africa, when the British acquired sovereignty over the Cape colony, they affirmed, in the *Articles of Capitulation*, the protection of the rights of all "burghers and inhabitants" of the Cape. However, such rights were extended only to rights that existed under "civilised" laws, and in this regard only properties held under Roman-Dutch law were recognised.[79] In the *Southern Rhodesia* case of 1919, the Judicial Committee of the Privy Council had to deal with a case concerning the opposing territorial rights of the British South Africa Company and the Crown. The central issue was to determine whether the conquest of native territory by a British chartered company made on the behalf of the Crown gave rights of ownership to that company. The Committee decided that an explicit proclamation was not necessary. Even though this case involved a dispute between a charter company and the Crown, the Committee heard counsel for the natives as the judges explored the impact of the British conquest on indigenous rights of ownership. The counsel of the natives argued that their right to lands had survived conquest. The judges recognised that the concerned indigenous peoples were the natural owners of all the lands that had neither been ceded nor officially claimed through legislation. The judges stated:

> It seems to be common ground that the ownership of the lands was 'tribal' or 'communal,' but what precisely that means remains to be ascertained. In any case it was necessary that the argument should go to the length of showing that the rights, whatever they exactly were, belonged to the category of rights of private property, such that upon conquest it is to be presumed, in the absence of express confiscation or of subsequent expropriatory legislation, that the conqueror has respected them and forborne to diminish or modify them.[80]

The view of the Judicial Committee of the Privy Council was that indigenous inhabitants had a full right of ownership prior to the conquest of their territory by the company acting on behalf of the Crown. With conquest this right

78 *See*, for example, Vajesingji Joravarsingji v. Secretary of State for India, 51 Ind. App. 357 (1924).

79 *See* Özlem Ülgen, *Developing the Doctrine of Aboriginal Title in South Africa: Source and Content*, 46(2) J. Afr. L. 137 (2002).

80 *In re* Southern Rhodesia, [1919] A.C. 211—Privy Council.

became a private right of ownership that the Crown could alienate at any time by legislation. Thus, even though the Privy Council held that property rights would survive conquest in the absence of express confiscation, the rule was not applicable to the native population. By conquest "the aboriginal system gave place to another prescribed by the Order in Council," as "the maintenance of their rights was fatally inconsistent with white settlement of the country, and yet white settlement was the object of the whole forward movement." Therefore, the Committee concluded that "[W]hoever now owns the unalienated lands, the natives do not."[81] Conquest gave the Crown full title to territory of the land, when the Crown became the conquering power with a right to establish a "land system of white settlement and of native reserves," the Crown having "the right to dispose of the whole of the land."[82] Thus, in this case, the Privy Council clearly applied a double standard regarding the effect of conquest on "acquired rights," as it was held that the British Company was entitled to reimbursement, whereas the indigenous peoples did not get their rights recognized. This was justified by recourse to the notion of "civilization."

A decision of the British-American Claims Tribunal in the case of *George Rodney Burt* also highlighted this dichotomy between the rights of property that are preserved in the case of conquest of so-called "civilised" peoples and not respected for so-called "savages." In this case, George Burt, an American citizen, had bought a piece of land from the native chiefs of the Fiji Islands before Britain's annexation of Fiji. The Tribunal stated that Britain had to respect Burt's property rights even though the islands were acquired by Britain on the grounds of *terra nullius* territory.[83] Thus, an American citizen had a right to property on an island that was acquired under the legal theory of *terra nullius*, but indigenous communities who lived there and had sold a piece of land to the American citizen had no right of ownership. This decision shows one of the most paradoxical consequences of the distinction between the impact of conquest on indigenous peoples and non-indigenous proprietary rights. As in the case of indigenous peoples, an exception to the rules of international law was made, as the acquired rights of property of indigenous peoples has never been respected.

Although the purpose here is not to rewrite history when considering the so-called conquest of indigenous territories, two important points have to be made. First, it is crucial to highlight the abuse and misuse of the term conquest

81 *Id.*

82 *Id.*

83 George Rodney Burt v. Great Britain, *in* Report on American and British Claims Arbitration 588–98 (F.K. Nielsen ed., 1926).

when referring to indigenous colonisation; indeed the use of the term "conquest" does not reflect the reality of the massacre of indigenous populations. As recently pointed out by Epstein, the misused term "conquest" to describe the "wholesale killing of entire populations, men, women, and children—is absurd and pernicious, lending a legitimacy to a holocaust."[84] While conquest is no longer regarded as a valid mode of acquisition, it is still used as a legal justification for proving the territorial possession of indigenous territories. As stated above, the US courts have often made reference to the historical rights of conquest to deny indigenous peoples' present day claims. It is also worth bearing in mind that across the globe, several indigenous communities are under serious military pressure,[85] and even though such internal conflicts are not formulated as "wars of conquest," the aims and the results are quite similar to the wars of colonial conquest, since the aim often remains a bid for control of indigenous territories. In the end, it is military control of indigenous territories that would provide the title to occupy their lands; therefore it is still vital to highlight that such acquisitions of territory do not fit within the legal framework of the right of conquest. The second important point relates to the discriminatory approach towards indigenous peoples. As highlighted above, in many cases the rules regarding conquest have not been applied in the case of conquest of indigenous territory. Therefore, there is an issue of discrimination in the application of the rules of international law. Such abuse can be a matter of contemporary litigation. For example, in March 2003, the Supreme Court of Appeal of South Africa looked at the rules governing conquest to decide in favour of indigenous peoples' right of land ownership.[86] These contemporary forms of litigation are just starting, and indigenous peoples should be invited to push for litigation relating to the discriminatory application of the rules of conquest. In terms of indigenous land rights, it is important to understand that this theory of conquest encompasses the recognition of a certain degree of

---

84 Robert J. Epstein, *The Role of Extinguishment in the Cosmology of Dispossession, in* Justice Pending: Indigenous Peoples and Other Good Causes, Essays in Honour of Erica-Irene A. Daes (Gudmundur Alfredsson & Maria Stavropoulou eds., 2002).

85 In 1993, Nietschmann found out that of the 122 armed conflicts recorded on the planet, 97 involved conflict between states and indigenous peoples. *See* Bernard Nietschmann, *The Fourth World: Nations Versus States, in* Reordering the World: Geopolitical Perspectives on the Twenty-First Century 237 (G.J. Demko & W. Wood eds., 1994). Since 1945, 20 million indigenous peoples had been turned in refugees, 73.5 millions had been killed.

86 The Ritchersveld Community and Others and Alexkor Limited and the Government of South Africa, Case No. 488/2001 (Mar. 24, 2003)—Supreme Court of Appeal of South Africa; this case is discussed in length in Chapter 3.

indigenous right of possession, especially through the doctrine of continuity, a rule that has been gradually recognized by several national courts.[87]

B The Occupation of Indigenous Territories

At the end of the 18th and early 19th centuries, a new phase in the evolution of international law began—witnessing the rejection of the existence of indigenous territorial rights. This view was based on the idea that indigenous peoples did not legally exist; thus they did not have any right to territorial ownership. Different geo-political, historical, sociological or ethnological factors could explain this evolution.[88] Legally this change of approach is visible through the development of the doctrine of *terra nullius* and through the evolution of the rules of territorial acquisition with the requirement of "effective occupation." Another factor in the evolution of the norms regarding acquisition and possession of territory was the commencement of a vast movement of decolonisation, especially in the Americas. During this first wave of decolonisation the new emerging States reclaimed territory against the former colonial powers. Hence, there was suddenly a need to redefine the rules of territorial possession for those new States within the framework of international law created by the colonisers. The transfer of territory between ex-imperial European colonisers and newly independent States transpired without reference to indigenous peoples who had been ignored during the process. Throughout the decolonisation process, the aim that was ascribed to international law was "the preservation of order," meaning the stabilization of the boundaries defined by the imperial colonisers under the power of the new States. This is manifest through the reference to the rule of *uti possidetis*, which allowed States to neglect the decolonisation of indigenous territories. Thus, one can argue that whereas early international law was aimed at providing the colonisers with a legacy for their conquest, modern international law aimed at justifying the stability of these conquests for either the colonisers or their descendant States.

This is evident through the evolution of three doctrines, the development of which are clearly interlinked: the *terra nullius* doctrine, the requirement of "effective occupation" and the *uti possidetis* doctrine. These norms implied the rejection of indigenous peoples' territorial rights by denying the legal existence of indigenous claims over their territories. These three norms implicitly

87 *Id*, at 52–62; *see* discussion in Chapter 2.

88 *See* Michel Morin, L'Ursupation de la Souveraintè Autochtone (1997).

resulted in the spoliation of indigenous peoples' territories based on the idea that indigenous peoples did not exist, and thus their territories were open to occupation. Under international law, occupation is "the act of appropriation by a state by which it intentionally acquires sovereignty over such territory as is at the time not under the sovereignty of another state."[89] As Jennings and Watts added: "[T]he only territory which can be the object of occupation is that which does not already belong to any state, whether it is uninhabited, or inhabited by persons whose community is not considered to be a state."[90] In this sense, the doctrines of *terra nullius*, effective occupation and *uti possidetis* all related to the occupation of indigenous territories under the legal fiction that indigenous peoples were either unable or not "civilised" enough to occupy their lands, while States could. Before exploring the doctrines that allowed the occupation of indigenous peoples' territories, the subsequent discussion will venture into the legal theories and sources that led to the total ignorance of indigenous peoples' occupancy of their lands. Then, based on such analysis, it will examine in detail the doctrine of *terra nullius* and the theory of effective occupation.

1 *The Post-Westphalian Order: Dichotomy between Nations and Indigenous Communities*

With the Treaty of Westphalia of 1648 a new historical period began: as well as ending the Thirty Years War, it also put an end to the Roman Catholic Church political hegemony and marked the emergence of the modern system of States in Europe.[91] The Treaty of Westphalia also had a crucial and revolutionary impact on the evolution of the rules governing territorial sovereignty. Following the Treaty of Westphalia, the issue of sovereignty became the pivotal idea of international law.[92] It is generally accepted that the Treaty of Westphalia articulated the turning point of a new order, as sovereign territorial States replaced the feudal order. This revolution had a deep impact on theories of title to territory and on indigenous peoples' territorial right, as after Westphalia a body of law was set up with only one subject: the "nation-state."

89 Robert Jennings & Arthur Watts, Oppenheim's International Law 686 (9th ed. 1996) [hereinafter Jennings & Watts].

90 *Id.*, at 687.

91 On this issue, *see* Adam Watson, The Evolution of International Society; A Comparative, Historical Analysis (1992).

92 Peter Fitzpatrick, *Terminal Legality: Imperialism and the (De)composition of Law, in* Law, History, Colonialism, The Reach of Empire (D. Kirkby & C. Coleborne eds., 2001) [hereinafter Fitzpatrick].

With regard to indigenous peoples' relationship with "European sovereign States," one of the most influential theorists of those new rules was Emmerich de Vattel (1714–1769). One of the legacies of Vattel's theory is to be found in the rules governing territorial sovereignty. Vattel affirmed that States, like individuals, have natural rights and obligations flowing from natural law. In addition to natural law, States have some positive obligations that are to be found in the law of treaties and customs. Vattel's theory is noteworthy for its contribution to the doctrine of State territorial sovereignty, each "nation-state" having exclusive jurisdiction over its territory. For example, in *The Law of Nations* Vattel wrote:

> When a Nation takes possession of a country which belongs to no-one, it is considered as acquiring sovereignty over it as well as ownership; for, being free and independent, it cannot intend, when it settles a territory, to leave to others the right to rule it, nor any other right which belongs to sovereignty.[93]

In his theory of nation-state territorial sovereignty, Vattel touched on the problem of the place of indigenous communities within the Law of Nations. The fundamental question in this discourse is to assess whether indigenous communities can be considered "nation-states" or whether they were to be considered as inhabitants of the "country which belongs to no-one." This issue is fundamental, as only "nation-states" were entitled to territorial ownership. It is worth noting that several indigenous communities defined themselves as nations, especially some of the tribes in North America who referred to themselves as "nation."[94]

Vattel defined nation-states broadly as "political bodies, societies of men who have united together and combined their forces, in order to procure their mutual welfare and security."[95] Vattel's central argument was the link between territory and nation-state; a nation can only become a State when attached to a specific territory in which such a nation exercises its exclusive sovereignty, the notion of territorial occupation being an essential element of sovereignty. In this sense, by referring to the nation-state's territorial sovereignty, Vattel followed the legacy of Grotius and reaffirmed the modern territorial-based

93 Emmerich De Vattel, The Law of Nations 84 (1758 *translated* 1916) [hereinafter Vattel].

94 For an informed discussion on the terms "Nation," "Tribe" and "State," *see* Thomas M. Franck, *Clan and Superclan: Loyalty, Identity and Community in Law and Practice*, 90 Am. J. Int'l L. 359 (1996).

95 Vattel, *supra* note 93.

system of international law. Relating to the territorial organisation of a nation, Vattel wrote: "[T]he territory in which a Nation inhabits, whether the Nation moved into it as a body, or whether the families scattered over the territory came together to form a civil society, forms a national settlement, to which the Nation has a private and exclusive right."[96] Thus, *a priori*, indigenous nations were not rejected from such a system of nation-states' territorial sovereignty. However, even though Vattel left a space for indigenous political and social organizations to be recognised as "nation-states," the door was nearly closed by the distinction he made between sedentary and hunter-gatherer societies. He affirmed that non-agricultural societies "can not populate the whole country" as their occupancy cannot be "a real and lawful taking of possession." Therefore it was entirely lawful to occupy such a country.[97] Relating to the colonisation of North America, Vattel wrote that Indian nations:

> cannot appropriate to themselves more land than they have occasion for, or more than they are able to settle and cultivate. Their unsettled habitation in those immense regions cannot be accounted a true and legal possession; and the people of Europe, too closely pent up at home ... were lawfully entitled to take possession of it, and settle it with colonies. The earth ... belongs to mankind in general, and was destined to furnish them with subsistence: If each nation had ... resolved to appropriate to itself a vast country, that the people might live only by hunting, fishing, and wild fruits, our globe would not be sufficient to maintain a tenth part of its present inhabitants.[98]

Vattel affirmed that the European nations did not have a right to steal lands that were owned by the Indians under the claim that they were civilising them. Conversely, he also affirmed that natural law obliged the Indians to adopt agriculture. Thus, even though Vattel did not legally justify colonisation, arguments supporting some of the rules utilised in the territorial conquest of indigenous territories are evident in his theory. In fact, Vattel's theory of sovereignty sowed the seeds of a system, the "Laws of Nations," which fundamentally rejected the territorial sovereignty of nations that were not organised on a European model of settled agriculture.[99]

---

96 *Id.*

97 Emmerich de Vattel, *quoted in* Fitzpatrick, *supra* note 92, at 14.

98 Vattel, *supra* note 93, at 100.

99 For example, in analysing Vattel's theory of territorial sovereignty, Anaya pointed out that "[A]lthough he did not hold expressly that a society based on sedentary pursuits was

Vattel's idea of the superiority of settled agricultural societies was a reflection of the general literature of this period.[100] From Locke to Hegel, several major authors have argued for what can be described as the "agricultural argument."[101] The general idea was that only agriculture could be regarded as a basis of a real land tenure system, the central argument being that because the indigenous did not improve the soil by cultivating it, "they did not assert exclusivity; therefore, (…) their rights were so negligibly thin as to disintegrate automatically wherever the European invader set literal or constructive foot."[102] The father of the "agricultural argument" is often recognised to be Locke. In his *Essay Concerning the True Original, Extent, and End of Civil-Government*, Locke expressed the idea that uncultivated land was not possessed closely enough to constitute property. Locke recognised that the "Indians" had some usufructuary rights over their hunting products, but that they are "commonly without any fixed property in the ground."[103] Thus, territories used by hunters and gatherers or non-sedentary agriculturists were to be regarded as vacant. The Lockean argument that rights in land arose only from appropriation and improvement of the land by agriculture was accepted widely. For example, Rousseau in his *Discours sur l'origine de l'inégalité* explained the origin of private property by using the model of the development of agriculture.[104]

These theories of the 18th century fostered the idea that ownership of the land could only be based on the definite occupancy of such land, and that agriculture was the only means to define the terms of occupation. The agricultural argument had a crucial impact on indigenous rights within the Law of Nations. First, it justified the colonisation of non-agricultural lands, and, secondly it

a prerequisite for statehood, he did accept the view that cultivating land established a greater right to the land than did hunting or gathering." James Anaya, Indigenous Peoples in International Law 23 (2d ed. 2004) [hereinafter Anaya].

100 One of the only exceptions being Christian Wolff. *See* Christian Wolff, Jus Gentium Methodo Scientifica Pertractum (Translation 1934), as Wolff held that single families and nomadic tribes had a right to the land they inhabited.

101 Thomas Flanagan, *The Agricultural Argument and Original Appropriation: Indian Lands and Political Philosophy*, 22 Can. J. Pol. Sci. 589 (1989).

102 David G. Bell, *Was Amerindian Dispossession Lawful? The Response of 19th Century Maritime Intellectuals*, 23 Dalhousie L.J. 168 (2000).

103 *See* James Tully, Strange Multiplicity: Constitutionalism in an Age of Diversity 72 (1995) [hereinafter Tully].

104 Jean-Jacques. Rousseau, Discours sur l'origine de l'inégalité (1963); *see also* Jean-Jacques. Rousseau, Du Contrat Social (1762): "to authorize a right to first occupation, you have to take possession not through formal ceremony, but through work and cultivation."

carried the idea that a community cannot be considered as sovereign if such a community is not composed of settled inhabitants with a "proper" land tenure system. The agricultural argument implied that sovereign nation-states can only be defined on the basis of a definite territory, a requirement that rejects all other systems, not only nomadic, but is also based on kinship or systems of ownership of land not based on the notion of defined boundaries in the European sense. After Westphalia most Western theorists of international law affirmed that the only valid territorial rights were those organized within the boundary of a modern political organised society—in other words, a State.[105] The notion statehood rapidly developed, based on the framework of the European model of political and social organization; such a model was thus difficult to transpose outside the boundaries of Europe. As Anaya pointed out: "indigenous peoples of the Western Hemisphere and elsewhere, at least prior to European contact, typically have been organized primarily by tribal or kinship ties, have had a decentralized political structure often linked in confederations, and have enjoyed shared or overlapping spheres of territorial control."[106]

One of the attributes of the "nation-state" was that only the government of the State exercised the territorial ownership of land.[107] Therefore, with the emergence of a new international order based on the Laws of Nations, a system was born "that distinguished between only two types of entities that could hold rights—sovereign states and individuals—each with a different set of natural rights."[108] Within this new order, based on the idea of territorial sovereignty of "nations-states" only, the place of indigenous communities was to be defined. To be recognised as a group entitled to collective ownership of a territory meant being recognised as a "sovereign nation-state." At this stage, the central feature, which would have profound impact on indigenous rights of ownership, was framed with the establishment of a distinction between the two sets of rights: the individual right to property, and the States' right to territory. Legally, the impact of such distinction is that whereas territorial sovereignty, which concerns the issue of jurisdiction over a specific area of territory, is an issue of international law, "title to land is a matter of proprietary

105 Norbert Rouland, Stéphane Pierré-Caps & Jacques Poumarède, Droit des minorités et des Peuples Autochtones 362 (1996).

106 Anaya, *supra* note 99, at 22.

107 On this issue, *see* Tully, *supra* note 103, at 78.

108 Catherine J. Iorns Magallanes, *International Human Rights and their Impact on Domestic Law on Indigenous Peoples' Rights in Australia, Canada, and New Zealand, in* Indigenous Peoples' Rights in Australia, Canada and New Zealand 236 (Paul Havemann ed., 1999).

rights, which depend for the most part on the municipal law of property."[109] This distinction between the individual property rights and State territorial rights created a disparity in which the indigenous notion of territorial collective ownership was lost, as it fell between those two sets of rights.[110] At this point, the doctrine of international law closed the door on the existence of an indigenous notion of communal land ownership. Accordingly, two predominant notions, stemming from the early theorists of the 18th and 19th centuries, had a deep impact on indigenous land rights, the idea of the superiority of settled agricultural societies and the idea that only "nation-states" have a right of territorial sovereignty, which includes the sacrosanct individual right to property.[111] These notions dominated the evolution of international law during an epoch that witnessed the colonisation of most of the indigenous territories. One of the major consequences of this approach, based on the superiority of the European "agricultural" system, was the reference to the doctrine of *terra nullius*. In addition to affirming the superiority of the colonisers over indigenous inhabitants of colonized territories, *terra nullius* simply denied their existence.

2 *Occupation of "Vacant" Territories:* Terra Nullius *as a Legal Fiction*

The doctrine of *terra nullius* comes from Roman law and has evolved across the centuries to become part of the modern theory of international law. Theoretically, when applied to the acquisition of territory, *terra nullius* refers to territory that is not subject to any sovereignty "either because it has never been so subject, or, having once been in that condition, has been abandoned."[112] Originally, the Latin sense of the principle referred to "empty territory." However, this notion of empty territory has been used in a political manner. The doctrine evolved with the increased competition between the colonial powers. At this stage, *terra nullius* territories were all the territories with no form of "civilised" and recognisable government. The colonial powers did not recognise the territorial sovereignty of indigenous communities, as territorial rights were deemed valid only within a state-run organization. This application of *terra nullius* was not based on the idea that the territory was uninhabited but

109 Kent McNeil, Common Law Aboriginal Title 108 (1989); on this issue, *see* Hugo Grotius, DeJure Belli 206–07 (Francis W. Kelsey trans., 1925); Emmerich de Vattel, Droit des Gens, ou les principles de la loi naturelle, Livre 1, Ch. 18 (1983).

110 This point is discussed later in Chapter 3.

111 *See* Crawford B. Macpherson, The Political Theory of Possessive Individualism: Hobbes to Locke (1962).

112 Lindley, *supra* note 29, at 10.

on the idea that indigenous societies could not exercise proper territorial sovereignty, as only States organised in the form of a civil government could do so.

The influential jurist Oppenheim, in his treatises, pointed out that only the members of the "Family of Nations" could access statehood, and that the Law of Nations only applies to those members that he defined as being "old Christian States of Western Europe" and "the body of Christian States which grew up outside Europe."[113] Since only States were able to recognise another State as a member of the "family," it was certain that international law would not apply to indigenous communities. Oppenheim added that "occupation can only take place by and for a State; it must be a State act, that is, it must be performed in the service of a State, or it must be acknowledged by a State after its performance."[114] As Martens, another influential jurist put it: "one can only occupy lands that do not belong to anyone or are inhabited by barbarous tribes."[115] From this perspective, *terra nullius* did not mean that a territory should be empty but that a territory should not be under the control of one of the so-called "civilised" States. Thus, the colonial powers themselves decided whether a territory was to be regarded as legally empty or not. This principle implied a total disregard for the concerned peoples.

Applied in this context the principle of *terra nullius* meant that any territory that was not under the jurisdiction of a State, in the sense defined by the actors of international law, was an empty territory. Therefore, at the time of the European colonisation, most of the world was "legally" empty and free for conquest and occupation; legally the "new world" was "vacant." In this sense, the concept of *terra nullius* was based on a fiction created by the colonial powers, enabling them to ignore indigenous peoples' territorial rights and to acquire territory by simple occupation. This judicial fiction was used all over the world by the European imperial colonisers at different stages of the history of colonisation. For example, the Berlin Conference, which systematised the "Scramble for Africa"[116] between the European powers in 1884–1885, was clearly based on the assumption that most of Africa was *terra nullius*.[117] The *terra nullius* doctrine has been used throughout the history of colonisation, and became

113 The only exceptions to the "non-Christians states," were Turkey and Japan. *See* Lassa Francis Oppenheim, International Law (3d ed. 1920).

114 Lassa Francis Oppenheim, International Law: A Treatise 507 (6th ed. 1947).

115 "On ne peut occuper que des terres n'appartenant à personne et habitées par des tribus barbares" (my own translation). Frederic de Martens, Traite de droit international 464 (1886).

116 Thomas Pakenham, The Scramble for Africa (1992).

117 Jörg Fisch, *Africa as Terra Nullius: The Berlin Conference and International Law, in* Bismarck, Europe, and Africa 347–75 (Stig Förster et al. eds., 1988).

more and more refined as it was driven by the genuine belief in "civilisation," all the "non-civilised" lands being *terra nullius*. Even though, the fundamental spirit of this doctrine has always been to afford the European imperial powers immunity from the rules of acquisition by occupation or conquest without a just cause, the doctrine has evolved in its phrasing. This "maturing" of the doctrine of *terra nullius*, depending on the geopolitical situation, shows how this judicial concept could be manipulated depending on the political wishes of the colonial States.[118]

It is specifically in the context of the transfer of territories during the decolonisation process that international law was invited to reflect on the legitimacy of the *terra nullius* doctrine. One of the first contemporary international cases that had to explicitly deal with the issue of *terra nullius* is the case of the *Western Sahara* in 1975.[119] In this case, the International Court of Justice (ICJ) was notably asked to give an advisory opinion on the issue of determining whether the Western Sahara (Rio de Oro and Sakiet El Hamra) was *terra nullius* at the time of its colonisation by Spain. In its ruling, the ICJ highlighted that, at the time of its colonisation, the Western Sahara was inhabited by nomadic peoples with a specific political and social system of tribes with competent chiefs to represent them, and therefore could not been regarded as a *terra nullius*. This advisory opinion represented one of the first instances where international law recognised that because indigenous political and social organisations have had "legal ties" with colonial States, a territory could not be regarded as *terra nullius*. One of the key factors in this opinion was that Spain had concluded treaties with the local chiefs, so in the view of the Court, Spain did not see the Western Sahara as *terra nullius*.[120] However, even though the ICJ acknowledged the existence of "legal ties" between indigenous communities and the colonial rulers, the issue was to define which of the two claiming States owned this territory. The ICJ adopted the position that only States were of concern when the issue of territorial sovereignty arose; as for the Court the political ties that existed between the nomadic tribes and other powers in the region were to be regarded as proof of allegiance to the colonial State.[121] The ICJ implicitly maintained the traditional view that only States can exert territorial sovereignty,

118 For an overview of the historical application of the doctrine, *see* Mohammed Bedjaoui, *Terra Nullius, 'droits' historiques et autodétermination* (exposés oraux prononcés devanr la Cour Internationale de Justice en l'affaire du Sahara Occidental, La Haye, 1975).

119 Western Sahara (Request for Advisory Opinion), 1975 I.C.J. 12 (Oct. 16).

120 *See also* the Separate Opinion of Judge Ammoun who referred to Victoria's theory to reject the concept of *res nullius*, *id.*, at 6 (paras. 86–87).

121 *Id.*, at 43–44.

not local nomadic, political and social organisations. As noted by Starke, this advisory opinion supported the view that "legal ties of territorial sovereignty over peoples or land must be distinguished from ties of allegiance, in the case of persons, and mere customary rights in relation to land."[122] Clearly, despite the revolutionary acknowledgment from the Court that a territory inhabited by tribes, which have a social and political organisation, cannot be, by nature, considered *terra nullius;* only State activities over a defined territory could give rise to the recognition of territorial sovereignty.[123]

The ICJ only addressed the issue of defining whether indigenous peoples' nomadic organisation could constitute a political organization. Thus, the Court did not deal with the legacy of the *terra nullius* principle itself, as it would take more than 20 years before a ruling finally acknowledged that the *terra nullius* doctrine was a "racist" fiction. That did not occur at the international level, but in a significant national context with respect to *terra nullius*. One of the most striking applications of the *terra nullius* doctrine took place in Australia. When the British arrived in 1788, the colonisers took possession of the country based on the fictitious legacy that the country was uninhabited. This is reflected by the decision of 1836 of the Supreme Court of New South Wales in the case of *R. v. Murell,* in which Justice Burton stated that: "although it might be granted that on first taking possession of the Colony, the Aborigines were entitled to be recognised as free and independent, yet they were not in such a position with regard to strength to be considered free and independent tribes. They had no sovereignty."[124] Similarly, the Privy Council in 1889 in the case of *Cooper v. Stuart* reaffirmed that at the time of colonisation of the country, "there was only one sovereign, namely the King of England, and only one law, namely English law."[125] This non-recognition of any existing form of human organisation in the country allowed the English Crown to take ownership of all the lands. Hence, Australia offers a significant historical example of indigenous peoples' lands being acquired by the application of "an enlarged *terra nullius* doctrine" in the sense that no treaty or any other act was undertaken.[126] The only justification for British, and subsequently, Australian ownership was based on the idea that

122 Joseph Gabriel Starke, Introduction to International Law 183 (1977).

123 On this issue, *see* Michael Reisman, *Protecting Indigenous Rights in International Adjudication,* 89(2) Am. J. Int'l L. 354–55 (1995).

124 R. v. Murrell and Bummaree, Forbes C.J., Feb. 5, 1836—Supreme Court of New South Wales; *see also* 1976 N.S.W.L.R. 581.

125 Cooper v. Stuart, (1889) 14 App. Cas. 286—Privy Council.

126 Siegfried Wiessner, *Rights and Status of Indigenous Peoples: A Global Comparative and International Legal Analysis,* 12 Harv. Hum. Rts. J. 57 (1999).

the original inhabitants of the country did not legally exist. Therefore, the rejection of the doctrine of *terra nullius* by the Australian High Court in 1992 in the *Mabo* case was a significant development, not only within the boundaries of Australia, but in terms of international law as, in a sense, it saw "the fall of the ultimate fortress." In this judgment, largely based on comparative and international law, Justice Brennan stated:

> the fiction by which the rights and interests of indigenous inhabitants in land were treated as non-existent was justified by a policy which has no place in the contemporary law of this country. (…) Whatever the justification advanced in earlier days for refusing to recognise the rights and interests in land of the indigenous inhabitants of settled colonies, an unjust and discriminatory doctrine of that kind can no longer be accepted.[127]

The majority of the judges also rejected the proposition that after the occupation of the territory, the Crown gained absolute ownership of the land. Consequently, the Australian High Court recognised that the indigenous population had a pre-existing system of law, which, unless specifically modified or extinguished, would have to be recognised.[128] In its reasoning, the Court relied heavily on international law and specifically the prohibition of racial discrimination contained in the International Convention on the Elimination of All Forms of Racial Discrimination. Australia ratified the Convention in 1975 and incorporated it into Australian law, enacting the Racial Discrimination Act 1975 (Cth) (RDA). In many ways, this overturning of the *terra nullius* doctrine was influenced by international contemporary human rights standards on non-discrimination.

Overall, contemporary international law has addressed the legacy of the *terra nullius* doctrine through two angles. The first angle was to recognise that indigenous peoples' political organisations may have had sufficient "legal ties" with other powers not to be considered as *terra nullius* (without entering the debate whether indigenous communities should be regarded as exercising territorial sovereignty). The second angle is based on a non-discriminatory approach and affirms that the concept itself is a "discriminatory fiction" and should not be regarded as a contemporary rule of international law. However, the legacy of territorial acquisition based on the non-existence of indigenous peoples has taken other forms, as the rules of "effective occupation" and *uti possidetis* also amount to similar denials of indigenous peoples' capacity to

127 Mabo v. Queensland [No. 2] (1992) 175 C.L.R. 1, 107 A.L.R.—High Court of Australia.

128 This aspect is discussed in Chapter 2.

possess territory. In this regard, these contemporary forms of denial are a continuation of *terra nullius,* or *terra nullius* by other means.

3 Terra Nullius *by Other Means: Contemporary Forms of Denial*

The *terra nullius* doctrine was significantly enhanced with the development of colonisation. There was a need to redefine the doctrine because of the increased competition between the colonial powers in Africa and Asia, and because of the emergence of new actors, namely the new States arising from the first wave of independence, specifically the new States of North and South America. As pointed out by Castellino and Allen: "in seeking to declare that all Latin American territories were considered occupied territory the Creoles made some salient points that directly challenged and undermined the international perception of *terra nullius*."[129] The Creole emancipation has to be seen as the first denial of *terra nullius*. Suddenly, new identities claimed that "no part of their territory however unexplored it might be, would be allowed to be open to European annexation or acquisition."[130] Clearly, at this stage, international law accepted the idea that even though the new South American States did not "effectively control" their national territories, their territories could no longer be considered as *terra nullius*. In this regard, the new South American States gained their recognition as territorially defined States to the detriment of the indigenous communities' territorial entitlements. This has to be read in conjunction with the Monroe Doctrine of 1823, in which the U.S. President stated that "[T]he American continents ... are henceforth not to be considered as subjects to future colonisation by any European powers."[131]

During this period, there was a territorial transfer between the "old" and "new" worlds. There was a need for the new world to ensure the transfer of title from the previous European colonisers. Therefore, it was officially declared that no lands were to be considered as *terra nullius* for the Europeans in the Americas. However, at this point, large parts of North America and Latin America were still regarded as open to conquest by the new independent States. The Creole emancipation and the independence of the United States were symptomatic of what would occur in the future—the rejection of a European right of colonisation coupled with a domestic right to acquire indigenous territories not yet under State control. This can be considered as a move to a domestic application of *terra nullius*—with external boundaries starting to

129 Castellino & Allen, *supra* note 5, at 64.

130 *Id.*, at 65.

131 President Monroe's Seventh Annual Message to Congress, Dec. 2, 1823, *in* Compilation of the Messages and Papers of the Presidents 287 (J.D. Richardson ed., 1907).

be fixed while internally conquest was still based on the idea that indigenous territories were *terra nullius* open to colonisation by the emerging States, even if the process was never identified in those terms. This process was also used during decolonisation in Africa and Asia. Indigenous peoples would not be considered in the succession between European colonisers and the new States that followed decolonisation in Africa and Asia, but would be subject of continuing, albeit newer colonisation. In this process, even though not specifically mentioned, the new States often regarded the territories owned by indigenous communities as empty territories or territories under no control, concepts that are close to the notion of *terra nullius*. Two rules of international law are at the heart of the denial of indigenous peoples' capacity to territorial ownership: the requirement of effective occupation and the doctrine of *uti possidetis*. It is through these rules that indigenous peoples were effectively ignored as potential holders of territorial rights.

The Positivist Requirement of "Effective Occupation"

Since the 18th century, the discovery of a territory had to be followed by the "effective occupation" of that territory.[132] With the emergence of new actors, as potential successors to the colonial powers, arose the need to reorganise international relations concerning the transfer or annexation of territories. The solution came in the reaffirmation of the rules regarding "effective occupation" of a territory. The meaning of "effective occupation" was defined through different international arbitrations and tribunals during the 1920s that had to deal with the issue of the competition between competing claims of ownership and possession over an area. The central principle developed by these tribunals was that the conqueror, after arriving in a "free" territory, must have organised its "effective" occupation. This could be done through a variety of different actions, such as the planting of a settlement, the building of a fort or any other act that could show that the conqueror State "can and does, control the territory claimed."[133] In this process, the role of international law was to evaluate the degree of occupation of the claimed territory. The rule of "effective occupation" involved organising generally accepted rules of colonisation between the powers. International law thus became the tool to resolve disputes between

132 On effective occupation, *see* Jennings & Watts, *supra* note 89, at 687–96.

133 James L. Brierly, The Law of Nations 164–65 (Humphrey Waldock ed., 6th ed., 1963). These requirements are not necessary when the territory claimed is uninhabited; in such cases the requirement of effective occupation is not necessary. *See* Clipperton Island Arbitration (Fr. v. Mex.) 2 R.I.A.A. 1105 (1931), *reprinted in* 26 Am. J. Int'l L. 390, 394 (Supp. 1932).

colonial imperial powers.[134] Only colonial States were concerned by this rule of effective occupation, as they were the only ones capable of such acts of occupation. As succinctly captured by Jennings: "Natives living under a tribal organization were not regarded as a State for this purpose, and though force, even considerable force, might be used for the establishment of the settlement, the result in law was not conquest but occupation."[135] Thus, at the heart of this principle of effective occupation was the suggestion that indigenous communities could not "effectively" own their lands because their systems of ownership were not "civilised" enough to enable them legal occupation of their homelands.[136] It is important to bear in mind that the end of the 19th century was deeply marked by the notion of guardianship.[137] For example, during the debates for the adoption of the Declaration of the Berlin Conference of 1885, the place of the indigenous communities was questioned, as some delegates suggested that native tribes should be taken into consideration. However, Articles 34 and 35 made clear that regarding the rules of effective occupation, the requirements were public notification of annexation (or protectorate) and exercise of sufficient authority, requirements that only colonial States could reach.[138]

Consequently, this notion of "effective occupation" as a necessary basis for title to territory had a deep impact on indigenous rights to territorial ownership. Under this rule, indigenous peoples were not capable of occupation. The case of the *Island of Palmas* of 1928,[139] which is today regarded as one of the decisions that founded contemporary international law on the subject, expresses the idea that indigenous socio-political organisations could not be part of the law of nations and therefore could not exercise "effective occupation" of a territory. In this case, the United States and the Netherlands were claiming sovereignty over the island. The United States, being the successor to Spain on the island, based its title on the Spanish discovery of the island. The Netherlands in contrast to, based its title on its effective occupation of the island. Huber, the international arbitrator, examined the treaties between the colonisers and the indigenous inhabitants for proof of "effective

134 However, later international law refer to indigenous peoples' traditional occupation under ILO Convention 169 72 ILO Official Bull. 59 (1989), *reprinted in* 28 I.L.M. (1989). This is analysed in Chapter 3.

135 Jennings & Watts, *supra* note 89, at 20.

136 On this issue, *see id.*

137 *See* Gordon Bennett, Aboriginal Rights in International Law (1978).

138 *See* James Crawford, The Creation of States in International Law (1979); Charles Henry Alexandrowicz, The European-African Confrontation (1973).

139 Island of Palmas (U.S. v. Neth.), 2 R.I.A.A. 831 (1928).

occupation" but "considered them only as 'facts' relevant to the Netherlands' assertion of sovereignty."[140] These treaties between indigenous representatives and the Netherlands proved only the "effective occupation" of the territory by the colonisers, not the "effective occupation" by the indigenous population, an issue that was not even addressed in this ruling. A few years later, the Permanent Court of International Justice (PCIJ) in the Eastern Greenland case between Denmark and Norway endorsed the same position.[141] In this case, to define the territorial sovereignty of this part of Greenland, the judges only explored the "effective occupancy" of Denmark and Norway. The fact that several indigenous Inuit communities inhabited the concerned territory was completely ignored by the Court. Thus, from the perspective of indigenous peoples, the positivist doctrine of effective occupation appears as a legal mechanism ensuring the consolidation of the colonisation of indigenous peoples' territories with a complete disregard to their existence on these lands.

More recently, the ruling of the ICJ in the *Territorial Dispute* case between Libya and Chad confirmed this position.[142] This 1994 case is based on a territorial dispute over the Aouzou strip, a tract of land supposedly full of uranium, inhabited by the Toubou, an indigenous community.[143] The Court found that neither Libya nor Chad had exercised effective occupation of the concerned land. However, the Court accepted the agreement made between the parties and concluded: "the effectiveness of occupation of the relevant areas in the past, and the question whether it was constant, peaceful and acknowledged, are not matters for determination in this case."[144] Despite being virtually the only inhabitants living in the concerned territory, the indigenous tribes were not regarded as potential occupiers of the land in dispute because only states can qualify as effective occupiers.[145]

Overall, these decisions reflected the idea that only so-called "civilised" States could "effectively" hold territory, and, therefore, only States were allowed to claim territorial sovereignty. Hence, only States with an established

---

140 *Id.*, at 856, 865.

141 Legal Status of Eastern Greenland (Den. v. Nor.), 1993 P.C.I.J. (ser A/B) No. 53.

142 Territorial Dispute (Libya v. Chad), 1994 I.C.J. 6 (Feb. 3), *reprinted in* 33 I.L.M. 571 (1994).

143 *See* Matthew M. Ricciardi, *Title to the Aouzou Strip: A Legal and Historical Analysis*, 17(2) Yale J. Int'l L. 301–488 (1992).

144 Territorial Dispute (Libya v. Chad), 1994 I.C.J. 6 (Feb. 3), *reprinted in* 33 I.L.M. 571 (1994).

145 In his comments on the case, Reisman stated "[W]hat is particularly striking in this case is that the Court virtually acknowledged that no one but the indigenous inhabitants had the degree of contextually relevant effective occupation that is required by international law." *See* Michael Reisman, *Protecting Indigenous Rights in International Adjudication*, 89 Am. J. Int'l L. 350 (1995).

government can claim effective occupation of a territory. In defining what effective control consists of, Lindley highlighted that the general agreement is to appreciate "whether there has been established over it [the territory] a sufficient governmental control to afford security to life and property there."[146] Likewise, Schwarzenberger pointed out that "effective possession manifests itself by the establishment of proper state machinery for purposes of defense and administration."[147] Therefore, this theory of "effective occupation" as proof of ownership of a territory was not applicable to indigenous peoples, but only applicable against them, as indigenous peoples were not regarded as being able to establish such "State machinery." Those views were reflected in the Covenant of the League of Nations in its "Native inhabitants clause." In this clause, the State parties obliged themselves "to secure the just treatment of the native inhabitants of territories under their control."[148] Indigenous peoples were only considered as peoples "under control"—the State being the only one that can effectively occupy a territory under the canon of the law of so-called "civilised" States. Behind the idea that indigenous communities could not "effectively" occupy their territory transpires the same legal fiction that was at the basis of *terra nullius*. Both are based on the discriminatory view that indigenous peoples are not adequately organised politically and socially to effectively occupy their own territories. Under the rule of effective occupation, indigenous territorial rights have been deliberately ignored on the same basis, i.e., that indigenous communities or nations are not "civilised" enough to occupy their lands and thus have no right of ownership. In this sense, the doctrine of "effective occupation" as applied to indigenous peoples is just one of the modern legal expressions of the doctrine of *terra nullius*. The only difference is that contrary to the *terra nullius* doctrine, which is now rightly regarded as a discriminatory theory when applied to territory occupied by indigenous peoples, there are no legal decisions that reject the discriminatory application of the rule of effective occupation. Even though the notion of "civilised" States has been disregarded, the notion of effective occupation remains a vestige of such a view.

Impact of *Uti Possidetis* on Indigenous Territorial Ownership

Post-1948, one of the pillars of the U.N. system was the creation of the Fourth Committee on Decolonisation. The movement of decolonisation that followed the Second World War was based on the ideal of democracy and civil

146 Lindley, *supra* note 29, at 141.

147 Georg Schwarzenberger, *Title to Territory: Response to a Challenge*, 51 Am. J. Int'l L. 316 (1957).

148 Covenant of the League of Nations, art. 23(a) (1920).

liberties for the colonised peoples.[149] During this era, the ideal that colonialism should be abolished and that people should be free to determine their destiny and have access and use of their lands and resources, formed part of the U.N. mandate.[150] Thus, from a theoretical perspective, the movement towards decolonisation contained the answer to the demand of indigenous peoples for recognition of their fundamental rights, and specifically the right to own their homelands.[151] However, as described by Reisman: "[D]espite the moral relevance of decolonisation to the situation of indigenous peoples, decolonisation rarely encompassed indigenous peoples. In the New World, decolonisation benefited mostly so-called Creole or local elites of European extraction."[152]

Politically, one of the main reasons remains the reference to the "Blue Water Thesis" or "Salt Water Thesis," which limited the application of the term "colony" to countries or peoples separated from their colonisers by miles of salt water.[153] Yet, one of the main legal explanations for this rejection of indigenous peoples' rights to territorial ownership during the decolonisation process is the extensive recourse to the notion of *uti possidetis*. As well as *terra nullius*, the doctrine of *uti possidetis* has its origin in Roman law. The phrasing comes from *uti possidetis, ita possideatis* meaning "as you possess, so may you possess." This edict was used in *jus civile* as a method of resolving litigation when two parties were claiming ownership to a real property.[154] International law recycled

149 *See* Myres S. McDougal, Harold D. Lasswell & Lung-Chu Chen, Human Rights and World Public Order (1980).

150 *See* U.N. Charter art. 1 and U.N. GAOR 1514(XV) (1960), which link the U.N. Charter with decolonisation.

151 A large number of indigenous communities entered the fight for decolonisation. *See*, for examples, the Nagas against India, the Karens in Myanmar, the so-called *Montagnards* of upland Vietnam, the Hmongs in Laos, the Miskito in Nicaragua, the Berbers in Western Sahara, etc.; on this issue, *see* Ted Robert Gurr, Minorities at Risk: A Global Survey of Ethnopolitical Conflicts (1993); *see also* War in the Tribal Zone: Expanding States and Indigenous Warfare (Brian Ferguson & Neil Lancelot Whitehead eds., 1992).

152 Michael Reisman. *Protecting Indigenous Rights in International Adjudication*, 89 Am. J. Int'l L. 350 (1995).

153 During the debates, Belgium tried to expand the scope of the obligations under Chapter XI of the U.N. Charter to include enclave indigenous populations. This was rejected, but was however reflected in the General Assembly Resolution 1541 in its Principles IV and V, which invite States to "transmit information in respect of a territory which is geographically separate and is distinct ethnically and/or culturally from the country administrating it." On this issue, *see* Government of Belgium, *The Belgian Thesis: The Sacred Mission of Civilazation, To Which Peoples Should the Benefit be Extended?* (1953). Belgium defended this thesis for the wrong reasons; *see* discussion on this issue in Chapter 5.

154 On the Roman origins of *uti possidetis, see* Castellino & Allen, *supra* note 5.

this edict of private law into a doctrine of territorial possession in the view of "preserving order." As stated by the ICJ in the *Frontier Dispute* case (*Burkina Faso v. Mali*):

> the essence of the principle lies in its primary aim of securing respect for the territorial boundaries at the moment when independence is achieved. Such territorial boundaries may be more than delimitation between different administrative divisions or colonies all subject to the same sovereign. In that case, the application of the principle of uti possidetis resulted in administrative boundaries being transformed into international frontiers in the full sense of the term.[155]

The first use of this doctrine in international law took place with the Creole emancipation in Latin America. With independence from Spain and Portugal came the issue of the drawing of the new countries' boundaries: were they to be based on the previous colonial administrative divisions or on the ethnic and social divisions that existed prior to colonisation? The new leadership adopted the view that the administrative lines created during colonisation were sacrosanct and should be preserved. This position had several consequences in the drawing of boundaries between the main provinces that were created on the basis of the Spanish and Portuguese occupations. One major consequence, which is often ignored, was that there was no express recognition of indigenous peoples' territorial entitlements, and that all the lands occupied by indigenous peoples were included within the boundaries of the new States. This is reflected in the *Gulf of Fonseca* case of the ICJ. In this case El Salvador drew the Chamber's attention to the potential conflict between claims based on Spanish documents and those of earlier "Indian" rights. The Chamber of the ICJ stated that: "[I]t was the administrative boundaries between the Spanish colonial administrative units, not the boundaries between the Indian settlement as such, that were transformed by the operation of the *uti possidetis juris*, into international boundaries in 1821."[156] Through this, the ICJ legally endorsed the political decision that was made by the Creole *élite* in rejecting indigenous ethnic territorial division in favour of the colonial administrative one.

The references to the doctrine of *uti possidetis* are not limited to Latin America; the drawing of boundaries during the decolonisation process was also a crucial issue in Africa and, to a lesser extent, in Asia. Even though before

155 Frontier Dispute (Burkina Faso v. Mali), 1986 I.C.J. 554, 586.

156 Land, Island and Maritime Frontier Dispute (El Salvador/Honduras: Nicaragua intervening), Judgment of Sept. 11, 1992, 1992 I.C.J. paras. 95–96.

the arrival of the Europeans colonisers the social and ethnic structures had some territorial basis across the African continent, there was no concept of frontiers in the European sense.[157] At the time of colonisation, the drawing of the boundaries by the colonisers was mostly based on the logic of regulating "spheres of influence" between the different colonial powers. Hence, at the time of decolonisation, there was no logic in maintaining the boundaries drawn by the colonisers.[158] Yet, the *uti possidetis* doctrine was recognised as one of the rules of modern decolonisation, and the United Nations endorsed this rule in the interests of order.[159] General Assembly Resolution 1514(XV) of 1960 implicitly favours the preservation of the boundaries as drawn by the colonial powers regardless of their arbitrary character. Even though the resolution is aimed at "granting of independence to colonial territories and peoples," the resolution prohibits "the partial or total disruption of the national unity and territorial integrity of a country."[160]

The doctrine of *uti possidetis* has to be read in its socio-political context. From a legal point of view, it is certain that the doctrine has been recycled from Roman law for the purpose of maintaining "order" during the transition period of decolonisation.[161] Going back to the real significance of the doctrine of *uti possidetis* in Roman law shows that its actual meaning was to provide the conflicting parties with a means of resolving their ownership rights. In this sense, as Ratner highlighted: "uti possidetis did not address the final disposition of the property but, rather, shifted the burden of proof during the proceedings to the party not holding the land."[162] As in *jus civile*, the burden of the proof lay with the party that did not currently possess the land, whereas a straight application of the Roman law principle would have given the indigenous communities, as *de facto* possessors, the advantage. As Ratner

157 Romain Yakemtchouk, *Les Frontières Africaines*, 74 R.G.D.I.P. 27 (1970); *see also* Marc Ferro, Histoire des Colonisations 252 (1994); Ian Brownlie, African Boundaries, A Legal and Diplomatic Encyclopedia (1979). More specifically, on the issue of boundaries and indigenous peoples, *see* Colonial Frontiers, Indigenous-European Encounters in Settler Societies (Lynette Russell ed., 2001).

158 *See* Thomas Pakenham, The Scramble for Africa (1991); Malcolm Shaw, Title to Territory in Africa (1986).

159 *See* Rigo Sureda, The Evolution of the Right to Self-Determination: A Study of the United Nations Practice (1973).

160 G.A. Res. 1514(XV), para. 6, U.N. GAOR, 15th Sess., Supp.16, U.N. Doc. A/4684 (1960).

161 On the issue of order, *see* Hedley Bull, The Anarchical Society: A Study of Order in World Politics (1977).

162 Steven Ratner, *Drawing a Better Line: Uti Possidetis & the Borders of New States*, 90 Am. J. Int'l L. 590 (1996).

concluded: "[T]his adaptation, of course, proved a complete reversal from the Roman law concept, which excluded even provisional possession to a party who accomplished it by violence, and which would have suggested a return to the status quo ante bellum."[163] By translating this doctrine into a doctrine of territorial possession, international law altered its essence and shifted its private law origins to territorial claims between States only (i.e., with the exclusion of non-State parties). In terms of indigenous peoples' land rights, Shaw concluded, the doctrine "bestowed an aura of historical legality to the expropriation of the lands of indigenous peoples."[164]

With respect to the foundations and justifications of this process, two arguments can be made regarding indigenous peoples' land rights. First, it can be argued that *uti possidetis* implies the idea that territory is merely a portion of land between boundaries drawn by the colonial powers, rather than a space where a specific culture is rooted. The doctrine was used to organise the creation of successor States, and to allow the process of State consolidation within the boundaries drawn by the colonial interests. From this perspective, the doctrine increased the dichotomy between territory seen as a space where a culture is rooted, and territory as solely a question of possession. A closer scrutiny of the justifications of the norm shows that one of the justifications for disregarding cultural and ethnic territorial connections is the assumption that "a cosmopolitan democratic state can function within any borders."[165] The idea is that within the boundaries of any democratic State, indigenous peoples will find a way to express their specific wishes. In this arguably idealistic approach, international law neglected the fact that indigenous peoples' identities are closely linked with territory, and that States, even though democratic, may not respect indigenous cultural approaches to territory. The fundamental importance of land and territorial possession was left in the hands of "democratic states," which were not compelled to leave any space for the recognition of indigenous territorial customs. In sum, the first objection to the legitimacy of *uti possidetis* is that, implicitly, the norm is a rejection of the idea that territory has a deeper cultural significance for indigenous peoples living in the "new democratic" States. Part of this assumption is based on the idea that those States, being democratic, would provide indigenous communities with democratic entitlements. However, the fact that territorial ownership was a cornerstone of indigenous cultures was ignored.

---

163 *Id.*

164 Malcolm Shaw, *The Heritage of States: The Principle of Uti Possidetis Juris Today*, 67 Brit. Y.B. Int'l L. 97 (1996).

165 Ratner, *supra* note 162, at 591.

This point is linked with a second criticism that can be addressed to the recycling of the Roman law principle into modern international law. The doctrine contains the implicit idea that in the name of order, the territorial identity of a people should be defined by the geographical legacy of the colonial powers, and that previous territorial links are not relevant in the drawing of boundaries. Thus, the legacy of the *uti possidetis* doctrine should be challenged, as it blindly denies indigenous claims over certain parts of territories that were included within the new postcolonial States. As stated by the judges of the ICJ in the ruling of the *Frontier Dispute* case: "[T]he principle of uti possidetis freezes the territorial title; it stops the clock but does not put back the hands."[166] This issue is linked to the concept of a "critical date." In the words of Shaw:

> the critical date as a legal concept posits that there is a certain moment at which the rights of the parties crystallize, so that acts after that date cannot alter the legal position. It is this moment which is more decisive than any other for the purpose of the formulation of the rights of the parties in question.[167]

This issue of "critical date" is particularly relevant in the case of Latin America and Africa. At the time of independence from Spain and Portugal, much of Latin America was still controlled by indigenous peoples (e.g., south part of the Southern cone, Western Amazon basin and American Southwest). From this perspective, one can argue that the law regarding title to territory at the end of the 19th century recognised the effective occupation of a territory as criteria for legal territorial ownership.[168] Based on this principle, it was clear, at the time, when more than half of the Western territories of North America and more than two-thirds of the territories in South America were not under an "effective occupation" of the newly created States, international law was not sufficiently providing justification for the territorial transfer. With respect to the rule of "effective occupation" as a basis for legal title to territory, the norm of *uti possidetis* seems to contradict it. Even though it is clear that the new States of the Americas did not exert "effective occupation" over most of the territories that were assigned to them, the international community acted as if this was the case. International law, through the adaptation

166 Frontier Dispute (Burkina Faso v. Mali), 1986 I.C.J. 554, 586.

167 Shaw, *supra* note 164.

168 *See* earlier discussion of the principle of "effective occupation."

of *uti possidetis*, thus built a bridge between the rules of *de jure* and *de facto* occupation.[169] It can be argued that there remains a contradiction between the rule of "effective occupation," which stands for a *de facto* occupation, and the norm of *uti possidetis*, which implicitly recognises a *de jure* occupation. In this legal juggling, indigenous peoples could not claim territories in the process of the transfer of title of their territories between newly emerging States. This is why it is important to appreciate the impact of the "recycling" of the *uti possidetis* norm on the rule of title to territory regarding occupation. As well, as *terra nullius* and the rule of effective occupation, *uti possidetis* ignores both the existence of indigenous peoples and their territorial attachments. The only difference is that *uti possidetis* does so in the name of order, even though, in the light of the current territorial disputes between indigenous communities and States, such a notion of order can legitimately being questioned.

Conclusion

International law has played an important role in the colonial acquisition of indigenous territories. The international regime regarding title to territory, which emanates from the Roman property rights regime, has had some devastating effects on indigenous peoples' right to safeguard their territories. This chapter has highlighted that the rules governing the conquest of territories have been applied in a particularly discriminatory manner against indigenous peoples. Based on the notion of "civilisation," international law has failed to acknowledge the territorial identity of indigenous peoples. These rules of colonisation have been corrected through the decolonisation process, but indigenous peoples have not benefited from such changes. Decolonisation had a limited effect due to the fact that only States, which respected the boundaries established by the colonial powers, benefited from this movement. Through the doctrine of *uti possidetis* and the notion of "critical date," international law has affirmed the maintenance of colonial boundaries. Even though the application of the doctrine of *terra nullius* has been rejected for its discriminatory nature, it has been highlighted that through the principle of effective occupation, indigenous peoples are still not considered as actors and have not been considered as having effectively "occupied" their territories for the purpose of international

169 For a discussion on *uti possidetis de facto* and *de jure*, *see* Castellino & Allen, *supra* note 5, at 11–12.

law. Nonetheless, despite this self-serving interpretation of the rules of acquisition, which established indigenous peoples as victims, they represent only one aspect of the theories of dispossession. Adjoining the rules regarding the right of acquisition, another pillar of the colonisation of indigenous territories is the notion of extinguishment of indigenous peoples' sovereignty and territorial rights—an issue that is addressed in the following chapter.

CHAPTER 2

Means of Extinguishment

> What is the Indian title? It is mere occupancy for the purpose of hunting. It is not like our tenures; they have no idea of a title to the soil itself. It is overrun by them rather than inhabited.
>
> United states supreme court, 1810[1]

Adjoining the rules regarding the right of acquisition, another pillar of the colonization of indigenous territories is the notion of extinguishment of indigenous peoples' territorial rights. Legally, extinguishment is defined as "the destruction or cancellation of a right, power, contract, or estate. The annihilation of a collateral thing or subject in the subject itself out of which it is derived."[2] In the case of indigenous peoples, it suggests that a government would unilaterally extinguish the right of indigenous peoples to use and occupy their ancestral lands. Historically, this relies on the idea that indigenous peoples had suddenly lost their territorial sovereignty: it had been "extinguished" by the arrival of the European imperial colonial powers. While the practice of extinguishment was predominant at the time of colonization, the present chapter suggests that States have not rejected this practice in their contemporary approach to indigenous peoples' territorial rights. In divergence with the previous chapter, where the focus lays on States ignoring the very existence of indigenous peoples, this chapter examines the cases in which international law established that indigenous peoples might have exercised some form of territorial rights, but that such rights have been extinguished either by colonial treaties or through national legislations. Accordingly, the following chapter is divided into two different sections. The first section explores how the establishment of colonial treaties between States and indigenous peoples resulted in the extinguishment of indigenous peoples' land rights, and how, through these treaties, international law has provided resources to justify the extinguishment of indigenous territorial sovereignty over their own lands.[3] Then, the second

1 Fletcher v. Peck, 10 U.S. 87, 121 (1810).

2 Henry Campbell Black, Black's Law Dictionary 524 (1979).

3 The issue of indigenous peoples' sovereignty is certainly one of the most controversial and unresolved. While it deserves attention, the purpose here is not to concentrate on whether indigenous peoples did, and do, possess sovereignty, but to critically evaluate the extent to which States have extinguished indigenous peoples' territorial sovereignty, i.e., the independent occupation of a territorial area. On the issue of sovereignty, *see* Indigenous Peoples'

 | DOI 10.1163/9789004323254_005

section addresses the issue of extinguishment of indigenous title to territory through national laws and domestic case law using reference to international law. More particularly, it examines the doctrine of "discovery" under which indigenous peoples' territorial sovereignty was extinguished while a right of occupancy was established for settlers. Subsequently the section considers the contemporary application of the practice of extinguishment in common law countries through an analysis of the doctrine of extinguishable aboriginal title. While the present chapter is aimed at exploring the rules of international law regarding the extinguishment of indigenous peoples' land rights, domestic examples, mainly from common law countries, will also be explored and compared to the norms of international law with the aim of understanding how the international legal discourse addresses such national developments putting forward extinguishment.

A The Extinguishment of Indigenous Territorial Sovereignty by Colonial Treaties

Treaties are a prominent source of the legal relations between indigenous nations and States.[4] International law defines treaties as "consensual agreements between two or more subjects of international law intended to be considered by the parties as binding and containing rules of conduct under international law for at least one (normally for all) of the parties."[5] It is admitted that with regard to treaties between indigenous peoples and States, the notion of treaties generally encompasses notions of agreements and other constructive arrangements between States and indigenous peoples.[6] Treaty-making was

Rights in Australia, Canada and New Zealand (P. Havemann ed., 1999); Makere Stewart-Harawira, The New Imperial Order: Indigenous Responses to Globalization (2005).

4 For example, in Canada, between 1871 and 1921, of the 11 treaties that were signed between the government and indigenous nations, all engender some territorial consequences. In the United States, over 371 treaties were signed between the governments and Indian tribes, 76 of them called for removal of indigenous nations from their lands and [illegible] dealt with land cession. For an overview, *see* Final Report presented by Mr. Miguel Alfonso Martinez, *Study on Treaties, Agreements and Other Constructive Arrangements between States and Indigenous Populations*, U.N. Doc. E/CN.4/Sub.2/1999/20 [hereinafter Martinez, Final Report]; *see also* Charles H. Alexandrowicz, An Introduction to the History of the Law of Nations in the East Indies (1967).

5 Rudolf Bernhardt, *Treaties*, *in* Encyclopaedia of Public International Law 459 (Rudolf Bernhardt ed., 1992).

6 *See* U.N. Doc. E/CN.4/Sub.2/1992. The Special Rapporteur notes that treaties between States are also to be considered in their impact on indigenous peoples' land rights. For example,

often one of the first encounters between two very different legal systems. The first treaties between indigenous peoples and European imperial powers were mostly based on the need for commerce and peace, and for this purpose trade companies were given extensive powers to enter into treaty relationships with indigenous peoples in the name of their respective State.[7] During the early encounters between European colonial powers and indigenous communities, treaties were often viewed as the peaceful legal instruments used to establish either friendly relations or commerce.[8] However, behind such a facade, even when aimed at peace or commerce, colonial treaties often provided for the cession of indigenous territories, payment of some compensation and promise to protect the tribe's ownership over the remaining territory. The consent of the indigenous representative to transfer the property of their lands to one of the colonial powers was considered the "ultimate" proof of territorial ownership over indigenous land. For the European colonizers, treaties were binding contracts guaranteeing their political and territorial authority over the newly "discovered" territories (especially against rival colonial powers); whereas, for the indigenous peoples, treaties signified their status as nations and suggested implicit recognition by the colonizers of the validity of their legal and political organization.[9] Thus, even though colonial treaties appeared as proof of a clear dialogue between indigenous nations and colonial States, with the documents being the historical record of such dialogue, it was often based on an illusion for the indigenous peoples, as such treaties have rarely been honored and often resulted in the extinguishment of their territorial entitlements. The following analysis explores how colonial treaties established a progressive alienation of indigenous peoples' land rights.

International legal doctrine and jurisprudence have changed on the issue of the nature of the treaties between governments and indigenous peoples. There was a period where these treaties were regarded as valid and part of the Laws of Nations. Indigenous nations were deemed to have the legal capacity to sign treaties until the interests of States parties changed and these treaties were simply disregarded. A shift took place during the 19th century,

---

the Lapp Codicil adopted by the kingdoms of Sweden and Norway in 1751 had some direct consequences on the territorial rights of Saami communities in both countries, even though they were not a party to the treaty.

7 *See*, for examples, Edits, ordonnances royaux, déclarations et arrets du Conseil d'e tat du Roi concernant le Canada (1854), which reproduces the documents establishing *la Compagnie des Cents Asssociés and la Compagnie des Indes Orientales*.

8 *See* Robert A. Williams, Linking Arms Together: American Indian Treaty Visions of Law and Peace, 1600–1800 (1997); *see also* Robert S. Allen, His Majesty's Indian Allies: British Indian Policy in the Defence of Canada, 1774–1815 (1992).

9 *See* Martinez, Final Report, *supra* note 4, at 117.

when indigenous peoples were not considered sovereign entities anymore; thus, treaties with indigenous peoples were suddenly regarded as domestic matters rather than issues concerning international obligations. Consequently, these treaties had the effect of depriving indigenous peoples not only of their lands but also of their sovereignty, as indigenous nations were made subjects of the colonial powers. Thus, the following discussion examines how this shift from peace and land-sharing treaties to extinguishment of territorial sovereignty took place. Based on such analysis it then considers the consequences of these treaties within the contemporary discussion on indigenous peoples' land rights. One of the legal challenges is to determine whether these treaties are still valid at present. The issue of the nature and validity of these "historical colonial treaties" is crucial in terms of contemporary indigenous peoples' land rights. If these treaties were to be regarded as valid under international law, States would have to respect the promises made regarding indigenous peoples' territorial rights. Indigenous groups, especially in the United States, Canada and New Zealand, often refer to their treaty rights as a means to call attention to human rights abuses they have suffered and to define their political rights *vis-à-vis* the States that colonized their lands.[10] Some indigenous groups argue that treaties are to be considered valid international treaties and should be governed by the fundamental principle of *pacta sunt servanda*, whereas governments often defend the thesis that these treaties have to be regarded as matters of purely domestic law. This issue is central in terms of treaty-based land cession that occurred in the past, because if these treaties were of an international nature, they would give indigenous peoples access to rules of international law and may open the door to international adjudication. One of the fundamental issues is its validity at the time of signature and also, through the intertemporal rule of law, its contemporary validity. Accordingly, the following analysis interlinks historical as well as contemporary facts, as an intertemporal analysis is imperative.[11]

1 *A Process of Retrogression: From International Law to "Domestic Dependent Nations"*

One of the central notions with regard to treaties is the requirement of consent between two or more parties. This notion of consent was central in treaties

---

10 Rebecca Tsosie, *Sacred Obligations: Intercultural Justice and the Discourse of Treaty Rights*, 47 UCLA L. Rev. 1615 (2000).

11 The Laws of Treaties is very ancient, and one can find traces of the international law of treaties far back in history. The Vienna Convention is usually regarded as the codification of these customary international law regarding treaties. *See* Paul Reuter, Introduction au droit des traités (1985); Ian Sinclair, The Vienna Convention on the Law of Treaties (1973).

between States and indigenous nations, as between the 16th and 19th centuries there was a strong legal agreement in North America that indigenous peoples' territories could not be acquired without their consent.[12] By entering into a treaty with indigenous peoples, colonial powers sought to ensure the legal transfer of territories. The main purpose of such treaties was to give proof of occupation to the colonizers rather than provide rights to the indigenous peoples who, in most cases, received derisory consideration for ceding land.[13] In these treaties, indigenous nations never fully consented to cession of their territorial sovereignty; this loss is mostly the result of what has been designated the "domestication" of indigenous nations. Under such domestication, treaties were disregarded, and even though, as Wiessner's suggests, one of the "rocks" on which international law stands is the principle of *pacta sunt servanda*, the notion that nation-states are bound to keep their word,[14] indigenous peoples have been the victims of the non-respect and violation of treaty obligations by colonizers.

The first crucial issue when dealing with colonial treaties between States and indigenous peoples is the question of the nature of these treaties. The issue is to appreciate the role of international law, as for example the Vienna Convention on the Law of Treaties defines international treaties as agreements between States only,[15] and thus, *a priori*, excludes indigenous peoples. Of course the validity of these treaties as "international" would arguably bring them within the framework of international law.[16] As discussed in the previous chapter, early international legal doctrine acknowledged the capacity of indigenous peoples' representatives to enter into treaty relationships with colonial powers. Vittoria, Grotius and Vattel all recognized such capacity and considered treaties as a regular means of establishing a legal relationship with indigenous nations.[17] It is particularly obvious in the case of the United States,

12 For example, *see*, Mitchel and Others v. United States. 34 U.S. (9 Pet.) 711, 745 (1835).

13 Bedjaoui has portrayed colonial treaties as "*traités de verroterie*," as such treaties were concluded only as proof for the European colonial powers of their rights over certain territories against other colonial powers. *See* Mohammed Bedjaoui, *Terra Nullius, 'droits' historiques et autodétermination* (exposés oraux prononcés devanr la Cour Internationale de Justice en l'affaire du Sahara Occidental), at 32 (La Haye, 1975).

14 Siegfried Wiessner, *American Indian Treaties and Modern International Law*, 7 St. Thomas L. Rev. 567 (1995) [hereinafter Wiessner].

15 *See* art. 2(a): "treaty means an international agreement concluded between States in written form and governed by international law"; Vienna Convention on the Law of Treaties, U.N. Doc. A/CONF.39/26, *reprinted in* 8 I.L.M. 679 (1969).

16 On the eventual consequences of the recognition of the international nature of these treaties, *see* Wiessner, *supra* note 14.

17 *See* Chapter 1.

which illustrates the international value that was recognized to these treaties. These treaties were public and registered documents, for example the National Archives of the United States has copies of all the treaties signed. Wiessner distinguished three major phases relevant to the history of American Indian treaties. The first phase corresponds to the time prior to the independence of the United States, when Indians signed treaties with all the major European colonial powers. These treaties are known as "alliance" or "friendship" treaties. The second phase relates to the independence of the United States when the new nation needed "useful allies." Several treaties were signed between the government and Indian tribes to this purpose. Wiessner highlighted that during those two periods, treaties were signed "using the language of international law."[18] In 1789, President George Washington declared that, with respect to treaties between the United States and "the Natives," the Senate should adopt the same procedure as was practiced in treaties with European nations.[19] Thus, as with any other international treaty, treaties made with Indians required formal ratification by Congress. This position was reflected in the U.S. Supreme Court case of *Worcester v. Georgia*, in which Chief Justice Marshall stated:

> The Constitution, by declaring treaties already made, as well as those to be made to be the supreme law of the land, has adopted and sanctioned the previous treaties with the Indian nations and consequently admits their rank among those powers who are capable of making treaties. The words "treaty" and "nation" are words of our own language, selected in our diplomatic and legislative proceedings, by ourselves, having each a definite and well understood meaning. We have applied them to Indians, as we have applied them to other nations of the earth. They are applied to all in the same sense.[20]

However, this position was rapidly replaced by one in which "[T]he instrument of treaties was now used predominantly to regularize the removal of Indians from their traditional vast hunting and fishing grounds to ever smaller, ever more barren areas of land called reservations."[21] This phase corresponds to the time when the Monroe Doctrine was framed: with the battle between the European colonial empires in North America over, it was time for the internal colonization of the country; a new policy of assimilation of the Indian

18 Wiessner, *supra* note 14.

19 1 Annals of Congress 80–81 (1789).

20 Worcester v. Georgia, 31 U.S. 515, 559–60 (1832).

21 Wiessner, *supra* note 14, at 577.

tribes started, resulting in the rejection of treaties previously signed. This was done through what was known as the "domestication" of the Indian nations as Indian tribes suddenly became "domestic dependent entities." This process of domestication was supported by the jurisprudence of the Supreme Court.[22] Finally, treaty making disappeared completely with the 1871 Indian Appropriation Act, which ended the practice of making treaties with Indian nations in the United States.[23]

In summary, during the period that witnessed the battle between the European imperial powers, especially in North America, these powers and their "descendants" recognized indigenous communities as international actors capable of entering into a treaty relationship for the purposes of peace and the establishment of safe boundaries. However, after this first phase of colonization, the European and new American States stopped considering their treaty engagements with indigenous peoples as falling under the category of international treaties. The case of the United States illustrates that at the time of their signature, treaties between States and indigenous peoples were of an international nature. This suggests that at a certain period in history, indigenous communities were endowed with an international personality and possessed territorial sovereignty. As pointed out by Martinez, the former U.N. Special Rapporteur on the issue of treaties between States and indigenous populations, in his final report: "[I]n establishing formal legal relationship with peoples overseas, the European parties were clearly aware that they were negotiating and entering into contractual relations with sovereign nations, with all the international legal implications of that term during the period under consideration."[24]

States unilaterally changed the nature of the treaties with indigenous peoples from international treaties to domestic matters. This phenomenon of "domestication" was not only taking place in the United States but also in Canada and New Zealand, and this regression can be found in both internal and international judicial decisions. One of the most blatant judicial illustrations of this shift is to be found in the signature of the Treaty of Waitangi between the British Crown and some of the Maori chiefs in 1840, as in 1877, in a

22 *See* Johnson and Braham's Lessee v. M'Intosh, 21 U.S. (8 Wheat.) 543 (1823).

23 "No Indian nation or tribe within the territory of the United States shall be acknowledged or recognized as an independent nation, tribe or power with whom the United States may contract by treaty; but no obligation of any treaty lawfully made and ratified with any such Indian nation or tribe before prior to March 3, 1871, shall be hereby invalidated or impaired." Indian Appropriations Act 1871 (25 U.S.C.), at 71.

24 Martinez, Final Report, *supra* note 4, at para. 110.

Supreme Court case, Judge Prendergast suggested that the Treaty of Waitangi between the Maori and the British Crown was "a simple nullity" based on the Maoris' lack of sovereignty at the time of the signature.[25] This "domestication" of treaties, which were previously regarded as international treaties, was also endorsed at the international level. A British-American arbitration panel, in the *Cayguya Indians* case, confirmed that treaties concluded with indigenous peoples could not be regarded as having international nature, but represented unilateral acts pertaining to domestic law.[26] The same position was implied in the *Island of Palmas* case, in which treaties between the imperial colonial powers and the indigenous inhabitants were not even considered for not being regarded as "international."[27] In this case, the international arbitrator considered the treaties signed between the representatives of the indigenous populations of the island and the West Indies Dutch company in 1677, only as an eventual basis for the establishment of Dutch sovereignty over the island. The reasoning was based on the idea that treaties between the indigenous population and the colonizers only dealt with internal matters and, consequently, were of domestic value only. Thus, even though the term "domestication" comes from the jurisprudence of the U.S. Supreme Court, this "theory" has been used internationally allowing States parties to disregard their treaty obligations towards the indigenous party to the treaties. The process of "domestication" was described by Martinez as "a process of retrogression" as indigenous peoples were "deprived of (or saw greatly reduced) three of the four essential attributes on which their original status as sovereign nations was grounded, namely their territory, their recognized capacity to enter into international agreements, and their specific forms of government."[28]

This shift in nature had a deep impact on indigenous peoples' land rights as they were abruptly submitted to States' unilateral decisions, and the notion of their prior consent to acquisition of their territories was suddenly totally disregarded. It is only in the light of more contemporary legal decisions that it is possible to comprehend all the consequences of this "domestication" process in terms of indigenous peoples' land rights. In the case of *Ex parte Indian Association of Alberta* of January 1982, the British Court of Appeal was invited to define whether treaty obligations signed by the British Crown became obligations for the Canadian government. The Court of Appeal rejected the appeal of the Indian Association of Alberta by considering that

25 Wi Parata v. Bishop of Wellington [1877] 3 N.Z. Jur. (N.S.) S.C. 72.

26 Cayuga Indians (Great Britain) v. United States, 6 R.I.A.A. 173 (1926).

27 Island of Palmas case (Neth. v. U.S.) (1928), 2 R.I.A.A. 829 (1949).

28 Martinez, Final Report, *supra* note 4, at para. 105.

the British Crown was in charge of the treaty obligations that it had signed.[29] This decision was based on the fact that, for the Court, the treaty signed was not of an international nature because it was not signed between States.[30] In a similar vein, the Supreme Court of Canada in *R. v. Horseman*, addressing the issue of the modification of Treaty 8 by the government, stated: "[T]he power of the Federal Government to unilaterally make such a modification is unquestioned."[31] Finally, in 1999, the Canadian Supreme Court in the case of *Marshall*, reaffirmed the government's power to regulate treaty rights.[32] The Supreme Court affirmed that the rules governing the establishment and the extinction of these treaties were not to be determined by international law. As a result, the government could infringe, modify or extinguish the Crown's treaty obligations as long as it was justified by national interest.[33]

In terms of the validity of the content of the treaties, one of the central issues is the question of the understanding of the agreements between the parties, the existence of "a meeting of minds." In North America, it was common for indigenous peoples to conclude treaties between their nations to establish relationships with one another and their lands.[34] For indigenous peoples of North America, treaties were not instruments imposed by Europeans, but were part of their own practices as treaties "were sacred and were often given the highest regard and respect."[35] Nevertheless, even though the meaning of treaty relations was not foreign to indigenous peoples, in most cases the indigenous party "did not understand the principle of alienation of title to land; to them

---

29 R v. Secretary of State for Foreign and Commonwealth Affairs, *Ex parte* Indian Association of Alberta, [1982] Q.B. 892, 912—House of Lords.

30 The same reasoning was developed in *Manuel and Others v. Attorney General and Noltcho and others*. One of the consequences of the domestication process of the treaties is to be found in the interpretation of treaty rights. Borrows' analysis of the Supreme Court jurisprudence shows that "visible non-Aboriginal development is sufficient to defeat the treaty rights." *See* John Borrows, *Domesticating Doctrine: Aboriginal Peoples after the Royal Commission*, 46 McGill L.J. 615 (2001).

31 R. v. Horseman, [1990] 1 S.C.R. 901, 934, 108 N.R. 1.

32 R. v. Marshall, [1999] 3 S.C.R. 533, 179 D.L.R.(4th) 193, at paras. 24–28.

33 *See* Mark D. Walters, *Brightening the Covenant Chain: Aboriginal Treaty Meanings in Law and History After Marshall*, 24 Dalhousie L.J. 75 (2001).

34 A classic example of treaties among the indigenous peoples is the Haudenasaunee or Six Nations League of the Iroquois, a treaty-based confederation founded around 1570; *see* Victor Lytwyn, *A Dish with One Spoon: The Shared Hunting Grounds Agreement in the Great Lakes and St. Lawrence Valley Region, in* Papers of the Twenty-Eighth Algonquian Conference (David H. Pentland ed., 1997).

35 John Borrows, *Domesticating Doctrine: Aboriginal Peoples after the Royal Commission*, 46 McGill L.J. 615 (2001).

it was not dissimilar to a deist being expected to sell his interest in God."[36] As Newton noted: "[A]lthough the treaty terms were translated from the English language, even well-meaning translators had trouble accurately rendering feudal concepts of fee simple title to peoples who believed in the common ownership of land."[37] In most cases, indigenous peoples understood that they were entering an agreement for sharing the use of the lands, whereas they were actually ceding their territories based on the use of dishonest and fraudulent translations.[38] In the 1919 case of *Southern Rhodesia*, the Judicial Committee of the Privy Council stated on the issue of indigenous view of territorial cession:

> As well might be said that a savage who sold ten bullocks, being the highest number up to which he knew how to count, had thereby sold his whole herd, numbering, in fact, many hundreds. In the questions referred to the broad ownership and property mean ownership and property as civilized people understand these words.[39]

The misunderstanding between so-called "civilized" and "non-civilized" notions of territorial ownership certainly reached its peak with the Treaty of Waitangi in New Zealand. The official bilingual Treaty of Waitangi in New Zealand is the most well known illustration of these repeated misunderstandings. The term "sovereignty," used in the English text, is referred to as *Kawanatanga* in the Maori text, which literally means "governorship." Thus, in the English language version of the treaty, the Maori ceded to the Crown their sovereignty over their lands, whereas in the Maori language version, they agreed to give the Crown the right to govern. In 1941, the Privy Council affirmed that the treaty "had been a complete cession of all rights and powers of sovereignty of the chiefs."[40] This treaty is one of the clearest examples of the distinction between indigenous nations and State parties regarding territorial treaties. The indigenous nations have never given up their territorial sovereignty by treaties but only some specific parts of their lands in exchange for peace, protection, money or other valuables. To the indigenous parties, these exchanges usually meant recognition of their territorial ownership. In Canada, Leroy Little Bear has pointed out that

36 Michael Craufurd-Lewis, *Treaties with Aboriginal Minorities*, 15(1) Can. J. Native Stud. 1 (1995).

37 Nell Jessup Newton, *Compensation, Reparations, & Restitution: Indian Property Claims in the United States*, 28 Ga. L. Rev. 453, n. 20 (1994).

38 *Id.*

39 *In re* Southern Rhodesia [1919] A.C. 211—Privy Council.

40 Hoani Te Heuheu Tukino v. Aotea District Maori Land Board [1941] 2 All E.R. 93—Privy Council.

the concepts of land alienation and land transfer were alien concepts to most Aboriginal communities, as "the standard or norm of the Aboriginal peoples' law is that land is not transferable and therefore inalienable." He concluded that when Indian nations entered into treaty relationships with Europeans nations "the subject of the treaty, from the Indian's viewpoint, was not the alienation of the land but the sharing of the land."[41] This view has been affirmed by the Royal Commission on Aboriginal Peoples, which found that Aboriginal customs excluded "the right to alienate or sell land to outsiders, to destroy or diminish lands or resources, or to appropriate lands or resources for private gain without regard to reciprocal obligations."[42] In Canada, strong Aboriginal customary laws prohibited the absolute transfer of title to land, and the notion of extinguishment of an Aboriginal community's right to its lands was foreign, as it was not permissible under Aboriginal law.[43] It remains crucial to bear in mind that that indigenous peoples have also often been the victims of treaties imposed upon them by force, duress or fraud.[44]

Legally, treaties were used as a means of extinguishing indigenous territorial sovereignty. In most cases, the extinguishment of indigenous territorial sovereignty resulted in the unilateral decision of State parties to consider indigenous communities as domestic nations—the treaties being the evidence that indigenous nations had given up their territorial rights. In terms of litigation against such alienation of territorial sovereignty, the principal obstacle for indigenous peoples is based on the notion of "act of State." In several cases, national and international jurisdiction have reaffirmed that the acquisition of territorial sovereignty by treaty is an act of State that cannot be challenged in courts. The Privy Council in *Vajesingji Joravarisingji v. Secretary of State for India* stated: "even if in a treaty of cession it is stipulated that certain inhabitants should enjoy certain rights, that does not give title to those inhabitants to enforce these stipulations in municipal courts."[45] Such a statement is not

41 Leroy Little Bear, *Aboriginal Rights and the Canadian Grundnorm, in* Arduous Journey: Canadian Indians and Decolonization 243 (J. Rick Pointing ed., 1986).

42 *Report of the Royal Commission on Aboriginal Peoples*, Restructuring the Relationship, at 459 (Minister of Supply and Services Canada, Ottawa, 1996).

43 *See* Kent McNeil, *Extinguishment of Aboriginal Title in Canada: Treaties, Legislation, and Judicial Discretion*, 33 Ottawa L. Rev. 301 (2001–2002).

44 *See* Charles F. Wilkinson & John M. Volkman, *Judicial Review of Indian Treaty Abrogation: "As Long as Water Flows, or Grass Grows Upon the Earth"—How Long Time is that?* 63 Cal. L. Rev. 601 (1975).

45 Vajesingji Joravarisingji v. Secretary of State for India, LR 51 Ind. App. 357 (1924); *see also* Secretary of State for India v. Kamachee Bai Rajbai, 42 Ind. App. 229 (1915); and Hoani Te Heuheu Tukino v. Aotea District Maori Land Board, 2 All E.R. 93 (1941).

isolated and reflects the view of all national jurisdictions, as judges are generally reluctant to rule on the issue of interpreting whether treaties meant the transfer of territorial sovereignty. However, as a result of pressure from several indigenous communities, judges have been invited to appreciate the extent to which States must respect their treaty obligations regarding indigenous peoples' land rights.

2 *The "Trail of Broken Treaties": Contemporary Enforcement of Colonial Treaties*

In 1972, a group of indigenous peoples from North America occupied the Bureau of Indian Affairs in Washington, seeking the recognition of the validity of the treaties signed in the past. That occupation gave rise to the movement of the "trail of broken treaties."[46] There is a strong movement, especially in North America, in favor of the recognition of States' obligations contained in the treaties signed a long time ago. For indigenous peoples, the politics of recognition extends to both national and international spheres and entails the recognition of their territorial rights. A closer scrutiny of national and international jurisprudence shows that the appreciation of the international nature of treaties between States and indigenous peoples is not as legally clear as it may seem at first glance. For example, in 1881, the Austrian Emperor Franz Josef, acting as an international referee between Great Britain and Nicaragua, rendered a decision ruling that the Treaty of Managua between the Miskito Indians and Great Britain was of an international nature.[47] In a decision of the Court of Appeal for Eastern Africa in 1913, the nature of a treaty between indigenous peoples and States was one of the central issues of the ruling.[48] In a case involving Maasai leaders and the colonial authority administrating Kenya, the Court had to deal with the issue of the violation of the obligations of a treaty signed with the British colonial authority. This treaty, signed in 1904,

---

46 *See* Vine Deloria, Behind the Trail of Broken Treaties (1974). Such terminology is linked with the "trail of tears," when one-fifth of the Cherokee Nation died when the army forcibly marched the tribe from their lands in Georgia to a reservation. *See* John Ehle, Trail of Tears: The Rise & Fall of the Cherokee Nation (1988).

47 *See* U.N. Doc. E/CN.4/Sub.2/1996/23, at 23–24, at paras. 120–122. Likewise, in 1907 a decision of the Court of Appeal of French Western Africa considered that the treaties signed between France and the Damels of Cayor were of an international nature. *See* Nassira Belkacemi, *Contribution a l'étude des peuples autochtones en droit international et en droit interne* (Unpublished Thesis, Université de Montpellier, 1996) (on file with author).

48 Ol Le Njogo and Others v. The Attorney General and Others [1913], 5–7 E. Afr. Protectorate L. Rep. 92 (1913–1918)—Court of Appeal for Eastern Africa.

established the protection of the Maasai land rights to some of their territories. It stated that "as long as the Maasai as a race shall exist, (…) Europeans or other settlers shall not be allowed to take up land in the settlement."[49] However, despite this clause, another treaty was subsequently signed in 1911 removing the Maasai from their lands. Some Maasai leaders went to court, arguing that such a treaty was a violation of the previous treaty, and that the new treaty had been obtained by duress without the approval of the tribe. The Court of Appeal decided that the agreements between the Maasai and the British colonial administration were not domestic matters and could not be enforceable in municipal courts; it was recognized as a matter of international law.[50] However, it is mostly in contemporary judicial decisions that the progressive recognition of the validity of the historical treaties between indigenous peoples and States can be found.

Regarding the enforcement of States' treaties obligations, some countries have established specific judicial or quasi-judicial bodies in charge of treaty interpretation. For example, in New Zealand, one of the functions of the Waitangi Tribunal is to inquire into and make recommendations on claims submitted to the Tribunal with respect to breaches of the principles of the treaty. In Canada, the government established a Treaty Commission, and in 1946, the U.S. Congress passed the Indian Claims Commission Act to establish a body competent to hear and settle grievances. The Canadian Supreme Court, in *Sioui* of 1990,[51] and in *R. v. Howard* of 1994,[52] affirmed the validity of treaties signed respectively by the British Crown and the Canadian government, concluding that the Crown must honor its treaty obligations.[53] Other national cases highlighted the fact that treaties between indigenous peoples and States are to be considered as valid treaties. In New Zealand, the obligations contained in the 1840 Treaty of Waitangi were largely ignored until the 1970s, when indigenous activism pushed the government to set up the Treaty of Waitangi Commission to enforce the treaty. In 1983, the New Zealand government amended the

49 *Id.* at 73.

50 *See* Joseph Ole Simel, *The Anglo-Maasai-Agreements/Treaties—A Case of Historical Injustice and the Dispossession of the Maasai Natural Resources (Land), and the Legal Perspectives*, U.N. Doc. HR/GENEVA/TSIP/SEM/2003/BP.7. *See also* Regina Jefferies, *The Equitable Application of International Law: Revised Principles for a Solution to the Maasai Land Dispute*, 37 Ariz. St. L.J. 973 (2005).

51 Attorney-General of Québec v. Sioui et al., [1990] 1 S.C.R. 1025.

52 R. v. Howard, [1994] 2 S.C.R. 299.

53 *See also* R. v. Badger, [1996] 1 S.C.R. 771; R. v. Marshall, [1999] 3 S.C.R. 533.

Fisheries Act so that nothing would prejudice Maori fishing rights granted by the Treaty of Waitangi of 1840.[54]

Regarding international norms, the clearest expression of States' obligations to respect colonial treaties is expressed in the U.N. Declaration on the Rights of Indigenous Peoples which states in its article 37:

> Indigenous peoples have the right to the recognition, observance and enforcement of treaties, agreements and other constructive arrangements concluded with states or their successors, and to have States honour and respect such treaties, agreements and other constructive arrangements.[55]

This article has been subject to lingering negotiations during the drafting of the declaration. The government of New Zealand stated that it had "considerable difficulty with the suggestion that domestic issues under such treaties and arrangements should be subject to international arbitration."[56] Canada insisted that treaties with indigenous peoples of Canada are domestic rather than international agreements, and Venezuela expressed reservations in relation to the expression "to competent international bodies," stating that agreements with indigenous peoples are national agreements to be settled by national bodies. However, Brazil, Colombia and Finland supported the article.[57] At the regional level, Article XXII of the Proposed American Declaration states: "Indigenous peoples have the right to the recognition, observance and enforcement of treaties, agreements and constructive agreements, that may have been concluded with states or their successors."[58] Another indicator of the evolution towards the recognition of colonial treaties came from the European Parliament, which endorsed a resolution calling "states which in the past have signed treaties with indigenous peoples to honour their undertakings, which remains imprescriptible."[59] Despite their non-binding effects, these international documents reflect the growing concern of the international community to recognize the effect of the treaties that were signed a long time ago between

54 On the contemporary consequences of the 1840 treaty, *see* Ian Brownlie, Treaties and Indigenous Peoples (1992).

55 United Nations Declaration on the Rights of Indigenous Peoples, General Assembly, A/RES/61/295, Adopted on 13 September 2007, Article 37.

56 *See* U.N. Doc. E/CN.4/2004/81, at 16.

57 *See* U.N. Doc. E/CN.4/2004/81, at 16.

58 Draft Inter-American Declaration on the Rights of Indigenous Peoples, Doc. OEA/Ser/L/V/II.90, doc. 9, rev. 1 (1995).

59 *Resolution On Action Required Internationally to Provide Effective Protection for Indigenous Peoples*, Eur. Parl. Doc. PV 58(II), (Feb. 9, 1994), para. 10.

States and indigenous nations, notwithstanding the passage of time and the domestication theory.

In terms of international law, one of the central rules of interpretation for historical treaties is the notion of intertemporal law.[60] Under such doctrine, the interpretation of a treaty should be done on the basis of the law existing at the time the act was concluded; however, such application should be done with regard to the law existing at the time of application.[61] National courts have begun to examine the legality of colonial treaties based on such rules. For example, in 1980, the U.S. Supreme Court recognized "the pattern of duress practiced by the Government on the starving Sioux to get them to agree to the sale of the Black Hills."[62] In 2001, it was recognized that the Cayuga Ferry Treaty of 1795 was illegal, resulting in the invalidity of the transfer of land obtained from the Cayuga. As stated above, these treaties were originally valid in terms of the international law of the time, but one central issue is to determine whether the move from the "rule of law" to the "law of the rulers" was legal under the international law regime. Under the traditional rules governing treaty relationships, a party cannot unilaterally abrogate from a treaty unless treaty provisions are duly declared null and void. Consequently, States could not have unilaterally abrogated treaties by applying the theory of domestication. Even with due deference to the rule of intertemporal law, such unilateral abrogation would be illegal. Even though the indigenous party became a so-called "domestic dependent" entity, at the time when the treaties were signed, the indigenous party was considered as a sovereign party capable of entering into treaty relations. Thus, it can be advanced that if the criterion of intertemporal law is followed, historical treaties should be regarded as valid and applicable. These treaties were originally regarded as giving rise to international obligations, and both the U.N. Declaration and the Proposed American Declaration promote the respect of these treaties by States. Based on the aforementioned national case law and on the text of both the U.N. and the Proposed American Declarations on the rights of indigenous peoples, it can be argued that there is an evolution in favor of the full legal reassessment of these colonial treaties,[63]

60 On the issue of intertemporal law, *see* Taslim O. Elias, *The Doctrine of Intertemporal Law* 74 Am. J. Int'l L. 285 (1980).

61 *See* Island of Palmas (U.S. v. Neth.) 2 R.I.A.A. 831 (1928).

62 United States v. Sioux Nation of Indians et al., 448 U.S. 37 1 (1980).

63 The Economic and Social Council has endorsed a recommendation from the Commission on Human Rights to organize an expert seminar on treaties between States and indigenous peoples. *See* U.N. Doc. E/2003/271; *see also Report of the Seminar on Treaties, Agreements and other Constructive Arrangements between States and Indigenous Peoples*, U.N. Doc. E/CN.4/Sub.2/AC.4/2004/7; U.N. Doc. E/CN.4/Sub.2/AC.4/2002/WP.9.

and such movement could have some important consequences on indigenous peoples' land rights. Yet, at present, it is difficult to foresee what would be the effects of such development, as under the theory of the domestication of the treaties, indigenous peoples are still the victims of a system that has resulted in the extinguishment of the territorial rights that were recognized in the historical treaties.

B Theories of Extinguishable Indigenous Land Rights

The extinguishment of indigenous peoples' land rights through the process of "domestication" of historical treaties represents only one aspect of the theories on extinguishment. A second aspect of extinguishment can be found through the theories of extinguishable land rights for indigenous peoples. This reference to extinguishable rights refers to the recognition by States authority of an 'extinguishable' right for indigenous peoples to occupy their traditional land. One of the first references to such an extinguishable right of occupancy came through the reference to the doctrine of discovery. This doctrine was based on the assumption that even tough indigenous peoples had rights over their territories before their so-called "discovery"; such rights were extinguished with the "arrival" of the colonial powers. Yet, in a second movement, the existence of such pre-existing land right gave rise to the recognition of a new doctrine on indigenous title that recognizes a limited form of extinguishable land ownership. Accordingly, the following discussion is twofold. First it examines the doctrine of discovery with its attached right of occupancy for indigenous peoples, and then it explores the contemporary notion of extinguishable indigenous title. In doing so, it focuses on the common law jurisprudence on Native and Aboriginal title that has been developed by courts in Canada and Australia. The aim is not to analyse the jurisprudence of Native/Aboriginal title in itself, but to appreciate to what extent such common law doctrine is the prolongation of international legal theories on extinguishment. Based on such analysis, it questions the development of an international trend towards indigenous title in other parts of the globe, as arguably the development of a theory on Aboriginal and Native title is gradually becoming a global phenomenon.[64] In this regard, the following discussion seeks to examine how such development paradoxically relies on theories of extinguishment that have been labelled as discriminatory by different international human rights treaty monitoring bodies.

64 *See* Jérémie Gilbert, *Historical Indigenous Peoples' Land Claims: A Comparative and International Approach to the Common Law Doctrine on Indigenous Title* 56 International and Comparative Law Quarterly pp. 583–611 (2007).

1 *Discovery: A Theory of Extinguishable Right of Occupancy*

During the colonization of indigenous territories, one of the crucial issues was the eventual conflict between the rights of settlers and those of indigenous peoples. Even though indigenous peoples lost their sovereignty, this did not mean that indigenous territories were inhabited. For this reason, indigenous right of ownership, as opposed to that of settlers, remained to be defined. The resolution of this came through what has been termed the "doctrine of discovery."[65] The early judgments of the U.S. Supreme Court at the commencement of the 19th century provided one of the first sources of legal litigations between indigenous nations and national courts. The impact of the theorists on the Laws of Nations on the evolution of what became international law is evident in the "Marshall's cases," named after Chief Justice John Marshall.[66] Half a century after Vattel's theory, these five crucial judgments of the U.S. Supreme Court, relating specifically to indigenous issues, made clear reference to the theories developed by the fathers of the Law of Nations. These judgments laid down the theory of international law regarding indigenous peoples' extinguishable land rights. More specifically, the case of *Johnson v. M'Intosh* of 1823 drew the foundations and justifications of what is designated as the "doctrine of discovery."[67] This case was based on a property dispute between two parties claiming their right of ownership of a piece of land originally located on Indian land. The defendant, William M'Intosh, legitimated his title to the Cabot grant,[68] whereas the plaintiff based his title on the purchase of the concerned land from the Pinkeshaw Indians. The Supreme Court ruled in favor of M'Intosh, declaring the "superiority" of the title of the discoverer over the rights of the plaintiff who bought the land from the Indians. This ruling was clearly based on references to the earlier doctrinal position of international law as the judge stated:

> The character and religion of [the New World's] inhabitants afforded an apology for considering them as a people over whom the superior genius

65 *See* David Wilkins, *Bridging Theory and Practice: Quit-Claiming the Doctrine of Discovery: A Treaty Based Reappraisal*, 23 Okla. City U.L. Rev. 277 (1998); *see also* Larry Sager, *Rediscovering America: Recognizing the Sovereignty of Native American Indian Nations*, 76 U. Det. Mercy L. Rev. 745 (1999).

66 For detailed analysis of the so-called Marshall's cases, *see* Robert Faulkner, The Jurisprudence of John Marshall (1968).

67 Johnson and Braham's Lessee v. M'Intosh, 21 U.S. (8 Wheat.) 543 (1823).

68 In 1497, Tudor King Henry VII issued the "Charter of Conquest," which granted John Cabot a right of conquest. *See* Robert A. Williams, *Colombus's Legacy: Law as an Instrument of Racial Discrimination Against Indigenous Peoples' Rights of Self-Determination*, 8 Ariz. J. Int'l & Comp. L. 51–68 (1991).

> of Europe might claim ascendancy. To leave them in possession of their country was to leave the country a wilderness (…) Agriculturalists, merchants, and manufacturers, have a right, on abstract principles, to expel hunters from their territory (…) Excuse, if not justification, [could be found] in the character and habits of the people whose rights had been wrested from them (…) The potentates of the Old World (…) made ample compensation to the inhabitants of the new, by bestowing upon them civilization and Christianity.[69]

In these few paragraphs, the judge deployed all the racist clichés that were developed by Eurocentric views of the "savages" and all the justifications offered by the theorists of early international law, i.e., the right of conquest based on Christianity and civilization, in conjunction with the agriculturist argument. These clichés were given legal consequences as the Court ruled:

> However extravagant the pretension of converting the discovery of an inhabited country into conquest may appear; if the principle has been asserted in the first instance, and afterwards sustained; if a country has been acquired and held under it; if the property of the great mass of the community originates in it, it becomes the law of the land, and cannot be questioned.[70]

Herein lies the heart of the legal fiction that was to have a very profound impact on indigenous dispossession. The judge clearly declared that "discovery" gave title to the discovering nation; even though the Court implicitly recognized that the country had been inhabited before its colonization. On the fundamental issue of the relationship between the Indian and the colonizers' laws regulating land ownership, the Court rejected the application of the law "which regulates … the relation between the conqueror and the conquered," as the circumstances required "resort to some new and different rule, better adapted to the actual state of things."[71] Marshall conceded that the "character and religion … afforded an apology for considering them as a people over whom the superior genius of Europe might claim an ascendancy." Bartlett referred to this ruling as a "pragmatic compromise," as "[T]he Court did not suggest that such rule was just. Rather the Court opined that it was the only possible accommodation of the interests of the settlers and of the Aboriginal

69 Johnson and Braham's Lessee v. M'Intosh. 21 U.S. (8 Wheat.) 543. at 573–90 (1823).

70 *Id.* at 591.

71 *Id.*

people."[72] The landmark decision of *Johnson v. M'Intosh* has to be read in conjunction with two other cases in which Judge Marshall completed his theory on the Indians' rights of ownership and sovereignty. In 1830, in the case of the *Cherokee Nation v. Georgia*, and in the 1832 case of *Worcester v. Georgia*, the U.S. Supreme Court recognized the Cherokee Nation as a "distinct community, occupying its own territory, with boundaries accurately described."[73] In the first case, based on the fact that the Cherokee had signed a number of treaties with the government of the United States, the judge ruled that "[T]he acts of our government plainly recognize the Cherokee nation as a state, and the courts are bound by those acts."[74] However, instead of concluding on the territorial sovereignty of the Cherokee Nation over their traditional homelands, Marshall concluded:

> The Indian territory is admitted to compose a part of the United States (…) Though the Indians are acknowledged to have an unquestionable, and, heretofore, unquestioned right to the lands they occupy, until that right shall be extinguished by a voluntary cession to our government; yet it may well be doubted whether those tribes which reside within the acknowledged boundaries of the United States can, with strict accuracy, be denominated foreign nations. They may, more correctly, perhaps, be denominated domestic dependent nations. They occupy a territory to which we assert a title independent of their will, which must take effect in point of possession when their right of possession ceases. Meanwhile they are in a state of pupilage. Their relation to the United States resembles that of a ward to his guardian.[75]

In addition to its clear reference to the Bible,[76] this decision was based on the notion developed earlier by international legal theorists that the "savages" could not "properly" hold on to the land, and therefore there was a duty to civilize them by imposing a proper land tenure system.[77] This decision outlined the means by which international law proposed to deal with the issue of indigenous

---

72 Richard Bartlett, *Native Title: From Pragmatism to Equality before the Law*, 20 Melb. U.L. Rev. 284 (1995).

73 Worcester v. Georgia, 31 U.S. (6 Pet.) 515, 8 L. Ed. 483 (1832), para. 561.

74 Cherokee Nation v. Georgia. 30 U.S. (5 Pet.) 1, 2 (1830).

75 *Id.*, at 16.

76 On the link between the Bible and the legal reasoning of the U.S. Supreme Court, *see* Steven Paul McSloy, *"Because the Bible Tells Me So": Manifest Destiny and American Indians*, 9 St. Thomas L. Rev. 37 (1996).

77 *See* Chapter 1.

territorial sovereignty, namely through the doctrine of guardianship and trusteeship. In this case, even though the Cherokee were recognized as having all the characteristics of an independent nation, they did not possess territorial sovereignty, as they were considered a "domestic dependent nation." The U.S. Supreme Court recognized that Indians communities constituted independent and autonomous organizations that could legally enter into treaty relationships with the United States, but it also held that such communities could not be considered as sovereign in the sense of international law. On this paradoxical issue, the U.S. Supreme Court relied on the notion of "quasi-sovereignty," meaning that Indian nations could have entered into a formal international treaty of land cession but could not exercise territorial sovereignty. In the words of former Special Rapporteur Martinez, indigenous peoples "are sovereign enough to enter into treaties with the purpose of ceding title to their territory, but they are not sovereign enough to function as independent political entities or, for that matter to protect the remnants of their sovereignty."[78] Thus, on the one hand, Indian communities possessed enough sovereignty to sign treaties to cede their territories, while, on the other hand, not being sovereign enough to hold territorial rights except the right to cede their lands. This reasoning is based on the second aspect of the doctrine of discovery—the notion of extinguishable right of occupancy. According to Marshall's views, Indian communities might have been sovereign nations, i.e., with territorial ownership over their homelands, but since their "discovery" by the European explorers, they became "domestic independent nations," i.e., with a residual right of occupancy. In terms of indigenous peoples' land rights, Marshall was willing to recognize only their "right of occupancy." He argued that Indian nations had a right of occupancy of their lands "until their occupancy right was consensually given up, sold for consideration or taken by 'conquest'."[79] In another case from the U.S. Supreme Court, the judge described the causes of extinguishment:

> their rights to its exclusive enjoyment in their own way and for their own purposes (…) until they abandoned them, made a cession to the government, or an authorized sale to individuals. In either case their right became extinct, the lands could be granted disencumbered of the right of occupancy, or enjoyed in full dominion by the purchasers from the Indians.[80]

---

78 *Study on treaties, agreements and other constructive arrangements between States and indigenous populations*, Third Progress Report, U.N. Doc. E/CN.4/Sub.2/1996/23, para. 54.

79 *See* Anthony Peirson & Xavier Bothwell, *We Live on the Land: Implications of Long-Ago Takings of Native American Indian Property*, 6 Ann. Surv. Int'l & Comp. L. 175 (2000).

80 Mitchel and Others v. The United States, 34 U.S. (9 Pet.) 711, 745 (1835).

The causes of extinguishment mentioned by the U.S. Supreme Court should not be seen as exhaustive, as in 1887 the government was authorized to sell lands reserved to the Indians without their consent. However, it would be wrong to view such doctrine only through Marshall's prose. Even though, as stated previously, early writers of international law, such as Vitoria and Grotius, agreed that discovery could not vest a legal title over the "discovered" land to the colonizers, Marshall based his ruling on the assertion of a consensus among European nations that discovery provides a legal title of ownership. The U.S. Supreme Court cases are not isolated and reflect the position of international law at the end of the 19th century as represented by the positivist school. The positivist school, which certainly represented one of the most blatant expressions of Euro-centricity within international law, held that non-European societies possessed no sovereign rights over the territory they inhabited.

Such influence is visible in the 1847 case of *R. v. Symonds* in which the New Zealand Supreme Court affirmed that "the right of the native title owner is withdrawn, the soil vests entirely in the Crown for the behalf of the nation"[81] Similarly, the Supreme Court of New South Wales in *Attorney-General v. Brown* (1847) asserted the acquisition of title by the Crown upon discovery and settlement.[82] In the 1901 *Nireaha Tamaki v. Baker* case, despite pointed that the judgments of Marshall Chief Justice were not binding on a British Court, the Privy Council did refer to the U.S. decisions highlighting that these judgments were entitled to the greatest respect.[83] The notion of right of occupancy was also used in South Africa, for example, following the 1828 Cape Ordinance; the British colonial power issued "tickets of occupation" to permit occupation of the lands of the indigenous communities of the Cape. Such lands were then vested to the government and to missionaries "in trust" for indigenous peoples.[84] It is the Judicial Committee of the Privy Council that best defined the substantial consistency of the indigenous right of occupancy. In the 1888 case of *St. Catherine's Milling and Lumbert Co. v. The Queen,* the Privy Council relied on the Royal Proclamation of 1763 by which the British Crown prohibited Indian land cession by any other party than the Crown, adding that all purchases had to be made on behalf of the Crown. Under the Royal Proclamation, Aboriginal peoples retained an "absolute proprietary right" only limited by their right of alienation to the Crown.[85] Even though the judges refused to

81 R v. Symonds [1847] N.Z.P.C.C. 387 (S.C.).

82 Attorney General v. Brown (1847) 1 Legge 312—Supreme Court of New South Wales.

83 Nireaha Tamaki v. Baker, [1901] A.C. 561, 579—Privy Council.

84 *See* Özlem Ülgen, *Developing the Doctrine of Aboriginal Title in South Africa: Source and Content,* 46(2) J. Afr. L. 138 (2002).

85 St. Catherine's Milling, and Lumber Co. v. The Queen, 14 A.C. 46 (1888)—Privy Council.

define the precise quality or substantive content of this Indian right, the Committee held that: "the tenure of the Indians was a personal and usufructuary right, dependent upon the good will of the sovereign."[86] In the 1926 *Cayuga Indians* case, an international arbitration tribunal also based its decision on the doctrine of discovery.[87] On behalf of the Cayuga Indians, Great Britain brought a claim against the United States for breach of its treaty obligation. In this case the tribunal declared:

> From the time of the discovery of America the Indians tribes have been treated as under the exclusive protection of the power which by discovery or conquest or cession held the land which they occupied. ... The power which had sovereignty over the lands has always been held the sole judge of its relations with the tribes within its domain. The right in this respect acquired by discovery have been held exclusive.[88]

One of the crucial aspects of these early judgments was the reference to the "doctrine of discovery," as through this legal construction the colonizers found the legal basis for the recognition of the superiority of their rights of ownership over the rights of the original inhabitants. As Lee put it, the essence of discovery is "the intentional appropriation of sovereignty over territory treated as a *terra nullius*, which is territory that does not belong to any state."[89] The doctrine of discovery provided the "discovering" power with exclusive sovereign title, as discovery extinguished indigenous peoples' territorial sovereignty, leaving them with a residual right of occupancy. This right of occupancy was itself extinguishable by subsequent cession or conquest. The right of occupancy should consequently be apprehended as a "gift" that recognizes indigenous peoples' right to use their lands, but preserved the superior colonial power to terminate this right in favor of the settlers. In this sense, the notion of the right of occupancy has been mostly developed in the countries where a large European community settled within indigenous territories. The right of occupancy left to the indigenous communities has often been best described as an "imperial right," as captured by Fitzpatrick:

> When peoples impertinently resisted conquest or where colonial occupation was tenuous, the savages were often found to have proprietary rights

86 *Id.; see also* Campbell v. Hall, 1 Cowp. 204 (1774).

87 Cayuga Indians (Great Britain) v. United States, 6 R.I.A.A. 173 (1926).

88 *Id.*, at 176.

89 Seokwoo Lee, *Continuing Relevance of Traditional Modes of Territorial Acquisition in International Law and Modest Proposal*, 16 Conn. J. Int'l L. 1 (2000).

> after all, rights which could then be transferred to settlers. Yet imperial right was still founded on the negating of the same people, with the result that their 'rights' were thoroughly subordinate and could never amount to or reflect that 'holding ... the land' which grounds the occidental 'right of sovereignty.'[90]

It has to be highlighted that the theory of a right of occupancy left the issue of indigenous rights to territory outside the scope of international law, as it implied that ultimately only sovereign States in which the indigenous territories were included could determine the existence and the termination of the indigenous right of occupancy, a right that was ultimately subordinated to the superiority of the State territorial sovereignty. This recognition of a right of occupancy thus signified that indigenous communities lost access to international law, as only sovereign States had a right to territory with Indians tribes afforded a mere "privilege" to occupy the land, without territorial sovereignty, at the behest of the government, who reserved the right to abolish it at any time. As well as the issue of indigenous sovereignty, it is important to comprehend the impact of these judgments on indigenous peoples' land rights in international law, since the legal precedent of the extinguishable rights of occupancy of the Indians had a direct impact on the modern jurisprudence across common law countries.[91]

While in the early judgments of the U.S. Supreme Court, the grounds for extinguishment were either cession or conquest,[92] these causes rapidly expanded. For example, in Southern Rhodesia it was accepted that the British South Africa Company could acquire lands that were reserved to the indigenous tribes "for the purpose of mineral development or as sites of townships, or for railways or other public works."[93] The doctrine of discovery and its accompanying theory of extinguishable rights of occupancy gave birth to legal theories, such as "plenary power," and other forms of imposition of States' legislative and executive bodies, all aimed at extinguishing indigenous peoples' right of occupancy. From this perspective, the early judgments of the U.S. Supreme Court played an important role in defining the doctrine of discovery, and the ultimate superiority of the so-called discovering power over the discovered

---

90 Peter Fitzpatrick, *Terminal legality: Imperialism and the (de)composition of law, in* Law, History, Colonialism, The Reach of Empire 17 (D. Kirkby & C. Coleborne eds., 2001).

91 *See*, for examples, Calder v. Attorney-General of British Columbia, [1973] S.C.R. 313–20—Supreme Court of Canada; Mabo v. Queensland [No 2] (1992) 175 C.L.R. 1., 107 A.L.R. 1—High Court of Australia.

92 *See* Johnson and Braham's Lessee v. M'Intosh, 21 U.S. (8 Wheat.) 543, 574 (1823)—U.S. Supreme Court; *see also* Chapter 1.

93 *In re* Southern Rhodesia [1919] A.C. 211, at 223—Privy Council.

provided some solid foundations for the three pillars that constitute the legal theory regarding indigenous rights in the United States:

> the Congressional Plenary Power Doctrine, which holds that Congress exercises a plenary authority in Indian affairs; the Diminished Tribal Sovereignty doctrine, which holds that Indian tribes still retain those aspects of their inherent sovereignty not expressly divested by treaty or statute, or implicitly divested by virtue of their status; and the Trust Doctrine, which holds that in exercising its broad discretionary authority in Indian affairs, Congress and the Executive are charged with the responsibilities of a guardian acting on behalf of its dependent Indian wards.[94]

In this regard, the theory of extinguishable right of occupancy had gained some maturity and permeated modern legal theory despite its clearly discriminatory foundations. In *United States v. Santa Fe Pacific Railroad*, the Supreme Court declared:

> The manner, method and time of such extinguishment raises political not justiciable issues. … And whether it be done by treaty, by sword, by purchase, by the exercise of complete dominion adverse to the right of occupancy, or otherwise, its justness is not open to inquiry in the courts.[95]

In 1955, the U.S. Supreme Court stated: "Indian occupation of land without government recognition of ownership creates no rights against taking or extinction by the United States."[96] In the same judgment, the U.S. Supreme Court affirmed that extinguishment of Indian title does not even give right to compensation. The Supreme Court stated:

> No case in this Court has ever held that taking of Indian title or use by Congress required compensation. The American people have compassion for the descendants of those Indians who were deprived of their homes and hunting grounds by the drive of civilization. They seek to have the Indians share the benefits of our society as citizens of this nation.

94 Robert A. Williams, *Colombus's Legacy: Law as an Instrument of Racial Discrimination Against Indigenous Peoples' Rights of Self-Determination*, 8 Ariz. J. Int'l & Comp. L. 51–68 (1991).

95 United States v. Santa Fe Pacific Railroad, 314 U.S. 339. 347 (1941).

96 Tee-Hit-Ton Indians v. United States, 348 U.S. 272, 285 (1955).

> Generous provision has been willingly made to allow tribes to recover for wrongs, as a matter of grace, not because of legal liability.[97]

In the United States it is the federal government, through an act of Congress, that has the power to extinguish Indian titles and alienate Indian rights of ownership.[98] However, the doctrine of sovereign immunity under U.S. law automatically barred Indians from suing the federal government for the loss of their lands unless Congress passed a specific law permitting such claims.[99] As pointed out by Epstein, with respect to the supreme authority of the U.S. Congress: "[T]his is the assertion of a State sovereignty and law that, indifferent to justice and morality, displaces or at least prevails over any and all other sovereignties."[100] In this sense, the "Marshall trilogy" of the 19th century has to be regarded as one of the first definitions of what is now known as Native or Aboriginal title doctrine in common law countries.[101] This doctrine, which has been applied in New Zealand, Australia and Canada,[102] established the basis of Native or Aboriginal title doctrine—a doctrine that represents one of the main focus points of the contemporary legal battle over indigenous peoples' land rights.

2 *Contemporary Theories of Extinguishable Indigenous Title*

"Indigenous title" here is used generically as a term that includes both "Native Title" and "Aboriginal Title"—terminology used in different parts of the world.[103] Indigenous title is a right to the land itself as well as the resources of the land, and is based on the presumption that colonial assertion of sovereignty did not necessarily extinguish indigenous peoples' right to land

97 *Id.*

98 *See* Felix S. Cohen, Handbook of American Indian Law (1982).

99 United States v. Dann, 470 U.S. 36, 45 (1985).

100 Roben Epstein, *The Role of Extinguishment in the Cosmology of Dispossession, in* Justice Pending: Indigenous Peoples and Other Good Causes 47 (Gudmundur Alfredsson & Maria Stavropoulou eds., 2002).

101 *See:* Blake A. Watson, *The Impact of the American Doctrine of Discovery on Native Land Rights in Australia, Canada, and New Zealand,* Seattle Ul Rev. 34 (2010): 507.

102 R. v. Symonds [1847] N.Z.P.C.C. 387—Supreme Court; and St. Catherine's Milling and Lumber Co. v. The Queen, [1887] 13 S.C.R. 577—Privy Council. See: Louis A. Knafla, Haijo Westra (eds), Aboriginal Title and Indigenous Peoples: Canada, Australia, and New Zealand (2011).

103 *See* Jérémie Gilbert, *Historical Indigenous Peoples' Land Claims: A Comparative and International Approach to the Common Law Doctrine on Indigenous Title* 56 International and Comparative Law Quarterly pp. 583–611 (2007).

ownership.[104] Indigenous title is what was left to indigenous peoples when colonial powers established their territorial sovereignty. As stated by Justice Brennan in the Australian High Court *Mabo (No. 2)* case: "[O]n acquisition of sovereignty over particular parts of Australia, the Crown acquired a radical title to the land in that part. Native title survived the Crown's acquisition of sovereignty and radical title."[105] As pointed out in Chapter 1, the *Mabo* decision was welcomed as a revolution in the legal theory of dispossession in Australia; then again every revolution contains its own limitations. In affirming that *terra nullius* was a "fiction" that was no more acceptable, the High Court of Australia also asserted the authority of the Crown to extinguish Native title. In his ruling, Justice Brennan stated that the Queensland Parliament retained the legislative power to extinguish Native title.[106] As highlighted by Powell and Bennett: "[T]he doctrine of Aboriginal title proposes that, while pre-colonial rights survive colonisation, they are liable to extinguishment by the new government."[107]

Broadly defined, indigenous title is a right for indigenous peoples to the exclusive use and occupation of their ancestral lands until such right is extinguished either voluntarily or by an act of the national parliament. In most common law countries the theory of indigenous title predominates. The following discussion focuses mostly on Australia and Canada, countries that arguably offer the most developed debate regarding indigenous title and, as Darren Dick puts it, where there has been "an interplay between decisions of the Canadian Supreme Court and the High Court of Australia in developing the doctrines of Aboriginal and Native title."[108] This discussion, though based on a comparative approach, seeks to reflect on key elements of the doctrine of indigenous title to analyse how it undermines indigenous peoples' rights to land as defined under international law. Two particularly contentious issues regarding indigenous title deserve specific attention. The first issue related to the proof of the existence of a title (discussed in Section a), and the second relates to the rules governing the extinguishment of indigenous title (discussed in Section b). Again the following discussion does not aim at offering a comprehensive analysis of the common law doctrine regarding Aboriginal title, but

104 *See* Delgamuukw v. British Columbia, [1997] 3 S.C.R. 1010—Supreme Court of Canada.

105 Mabo & v. Queensland [No 2] (1992) 175 C.L.R. 1, 107 A.L.R. 1; Native title is based on "the traditional laws acknowledged by and the traditional customs observed by the indigenous inhabitants of a territory," *id.* at. 44.

106 *Id.* at 29 and 97.

107 T.W. Bennett & C.H. Powell, *Aboriginal Title in South Africa Revisited*, 15 S. Afr. J. Hum. Rts. 449 (1999) [hereinafter Bennett & Powell].

108 Darren Dick, *Comprehending 'the genius of the common law'—Native Title in Australia and Canada compared post-Delgamuukw*, 5 Australian J. Hum. Rts. 1 (1999).

rather to offer an insight on how this dominant legal theory in the common law world is dominating indigenous peoples' rights, undermining some their rights to land under international law.[109]

a Content and Sources of Indigenous Title: The Burden of Proof

The roots of indigenous title are to be found in the indigenous customs and laws that preceded the acquisition of sovereignty by colonizers. In Canada, courts have highlighted that Aboriginal titles are based on pre-existing Aboriginal laws and on the principle of common law that occupation is proof of possession.[110] Thus, Aboriginal title is a right that has its source in the occupation of land prior to the Crown's assertion of sovereignty. One of the consequences drawn by the Chief Justice in the 1997 case of *Delgamuukw v. British Columbia* is that "an Aboriginal group asserting the claim must establish that it occupied the lands in question at the time at which the Crown asserted sovereignty over the land subject to the title."[111] In this case, the Supreme Court was invited to take into consideration two approaches. The first, proposed by the government of British Columbia and the Federal Government of Canada, asserted that Aboriginal peoples have to prove the physical occupation of the land at the time of sovereignty, whereas the Aboriginal party argued that proof of title should be rooted by reference to Aboriginal law. The decision of the Supreme Court was to take into consideration both pre-sovereignty occupation and Aboriginal laws.[112] In terms of the nature of Aboriginal title, the Supreme Court emphasized the collective proprietary status of the land title.[113] However, even though recognizing the proprietary force of Aboriginal title, the Supreme Court also reaffirmed the power of the government to extinguish such title.[114]

In Australia, the legislature has played an important role in defining Native title. Following the recognition of Native title in the *Mabo* case, the Native Title Act 1993 (NTA) established a legal procedure to determine the existence of Native title in Australia.[115] Based on Section 223 of the NTA, Native title can be defined as a right and interest that is possessed under traditional Aboriginal law. As in Canada, Native title has its origin both in Aboriginal laws and

109 For a rich and comprehensive analysis of common law Aboriginal Title, see: P.G. McHugh, Aboriginal Title: The Modern Jurisprudence of Tribal Land Rights (2011).

110 Delgamuukw v. British Columbia, [1997] 3 S.C.R. 1010—Supreme Court of Canada.

111 *Id.*, para. 144.

112 This is discussed in depth in Chapter 3.

113 Delgamuukw v. British Columbia, [1997] 3 S.C.R. 1010, at para. 115.

114 *Id.*, para. 173.

115 *See* Native Title Act 1993, § 225 of the Act, *available at* www.austlii.edu.au. See also: Lisa Strelein, Compromised Jurisprudence: Native Title Cases since Mabo (2009).

common law; however, the NTA envisages the right to fish or to hunt as part of Native title rights. Thus, there is no formal distinction between indigenous rights and indigenous title in Australia; as a result, rights, such as fishing and hunting, are legally equivalent to the right of ownership. The consequence of this approach is that it is easier to extinguish indigenous peoples' ownership, as it involves the same procedure as any other right.[116] In New Zealand, indigenous title is also based on a similar approach, as in *Te Weehi v. Regional Fisheries Officier* judges held that fishing, as a traditional economic activity, was part of the Maori title.[117] Overall, despite slightly differing, the three national approaches adopt the same approach as regards the nature and sources of indigenous title, which is based both on indigenous customs and common law.

The doctrine on indigenous title is gradually becoming a global phenomenon. Bennett and Powell have pointed out that even though the doctrine of Aboriginal title has been mainly developed in common law countries, the doctrine is not limited to countries that inherited English common law. They argue that Aboriginal title is *sui generis*; therefore "Aboriginal title lies at an intersection between indigenous laws and received systems of colonial law."[118] Courts in Canada and Australia have declared that Aboriginal title is not part of English common law in the narrow sense of that term.[119] Proof of such applicability can be found in the application of Aboriginal title in Quebec where, despite French rules of colonization, Canadian courts applied Aboriginal title doctrine.[120]

In some African states, besides early references to the notion of Native title in Privy Council decisions,[121] national courts have tended to refer to the contemporary doctrine of indigenous title. In the Supreme Court of Appeal of South Africa case of *The Richtersveld Community and Others*, the appellant relied on the doctrine of Aboriginal title. Even though the Court decided that "it is not necessary to pursue the matter any further and it becomes unnecessary to

116 For example, the High Court in *Ward v. Western Australia* developed the idea of partial extinguishment based on the "bundle of rights" approach. As native title is a bundle of rights, partial extinguishment does not have the effect of extinguishing the overall title, but only the concerned part. Ward v. State of Western Australia (1998) 159 A.L.R. 483.

117 Te Weehi v. Regional Fisheries Officer [1986] 1 N.Z.L.R. 680. However, *see* Claire Charters and Andrew Erueti, *Report from the Inside: the CERD Committee's Review of the Foreshore and Seabed Act 2004*, 36 Vict. U. Wellington L. Rev. 257 (2005).

118 Bennett & Powell, *supra* note 107, at 462.

119 *Id.*

120 *See* R. v. Côté, [1996] 3 S.C.R. 139—Supreme Court.

121 *See* the aforementioned case of Amodu Tijani v. The Secretary of Southern Nigeria, 2 A.C. 399 (1921).

decide whether the doctrine forms part of our common law or whether common law should be developed to recognise Aboriginal rights,"[122] the judges relied on the existence of a customary law interest for the indigenous community. Thus, despite the judges' refusal to enter the debate on whether Aboriginal title doctrine was applicable in South Africa, the court relied on indigenous title theory in its finding, and several references to cases dealing with Aboriginal/Native title were made through the judgment. Indeed, the judges found that the Richtersveld community's customary right of ownership had survived the annexation by the British Crown as "these rights constituted a 'customary law interest' and consequently a 'right in land'."[123] On the content and source of such a right, the Supreme Court of Appeal said that "[A]n interest in land held under a system of indigenous law is thus expressly recognised as a 'right in land,' whether or not it was recognised by civil law as a legal right."[124] The approach adopted corresponds to that taken by the Canadian courts regarding Aboriginal title, for the South African Court ultimately recognized the Richersveld right of ownership based on their "customary law interest under their indigenous customary law entitling them to exclusive occupation and use of the subject land and that its interest was akin to the right of ownership held under common law."[125]

To some extent, the "customary law interest" found in this case is equivalent to the notion of Aboriginal/Native Title. As pointed out by Vivier ADP, quoting an Australian decision, such right is also a "creature of traditional laws and customs."[126] In its decision, the Supreme Court of Appeal also focused on the notion of discrimination in its finding of the indigenous community right of ownership. In the judgment, a large emphasis was placed on the fact that the practices used for the dispossession of indigenous territory "were racially discriminatory because they were based upon the false, albeit unexpressed premise that because of the Richtersveld community's race and lack of civilization, they had lost all rights in the land upon annexation."[127] The view of the Court is that even though the undisturbed possession of the land by the concerned indigenous community was ignored on discriminatory grounds, indigenous

122 The Richtersveld Community and Others v. Alexkor Limited and the Government of the Republic of South Africa, Case No. 488/2001 (Mar. 24, 2003).

123 *Id.* at para. 8.

124 *Id.* at para. 9.

125 *Id.* at para. 27.

126 *Id.* at para. 37; *see* Members of the Yorta Yorta Aboriginal Community v. State of Victoria & Ors (2002) H.C.A. 58—High Court of Australia.

127 The Richtersveld Community and Others v. Alexkor Limited and the Government of the Republic of South Africa, Case No. 488/2001, at para. 8 (Mar. 24, 2003).

law regarding land ownership had survived and extended to the common law regime. This approach to indigenous title based on indigenous law that existed prior to annexation was confirmed by the Constitutional Court, which stated that "indigenous law feeds into, nourishes, fuses with and becomes part of the amalgam of South African law."[128] Barume has argued that the doctrine of Aboriginal title is relevant in commonwealth African countries.[129] Elsewhere he has highlighted that Native title theory would be particularly relevant in Kenya.[130]

This evolution is not limited to Africa, as, in Asia, national courts have also referred to the doctrine of Native and Aboriginal title in their decisions. The Federal Court of Malaysia, in a decision of March 2000, reaffirmed a High Court ruling that the doctrine of Native title applies in Malaysia.[131] In this case, involving some members of the Orang Asli community, Mokhtar Sidin JCA recognized that indigenous peoples have specific rights to their lands on the basis of the common law doctrine of Native title. Referring to leading cases on Aboriginal title from the Canada and Australia, the High Court affirmed that "Native title" is a right of the natives to live on their land. The judge applied such a right to the indigenous peoples of Malaysia to affirm the Orang Asli community's common law right to their lands. The judge stated:

> I believe this is a common law right which the natives have and which the Canadian and Australian courts have described as native title. I would agree that in Malaysia the aborigines' common law rights include, inter alia, the right to live on their land as their forefathers had lived and this would mean that even the future generations of the Aboriginal people would be entitled to this right.[132]

In this case, the judge also ruled that Aboriginal common law rights co-exist with other statutory rights guaranteeing indigenous peoples' land rights.[133]

---

128 Alexkor Limited and the Government of South Africa v. The Ritchersveld Community and Others, Case CCT 19/03, at 51 (Oct. 14, 2003).

129 Albert Barume, *Constitutional Protection and Aboriginal Title in Commonwealth African Countries*, Indigenous Rights in the Commonwealth Project (Oct. 2002), *at* www.cpsu.org.

130 Albert Barume, *Indigenous Battling for Land Rights: The Case of the Ogiek of Kenya, in* International Law and Indigenous Peoples 365 (Joshua Castellino & Niamh Walsh eds., 2005).

131 *See* Adong bin Kuwau v. Kerajaan Negeri Johor, [1997] 1 M.L.J. 418, [1998] 2 M.L.J. 158—Federal Court of Malaysia.

132 *Id.*, at 430.

133 On this issue: Ramy Bulan, *Native Title as a Proprietary Right Under the Constitution in Peninsula Malaysia: A Step in the Right Direction?* 9(1) Asia Pac. L. Rev. 83 (2001).

The Sabah and Sarawak High Court in *Nor Anak Nyawai et al.* followed the decision by observing that "the common law respects the pre-existing rights under native law or custom." Relating to the content and the nature of the indigenous title, the Court stated:

> It (native title) is therefore not dependent for its existence on any legislation, executive or judicial declaration ... though they can be extinguished by those acts. (...) They exist long before any legislation and the legislation is only relevant to determine how much of those native customary rights have been extinguished.[134]

This case is illustrative of the larger phenomenon of the diffusion of the theory of indigenous title all over the world.

Despite the different national approaches to indigenous title, overall, regarding the nature and sources of indigenous title, several national courts have adopted a similar attitude in considering that indigenous peoples' land rights have their sources in pre-existing indigenous customs. It is worth noting that this recognition of both the collective nature and the value of indigenous customs regarding their lands are satisfying the requirement of ILO Convention No. 169 on indigenous peoples' land rights.[135] Indigenous title is also meeting the international standards on traditional occupation, as for example, Article 14 of ILO 169, which states: "[T]he rights of ownership and possession of the peoples concerned over the lands which they traditionally occupy shall be recognised."[136] However, if the development of a global doctrine on indigenous title is to be welcomed for its recognition of indigenous customary land rights, it should be asked whether the indigenous title approach is as positive as it seems at first glance. As stated by the judges in the *Ward* case in Australia, it has to be borne in mind that native title is "especially fragile."[137] Indigenous title is indeed very fragile because it is extinguishable and very difficult to prove.

In the *Study of the Problem of Discrimination against Indigenous Populations* undertaken by former UN Special Rapporteur Cobo, one of his key conclusions was that "land occupied and controlled by indigenous populations should be presumed to be indigenous land. In case of doubt or dispute the *onus probandi*

---

134 Nor Anak Nyawai et al. v. Borneo Pulp Plantation Sdn Bhd, [2001] 2 Current L.J. 769 (Malaysia)—Sabah and Sarawak High Court.

135 *See* especially art. 13, Convention Concerning Indigenous and Tribal Peoples in Independent Countries, ILO No. 169, 72 ILO Official Bull. 59 (1989), *reprinted in* 28 I.L.M. 1382 (1989) [hereinafter ILO 169].

136 *Id.*, art. 14.

137 Ward v. Western Australia (2000) 170 A.L.R. 159, 179–80—High Court of Australia.

of the ownership of land should fall … on the non-indigenous populations who claim to have acquired a right to part of the land."[138] Any claimant to indigenous title has to prove the exclusive occupation of the land at the time of colonization. In *Van der Peet*, the Canadian Supreme Court established a test to prove the existence of Aboriginal rights.[139] Under this test, Aboriginal peoples are required to prove that their rights are based on pre-European contact practices, customs and traditions that are integral to the distinctive culture of the Aboriginal group claiming the recognition of Aboriginal rights.[140] In the 1997 *Delgamuukw* case, the governments of Canada and British Columbia invited the Supreme Court to rely on the test established in *Van der Peet* to identify Aboriginal rights when dealing with Aboriginal title. The test laid down by the Court to establish the existence of an Aboriginal title is as follows:

1. the land must have been occupied prior to sovereignty,
2. the occupation of the land must be continuous,
3. at sovereignty that occupation must have been exclusive.[141]

Thus, the courts require evidence of the exclusive occupation of the land at the time of colonization; where the claimants are relying on present occupation, the courts ask for continuity between prior and present occupation, even though "uninterrupted presence on the land need not amount to possession at common law for the purpose of an indigenous law right of occupation."[142] Dick has commented that "present occupation of the land could be relied upon as proof of occupation pre-sovereignty so long as continuity of occupation could be demonstrated."[143] The difficult task of proving the occupation of the land is therefore a burden on indigenous communities. The Canadian Supreme Court has reaffirmed the principles laid down in *Van der Peet*, that courts should receive oral histories as proof to establish occupation. Generally, courts have evolved in their ability to receive indigenous peoples' proof of occupation of the land.[144]

---

138 U.N. Doc. E/CN.4/Sub.2/1983/21/Add.8, para. 519.

139 R. v. Van der Peet, [1996] 2 S.C.R. 507.

140 *See* Russel Lawrence Barsh & James Youngblood Henderson, *The Supreme Court's Van der Peet Trilogy: Naive Imperialism and Ropes of Sand*, 42 McGill L.J. 993 (1997).

141 Delgamuukw v. British Columbia, [1997] 3 S.C.R. 1010., at para. 143.

142 The Richtersveld Community and Others v. Alexkor Limited and the Government of the Republic of South Africa, Case No. 488/2001, at para. 23 (Mar. 24, 2003).

143 Darren Dick, *Comprehending 'the genius of the common law'—Native Title in Australia and Canada compared post-Delgamuukw*, 5 Australian J. Hum. Rts. 1 (1999).

144 This is discussed in Chapter 3.

On the issue of exclusivity, the Assembly of First Nations in Canada has highlighted that "exclusivity does not refer to the absence of other groups on the land, but rather 'the intention and capacity to retain exclusive control'."[145] Australian courts have also admitted that exclusivity does not mean that the land cannot be shared between different communities.[146] In the *Richtersveld Community* case, the Supreme Court of Appeal of South Africa pointed out that "a nomadic lifestyle is not inconsistent with the exclusive and effective right of occupation of land by indigenous peoples."[147] The South African Court added that even though the concerned indigenous community need "not have occupied every bit of the subject land, and even if other indigenous peoples sometimes visited the territory, their exclusive beneficial occupation of the entire area was not affected."[148]

Besides the notion of exclusivity, the central plank to proving indigenous title is the requirement of continuity. Aboriginal peoples claiming ownership have to prove continuity in the occupation, use of the claimed land and a continuing system of customs and traditions since before sovereignty was claimed. In the *Delgamuukw* case, the judges specified that "[T]his requirement does not demand an 'unbroken chain of continuity' but 'substantial maintenance of the connection' between the people and the land."[149] In several cases, Australian and Canadian courts have affirmed that the requirement has to be based on a substantial maintenance of the connection between the people and the land.[150] However, difficulties arise in considering the notion of continuity when linked with the issue of how the land should be considered occupied. Should the land be occupied in the same "traditional" way as it was at the time of colonization or should the courts accept that such occupation may change over time? Justice Toohey in the *Mabo (No. 2)* case stated:

> modification of traditional society in itself does not mean traditional title no longer exists. Traditional title arises from the fact of occupation,

145 Assembly of the First Nations, *The Amicus Curiae Brief of the Assembly of First Nations*, 22 Hum. Rts. Q. 580 (2000).

146 Western Australia v. Ward, Attorney General (NT) v. Ward, Ningamara v. Northern Territory, Ward v. Crosswalk Pty Ltd. (2002) H.C.A. 28, at 502—High Court of Australia.

147 The Richtersveld Community and Others v. Alexkor Limited and the Government of the Republic of South Africa, Case No. 488/2001, at para. 23 (Mar. 24, 2003).

148 *Id.*, para. 24.

149 Delgamuukw v. British Columbia, [1997] 3 S.C.R. 1010—Supreme Court of Canada.

150 R. v. Van der Peet, [1996] 2 S.C.R. 507, at para. 65—Supreme Court of Canada; Delgamuukw v. British Columbia [1997] 3 S.C.R. 1010, at para. 153—Supreme Court of Canada; *see also* Western Australia v. Ward, Attorney General (NT) v. Ward, Ningamara v. Northern Territory, Ward v. Crosswalk Pty Ltd. (2002) H.C.A. 28—High Court of Australia.

> not the occupation of a particular kind of society or way of life. So long as occupation by a traditional society is established now and at the time of annexation, traditional rights exist. An indigenous society cannot, as it were, surrender its rights by modifying its way of life.[151]

The decision from the Australian High Court in the case of the Yorta Yorta peoples illustrates the impact of the high burden of proof on indigenous peoples' native title claims.[152] This case was one of the first to be filed after the federal parliament amended the NTA with the adoption of the Native Title Amendment Act of 1998 (NTAA). The NTAA shifted the burden of proof onto the Aboriginal people who have to provide evidence of their continuous occupation of their land. The Yorta Yorta people claimed ownership of some of their lands along the Murray River on the border between New South Wales and Victoria. Before the High Court, the Aboriginal peoples argued that by requiring positive proof of continuous acknowledgment and observance of traditional laws and customs in relations to land, the lower courts had misapplied the definition of native title. The High Court rejected the claim on the basis of a lack of proof that the claimants had maintained connections with their lands and carried out traditional practices on it since European invasion.

From this perspective, the burden of proof of continuity appears utterly biased, as it does not take into consideration the effects of forced removal of Aboriginal peoples that took place across Australia during the past centuries. Thus, forcible removal in itself could easily be a continuing source of extinguishment. As such extinguishment stands as a form of blanket amnesty for past dispossession. Paradoxically, even though Native title was not recognized in the past, it can be extinguished by grants that were given at a date where Native title was not recognized. This is the consequence of what has been designated the "temporal separation of recognition and extinguishment." In the words of the Aboriginal & Torres Strait Islander Social Justice Commissioner:

> while the legal category of native title is inserted into this history, the process of recognition is not. The legal requirement for recognition of native title is the maintenance of a 'continued connection.' While there is

151 Mabo v. Queensland [No 2] (1992) 175 C.L.R. 1, 192, 107 A.L.R. 1, 150—High Court of Australia.

152 Members of the Yorta Yorta Aboriginal Community v. State of Victoria & Ors (2002) H.C.A. 58.

> an 'historical' component to this requirement, the critical date for proof is the present; the contemporary connection.[153]

Once the existence of a right to the land in the form of an indigenous title has been proven, it still remains for indigenous claimants to prove that such title has not been extinguished. In its 2005 concluding observations on Australia, CERD has expressed its concerns on this issue and pointed out that "the high standard of proof required is reported to have the consequence that many indigenous peoples are unable to obtain recognition of their relationship with their traditional lands."[154] The Committee recommended "that the State party review the requirement of such a high standard of proof, bearing in mind the nature of the relationship of indigenous peoples to their land."[155] Similarly, regarding the international standards on indigenous peoples' land rights, this high standard of proof is contrary to ILO 169 as Article 14.1 of the Convention provides for the recognition of ownership rights over lands traditionally occupied by indigenous peoples.[156] The present standard, which does not take into consideration lands that were traditionally occupied, would be contrary to both the ILO Convention 169 and the UN Declaration on the Rights of Indigenous Peoples.

b International Law and Extinguishment

According to the current indigenous title doctrine, the process of extinguishment is in the hands of the executive or legislature.[157] Indigenous title could be explicitly extinguished by an act specifically adopted to this purpose or implicitly, by an act that creates a situation that would ultimately extinguish the title. Based on traditional doctrine of the separation of powers, the judicial power is limited to reviewing executive and legislative acts of extinguishment. Thus, courts have the power to control the legality of the extinguishment. Judicial control of the executive or legislative act of extinguishment is based on the requirement of a clear and plain intention. The general rule regarding extinguishment is that the legislative power should pass a valid act that exhibits a

153 Aboriginal and Torres Strait Islander Social Justice Commissioner, *Native Title Report 2000*, at 18.

154 *Concluding Observations of the Committee on the Elimination of Racial Discrimination:* Australia, U.N. Doc. CERD/C/AUS/CO/14, para. 17 (Apr. 15, 2005).

155 *Id.*

156 Art. 14, ILO 169, *supra* note 139.

157 However, *see* Kent McNeil, *Extinguishment of Aboriginal Title in Canada: Treaties, Legislation, and Judicial Discretion*, 33 Ottawa L. Rev. 301 (2001).

clear and plain intention to extinguish indigenous title. The requirement of a plain and clear legislative intention is a common feature of most of the jurisdictions recognizing indigenous title.[158] The legislature's intention would be determined by an objective test, as the intention has to be found in the words of the act itself and not in the state of mind of the legislators.[159] Secondly, extinguishment has often been achieved implicitly through legislative acts aimed at regulating the use of the land, potentially extinguishing indigenous title by "necessary implication." One of the issues for national courts is to appreciate whether legislation aimed at regulating activities, such as fishing, hunting or other laws whose purpose is to control use of natural resources, could extinguish indigenous title by ricochet. Indigenous title might be affected by regulations that do not address the existence of the title but that concern the same land for the purposes of conservation or even recreation.

Canadian courts have developed a test that could serve as a model in other parts of the world, using the indigenous title doctrine. In *R. v. Sparrow*, the Supreme Court of Canada established a "justification test" for determining the legality of governmental infringement of any Aboriginal right protected by the 1982 Constitution Act.[160] In this case, the Supreme Court required that the government justify the infringement by showing a substantial and compelling legislative objective, and by proving that the Crown's fiduciary obligations had been respected. The Supreme Court affirmed that the effects of such regulations infringing upon Aboriginal rights were to be assessed on a case-by-case basis, and that ultimately the government would have to show that the regulation was reasonable and justified by a valid legislative objective.[161] Ultimately, even though Aboriginal rights are not absolute (the government can infringe on those constitutionally recognized rights), such an infringement must be justified by the needs of society. The Supreme Court gave three examples of a valid objective that could extinguish Aboriginal rights: laws aimed at conserving and managing natural resources, laws preventing the exercise of Aboriginal rights that might cause harm to other segments of the population and any other reasons that are "compelling and substantial."[162] The courts would then seek to evaluate whether the government exercised a "plain and clear

158 *See* Shaunnagh Dorsett, *Clear and Plain Intention' Extinguishment of Native Title in Australia and Canada post-Wik*, 6 Griffith L. Rev. 96 (1997).

159 *See*, for example, Western Australia v. Ward, Attorney General (NT) v. Ward, Ningamara v. Northern Territory, Ward v. Crosswalk Pty Ltd. (2002) H.C.A. 28, at 502—High Court of Australia.

160 R. v. Sparrow, [1990] 1 S.C.R. 1075.

161 *Id.* at 411.

162 *Id.*

intention" to extinguish the Aboriginal right on a two-part test. The first part of the test is based on the assessment of whether the legislation that would infringe existing Aboriginal rights is justifiable as compelling and substantial (e.g., conserving or managing natural resources). In *Delgamuukw*, the Supreme Court reaffirmed that the justification test set-up in *R v. Sparrow* was applicable in cases of infringement of Aboriginal title. The Supreme Court ruled that provincial legislatures as well as the Canadian Parliament could infringe Aboriginal title.[163] Providing examples, the Supreme Court stated that the conservation of fisheries would be a compelling and substantial objective, whereas "sport fishing regulation without a significant economic component would fail this aspect of the test of justification."[164]

In Australia, the Full Federal Court in *Fourmile v. Selpam Pty Ltd.* held that the building of a public road created enforceable rights of free passage for the public that are wholly inconsistent with the continued existence of Native title; thus Native title was to be regarded as extinguished in this area.[165] Conversely in *Yanner v. Eaton*, the High Court held that while the Fauna Act regulated the exercise of Native title rights relating to the taking of crocodiles, it did not extinguish title. Scrutinizing the Fauna Act, the majority of the High Court determined that the act vested property in the Crown for the purposes of resource management and did not confer full beneficial ownership of fauna on the Crown.[166] However, taken as a whole, it seems that the control exercised by national courts over justifications for the infringements of indigenous title are defined too broadly to meet international legal standards. Based on the jurisprudence of the Human Rights Committee (HRC), Ülgen argued that the criterion used by the judges in Canada would not comply with the International Covenant on Civil and Political Rights (ICCPR), as to comply with Article 27 "development activities must allow for the continuation of the right to enjoy culture."[167] This led him to conclude that "the legality of government infringement on Aboriginal lands is determined by the sustainability of the traditional indigenous economy, rather than the economic benefit of the population as a whole from development activities."[168] The danger is that, in some

163 On this issue, *see* Kent McNeil, *Aboriginal Title and the Division of Powers: Rethinking Federal and Provincial Jurisdictions*, 61 Sask. L. Rev. 431 (1998).

164 Delgamuukw v. British Columbia, [1997] 3 S.C.R. 1010, at para. 161.

165 Fourmile v. Selpam Pty Ltd. (1998) 80 F.C.R. 151; on public roads and native title *see also* Ward v. State of Western Australia (1998) 159 A.L.R. 483—Federal Court (Lee J).

166 Yanner v. Eaton (1999) 201 C.L.R. 351.

167 Özlem Ülgen, *Aboriginal Title in Canada: Recognition and Reconciliation*, 42(2) Neth. Int'l L. Rev. 147, at 171 (2000).

168 *Id.*

cases, the infringement would be akin to extinguishment because of the wide legislative objectives the government can use to justify the infringement.

At the regional level, the Inter-American Commission of Human Rights (IACHR) has explored the relationship between the theory of extinguishable indigenous title to territory and human rights in the case of *Mary and Carrie Dann v. United States*.[169] In this case the petitioners, both members of the Western Shoshone indigenous community, alleged that the U.S. government had interfered with the use and occupation of their ancestral lands, thus violating some of their rights guaranteed by the American Declaration of the Rights and Duties of Man. More precisely, the petitioners challenged a decision of the Indian Claims Commission, which had concluded that Western Shoshone title to land had been extinguished.[170] The U.S. district court later confirmed the extinguishment of indigenous title and affirmed the acquisition of the Western Shoshone territory through the "estoppel effect of the ICC [Indian Claims Commission] judgment."[171] On appeal, the Ninth Circuit Court stated that the government had not shown clear evidence of its intent to extinguish Aboriginal title.[172] However, the Supreme Court ruled that such extinguishment had in fact occurred, with the payment of a sum of money to the tribe adduced as evidence of such extinguishment.[173] In this case, the United States recognized that the Western Shoshone nation had title to their ancestral lands, but that such title had been extinguished.[174] Thus, for the IACHR, the issue was not to determine whether the indigenous peoples have right to their lands, but rather to assess whether any part of such property rights remained unextinguished.[175] The Commission stated:

> While the State has suggested that the extinguishment of Western Shoshone title was justified by the need to encourage settlement and agricultural developments in the western United States, the Commission does not consider that this can justify the broad manner in which the State has purported to extinguish indigenous claims, including those of the Danns, in the entirety of the Western Shoshone territory.[176]

169 Mary and Carrie Dann v. United States, Report No. 113/01, Case No. 11.140 (Oct. 15, 2001).
170 *See* Shoshone Tribe v. United States, 11 I.C.C. 387 (1962).
171 United States v. Dann (Dann I), 572 F.2d 222, 223 (9th Cir. 1978).
172 United States v. Dann, 706 F.2d 919 (9th Cir. 1983).
173 United States v. Dann, 470 U.S. 39 (1985); *see also* United States v. Dann, 873 F.2d 1189, 1199 (9th Cir. 1989).
174 Mary and Carrie Dann v. United States, Report No. 113/01, Case No. 11.140 (Oct. 15, 2001).
175 *Id.* at para. 100.
176 *Id.* at para. 145.

In this process, the Inter-American Commission set out the guideline that any process of extinguishment should be in conformity with fundamental guarantees of equality before the law; and that such determination should consider both the collective and individual nature of property rights.

In most cases, courts have to determine the balance between indigenous titles and other non-indigenous land titles or grants against interests that are incompatible with the exercise of the indigenous title. Legally, the question is to evaluate whether non-indigenous title takes priority over the indigenous title. For judges the difficulty concerns whether indigenous title and other titles can co-exist or whether they are mutually inconsistent. The central issue that unpins this discussion is ultimately a question of equality: are indigenous titles equal to other titles or are they extinguishable by such other subsequent titles?

At the national level, courts have had to deal with the clash between notions of equality and indigenous title in seeking to determine, in cases of competing claims over the same piece of land, which title will prevail. One of the most passionate debates on the issue came from Australia where judges have been pushed to rule on this issue.[177] The relationship between the different land titles is a critical issue in Australia, as in several cases, Native titles are opposed to freehold, leasehold or mining lease interests. One of the critical issues was notably to determine whether pastoral leases extinguished Native title.[178] The difficulty in this case is to appreciate whether pastoral leases have the effect of extinguishing Native titles knowing that the purpose of the granting of these titles was not to extinguish Native title but rather to create interests in land over which it was assumed that there was no prior owner. In the case of the *Wik Peoples v. Queensland*, the High Court by a 4:3 majority, adopted a rationale based on equality and recognized that Native title was not necessarily extinguished by pastoral lease.[179] This was based on the idea that pastoral lease did not clearly and plainly show an intention to extinguish Native title. The significant outcome of the decision is its reference to the notion of "co-existence," meaning that Native title and pastoral lease could co-exist on the same land. However, the Court held that in cases of clear legal inconsistency between the two titles, Native title would be extinguished.

---

177 For a comparison between Canada and Australia, *see* Kent McNeil, *The Vulnerability of Indigenous Land Rights in Australia and Canada*, 42 Osgoode Hall L.J. 271 (2004).

178 *See* James Fitzgerald, *Effect of Pastoral Leases in Queensland: Wik Peoples v. State of Queensland & Ors*, 3 (78) Aboriginal L. Bull. 28 (1996).

179 Wik Peoples v. Queensland (1996), 141 A.L.R. 129. On this case, *see* Frank Brennan, The Wik Debate: Its Impact on Aborigines, Pastoralists and Miners (1998).

Hence, Native title could be extinguished by a Crown grant to a third party, which is inconsistent with the continued enjoyment of Native title. The High Court has gradually established an "inconsistency of incidents test." In *Mabo*, Brennan J stated that it was necessary to scrutinize whether the rights granted are inconsistent with native title. Relating to the relationship between native and other non-indigenous title, Brennan J explained: "[W]here the Crown has validly alienated land by granting an interest that is wholly or partially inconsistent with a continuing right to enjoy native title, native title is extinguished to the extent of inconsistency."[180] This inconsistency test removes judicial control of the intention, as ultimately courts would only appreciate whether there is another non-indigenous title. If there is such a title, then the question of the intention of the legislature to extinguish Native title need not be considered, because there is a presumption that the granting of a non-indigenous title signifies the will to extinguish the Native title. There have been many cases involving such balancing between other private interests and the extinguishment of indigenous peoples' title. For example, in *Fejo v. Northern Territory*, the Larrakia people claimed to own native title on a land that had once been granted to a private individual in the form of a fee simple (i.e., in freehold). The Court was asked to decide whether the Native title had been extinguished by freehold grant and if so, whether it could be revived when that grant ceased to exist. The judges decided that a grant of fee simple permanently extinguished all Native titles because the rights given under a freehold grant are wholly inconsistent with Native title rights. In this case native title had been extinguished and could not be revived, even though the freehold was subsequently suspended.[181] In *Ward* the High Court ruled:

> The test requires a comparison between the legal nature and incidents of the existing native title and the statutory grant … the question is not whether the estate or interest granted had been exercised in a way that was incompatible with the exercise of native title rights but whether it was legally capable of being so exercised.[182]

Consequently, the High Court had referred to Native title as a "bundle of rights" that could be partially extinguished.[183] Another blow was added to the content

180 Mabo v. Queensland [No 2] (1992) 175 C.L.R. 1, 69.

181 Fejo v. Northern Territory (1998) 195 C.L.R. 96—High Court of Australia.

182 Western Australia v. Ward, Attorney General (NT) v. Ward, Ningamara v. Northern Territory, Ward v. Crosswalk Pty Ltd. (2002) H.C.A. 28.

183 *Id.*

of Aboriginal title as the judges stated that indigenous peoples had no mineral rights in their land and confirmed that certain rights could be eliminated by other occupations/activities, such as mining. Therefore, extinguishment of the Native title would depend on the exercise of rights by a third party, and the burden to prove that the Native title is not inconsistent falls clearly on indigenous peoples.[184] As pointed out by Bennett and Powell, "extinguishment should not depend on the actual exercise of rights by a third party, because allowing private activities to decide the fate of an Aboriginal title would be in conflict with the rule that only the Crown has the power of extinguishment."[185] As stated by the Aboriginal and Torres Strait Islander Social Justice Commissioner: "[T]he principle of equality requires that the law accord native title holders the same level of protection and security in the enjoyment of title as that enjoyed by non-Indigenous title holders. The extinguishment of Indigenous interests in land for the benefit of non-Indigenous interests in land is racially discriminatory."[186]

Based on the notion of equality, another controversial legal issue is the question of the concurrence of rights. In her report on indigenous peoples and their relationship to land, Daes emphasized that extinguishment is a procedure only applied against indigenous peoples. She wrote: "Aboriginal title is normally subject to complete extinguishment by the Government of the State, without the legal protection and rights that in most countries protect the land and property of citizens."[187] Thus, she noted that the concept of Aboriginal title is by itself discriminatory as "it provides only defective, vulnerable and inferior legal status for indigenous land and resource ownership."[188] Extinguishment suppresses all the rights of indigenous peoples even those of occupation and the right to use their lands. Extinguishment is an act of total and absolute confiscation with no recourse, which goes against the increasing recognition in international law of the special and fundamental relationship that indigenous peoples have with their lands. Matthew Coone, a Cree Grand Chief, when addressing the Canadian Royal Commission on Aboriginal Peoples said "the

184 For comments on this case, *see* Lisa Strelein, *Western Australia v. Ward on Behalf Miriuwung Gajerrong, High Court of Australia, 8 August 2002: Summary of Judgement*, 2(17) Land, Rts., L.: Issue of Native Title (2002).

185 Bennett & Powell, *supra* note 108, at 478.

186 Aboriginal & Torres Strait Islander Social Justice Commissioner, *Native Title Report 2000* (2000).

187 Erica I. Daes, Special Rapporteur, *Human Rights of Indigenous Peoples: Indigenous People and their relationship to land*, Working Paper, U.N. Doc. E/CN.4/Sub.2/1997/17, at para. 29.

188 *Id.*, para. 31.

doctrine of *terra nullius* is being rejected as a racist construct and a breach of human rights. Extinguishment is simply *terra nullius* applied after the fact."[189]

The practice of extinguishment also appears to be in contradiction with the international instruments that insist on indigenous peoples' rights to participation and consultation in decisions affecting them. The right to participate in decisions affecting them constitute an important aspect of indigenous peoples' rights under international law (see Chapter 5 and 6). Relating to land rights, this translates into a duty to consult indigenous peoples in decisions affecting their land ownership and usage.[190] General Recommendation XXIII to ICERD states "that no decisions directly relating to their rights and interests are taken without their informed consent."[191]

Thus, under ICERD, regarding indigenous peoples' participatory rights, indigenous peoples should give their consent beforehand to any decisions directly affecting them. As decisions affecting their rights over land and natural resources would fall within this category, the standard for decisions regarding land rights would require such free and informed consent.[192] Thus, the practice of unilateral extinguishment would appear to be in contradiction to such standard. Similarly, the ILO Convention 169 clearly affirms that the prior and informed consent of indigenous peoples is legally necessary before states can exploit indigenous peoples' territories.[193] Article 7 states that "the peoples

---

189 Presentation to the Royal Commission on Aboriginal Peoples by the Grand Council of the Cree: Eeyou Astchee (Montreal, Québec, Nov. 18, 1993), at 7.

190 *See* James Anaya, *Indigenous Peoples' Participatory Rights in Decisions about Natural Resources Extraction: The More Fundamental Issue of What Rights Indigenous Peoples have in Lands and Resources*, 22 Ariz. J. Int'l & Comp. L. 7 (2005).

191 General Recommendation 23: Indigenous Peoples, CERD, U.N. Doc. A/52/18, Annex V; CERD/C/51/Misc.13/Rev.4, para. 4(d) (1997).

192 For example, the Committee clearly criticized the lack of participation of indigenous peoples in the formulation of the amendment, as the government should have ensured that all members of the indigenous community had equal rights in respect of effective participation in public life, and that no decision directly relating to their rights and interests were taken without their informed consent, as recommended under General Recommendation XXIII, *see* Decision 2(54) on Australia, 18/03/99, A/54/18, para. 21(2). On this issue, *see also* Special Rapporteur on contemporary forms of racism, racial discrimination, xenophobia and related intolerance, U.N. Doc. E/CN.4/2002/24/Add.1 (Feb. 26, 2002).

193 On national effects of the right to participation as enshrined in ILO 169, *see*, for example, Jaime Cordoba Trivino, Defensor Del Pueblo, en representation de varias personas integrantes del Grupo Etnico Indigena U'Wa, Colombia Corte Constitutional, Sentencia No. SU-039/97—Constitutional Court of Colombia (in which the Colombian Constitutional Court held that an exploration license should not have been granted because indigenous peoples had not been properly consulted contrary to the right of participation contained in ILO 169).

concerned shall have the right to decide their own priorities for the process of development." Article 6(1) requires that governments shall:

(a) consult the peoples concerned, through appropriate procedures and in particular through their representative institutions, whenever consideration is being given to legislative or administrative measures which may affect them directly;
(b) establish means by which these peoples can freely participate, to at least the same extent as other sectors of the population, at all levels of decision-making in elective institutions and administrative and other bodies responsible for policies and programmes which concern them.

Thus, unilateral extinguishment is certainly contrary to the ILO provisions on States' duty of consultation.

The practice of extinguishment is also in contradiction with the UNDRIP. The Declaration strongly insists on States' duty to consult indigenous peoples in decisions that may affect them and on the duty to ensure indigenous peoples' participation in decision making. Article 10 of the Declaration states: "Indigenous peoples shall not be forcibly removed from their lands or territories. No relocation shall take place without the free and informed consent of the indigenous peoples concerned." Articles 11, 28, 29 and 32 also mention free and informed consent, and Article 19 states:

> States shall consult and cooperate in good faith with the indigenous peoples concerned through their own representative institutions in order to obtain their free, prior and informed consent before adopting and implementing legislative or administrative measures that may affect them.

The Proposed American Declaration contains a similar provision in its Article 21(2), which also refers to indigenous peoples' right to free and informed consent.[194] It is worth noting that in the aforementioned case of *Mary and Carrie Dann v. United States*, on the issue of unilateral extinguishment by State's authorities, the IACHR highlighted that indigenous peoples should not be

194 Proposed American Declaration, art. 21(2) reads: "Unless exceptional circumstances so warrant in the public interest, the states shall take necessary measures to ensure that decisions regarding any plan, program or proposal affecting the rights or living conditions of indigenous peoples are not made without the free and informed consent and participation of those peoples, that their preferences are recognized and that no such plan, program or proposal that could have harmful effects on those peoples is adopted."

deprived of their land rights "except with fully informed consent."[195] Overall, based on ICERD, ILO 169, the UNDRIP, and the OAS proposed declaration, to be legal, extinguishment would have to be based on the informed consent of indigenous peoples; in this regards, the practice of unilateral extinguishment is contrary to the international standards on indigenous peoples' participatory rights.

In addition, it is suggested that the theory of unilateral extinguishable indigenous title is also contrary to indigenous peoples' rights to participation in decisions affecting them. This right to participation refers to a right for indigenous peoples to be consulted in decisions affecting them; thus, under such right, indigenous peoples do not have a right to consent but a lesser right to be consulted. Regarding indigenous peoples' participatory rights, the HRC refers to a larger right to participation, rather than a right to free and informed consent. In its General Comment on Article 27, the HRC affirmed that indigenous communities must have effective participation in decisions that affect the community, especially where culture manifests itself in a particular way of life associated with the use of land resources.[196] In the *Länsmann* case, the HRC affirmed that when undertaking acts that might infringe indigenous peoples' rights, States have a duty to consult indigenous peoples.[197] In its concluding observation concerning the report from Canada, the HRC recommended "that the practice of extinguishing inherent Aboriginal rights be abandoned as incompatible with article 1 of the Covenant."[198] Hence, extinguishment may clearly be found in opposition to the right of participation of indigenous peoples in decisions affecting them in relation to their lands and territories. Overall, the practice of unilateral extinguishment of indigenous peoples' rights to land is contrary to States' obligation to consult indigenous peoples in decisions affecting them, whether this obligation extends to indigenous peoples' right to informed consent or to a lesser right to participate in such decisions; in both cases extinguishment does not respect both obligations of participation.

195 Mary and Carrie Dann v. United States, Case No. 11.140, Report 75/02, at para. 131 (Oct. 15, 2001).

196 Human Rights Committee, General Comment 23, art. 27 (50th sess., 1994), Compilation of General Comments and General Recommendations Adopted by Human Rights Treaty Bodies, U.N. Doc. HRI/GEN/1/Rev.1 at 38, para. 7 (1994).

197 Länsman et al. v. Finland, Communication No. 511/1992, U.N. Doc. CCPR/C/52/D/511/1992, at para. 9.5. *See also* Apirana Mahuika et al. v. New Zealand, Communication No. 547/1993, U.N. Doc. CCPR/C/70/D/547/1993 (2000).

198 U.N. Doc. CCPR/C/79/Add.105, para. 8 (1999).

Conclusion

This chapter has taken an historical approach to analyze how international law, notably though the development of State practices, has developed a theory of extinguishable rights to land for indigenous peoples. As noted earlier this was first developed through the adoption of colonial treaties which were then disregarded and extinguished unilaterally by States. However as examined in this chapter it would be wrong to assume that the practice of extinguishment of indigenous peoples' land rights has disappeared from contemporary practice as many jurisdictions are still relying on legal theories of extinguishable rights for indigenous peoples. As noted earlier it is mainly developed under the common law theory of Aboriginal or Native title which leaves indigenous peoples at the mercy of a potential extinguishment of their rights to land. Indigenous title can be unilaterally extinguished without indigenous consent and just compensation. Extinguishment is a discriminatory practice at two levels. First, extinguishment is only applicable against indigenous title – no other titles to land ownership are extinguishable, and, in this regard, it is imperative that indigenous title be submitted to the same level of protection against expropriation. Secondly, the fact that indigenous title can be extinguished by other titles is clearly discriminatory, since it assumes that indigenous title is inferior and subordinated. Thus, the concept of indigenous title raises concerns about equality before the law, one of the most fundamental human rights issues.[199] This theory of extinguishable indigenous peoples' right to land is undoubtedly a vestige of the colonial notion of 'discovery' which relied on the vision that colonial law had the inherent effect of extinguishing any other form of land tenure. Whilst the common law theory supports the idea that some of the pre-existing land rights might have 'survived' colonization, the extremely high burden of proof put on the indigenous communities to prove the existence of such right to land, coupled with the extreme fragility of the such a right makes indigenous peoples victims of a legal system which does not recognize their full and natural rights to their lands and territories. While the common law doctrine on aboriginal title is not developed under the precepts of international law, it has been emerging as a spin off of the international colonial legal doctrine regarding title to territory. Moreover, it is a legal doctrine which has gained a certain universal recognition by being adopted by several national jurisdictions across the globe. As such when considering indigenous peoples' land rights under international law, it is important to keep

199 Richard Bartlett, *Mabo: Another Triumph for the Common Law*, 15 Sydney L. Rev. 178 (1993).

in mind that a large part of the globe is still governed by a legal theory which is relying on the notion of extinguishable indigenous peoples' rights as developed under colonial rules. On a perhaps more positive note, the common law doctrine on aboriginal title has raised several important issues; one of the most fundamental being the recognition that indigenous title is a collective and *sui generis* right fundamentally based on the customary practices of indigenous peoples. Bearing in mind the fierce debates at the international level on the issue of collective rights for indigenous peoples, the importance of the jurisprudence emerging from the common law courts on that issue provide some insightful legal elements, notably regarding the place of customary laws and the collective nature of indigenous peoples, attachment to their lands. This evolution from the theories of dispossession towards the gradual recognition of indigenous peoples' rights to own and use their lands forms the subject of the next part of this book.

PART 2

Indigenous Peoples as Subjects: Theories of Protection

Recent developments in international law have arguably signalled the end of the age of victimisation. Instead, with indigenous peoples in the forefront, it can be argued that we are witnessing the birth of a new era in which the recognition of indigenous peoples' land rights is gradually coming to occupy a central position in international legal discourse. In the words of Thornberry, after the ambiguous discourse of international law, indigenous peoples have now entered the age of rights.[1] Thus, after examining the international legal discourse on dispossession, the second part of the book enters into a more positive approach towards indigenous peoples' land rights by exploring whether after centuries of dispossession, international law, notably under the human rights framework, could ultimately make a positive difference for indigenous peoples. In so doing, it emphasises the changed status of indigenous peoples from victims to subjects of international human rights law, highlighting how their rights to land has find some protection under human rights law.

As highlighted in the introduction to this book, indigenous peoples' relationship with their territory is deeply embedded in their economic, social and cultural way of life. From this perspective, indigenous peoples' land rights are addressed through different lenses of the human rights discourse including civil, political, economic, social and cultural rights. The following discussion attempts an evaluation of the current legal routes through which indigenous peoples' land rights have been addressed under human rights law, notably focusing on the importance given property and cultural rights. One of the arguments made herein is that in terms of land rights and indigenous peoples there have been two main judicial approaches, one based on a right to property (Chapter 3) and the other based on cultural rights (Chapter 4). The first approach, the recognition of indigenous peoples' right to land ownership, is based on property rights, while the second, the right to use, is based on the view that indigenous peoples' survival, as distinct cultural entities, depends on the continued access to lands that they have occupied since time immemorial.

1 Patrick Thornberry, Indigenous Peoples and Human Rights 89 (2002); *see* Norberto Bobbio, The Age of Rights (1996).

 DOI 10.1163/9789004323254_006

CHAPTER 3

Land Rights as Proprietary Rights

> The violence of expelling indigenous peoples and taking the territory that gave them identity as well as feeding them was an injustice that should invalidate the moral argument for private property.
>
> ANDRO LINKLATER[1]

The right to property has played a tremendous role in the development of human norms and values.[2] As typical property law is primarily concerned with property in the form of land,[3] an appropriate framework for the recognition of indigenous peoples' land rights would be through the recognition of their right to property. Property generally refers to the "ownership over a thing or things," but the word is also often associated with the idea of property in land.[4] Legally, the category 'property law' also primarily refers to property in the form of land.[5] Hence, property rights often appear as the obvious place for the protection of land rights. Commonly, property rights have been a central feature of the affirmation of individual liberties against state authority.[6] As captured by Ederington: "the protection of private property from state interference has been one of the most pronounced themes throughout the history of modern international law since its inception in the seventeenth century."[7] Even though, under international law, provisions concerning property rights do not specifically focus on land rights, in the context

---

1 Andro Linklater, Owning the Earth: The Transforming History of Land Ownership 108 (2013).

2 See: Richard Schlatter, Private Property: The History of an Idea (1951); Lawrence Becker, Property Rights: Philosophical Foundations (1977); James Penner, The Idea of Property in Law (2000).

3 *See* Carol Rose, *Property as the Keystone Right*, 71 Notre Dame L. Rev. 329 (1996); for a discussion on property right and its evolution, *see* Michael A. Heller, *Property, in* The Oxford Handbook of Legal Studies 62–79 (Peter Cane & Mark Tushnet eds., 2003).

4 See *Oxford English Dictionary* (11th Ed., 2004).

5 Under most legal systems of the world property in land laws fall within the larger category of property rights. See: John Steven & Robert Pearce, Land Law (1999); A.W.B. Simpson, A History of the Land Law (1986); E.H. Burn, Cheshire & Burn's Modern Law of Real Property (16th ed., Butterworths, 2000).

6 *See* Jeremy Waldron, The Right to Private Property (1988).

7 Benjamin Ederington, *Property as a Natural Institution: The Separation of Property from Sovereignty in International Law*, American University International Law Review 13, no. 2 (1997): 263–331, at 263.

of indigenous peoples' rights this chapter explores how the discourse on property rights could relate to indigenous peoples' right to the ownership of their lands.

The notion of property is infused with philosophical and social-cultural notions; it is thus difficult to define a universal legal notion of property. As noted by Tsosie: "[P]roperty rights are, by nature, social rights; they embody how we, as a society, have chosen to reward the claims of some people to finite and critical goods, and to deny the claims to the same goods to others."[8] It is by way of this social rights approach to property rights that indigenous peoples' land claims are being brought to the forefront of the discussion on property rights. As it is examined in this chapter, when it comes to linking property rights and land rights, two majors challenges have emerged for indigenous peoples. First, property rights have largely been developed as individual rather than collective rights. Many indigenous communities across the globe have made it clear that from their perspective land rights are usually considered to be of a collective nature, but also not as an alienable, marketed orientated right. Many indigenous peoples refer to their collective rights as custodians rather than individual owners of the land.[9] In general, under international human rights law, States have been extremely reluctant to recognise collective rights.[10] Since collective forms of ownership are usually a central feature of indigenous peoples' attachment to their ancestral lands, this represent one of the first challenge in trying to integrate land rights within the property rights discourse. This dichotomy, or clash, between two different visions of what is meant by property is examined in the first part of the chapter. A second major difficulty relating the connection between property rights and land rights relates to the issue of remedies. Indeed, property rights are not absolute; therefore public authorities can, under specific conditions, expropriate them and have to

8 Rebecca Tsosie, *Land, Culture, and Community: Reflections on Native Sovereignty and Property in America*, 34 Ind. L. Rev. 1291 (2001).

9 See Jérémie Gilbert, *Custodians of the Land: Indigenous Peoples, Human Rights and Cultural Integrity*, in Cultural Diversity, Heritage and Human Rights Intersections in Theory and Practice (William Logan, Mairead NicCraith, Michele Langfield eds., 2010).

10 *See* Peter Jones, *Human Rights, Group Rights and Peoples' Rights*, 21(1) Hum. Rts. Q. 80–97 (1999); Michael Freeman, *Are there Collective Human Rights?*, 43 Pol. Stud. 25 (1995); Martin Scheinin, *How to Resolve Conflicts between Individual and Collective Rights?*, *in* Rethinking Non-Discrimination and Minority Rights 219–38 (Martin Scheinin & Reeta Toivanen eds., 2005); Geoff Gilbert, *Individuals, Collectivities and Rights*, *in* Minorities, Peoples and Self-Determination (Nazila Ghanea & Alexandra Xanthaki eds., 2005).

provide compensation. For indigenous peoples, since land rights are essential to their cultural, social, economic and spiritual survival, the removal from their lands might have some serious consequences. As such, specific approaches to remedies need to be developed. This is examined in the second part of the chapter which proposes an examination of theories of restitution.

A Property Rights: Sources and Content

To understand the content of property rights and the relationship with land rights, it is necessary to examine how the right to property has developed as a norm. Property rights have an important historical pedigree, notably linked with the emergence of liberal individual rights but also colonialism.[11] The historical evolution of property rights and how it might relate to indigenous peoples' land rights is examined in the first section. The aim is not only historical, as it is essential to understand how property rights have evolved to comprehend to what extent land rights for indigenous peoples can fit, or not, within such normative framework. In exploring the historical development of a right to property in land, the aim is to analyse how indigenous peoples have managed to gradually push for the recognition of their right to a collective form of property rights. Based on such analysis, the second section will then explore how a specialised body of law linking property rights and land rights for indigenous peoples has emerged. It will analyse the content of some of the more recent and specialized doctrine and jurisprudence which has put forward a more social, cultural and collective approach to property in land.

1 *Weaknesses and Promises of the Property Rights Discourse*

The origins of the right to property, and notably the protection of the institution of private property, has largely influenced the way property rights have been framed under international law. In terms of land ownership, property rights have been framed in a Western perspective that often disregards indigenous peoples' notions of property.[12] Nonetheless, the following discussion also examines how human rights law, notably based on the principle of non-discrimination, might have challenged this formal and individualistic approach to property rights.

---

11 *See* Andro Linklater, Owning The Earth: The Transforming History of Land Ownership (2013).

12 *See* Bryan Bradley, *Property as Ontology: On Aboriginal and English Understandings of Ownership*, 13 Can. J.L. & Juris. 3 (2002).

a The Western Framing of Individual Property Rights

It is hard to place the exact moment when property rights entered international law, but early international debates give us a good indication on how important the issue was in terms of the development of international law. One of the first recorded controversies on the origins of property was between Pope John XXII and William of Ockham based on Franciscan poverty; as for the Pope, property was brought in by divine positive law, whereas for Ockham, property was the result of human positive law.[13] Kilcullen, who has written extensively on the origin of property, concluded that most of the early theologians and early theorists of international law recognized that property in land is a matter of human convention and law and not a basic moral principle.[14] Many philosophers, such as Locke, have described individual private property as being a crucial element of the overall well-being of society.[15] Rousseau situated the origin of civil society with the establishment of private individual property in land.[16] For many centuries, property in lands has been the determining factor for the right to political participation. In both the Ancient Greek system of democracy and the Roman political organization, property in land was the basis to grant access to political participation.[17] In England and France political rights were also based on land ownership for many centuries.[18]

Historically, the guarantee of property rights in land was often one of the central issues that triggered the development of an emergent human rights

13 For translations from Ockham's Dialogue and other works *see* William of Ockham, Letter to the Friars Minor and Other Writings (Stephen McGrade & John Kilcullen eds., 1995); Charles Bayley, *Pivotal Concepts in the Political Philosophy of William of Ockham*, 10J. History Ideas 199 (1949).

14 John Kilcullen, The Origin of Property: Ockham, Grotius, Pufendorf, and Some Others (1995).

15 *See* the analysis of Crawford Brough McPherson, The Political Theory of Possessive Individualism: Hobbes to Locke (1962).

16 *See* Jean Jacques Rousseau, Discours sur l'inégalité (1754 *reprinted* 1963).

17 *See* Moses Finely, The Legacy of Greece: A New Appraisal (1981); Richard Saller, Patriarchy, Property and Death in the Roman Family (1994); The Cambridge History of Greek and Roman Political Thought (Christopher Rowe & Malcolm Scofield eds., 2000).

18 In England, it was only with the Reform Acts of 1830 that males without property were given franchise on a limited basis. *See* Léon Sheleff, The Future of Tradition: Customary Law Common Law and Legal Pluralism 218 (1999); this has some impacts on indigenous peoples, for example, under the 1852 New Zealand Constitution Act, suffrage was granted to males owning land; thus Maori were excluded since their ownership was communal and based on the Crown' right of pre-emption. *See* Steven Bourassa & Ann Louise Strong, *Restitution of Land to New Zealand Maori: The Role of Social Structure*, 75(2) Pac. Aff. 227 (2002).

system. Regarding land proprietary rights, the rule against executive expropriation can go back as far as the 1215 Magna Carta, as it is stated that "no Freeman shall ... be disseised ... but by lawful Judgement of his Peers, or by the law of the Land." The Magna Carta added: "[I]f anyone has been dispossessed or removed by us, without the legal judgment of his peers, from his lands, castles, franchises, or from his right, we will immediately restore them to him."[19] Such protection against arbitrary violation of property was also a central feature of the American and French declarations of the 18th century, the Virginia Declaration of Rights of 1776 and the French Declaration on the Rights of Man and the Citizen of 1789. These two declarations asserted the private right to property as one of the fundamental human rights. The 1776 Virginia Declaration of Rights stated:

> That all men are by nature equally free and independent, and have certain inherent rights, of which, when they enter into a state of society, they cannot, by any compact, deprive or divest their posterity; namely, the enjoyment of life and liberty, with the means of acquiring and possessing property, and pursuing and obtaining happiness and safety.[20]

The emphasis on the fact that private property should be free from any State interference was also reflected in the 1789 French Declaration on the Rights of Man and the Citizen, in which it was asserted: "[T]he end in view of every political association is the preservation of the natural and imprescriptible rights of man. These rights are liberty, property, security, and resistance to oppression."[21] The right to property thus came as the second most important right affirmed by the French revolutionary assembly. This illustrates how the right of individuals to own property and to be protected from State interference has been a central right in the development of law and the framing of what is now seen as constitutional human rights protection.[22]

---

19 *Reprinted in* The Human Rights Reader 102 (Walter Laqueur & Barry Rubin eds., 1989).

20 Virginia Declaration of Rights of 1776, *available at* www.yale.edu/lawweb/avalon/virginia.htm.

21 Declaration of the Rights of Man and the Citizen, *available at* www.yale.edu/lawweb/avalon/rightsof.htm.

22 It is worth noting that most contemporary national constitutions include property rights as part of the fundamental rights, one of the only exceptions being India where the 44th Amendment of the Constitution removed property rights from the part on fundamental rights, as "economic justice could not be achieved whilst property rights were fundamental"; *see* John Murphy, *Insulating Land Reform from Constitutional Impugnment: An Indian Case Study*, 8S. Afr. J. Hum. Rts. 362 (1992).

It is important to note that the view developed through these early declarations is that States have to respect individual property rights while exercising collective territorial sovereignty.[23] A conventional myth is that there has been a linear evolution of property rights, where, at the origins, property was communal, but humanity "evolved" and property became individual and more "civilized."[24] This distinction between individual property rights and communal State jurisdiction was found in Roman law, where a clear distinction was made between the *dominium*, the communal domain, and individual property.[25] Similarly, the European feudal system relied on the idea that the King (or Lord Paramount) was the ultimate owner of all the lands and that the Lords (Tenants in Chief) exercised the King's power over the actual occupants of the land, who were granted the individual right of possession.[26] In this regard, the two "revolutionary" declarations of the 18th century reflected upon the distinction between the individual right to property and governmental territorial sovereignty. These two important declarations, relied on the idea that a State, as representing a nation, exercised the collective ownership of the national territory, and its only obligation was to respect the individual right to property. Only States had collective ownership in the name of the nation, and the individual had a fundamental right to property. These two declarations, which were the result of the enlightenment, carried with them the ideal that "a constitutional state possesses an individual identity as a 'nation,' an imaginary community."[27]

The only considerable challenge to the individual approach to property rights came from a Marxist approach in which States would retain ownership while granting some right of use to individuals. However, the implementation of this approach to land property as "all peoples' property" in the former Soviet Union and other countries meant nationalization of the lands in a direction that made it "state property," and as Gutto noted: "state property does not

23 On this issue, *see* Benjamin Ederington, *Property as a Natural Institution: The Separation of Property from Sovereignty in International Law*, 13 Am. U. Int'lL. Rev. 263 (1997).

24 For references on this issue, *see* Samuel Pufendorf, De Jure Naturae et Gentium Libri Octo (1688 *reprinted* 1989); *see also* Gary Harding, *The Tragedy of the Commons*, 162 Sci. 1243–48 (1968).

25 Peter Birks, *The Roman Law Concept of Dominium and the Idea of Absolute Ownership*, Acta Juridica 1 (1985); for a discussion on the impact on the African system of this Western concept, *see* Hastings WO Okoth-Ogendo, *Property Theory and Land-use Analysis—An Essay in the Political Economy of Ideas, in* African Law and Legal Theory 291–303 (Gordon Woodman & Akintunde Obilade, 1995).

26 A.W. Brian Simpson, A History of Land Law (2d ed. 1986).

27 James Tully, Strange Multiplicity 68 (1995); on this issue, *see* Benedict Anderson, Imagined Communities: Reflections on the Origin and Spread of Nationalism (1983).

necessarily mean greater popular control and management by the people and for the people' direct enjoyment."[28] The result of such an approach in relation to land ownership has proved to be disillusive.[29] For indigenous peoples especially, the socialist approach to land ownership that was implemented in the Soviet Union resulted in the relocation of settlements and communities, and "in closing many smaller villages and commingling residents into fewer, larger settlements."[30] Ultimately, in terms of land rights, this approach also maintained a dichotomy between State territorial sovereignty and individual rights, and thus did not challenge the State's absolute territorial control over the community of rights exercised through collective land ownership.[31] In this regard, the socialist or communist approach to collective ownership did not contest the division between State territorial sovereignty and individual property land rights, for even though the notion of individual property in land was suppressed, the only collective ownership that was recognized was State ownership.[32] Thus, indigenous peoples' collective approach to territorial ownership was also suppressed.

The impact of this distinction between State territorial rights as the only form of collective territorial ownership and the fundamental individual right to property had some direct impact on indigenous peoples' land rights. During the colonial era it has usually been recognized that indigenous peoples had a system of land ownership based on a collective notion of ownership. In 1835 the U.S. Supreme Court stated:

> One uniform rule seems to have prevailed from the first settlement, as appears by their laws; that friendly Indians were protected in the possession of the lands they occupied, and were considered as owning them by a perpetual right of possession in the tribe or nation inhabiting them, as

28 Shadrack B.O. Gutto, Property & Land Reform: Constitutional and Jurisprudential Perspectives 10 (1995).

29 *See* K. Pleyer, *The Development of Ownership in the German Democratic Republic and in Eastern Europe, in* Land Reform and the Future of Landownership in South Africa 9–20 (A.J. Van Der Walt ed., 1991); Ugo Mattei, *Socialist and non-socialist approaches to land law: continuity and change in Somalia and other African States*, 16 Rev. Socialist L. 17 (1990); Christopher Osakwe, *General Principles of Soviet Land Law: Ownership and Use of Land in the Soviet Union*, Acta Juridica 147 (1985).

30 Gail Osherenko, *Indigenous Rights in Russia: Is Title to Land Essential for Cultural Survival?*, 13 Geo. Int'l Envt'l. L. Rev. 695 (2001).

31 On this subject, *see* Alan Gewirth, The Community of Rights (1996).

32 On the relationship between Marxist ideology and indigenous peoples' struggle, *see* the interview with Nilo Cayuquo reproduced in 9 Latin Am. Perspectives 100 (Spring 1982).

> their common property, from generation to generation, not as the right of the individual located on particular spots.[33]

The US Supreme Court acknowledged that the collective ownership of the lands by the "Indians" was once recognized, however when referring to such a collective right, the Court used the past tense showing that such a right was no longer recognized. For instance, an Act of Congress of 1887 only referred to the Indians individual right of property. This act stated that "reserved lands being allotted in suitable cases to members of a tribe in individual proprietorship, with a view to the proprietors being admitted to all the rights and obligations of United States citizenship."[34] The main purpose of such approach was clearly to divid land into parcels for individual ownership in order to "civilize and Christianize the Indians and ... Break up the authority of the tribe."[35] This period, referred to as the "allotment and assimilation era," was based on the "[R]easoning that communal ownership of land only exacerbated tribal Indian's uncivilized lifestyles."[36] As highlighted by Newton, this idea was that "ownership of private property alone would turn Indians into farmers and ranchers; Christianization and civilization were sure to follow."[37]

Similarly, in New Zealand, the colonial laws regarding Native lands (Native Title Lands Act 1862 and Native Lands Act 1865) brought about the extinction of communally held territories in order to weaken the Maori social structure. In 1987, the Waitangi Tribunal described the effects of such laws:

> It will be seen at once that tribal ownership and tribal authority and control were each done away with. Land was awarded to individuals and those individuals could sell their individual shares without reference to the tribe.... The consequences were far reaching. Individual claims and individual ownership exacerbated family disputes, always present but formerly controlled through the influence of chiefs and elders. The

---

33 Mitchel and others v. United States 34 U.S. (9 Pet.) 711, 745 (1835).

34 An Act to Provide for the Allotment of Lands in Severalty to Indians on the Various Reservations, and to Extend the Protection of the Laws of the United States and the Territories over the Indians, and for Other Purposes, 29 Stat. 388 (1887), *available at* http://www.yale.edu/lawweb/avalon/statutes/native/dawes.htm.

35 Jennifer Roback, *Exchange, Sovereignty, and Indian-Anglo Relations, in* Property Rights and Indian Economies: The Political Economy Forum (Terry L. Anderson ed., 1992).

36 Nell Jessup Newton, *Compensation, Reparations, & Restitution: Indian Property Claims in the United States*, 28Ga. L. Rev. 453 (1994).

37 *Id.*

> individual assumed an unaccustomed authority and traditional leadership waned.[38]

This will of the colonizers to impose individual property ownership has been the general feature of most colonial powers. As Barume noted in the case of Kenya:

> one of the colonial strategies for accessing native lands was to destroy any sort of collective holding of lands. This was done through a range of measures, such as the abolition of the traditional institutions on which the system was built, the individualization of land holding and similar measures.[39]

Similarly, as pointed out by Stavenhagen, former UN Special Rapporteur on the rights of indigenous peoples, during his official visit to the Philippines:

> In pre-Hispanic times indigenous communities held land collectively, but after the Spanish conquest all lands became the exclusive patrimony and dominion of the Crown. The colonial government, applying the theory of *jura regalia*, known as the Regalian Doctrine, distributed land grants to private individuals but also protected, under certain conditions, the pre-existing communal holdings. The American colonial administration inherited this system and the State's control over the public domain was reinforced, communal landholdings were not legally recognized and private land titles were issued in accordance with new legislation.[40]

The notion of regalian power, or regalian doctrine, comes from Roman law, the *jura regalia*. Under this doctrine, any private title to land had to emanate from the government. All lands not granted by the government to individuals are part of the public domain and remains the property of the government.

In this distinction between State territorial sovereignty and individual rights to property, indigenous peoples did not fall into either of the two

38 Waitangi Tribunal—*The Taranaki Report*, Wai 143, at 8–10 (1996).

39 Albert K. Barume, *Indigenous Battling for Land Rights: The Case of the Ogiek of Kenya, in* International Law and Indigenous Peoples 365 (Joshua Castellino & Niamh Walsh eds., 2005).

40 Report of the Special Rapporteur on the Situation of Human Rights and Fundamental Freedoms of Indigenous People, Mr. Rodolfo Stavenhagen, *Mission to the Philippines*, U.N. Doc. E/CN.4/2003/90/Add.3, para. 8.

categories. The corollary of the doctrine was that it was only through a State grant that land could pass into private ownership.[41] The imposition of this system of individual property land rejected indigenous notions of ownership that were usually based on a different approach. In the words of Meek describing the context of pre-colonial Africa:

> Summing up the characteristics of indigenous systems of land-holding, it may be said that these are devised to meet the need of subsistence agriculture and depend on a sufficiency of land to allow a rotation which includes a long period of fallow. Land is held on (a) kinship and/or (b) a local group basis. Individuals have definite rights but these are qualified by membership of a family, kindred and ward (or small village). (…) The chief is the custodian of land, but is not the owner. The normal unit of land ownership is the extended family, or kindred.[42]

This "normal unit of land ownership" has never been legally recognized. As one of the judges stated in the *Amodu Tijani* case of 1921: "[T]he next fact which is important to bear in mind in order to understand the native land law is that the notion of individual ownership is quite foreign to native ideas. Land belongs to the community, the village, or the family, never to the individual."[43] However, this does not preclude the fact that under customary indigenous laws, individuals usually also have rights and interests in the land. As Bentsi-Enchill points out, the group title to the land "is a sort of umbrella beneath which are the particular, distinct and exclusive interests of sub-groups and individuals in a portion of such land occupied by them or allotted to them."[44] It is this collective "umbrella" that the Western-based legal systems failed to recognize. For example, in *In re Southern Rhodesia* of 1919 Lord Sumner stated:

> Some tribes are so low in the scale of social organisation that their usages and conceptions of rights and duties are not to be reconciled with the institutions or the legal ideas of civilised societies. Such a gulf cannot

41 *See* Vattel on the distinction between title to territory which entails sovereignty and jurisdiction and title to land which is a proprietary right; Emmerich de Vattel, Le Droit de Gens (1758), *see especially* Bk. 1, Ch. 18, para. 204 "Aux depends de la compagnie."

42 Charles Kingsley Meek, Land Law and Customs in the Colonies 26–27 (1946).

43 Amodu Tijani v. Secretary, Southern Nigeria, 2 A.C. 399 (1921) (Rayner CJ)—Privy Council.

44 Kwamena Bentsi-Enchill, *Do African Systems of Land Tenure Require a Special Terminology?*, 9J. Afr. L. 114, at 127 (1965).

> be bridged. It would be idle to impute to such people some shadow of the rights known to our law and then transmute it into the substance of transferable rights of property as we know them.[45]

Indigenous notions of property were deemed too "primitive" to be recognized under "civilized" laws. One of the legal consequences of such a distinction was that the rules regarding the protection of individual property did not apply in the case of collective indigenous forms of ownership. Thus, legally, the notion of property undertook this liberalist approach to individual property.

This historical background is important to bear in mind when examining the evolution of the right to property under the contemporary system of international human rights law. After the Second World War, the Universal Declaration of Human Rights (UDHR) was envisaged as enshrining the most universal conception of values.[46] During the debates for the drafting of the UDHR, the definition of property rights formed an important part of the discussions.[47] One of the issues was to define whether property rights would be recognized as individual or as collective rights. In the course of the debates that lead to the adoption of the UDHR, the USSR delegation introduced the idea that the right to property should be granted to individuals as well as in association with others.[48] In what is known as the Pavlov proposal, the USSR insisted on phraseology that stated that no particular property ownership would be favoured.[49] Following disagreements between the different States delegations, a working group focusing on the issue of the right to property was established. As a result, Article 17 of the UDHR reads:

> 1. Everyone has the right to own property alone as well as in association with others.
> 2. No one shall be arbitrarily deprived of his property.

45 *In re* Southern Rhodesia [1919] AC 211, at 233—Privy Council.

46 Johannes Morsink, The Universal Declaration on Human Rights, Origins, Drafting and Intent (1999) [hereinafter Morsink]; Reflections on the Universal Declaration of Human Rights: A Fiftieth Anniversary Anthology (Barend Van Der Heijden & Bahia Tahzib-Lie eds., 1998).

47 United Kingdom and Australia were opposed to the recognition of a right to property, whereas Chile insisted on the need for a definition of property; *see*, U.N. Doc. E/CN.4/21, Annex F, at 76–77.

48 Report of the Drafting Committee on an International Bill of Human Rights, U.N. Doc. E/CN.4/21, Annex F, at 76–77.

49 *See* Morsink, *supra* note 47, at 147.

Therefore, as Article 17 recognizes a corporate as well as an individual approach to the right to property, the notion of property is not limited to the Western individualistic notion of property and could include collective property of land. Also, it is worth noting that the right to property is one of the only rights that cannot be classified both as either a political and civil right or an economic, social and cultural right.[50] The International Commission of Jurists has highlighted that Article 17 should protect indigenous peoples' land ownership even though "it may be that those indigenous people who never faced competition for their land will find it difficult to qualify for protection under Article 17, for they might never have found it necessary to develop any concept of property in land."[51] However, the social and cultural values of property, which are fundamental from an indigenous perspective, are not affirmed in the UDHR.[52] The drafting of such a right was controversial and gave rise to some serious debates and negotiations.[53] The controversy notably concerned the need to include such a right and the extent to which the right to property should be limited by national laws. Ultimately, there was an agreement on the need to include property as a fundamental human right. Cassin, one of the drafters, has later highlighted how such inclusion was the result of a compromise between two groups of countries with on the one hand States supporting the inclusion of an individual right and on the other States pushing for the recognition of the social collective values of property.[54] Consequently, the affirmation of a right to property in the UDHR has been labelled as "weak and unsatisfactorily flimsy."[55] While the particular issue of property in land was not itself a particular focus of the discussion, the divide between the individual and the more social and collective approach to property was going to mark the later debate on land rights.

50 Another example would be the right to form trade unions. On this issue, *see* Catarina Krause, *The Right to Property, in* Economic, Social and Cultural Rights—A Textbook 191 (Asbjørn Eide et al., 2d eds. 2005) [hereinafter Krause].

51 International Commission of Jurists, *Intervention before the WGIP, reprinted in* Int'l Comm. Jurists Rev. (1984).

52 During the debates leading to the adoption of Article 17 the focus was more on a liberal versus communist approach to the right to property, rather than on the cultural value of such a right, on this issue; *see* Morsink, *supra* note 47.

53 For a review and analysis, see: Theo Van Banning, The Human Right to Property (2002).

54 See: René Cassin, in Receuil Des Cours (The Hague Academy for International Law, 1972), p. 287.

55 William Schabas, *The Omission of the Right to Property in the International Covenants*, 4 Hague Yearbook of International Law (1991) 135–60.

The reference to the right to property was dropped in the two Covenants adopted in 1966, making property rights one of the only human rights affirmed in the UDHR which was not integrated into one of the legally binding Covenants. Several arguments have been advanced to explain the rejection of a property right from the two Covenants, notably the divide between the West and Eastern blocs. A more philosophical explanation has also been advanced by Van Banning highlighting that "a human right does not denote the relationship between an individual and a thing."[56] Ultimately, the two 1966 Covenants do not mention property rights as such;[57] a reference to property rights was dropped as being too controversial, since, despite the many proposals for an article on property rights, too many disagreements remained about the scope of such a right.[58] The debates focused on the notion of expropriation, due process of law, limitation and compensation, and, as no agreement was possible between the different views, the inclusion of a right to property was finally omitted.[59] As this debate shows, the right to property proved to be too controversial to be included in the two Covenants, an important aspect of such rejection related to the fact that no agreement could be reached on whether such a rights could be exercised in a collective form.

b Property Rights as Non-discrimination

One of the strongest connections between property rights and land rights has been emerging under the anti-discriminatory agenda of human rights law. The International Convention on the Elimination of all Forms of Racial Discrimination (ICERD), in its Article 5(d)(v), stipulates that States should guarantee "the right to own property alone as well as in association with others."[60] The reference to property rights, and notably the mention of its eventual collective nature is an important feature of the Convention. Based on its mandate to eliminate racial discrimination, the Convention has greatly contributed to the development of the specific body of indigenous peoples' human rights and to the interpretation of general human rights law to make it adequate and

56 Theo Van Banning, The Human Right to Property (2002), p. 168.

57 The only mention of property in the two Covenants is in Article 2 on non-discrimination; and Article 24 of the ICCPR, which protects children as well as Article 15, which concerns intellectual and industrial property. International Covenant on Civil and Political Rights (1966), *reprinted in* 6 I.L.M. 368 (1967).

58 On this issue, *see* Krause, *supra* note 51; U.N. Doc. A/2929; U.N. Doc. E/CN.4/SR.417 and 418.

59 *See* Official Records of the General Assembly, Tenth Sess., agenda item 28 (Part II), E/2573.

60 International Convention on the Elimination of All Forms of Racial Discrimination, (1965), 660 U.N.T.S. 195, *reprinted in* 5 I.L.M. 352 (1966).

relevant to indigenous peoples.[61] The Committee on the Elimination of Racial Discrimination (CERD) was notably the first human rights treaty monitoring body to adopt a specific general recommendation on the rights of indigenous peoples.[62] In this General Recommendation, CERD explained further the meaning of article 5 relating to property rights in relation to indigenous peoples' land rights, highlighting the need to protect communal ownership of territories. Based on article 5, the Committee has highlighted that States need to:

> (…) recognise and protect the rights of indigenous peoples to own, develop, control and use their communal lands, territories and resources and where they have been deprived of their lands and territories traditionally owned or otherwise inhabited or used without their free and informed consent, to take steps to return these lands and territories.[63]

Based on this approach, the Committee has developed a systematic jurisprudence inviting Sates to develop adequate protection for the rights of indigenous peoples to own, use, and control their traditional lands, territories, and resources. In the view of the Committee, the non-recognition of land rights for indigenous peoples constitutes in itself racial discrimination. Regarding indigenous peoples' land rights, CERD has made several references to Article 5 in its concluding observations.[64] For example, under Australian law, the Racial Discrimination Act 1975 (Cth), which implements ICERD at the national level, has had a significant impact on the recognition of indigenous peoples' rights to collective property of their traditional territories.[65] It is worth noting that

61 For an in depth analysis, *see*: Fergus Mackay, *Indigenous Peoples' Rights and the UN Committee on the Elimination of Racial Discrimination*, in 155–202 Perspectives on The Rights Of Minorities and Indigenous Peoples in Africa (Solomon Dersso, ed., 2010); and Jérémie Gilbert, *CERD's Contribution to the Development of the Rights of Indigenous Peoples under International Law*, in Eliminating All Forms of Racial Discrimination: 50 Years of ICERD (David Keane, ed, forthcoming 2016).

62 General Recommendation XXIII: Indigenous Peoples, CERD, U.N. Doc. A/52/18, Annex V; CERD/C/51/Misc.13/Rev.4, para. 4(d) (1997).

63 Ibid.

64 *See*, for examples, *Concluding observations of the Committee on the Elimination of Racial Discrimination:* Australia, U.N. Doc. CERD/C/AUS/CO/14; United States of America: U.N. Doc. A/56/18, paras. 380–407. On this issue, *see also* Early warning and urgent action procedures: Decision on Suriname, U.N. Doc. CERD/C/DEC/SUR/2.

65 *See* Koowarta v. Bjelke Petersen (1982) 153 C.L.R. 168; Mabo & Ors. v. State of Queensland (1988) 83 A.L.R. 14; Mabo v. Queensland [No. 2] (1992) 175 C.L.R. 1, 107 ALR 1—High Court. However, since the introduction of the Native Title Act 1993 (Cth) this recognition has

the reference to a right to own property "in association with other" in ICERD provides indigenous peoples not only with a right to a collective ownership of their lands but also guarantees some substantive collective rights over such territories. Based on Article 5 of the Convention, CERD pointed out that where traditional lands have been confiscated without free and informed consent of indigenous owners, such lands should be returned or, where return is not possible, it gives rise to a right to compensation.[66] Thus, by expressly requiring States parties to guarantee the right to everyone to own property without distinction as to race, color, or national or ethnic origin, ICERD significantly opens the door to indigenous peoples' collective approach to property in lands.

Another important contribution from CERD regarding land rights relates to the obligation for States to recognise indigenous peoples' own land tenure systems. On many occasions, CERD has highlighted that indigenous peoples' land rights derive from their own customary laws and forms of land tenure, and that as such they exist as valid and enforceable rights absent formal recognition by the government. For example, in the case of Canada, the Committee has expressed concerns about "the difficulties which may be encountered by Aboriginal peoples before the courts in establishing Aboriginal title over land." It recommended that Canada "examine ways and means to facilitate the establishment of proof of Aboriginal title over land in procedures before the courts."[67] The non-recognition of such systems of land tenure constitutes racial discrimination. Hence governments need to recognise customary land tenure systems as a source of right, highlighting that those customary rights must also be effectively protected under the national legal systems. The role and place of customary land tenure systems undoubtedly constitute an important contribution of the Committee, which has since then been extensively used as an important reference by the other human rights institutions, including within the Inter-American and African jurisprudence.[68] Overall, the Committee has played an important role in highlighting how property rights in land are essential for indigenous peoples, and by putting the emphasis on the fact that the non-recognition of land rights derived from customary tenure and law does

---

been undermined; *see* CERD, *Concluding Observations of the Committee on the Elimination of Racial Discrimination:* Australia, U.N. Doc. CERD/C/AUS/CO/14, para. 16.

66 On this issue, *see* the section on Restitution below.

67 Concluding observations: Canada, UN Doc, A/57/18 (2002), at para. 330.

68 See: Inter-American Court of Human Rights: *Sawhoyamaxa Indigenous Community v Paraguay*, 29 March 2006, para 248; the Mayagna (Sumo) Awas Tingni Community case, 31 August 2001. Series C No 79, paras 148–51; African Commission on Human and Peoples' Rights, *Centre for Minority Rights Development (Kenya) and Minority Rights Group International on behalf of Endorois Welfare Council v Kenya*, Communication 276/2003 (2010).

in itself constitute racial discrimination. Knowing that there is no main human rights treaty specifically including property rights in land for indigenous peoples, the Committee's approach linking discrimination, property rights and land rights has undoubtedly proven to be extremely important to make human rights law relevant to indigenous peoples.

Another relevant treaty for indigenous peoples is the Convention on the Elimination of All Forms of Discrimination against Women (CEDAW) which is also making a connection between property rights and non-discrimination. In inviting States Parties to take all appropriate measures to eliminate discrimination against women in rural areas, Article 14 calls on States to make sure that women "have access to agricultural credit and loans, marketing facilities, appropriate technology and equal treatment in land and agrarian reform as well as in land resettlement schemes."[69] Article 16 of CEDAW, focuses on the elimination of discrimination within the family, inviting State parties to take all necessary measures to ensure that both spouses have equal rights in the "ownership, acquisition, management, administration, enjoyment and disposition of property."[70] While not directly mentioning land rights, the reference to ownership and property is relevant to address property in lands. The Committee on the Elimination of Discrimination against Women (CEDAW Committee) has specifically highlighted such a connection in its General Recommendation No. 21 on 'Equality in marriage and family relations' which largely focuses on Article 16. The General Recommendation states: "In countries that are undergoing a programme of agrarian reform or redistribution of land among groups of different ethnic origins, the right of women, regardless of marital status, to share such redistributed land on equal terms with men should be carefully observed."[71] This focus on non-discrimination against women is extremely relevant for indigenous women, and the Committee has specifically addressed the discrimination faced by indigenous women in their access to land rights. For example, in its 2012 Concluding Observations regarding the situation in Mexico, the Committee invited the government "to adopt temporary special measures to address the disparities that indigenous rural women face with regard to access to land and property."[72] One of the central focuses of the Committee has been to ensure that women are not discriminated against in their access to land under both formal and informal (or customary) legal

69 CEDAW, Article 14(2)(g)).

70 CEDAW, art. 16.

71 General recommendation No. 21: Equality in marriage and family relations, para. 27.

72 Concluding Observations of the Committee on the Elimination of Discrimination against Women: Mexico, CEDAW/C/MEX/CO/7-8, 7 August 2012, at 35.

systems.[73] The Committee has also highlighted how the formal systems of land registration, which often provide some form of recognition to customary systems, either directly or indirectly support practices which favour males and put women in a disadvantaged position by notably perpetuating tenure regimes based on the assumption of household and community unity, resulting in de facto inequality.[74] Hence, the CEDAW committee has shown how property in land, both within formal and informal system of land tenure, is an essential element to address discrimination faced by indigenous women. Overall, the two international human rights treaties specifically focusing on the elimination of discrimination, ICERD and CEDAW, offer an important platform to challenge the western and individualistic approach to property in land which have marked the development of property rights. Under these two treaties the emphasis is put on the need to recognise indigenous peoples' own customary land tenure system as constituting property in land. The non-recognition of these traditional systems of land tenure would otherwise constitute discrimination.

2 *Indigenous Peoples' Right to Collective Land Ownership*

Adding to the development of a property rights to land for indigenous peoples under the mainstream human rights treaties, a more specific or *sui generis* approach has been developed. The following analysis examines how a specific body of law and jurisprudence has emerged to specifically protect the right to property in land for indigenous peoples. This has emerged under two main mechanisms, first as part of the increasing and expanding jurisprudence of regional human rights bodies, this is examines in the first sub-section. And also as part of the development of specific instruments dedicated to the rights of indigenous peoples, this is analysed in the second sub-section.

a Regional Jurisprudence: Possession as Property

Some of the most important developments regarding the recognition and affirmation of the connection between the right to property and land rights for indigenous peoples have emerged from the practice of regional human rights institutions. The Inter-American system of human rights, under the leadership

---

73 *See* for example, Concluding observations of the Committee on the Elimination of Discrimination against Women: Congo, UN Doc. CEDAW/C/COG/CO/6 (1 March 2012), para. 37–38.

74 For an in depth analysis, see: Ingunn Ikdahl, Anne Hellum, Randi Kaarhus, Tor A. Benjaminsen, Patricia Kameri-Mbote, *Human Rights, Formalisation And Women's Land Rights In Southern And Eastern Africa* (Studies in Women's Law No. 57, Institute of Women's Law, University of Oslo, 2005).

of both the Inter-American Commission and the Court has been particularly proactive on that front. Article XXIII of the American Declaration on the Rights and Duties of Man refers to private property "as meets the needs of decent living and helps to maintain the dignity of the individual and the home."[75] Article 21 of the American Convention on Human Rights states:

> Everyone has the right to the use and enjoyment of his property. The law may subordinate such use and enjoyment to the interest of society.... No one shall be deprived of his property except upon payment of just compensation, for reasons of public utility or social interest and in the cases and according to the forms established by law.[76]

This article on property rights has become a central feature of the jurisprudence relating to indigenous peoples' land rights. In many situations, the Inter-American Commission on Human Rights (IACHR) has highlighted the collective nature of indigenous peoples' right to land property.[77] It has also highlighted how indigenous peoples' approach to land usage need to be regarded as property rights. The Commission had once stated that "[F]rom the standpoint of human rights, a small corn field deserves the same respect as the private property of a person that a bank account or a modern factory receives."[78] The IACHR has been especially proactive in the promotion of the recognition of indigenous customary laws. On several occasions, the IACHR has insisted on the importance for States to receive indigenous customary laws as a source of rights under national systems. For example, in its report on the situation of human rights in Guatemala, the Commission pointed out that the non-recognition of custom-based indigenous local provisions considerably

---

75 American Declaration of the Rights and Duties of Man, OEA/serv.L/V/11.71 (1948).

76 In the *Awas Tingni* case, the Court pointed out that "During the study and consideration of the preparatory work for the American Convention on Human Rights, the phrase "[e]veryone has the right to the use and enjoyment of private property, but the law may subordinate its use and enjoyment to public interest" was replaced by "[e]veryone has the right to the use and enjoyment of his property. The law may subordinate such use and enjoyment to the social interest." In other words, it was decided to refer to the "use and enjoyment of his property" instead of "private property";" The Mayagna (Sumo) Awas Tingni Community v. Nicaragua, Inter-Am. Ct. H.R., (ser. C) No. 79, at para. 145 (Aug. 31, 2001)—Inter-Am. CHR.

77 See: IACHR, *Indigenous and Tribal Peoples' Rights over Their Ancestral Lands and Natural Resources: Norms and Jurisprudence of the Inter-American Human Rights System* (2009) OEA/Ser.L/V/II. Doc. 56/09.

78 IACHR, *4th Report on the Situation of Human Rights in Guatemala*, at 36, Mar. 12, 1993.

limited and blocked indigenous peoples' ability to assert rights over their traditional territories.[79]

An important momentum regarding the development of a strong jurisprudence linking property rights and land rights for indigenous peoples took place in a case regarding indigenous peoples' rights in Nicaragua. In the case of the *Mayagna (Sumo) Awas Tingni Community*, the Commission clearly established a link between collective communitarian ownership, consent and property rights as enshrined in Article 21 of the Convention.[80] Adopting a strong stance on non-discrimination, the Commission stated that "[N]on-recognition of the equality of property rights based on indigenous tradition is contrary to the principle of non-discrimination set forth in article 1(1) of the Convention."[81] Due to the failure of Nicaragua to comply with the Commission decision, the case was transmitted to the Inter-American Court of Court (IACtHR).[82] The ensuing ruling from the Court in 2001 quickly became a landmark decision regarding property rights in land for indigenous peoples. The Court observed that:

> Given the characteristics of the instant case, it is necessary to understand the concept of property in indigenous communities. Among indigenous communities, there is a communal tradition as demonstrated by their communal form of collective ownership of their lands, in the sense that ownership is not centered in the individual but rather in the group and in the community.[83]

The Inter-American Court added that traditional patterns of use and occupation of territory by indigenous peoples must be qualified as a right to property. The Court acknowledged that under the American Convention on Human Rights, customary indigenous collective ownership has to be regarded as a property right. Crucially, the Court highlighted that possession of the land

---

79 *Fifth Report on the Human Rights Situation in Guatemala*, OEA/Ser.L/V/II.111 doc.21 rev., para. 57 (Apr. 6, 2001).

80 Inter-American Commission of Human Rights, Report No. 27/98 (Nicaragua), at 115.

81 The Mayagna (Sumo) Awas Tingni Community v. Nicaragua, Inter-Am. Ct. H.R. (ser. C) No. 79, at para. 140 (b) (Aug. 31, 2001)—[hereinafter *Awas Tingni* case].

82 For an overview of national and international proceedings that lead to the Court, *see* James Anaya & Claudio Grossman, *The Case of Awas Tingni v. Nicaragua: A New Step in the International Law of Indigenous Peoples*, 19 Ariz. J. Int'l & Comp. L. 1 (2002).

83 *Awas Tingni* case, *supra* note 82, at para. 149; on the reception of indigenous customary law by the Court, *see also* Aloeboetoe et al. Case. Reparations (Art. 63(1) of the American Convention on Human Rights) Judgment, para. 46 (Sept. 10, 1993)—Inter-Am. CHR.

should suffice for indigenous peoples lacking real title to obtain official recognition of that property. This is an extremely important point, not only in this case, but more generally since in most situations indigenous peoples are lacking a formal title to prove their property rights to land. As Anaya highlights: "[T]he existence of indigenous property systems does not depend on prior identification by the state but rather may be discerned by objective evidence that includes indigenous peoples' own accounts of traditional land and resource tenure."[84] Since then, the Court has adopted several other rulings confirming this very strong connection between property rights and land rights for indigenous peoples, and also the fact that possession should constitute property.[85]

This marks an important and revolutionary step in the interpretation of property rights when it comes to land rights. Firstly it recognised that property rights to land could be collective, going against the general reluctance against collective rights and centuries of an individual approach to property rights. Secondly, it also put forward the importance of recognising indigenous peoples' own systems of land tenure as constituting property, and as such it also highlights that possession in itself constitute property. It is also important to note that the Court placed its interpretation of property rights as encompassing land rights for indigenous peoples within the natural evolution of international law, highlighting that it was part of "an evolutionary interpretation of international instruments for the protection of human rights."[86] This gave a clear international perspective to the issue grounding the connection between property rights and land rights within international human rights and not only in the context of the Americas. Since then the case has been used as a benchmark by several UN monitoring bodies, inter-governmental organisations, and also national cases, not only in the Americas but worldwide.[87]

84 James Anaya, *The Protection of Indigenous Peoples' Rights over Lands and Natural Resources under the Inter-American Human Rights System*, 14 Harv. Hum. Rts. J. 33, at 46 (2001).

85 For references and analysis, *see*: Inter-American Commission on Human Rights, *Indigenous and Tribal Peoples' Rights Over Their Ancestral Lands and Natural Resources: Norms and Jurisprudence of The Inter-American Human Rights System*, OEA/Ser.L/V/II. Doc. 56/09 (2009); and: Enzamaria Tramontana, *The Contribution of the Inter-American Human Rights Bodies to Evolving International Law on Indigenous Rights over Lands and Natural Resources*, 17 (2) International Journal on Minority and Group Rights (2010), pp. 241–63

86 *Awas Tingni* case, *supra* note 82, at para. 148.

87 For references see: Jonathan P. Vuotto, *Awas Tingni v. Nicaragua: International Precedent for Indigenous Land Rights*, 22 B.U. Int'lL.J. (2004) 219; Alexandra Xanthaki, *Indigenous Rights in International Law over the Last 10 Years and Future Developments*, 10 Melb. J. Int'lL. 27 (2009); Leonardo J Alvardo, *Prospects and Challenges in the Implementation of Indigenous Peoples' Human Rights in International Law: Lessons from the Case of Awas*

There are also been some important developments under the African system of human rights. Article 14 of the African Charter on Human and Peoples' Rights reads: "[T]he right to property shall be guaranteed. It may only be encroached upon the interest of public need or in the general interest of the community and in accordance with the provisions of appropriate laws."[88] This article was a at the heart of the 2010 decision form the African Commission on Human and Peoples' Rights (ACHPR) concerning the Endorois community in Kenya.[89] In its ruling, the Commission clearly highlighted that property right should apply to indigenous peoples, stating that for indigenous peoples traditional possession of land "has the equivalent effect as that of a state-granted full property title" and "entitles indigenous people to demand official recognition and registration of property title."[90] This recognition meant that the rights of the Endorois over their ancestral territory qualified as property as protected under Article 14 of the African Charter. More generally, the Commission highlighted that "the first step in the protection of traditional African communities is the acknowledgement that the rights, interests and benefits of such communities in their traditional lands constitute 'property' under the Charter and that special measures may have to be taken to secure such 'property rights.'"[91] This decision connecting property rights and land rights for indigenous peoples represents an important breakthrough, not only in the case of Kenya, but more generally for the whole continent as many indigenous communities are struggling to get the recognition of the right to property over their ancestral territories.[92]

At the European level, the European Convention on Human Rights does not mention property rights, but the first protocol to the Convention is especially

---

Tingni v. Nicaragua 24 Ariz. J. Int'l & Comp. L. 609 (2007); Mauro Barelli, *The interplay between global and regional human rights systems in the construction of the indigenous rights regime*, Human Rights Quarterly 32.4 (2010): 951–79.

88 African Charter on Human and Peoples' Rights, O.U.A. Doc. CAB/LEG/67/3, *reprinted in* 21 I.L.M. 58 (1982).

89 African Commission on Human and Peoples' Rights, Centre for Minority Rights Development (Kenya) and Minority Rights Group International on behalf of Endorois Welfare Council v Kenya, Communication 276/2003 (2010).

90 *Id*, at para. 209.

91 *Id*, para. 187.

92 See Solomon Dersso (ed) Perspectives on the Rights of Minorities and Indigenous Peoples in Africa (2010); Jerémie Gilbert, *Indigenous Peoples' Human rights in Africa: the pragmatic revolution of the African commission on human and peoples' rights* International and Comparative Law Quarterly 60, no. 01 (2011): 245–70; Albert Kwokwo Barume, Land Rights of Indigenous Peoples in Africa (2014).

dedicated to the issue.[93] Article 1 of the First Protocol to the European Convention states: "[N]o one shall be deprived of his possession except in the public interest and subject to the conditions provided for by law and by the general principles of international law."[94] The fact that, under the European Convention indigenous peoples issues are not specifically addressed limits the possibility for indigenous peoples to successfully use litigation under the ECHR.[95] However, the Commission has received some indigenous claims based on Protocol 1. In the *Könkämä* case, several Saami villages claimed that a new Swedish regulation, which controlled the licensing permits for small game hunting and fishing, was violating their right to property as protected under Article 1 of Protocol No. 1 to the Convention. The Commission acknowledged that "the exclusive hunting and fishing rights claimed by the applicant Saami villages in the present case can be regarded as possession within the meaning of Article 1 of Protocol No.1."[96] However, it pointed out that one of the central issues in this case was to determine whether the Saami villages were holders of such exclusive hunting and fishing rights. On this point, the Commission highlighted that the Swedish legislation did not provide for such an exclusive right but that the Saami based their claims "on various historical facts of considerable complexity." However, the Commission did not push its analysis of the Saami claims any further, as it found that the applicants had not shown that they had appealed properly at the national level before going to Strasbourg; therefore the case was deemed inadmissible.[97] However, as Thornberry suggests in the context of this decision, it "recognises that such specific indigenous rights fall within the ambit of the Protocol."[98] However, so far, this mechanism has had some very limited impact on indigenous peoples' land rights in

93 Attempts to include a right to property failed, as the Committee of Ministers felt that such an inclusion would delay the entering onto force of the Convention; *see* 6 Collected Edition of the Travaux Préparatories 156–90 (1986).

94 The Protocol adds that these provisions shall not "in any way impair the right of the state to enforce such laws as it deems necessary to control the use of property in accordance with the general interest or to secure the payment of taxes or other contributions or penalties"; in general, *see* Laurent Sermet, The European Convention on Human Rights and Property Rights (1990).

95 There is however a relevant jurisprudence regarding some of the rights relevant for indigenous peoples, see: Timo Koivurova, *Jurisprudence of the European Court of Human Rights Regarding Indigenous Peoples: Retrospect and Prospects*, International Journal on Minority and Group Rights, Vol. 18, pp. 1–37, 2011.

96 Könkämä and 38 other Saami Villages v. Sweden, App. No. 27033/95—ECOHR.

97 *Id.*

98 Patrick Thornberry, Indigenous Peoples and Human Rights 305–06 (2002).

Europe.[99] In other relevant cases, the Court has either rejected its jurisdiction, or not properly addressed property rights in land.[100] Due to the lack of a suitable regional system of protection of human rights in Asia or across the Pacific, there is no substantial jurisprudence that can be relied on to examine how the right to property could have evolved in other parts of the globe. However as highlighted in Chapter 2, it is worth highlighting that at the national level several courts in Asia have started to recognise the connection between property rights and land rights also highlighting that possession should be recognised as constituting property rights.[101]

b Specific Indigenous Property Rights

The right to property rights constitutes an important element of the specialised instruments dedicated to the rights of indigenous peoples. The International Labour Conventions concerning the rights of indigenous peoples put a great emphasis on property rights. ILO Convention No. 107 was the first instrument to specifically address the issue of land ownership rights for indigenous peoples. Article 11 states that "the right of ownership, collective or individual (…) shall be recognized."[102] However, as noted by Swepston: "[T]he land rights provisions in Convention No. 107 (articles 11 to 14) were designed—like the entire convention—to provide protection in the context of the 'inevitable' integration of indigenous and tribal people into national society."[103] In reaction, ILO Convention No. 169 recognises the right of indigenous peoples to exercise their own specific form of land ownership insisting on the collective aspect of such relationship. Article 13 indicates that in applying the Convention: "governments shall respect the special importance for the cultures and

99 See: Ghislain Otis and Aurélie Laurent, *Indigenous land claims in Europe: The European Court of Human Rights and the decolonization of property*, Arctic Review on Law and Politics, vol. 4, 2/2013 pp. 156–80.

100 See European Court of Human Rights, *Hingitaq 53 et al. v. Denmark*, No. 18584/04 (12 January 2006); *Handölsdalen Saami Village and others v. Sweden*, No. 39013/04 (3d sec.) [2009] ECHR 472 (17 February 2009).

101 *See also*: Land and Cultural Survival: The Communal Land Rights of Indigenous Peoples in Asia (Jayantha Perera, ed, Asian Development Bank, 2009); Human Rights Commission of Malaysia, Report of the National Inquiry into the Land Rights of Indigenous Peoples (2013).

102 Convention Concerning the Protection and Integration of Indigenous and other Tribal and Semi-tribal Populations in Independent Countries (ILO Convention No. 107), 328 U.N.T.S. 247 (1959), art. 11.

103 Lee Swepston, *A New Step in the International Law on Indigenous and Tribal Peoples: The ILO Convention 169 of 1989*, 15 Okla. City U.L. Rev. 677 (1990).

spiritual values of the peoples concerned of their relationship with the lands or territories, or both as applicable, which they occupy or otherwise use, and in particular the collective aspects of this relationship."[104] Regarding ownership rights, Article 14 reads: "[T]he rights of ownership and possession of the peoples concerned over the lands which they traditionally occupy shall be recognized." Even though Article 14 does not mention the collective or individual aspect of indigenous peoples' ownership, it affirms the rights of ownership and possession "of the peoples concerned," and thus suggests that if the peoples concerned do exercise a collective form of ownership, it should be recognised.

The language used in this article has been the subject of extensive debates leading to the adoption of the Convention. One of the issues was "whether a preference might be expressed for collective rather than individual forms of land ownership."[105] A justification for not retaining the words "collective" and "individual" in Article 14 was that the reference to both "ownership" and "possession" in this article would allow a flexible approach leaving "the people concerned to determine their own preferential form of land holding and ownership."[106] Thus, whereas ILO 107 only used the word "ownership," ILO 169 refers to both "ownership" and "possession." This was done in the view that the word "possession" is more flexible and thus encompasses traditional indigenous collective forms of ownership. The Committee of Experts indicated that with regard to the forms of land ownership, the purpose of the article is to recognise that indigenous peoples have a "right of land ownership, possession and use, in accordance with their own customs and traditions, even though these may be different from those prevailing for other members of national society."[107] The ILO Office also rejected the idea that a right to use the land could be acceptable, as it was stated: "to assimilate the term 'use' to ownership and possession would weaken the revised Convention by comparison to Convention No. 107, which recognizes the right to ownership."[108] Thus, a right to use the land would not fulfil the requirement of Article 14 of ILO 169, which recognises rights of ownership and possession.

---

104 Convention Concerning Indigenous and Tribal Peoples in independent Countries (ILO No. 169), 72 ILO Official Bull. 59 (1989), *reprinted in* I.L.M. 1382 (1989), art. 13.

105 International Labor Conference, *Partial Revision of the Indigenous and Tribal Populations Convention*, 1957 (No. 107), 75th Sess., Report VI(2), at 48.

106 *Id.* at 49.

107 *Id.*

108 International Labor Conference, *Partial Revision of the Indigenous and Tribal Populations Convention*, 1957 (No. 107), 76th Sess., Report IV(2A), at 36; However, the second part of Article 14.1 makes a clear distinction between land exclusively occupied by indigenous peoples and land that is shared to which indigenous peoples have a right to use.

Overall, despite not explicitly referring to a collective right to land ownership in Article 14, it is clear that Convention does recognise such a collective right to ownership. This is confirmed by the ILO Committee of Experts' practice. For example, in one of its examinations of a representation brought under Article 24 of the ILO Constitution, the Committee of Experts observed that:

> The ILO's experience with indigenous and tribal peoples has shown that when communally owned indigenous lands are divided and assigned to individuals or third parties, the exercise of their rights by indigenous communities tends to be weakened and generally they end up losing all or most of the lands, resulting in a general reduction of the resources that are available to indigenous peoples when they keep their lands in common.[109]

In this case, the General Confederation of Workers of Peru alleged that the government of Peru had failed to protect indigenous peoples' rights by converting communally held lands into individual titles. The Committee stated that:

> [T]he Convention recalls the special importance of the relationship of indigenous peoples with the lands or territories, and in particular the collective aspects of this relationship. The Committee notes further, from its experience acquired in the application of the Convention and its predecessor, that the loss of communal land often damages the cohesion and viability of the people concerned.[110]

Thus, ILO 169 clearly recognises the need to protect indigenous peoples' collective ownership and recognises such ownership as property right to land.

In terms of the sources of property, ILO 169 acknowledges indigenous peoples' specific approach to land ownership, as Article 14 recognises traditional occupation as a source of ownership. The ILO Committee of Experts has pointed out that such criteria would be reached when an indigenous community has traditionally had access for their subsistence and traditional activities to a particular land.[111] In the same way, ILO 169 particularly protects indigenous

109 *Report of the Committee set up to examine the representation alleging non-observance by Peru of the Indigenous and Tribal People's Convention, 1989 (No. 169), made under article 24 of the ILO Constitution by the General Confederation of Workers of Peru (CGTP)*, at para. 26.

110 *Id.* at para. 30.

111 For example, *see Report of the Committee set up to examine the representation alleging non-observance by Mexico of the Indigenous and Tribal Peoples Convention, 1989 (No. 169), made*

peoples' customary systems of land ownership by declaring that "[P]ersons not belonging to these peoples shall be prevented from taking advantage of their customs or of lack of understanding of the laws on the part of their members to secure the ownership, possession or use of land belonging to them."[112] Thus, the ILO takes into consideration that in most cases, indigenous peoples have an alternative conception of property rights, which could be based on a traditional collective form of ownership. ILO 107, in Article 14, stipulates that national agrarian programs should secure sufficient land to provide "the essentials of a normal existence" and "the means required to promote the development of the lands which these populations already possess."[113] This article is based on an equality approach to national development plans; the idea behind this is that indigenous populations should receive a treatment equivalent to the rest of the population. Article 19 of ILO 169 states:

National agrarian programmes shall secure to the peoples concerned treatment equivalent to that accorded to other sectors of the population with regard to:

(a) The provision of more land for these peoples when they have not the area necessary for providing the essentials of a normal existence, or for any possible increase in their numbers;
(b) The provision of the means required to promote the development of the lands which these peoples already possess.

Overall, regarding the relationship between property rights and land ownership, the ILO 169 recognizes indigenous peoples' traditional form of land ownership as a source of property, and clearly affirms that based on such traditions, States ought to protect indigenous peoples' right to a collective form of land ownership.[114]

The other important instrument regarding property rights in land is the U.N. Declaration on the Rights of Indigenous Peoples (UNDRIP) which contains

under article 24 of the ILO Constitution by the Trade Union Delegation, D-III-57, Section XI of the National Trade Union of Education Workers (SNTE), Radio Education.

112 Convention Concerning Indigenous and Tribal Peoples in independent Countries (ILO No. 169), 72 ILO Official Bull. 59 (1989), *reprinted in* I.L.M. 1382 (1989), art. 17.3f.

113 Convention Concerning the Protection and Integration of Indigenous and other Tribal and Semi-tribal Populations in Independent Countries (ILO Convention No. 107), 328 U.N.T.S. 247 (1957), art. 12(1), art. 14.

114 However it is important to bear in mind that until now only (Feb. 2016) only 22 States have ratified the Convention, see: http://www.ilo.org/dyn/normlex/en/f?p=1000:11300:0::NO:11300:P11300_INSTRUMENT_ID:312314.

numerous references to land rights, and more particularly to indigenous peoples' proprietary right to land.[115] The Declaration clearly highlights the importance for land rights which are mentioned throughout the text, but articles 25 to 30 are specifically dedicated to land rights. Article 26 of the Declaration takes a very wide approach by putting together notions of ownership, possession and use. Article 26.2 states that:

> Indigenous peoples have the right to own, use, develop and control the lands, territories and resources that they possess by reason of traditional ownership or other traditional occupation or use, as well as those which they have otherwise acquired.

Hence even though the Declaration does not specifically refer to collective property rights, it clearly recognises indigenous peoples traditional form of land tenure. Moreover, this part of Declaration, which deals with land rights, identifies indigenous peoples as rights holders, for all the articles use the formula "indigenous peoples have the right." However, the issue of collective rights was not uncontested during the drafting process; for example the U.K. government issued statement highlighting that it would not accept the concept of collective right.[116] The United States, Australia and New Zealand have expressed similar opposition to the recognition of collective rights.[117] Usually, States that resist the recognition of indigenous peoples' right to collective ownership argue for the recognition of the rights of persons belonging to indigenous groups based on the model of minority rights. Nevertheless, the text of the Declaration clearly affirms that States have to recognise indigenous peoples' customs, traditions and land tenure systems whether it is based on individual or collective rights.[118]

In terms of the content of indigenous peoples right to land, article 26 affirms that: "Indigenous peoples have the right to own, use, develop and control the lands, territories and resources that they possess by reason of traditional ownership or other traditional occupation or use, as well as those which they

115 G.A. Res. 61/295, annex, U.N. Doc. A/RES/61/295.

116 United Kingdom of Great Britain and Northern Ireland, explanation of vote on the Draft United Nations Declaration on the Rights of Indigenous Peoples, Human Rights Council, Geneva June 29, 2006.

117 Joint statement by Australia, New Zealand and the United States of America on the Chair's Text on the Declaration on the Rights of Indigenous Peoples, Human Rights Council, June 2006.

118 See especially art. 27 of the Declaration.

have otherwise acquired (…).” In making this broad affirmation the Declaration does not get into the debate on what indigenous peoples' land rights do or do not constitute. Traditionally on this issue there have been some debates on whether land rights for indigenous peoples meant a right to ownership or right to use the land. The Declaration avoids such issue by adopting a broad approach to the content of a right to land which means not only a right of ownership and use but also right to develop and control.

In terms of the substance of land rights, the Declaration makes some important contributions regarding the recognition of indigenous peoples' traditional customary land laws. It states that “States shall give legal recognition and protection to these lands, territories and resources. Such recognition shall be conducted with due respect to the customs, traditions and land tenure systems of the indigenous peoples concerned.” This is an important affirmation given that in most situations indigenous peoples are dispossessed of their lands as a result of state authorities' non-recognition of their traditional forms of land tenure systems. On this issue the Declaration goes even further by calling on states to recognise indigenous peoples' customary systems of laws when recognising and adjudicating land rights. Article 27 reads:

> States shall establish and implement, in conjunction with indigenous peoples concerned, a fair, independent, impartial, open and transparent process, giving due recognition to indigenous peoples' laws, traditions, customs and land tenure systems, to recognize and adjudicate the rights of indigenous peoples pertaining to their lands, territories and resources, including those which were traditionally owned or otherwise occupied or used. Indigenous peoples shall have the right to participate in this process.

Hence, this article provides for a sort of ‘guideline’ or ‘framework,’ inviting States to put in place a ‘transparent process’ at the national level that gives space to indigenous peoples' customary laws. It is important to highlight that such a process could play a role not only in the adjudication of land rights but also in the process of recognition of such rights. Regarding the operationalistion of such recognition, one might find this part of the Declaration disappointing: while it supports the establishment of a ‘transparent process’ it does not provide details on how such a process should work. At this stage it is important to bear in mind that the aim of the Declaration is to set basic minimum international standards and to affirm the need to give due recognition to indigenous peoples' own laws. However as examined in the next section below, international human rights law has also greatly evolved regarding the obligations of the States to protect and ensure the protection of indigenous peoples' land rights at the national level.

B Effective Measures of Protection and Demarcation

The recognition of property rights for indigenous peoples means that States have to adopt effective measures to ensure the protection of indigenous peoples' territories. There are different types of measures that government need to put in place to guarantee the protection of indigenous peoples' rights to property in land, these include measures to restrict the transfer or the alienation of indigenous peoples' lands, and measures to identify and demarcate indigenous lands. As noted by the former UN Special Rapporteur Cobo: "a protective regime should cover indigenous land (...) This regime should at least include restrictions on alienation, encumbrance, attachment and proscription."[119] This is reflected in Article 14 of ILO 169 which sets up a list of measures that governments shall undertake to secure indigenous peoples' land rights. This includes measures to identify indigenous lands, guarantee of their ownership and judicial mechanisms to resolve land claims. The present section explores and evaluates the theoretical and practical importance of these measures in the protection of indigenous peoples' right to their lands: first by examining measures that restrict the transfer and alienability of indigenous lands, and second by focusing on the measures for the demarcation of indigenous peoples' territories.

1 *Restriction on Land Transferability: The Danger of Paternalism*

One aspects of human rights protection of indigenous peoples' right to land is based on the idea that indigenous peoples need special protection from outside elements and, more specifically, from market forces. Many national systems have adopted an approach that places restrictions on indigenous peoples' capacity to alienate their lands.[120] There are two sides to this approach, a paternalistic historical view, and a modern approach that is based on the concept of special measures for the protection of specifically vulnerable groups. One of the questions relating to indigenous peoples' land rights is whether States should put in place separate systems to distinguish indigenous ownership of

119 U.N. Doc. E/CN.4/Sub.2/1983/21/Add.8, para. 526.

120 In the case of Latin America, *see* Roger Plant & Soren Hvalkof, *Land Titling and Indigenous Peoples*, (Inter-American Development Bank, 2001), *available at* www.iadb.org/sds/doc/IND-109E.pdf.

land from general ownership, especially when indigenous ownership is collective. In certain circumstances, the establishment of protective regimes often coincides with a paternalistic approach towards indigenous peoples. This is reflected in notions, such as "domestic dependent nations," as developed in the U.S. Supreme Court Marshall trilogy, i.e., indigenous nations are wards of the State, which has the duty to take care of indigenous nations who are not able to manage their own lands. Under this "trust" obligation, States established so-called "trust lands," which meant that a part of the land would be allocated to indigenous communities.[121] Based on this idea, several States have developed the notion of "reserved" or "trust" lands. The government owns the land but has a duty to put in place measures of protection of indigenous peoples' land rights. The State must administer indigenous peoples' lands for the benefit of its indigenous population, and the government may not alienate the land except in ways consistent with the trust relationship. Indigenous communities then have a right of occupancy of the land; however, such a right is precarious, as it remains subordinated to the decision of the governments.

These systems of trust or reserved lands have been developed in many places-examples of Indians reservations in North America are usually well known—but reserved lands were also a dominant feature of colonization in all the other regions of the globe.[122] The establishment of such reserved or trust lands were based on what McNeil has designated "the protection rationale" under which States protected land alienation in order to protect indigenous peoples.[123] Under international law, the idea that States have an obligation to protect indigenous peoples against land encroachment from other parts of the population is not recent. The assumed superiority of European settled societies and the trusteeship obligations towards Native populations were at the heart of both the Berlin (1884–85) and the Brussels (1889–90) Conferences on Africa, which dealt with the necessity of improving the conditions of the

121 *See* discussion on trust in Chapter 2.

122 There are several examples of such reserved lands in the Cobo Report: U.N. Doc. E/CN.4/Sub.2/1983/21/Add.4; *see also* the examples developed in International Labor Organization, Indigenous Peoples (1953); see also: Clement Ng'Ong'Ola, *Land Rights for marginalized Ethnic Groups in Botswana, With Special reference to the Basarwa*, 41J. Afr. L. 1 (1997); Sidney L. Harring, *The Constitution of Namibia and the 'Rights and Freedoms' Guaranteed Communal Land Holders: Resolving the Inconsistency Between Article 16, Article 100, and Schedule 5*, 12(3) S. Afr. J. Hum. Rts. 467 (1996); José O. Aylwin, *El Derecho de Los Pueblos Indigenas a la tierra y al territorio en America Latina: Antecedentes historicos y Tendencias Actuales*, O.E.A. GTDADIN Doc. 96/02.

123 Kent McNeil, *Self-Government and the Inalienability of Aboriginal Title*, 47 McGill L.J. 473 (2002).

Native populations.[124] Likewise, Article 22 of the League of Nations Covenant dealt with "peoples not yet able to stand by themselves under the strenuous conditions of the modern world."[125] Under Article 23, members of the League undertook "to secure just treatment of the native inhabitants of territories under their control."[126] Thus, the League of Nations perpetuated the paternalistic and colonial approach to indigenous peoples' rights on which reserved lands were based. Similarly, the Conferences of the Pan American Union in 1938, declared that:

> the Indians, as descendants of the first settlers of the Americas have a special right to the protection of the public authorities, in order to compensate for the inadequacy of their physical and intellectual development and, in consequence, all that may be done to improve the lot of Indians shall be just reparation for the lack of understanding with which they were treated in times past.[127]

The belief that governments should protect indigenous territories against alienation originated from the view that States have a duty to act for the well-being of their indigenous populations, as 'parents will do towards their children.'[128] This paternalistic approach towards land protection is not only historical as there are still traces of it in contemporary States practice. This is reflected in the so-called fiduciary approach developed in most common law countries towards indigenous nations that "enjoins one party to act in the interest of the other selflessly," thus placing indigenous peoples at the mercy of State action because of their "special vulnerability."[129] Another example

---

124 Berlin Conference, Final Act, Parry, 165 CTS (1885), Brussels Conference, General Act, 82 BFSP.

125 The Covenant of the League of Nations, June 28, 1919, 2 Bevans 48.

126 Art. 23, League of Nations Covenant. Generally, on the League of Nations and indigenous peoples, *see* Fernand Gouttenoire de Toury, *Les Revendications des Indigènes* 6 Les Cahiers des Droits de L'homme (1926); *see also* Félicien Challaye, *La Société des Nations et les Indigènes*, 5 Les Cahiers des Droits de L'homme (1928).

127 *Quoted in* IACHR, *The Human Rights Situation of the Indigenous Peoples in the Americas*, OEA/Ser.L/V/II.108, Doc. 62, Ch. 1 (Oct. 20, 2000).

128 On this issue, *see* Paul Keal, *'Just Backward Children' International Law and the Conquest on non-Europeans Peoples*, 49(2) Australian J. Int'l Aff. 191 (1995).

129 Paul D. Finn, *The Fiduciary Principle, in* Equity, Fiduciaries and Trusts 4 (Timothy G. Youdan ed., 1989). Se also: TW Bennett & CH Powell, *The State as Trustee of Land*, 16S. Afr. J. on Hum. Rts. 601 (2000); David W Elliott, *Aboriginal Peoples in Canada and the United States and the Scope of the Special Fiduciary Relationship*, 24 Man. L.J. 137

would be the approach of the Brazilian government under which indigenous territories are considered as the "endowment of the Federal Union" based on the idea that the government "assumes the responsibility to guarantee those lands to indigenous peoples, to protect them from attacks and usurpation from state agents and third parties, and to provide special measures necessary for indigenous welfare and survival."[130] From this perspective, one of the dangers is that these measures to protect land alienation contain within themselves a cultural imposition and a patronising and paternalistic approach. This danger was highlighted in the Cobo Report which specifically addressed the issue of reserved areas. On this issue, the former UN Special Rapporteur recommended that: "All indigenous reserved areas should be immediately handed over to the respective indigenous groups" and that "no intermediary institution of any kind should be created or appointed to hold the lands of indigenous peoples on their behalf."[131] The rejection of the trust system was also an important contribution of the decision of the African Commission in the Endorois case against Kenya. In this case, the territory of the indigenous Endorois community was classified as a 'Trust Land' in the period of post-colonial independence by the government. The trust creates an obligation for the government to act for the benefits of the communities living on 'Trust Land,' and also to ensure that their customary rights are protected.[132] In a statement which is worth quoting at length, the African Commission dismissed the whole system of trust land by stating:

> The African Commission is of the view that even though the Constitution of Kenya provides that Trust Land may be alienated and that the Trust Land Act provides comprehensive procedure for the assessment of compensation, the Endorois property rights have been encroached upon, in particular by the expropriation and the effective denial of ownership of their land. It agrees with the Complainants that the Endorois were never given the full title to the land they had in practice before the British colonial administration. Their land was instead made subject to a trust, which

---

(1996–1997); Garth Nettheim, Donna Craig, Gary D. Meyers (eds.), Indigenous Peoples and Governance Structures: A Comparative Analysis of Land and Resource Management Rights (Australian Institute of Aboriginal and Torres Strait Islander Studies, 2002).

130 Osvaldo Kreimer, *Indigenous Peoples' Rights to Land, Territories, and Natural Resources: A Technical Meeting of the OAS Working Group*, 10(2) Hum. Rts. Brief 13 (2003).

131 U.N. Doc. E/CN.4/Sub.2/1983/21/Add.8, paras. 520 and 524.

132 *See* O. Lumumba, *Who owns this land? A guide to understanding the law of trust lands in Kenya* (Kenya Human Rights Commission, 1997); see also: C. Juma C. and J.B. Ojwang (eds), In Land we Trust: Environment, Private Property and Constitutional Changes (1996).

> gave them beneficial title, but denied them actual title. The African Commission further agrees that though for a decade they were able to exercise their traditional rights without restriction, the trust land system has proved inadequate to protect their rights.[133]

Hence, the African Commission discards the system of 'Trust Land' for not providing real right of ownership. In the words of the Commission, only proper "ownership ensures that indigenous peoples can engage with the state and third parties as active stakeholders rather than as passive beneficiaries."[134] The affirmation that ownership only and not usage is protected under the right to property is an important statement, since most States usually favour a right of usage for indigenous peoples rather than a right of ownership over their traditional territories. Beyond the particular situation in this case, it is an important statement as several countries still hold land in trust for indigenous peoples, reminiscent of a colonial era with no standing under contemporary standards of international human rights law. Contemporary human rights law rejects the paternalistic approach of land reserves; however, it invites States to put in place special measures of restriction on the alienability of indigenous peoples' territories.

As the debates leading to the adoption of ILO 169 put in perspective, regarding special measures of protection for indigenous peoples' land rights, one of the central issues of discussion was on the establishment of national restrictive regimes on the alienation of indigenous peoples' lands. Originally, Recommendation No. 104 of the ILO Committee of Experts on Indigenous Labor, which led to the adoption of ILO 107, called for restrictions on the leasing and mortgaging of indigenous lands.[135] This issue of restriction on transferability of indigenous lands became extremely significant during debates leading to the adoption of ILO 169.[136] During the debates, indigenous representatives insisted that provision be made to ensure the inalienability of indigenous peoples' lands.[137] This was rejected, and instead the Convention only recognizes that States should respect specific procedures of transmission of land ownership.

---

133 African Commission on Human and Peoples' Rights, Endorois Decision, *supra* note 90, para. 199 (emphasis omitted).

134 Ibid, para. 204.

135 *See* International Labor Conference, *Living and Working Conditions of Indigenous Populations in Independent Countries*, Report VIII(1), 39th Sess., at 16 (Geneva 1956).

136 *See* International Labor Conference, *Partial Revision of the Indigenous and Tribal Populations Convention*, 1957 (No. 107), Report VI(1), 75th Sess., at 67–68 (1988).

137 The Worker' Members submitted an amendment, which stated that indigenous lands shall be recognized as inalienable; this amendment was rejected by 2,184 votes in favor,

Article 17 states that: "[P]rocedures established by the peoples concerned for the transmission of land rights among members of these peoples shall be respected."[138] As the report on the debates highlights, the inscription of inalienability of indigenous lands would have meant that "national governments would not relinquish their capacity to make ultimate decisions on matters of national interest or on the utilisation of natural resources."[139] Instead the Conference Committee decided "that Article 17 should continue the line of reasoning pursued in other parts of the Convention, according to which indigenous and tribal peoples shall decide their own priorities for the process of development (Article 7) and that they should be consulted through their representative institutions whenever consideration is being given to legislative or administrative measures which may affect them directly (Article 6)."[140] Thus, moving away from the paternalistic approach contained in the ILO 107, ILO 169 recognizes a central role to indigenous owned laws on land alienation. Article 17 establishes restriction on transferability of indigenous lands, and Article 18 states: "Adequate penalties shall be established by law for unauthorized intrusion upon, or use of, the lands of the peoples concerned, and governments shall take measures to prevent such offences."[141] Thus, ILO 169 clearly establishes that States have a duty to put in place effective measures for the protection of indigenous peoples' rights over their territories. This approach was illustrated in a situation brought to the ILO Committee of Experts against Mexico on behalf of the Huichol indigenous community, the Committee pointed out that Mexico should "take the necessary measures to guarantee effective protection of the rights of ownership and possession of the Huicholes, and in particular to protect them from possible intrusion by third parties."[142]

2,184 against under Article 65(10) of the Standing Order. *See* International Labor Conference, *Provisional Record 25*, 76th Sess., at 25–23 (1988).

138 Convention Concerning Indigenous and Tribal Peoples in independent Countries (ILO No. 169), 72 ILO Official Bull. 59 (1989), *reprinted in* I.L.M. 1382 (1989), art. 17.

139 International Labor Conference, *Partial Revision of Indigenous and Tribal Populations Convention*, 1957 (No. 107), ILO Conference, 75th Sess., Report V(1), at 46 (1988).

140 *Report of the Committee set up to examine the representation alleging non-observance by Peru of the Indigenous and Tribal People's Convention, 1989 (No. 169), made under article 24 of the ILO Constitution by the General Confederation of Workers of Peru* (CGTP), at para. 30.

141 *Id.*, art. 18.

142 *Report of the Committee set up to examine the representation alleging non-observance by Mexico of the Indigenous and Tribal Peoples Convention. 1989 (No. 169), made under article 24 of the ILO Constitution by the Trade Union Delegation, D-III-57, Section XI of the National Trade Union of Education Workers* (SNTE). *Radio Education*, Docs. GB.270/16/3, GB.272/7/2, para. 40 (1998).

This approach on protection against encroachment and alienability is also present in the UNDRIP. Article 26 of the Declaration specifically mentioned the duty of States to act to prevent land alienation, stating: "States shall give legal recognition and protection to these lands, territories and resources." Regional instruments also insist on States' obligations to act to protect indigenous peoples' territories form alienation. The Inter-American Charter of Social Guarantees makes specific references to indigenous peoples, and, in relation to land rights, the Charter states that "Institutions shall be created for the protection of Indians, particularly in order to ensure respect for their lands, to legalize their possession thereof, and to prevent encroachment upon such lands by outsiders."[143] The issue of protection is also an important feature of the current negotiations for the adoption of the OAS Declaration on the Rights of Indigenous Peoples in the Americas. During one of the meetings of the Working Group to Prepare the Draft American Declaration, participants have pointed out that States have to safeguard: "inembaragability, imprescriptibility and inalienabilty" of indigenous lands and territories.[144] It was pointed out that these three principles are crucial:

- *inembargability:* the principle that lands cannot be impounded or auctioned for debts;
- *imprescribility:* the theory that land rights cannot be subject to any statute of limitations, and;
- *inalienability:* the concept that land cannot be transferred to third parties outside the Indigenous peoples or collective.[145]

This debate is based on the fact that several national jurisdictions within the continent still defend the idea that there should be some special measures to prevent the alienability of indigenous peoples' lands. For example, in Canada, courts have recognized the fiduciary obligation of the State in the case of land alienation and concluded that the government had the power to alienate indigenous lands but must act in order to protect indigenous interests.[146] In the

143 Bogota Conference, 1948, Final Act of the Ninth International Conference, Res. XXIX, Annals, at 129.

144 *See* Meeting of the Working Group on the Fifth Section of the Draft Declaration, *Report of the Rapporteur* (Osvaldo Kreimer), OAS/Ser.K/XVI GT/DADIN/doc.113/03rev.1, at 5 (2003).

145 Osvaldo Kreimer, *Indigenous Peoples' Rights to Land, Territories, and Natural Resources: A Technical Meeting of the OAS Working Group*, 10(2) Hum. Rts. Brief 13 (2003).

146 *See* Kent McNeil, *Self-Government and the Inalienability of Aboriginal Title*, 47 McGill L.J. 473 (2002).

case of alienation, this includes the duty of consultation and the provision of adequate compensation. The content of Aboriginal title is limited by the States' right of pre-emption and inalienability. The right of pre-emption (pre-emptive right) refers to the State's exclusive right to purchase aboriginal lands. Inalienability refers to the fact that native title is an inalienable right to land that cannot be transferred, sold or surrendered to anyone other than the Crown. Thus, Aboriginal title provides indigenous peoples with a right of complete ownership against all but the government, as, in any case, the government retains the exclusive authority to terminate Native title. This exclusive right of the government has its root in the European rules of discovery and in the trusteeship doctrine that followed. In *R. v. Symonds* the Court stated: "To let in all purchasers, and to protect and enforce private purchase, would be virtually to confiscate the lands of the Natives in a very short time."[147] Overall, many countries have put in place such systems of restriction on the alienability of indigenous peoples reserved lands. As McNeil has pointed out, the reasons invoked for the establishment of such special measures on inalienability are only justified to the extent that governments do not recognize indigenous peoples' land tenure systems within Aboriginal nations. As he stated: "those reasons should not apply because no alienation of Aboriginal title is involved. If their own laws so permit, they could create interests in land within their own territories, while retaining their communal title to the whole of their territories."[148] The author then concluded that even though there is a need to preserve the land bases for indigenous peoples, the restrictions of the capacity of indigenous peoples to alienate their own lands should include and refer to their inherent right to self-government.[149] Even though it is necessary to ensure that indigenous peoples maintain control over the territories allotted to them, the approach, based on pre-emptive control of the government, is reminiscent of paternalism. It is to balance such dangers of paternalism that human rights legal discourse, as expressed in the African Commission decision in the Endorois case, is particularly relevant. Any meaningful system of protection should recognize indigenous customary laws regarding land alienation. Disregarding such customary systems of land tenure would amount to a discriminatory imposition of one legal system over another. It is for the establishment of this fine balance that the human rights system seeks the protection of indigenous peoples' lands from alienation, as well as the recognition of indigenous customary laws regarding such alienation.

---

147 R.v. Symonds [1847] N.Z.P.C.C. 387, 391—New Zealand Supreme Court.

148 McNeil, *supra* note 147, at 504.

149 *Id.*, at 509–10.

2 *Land Identification and Demarcation*

Another important consequence of the recognition of indigenous peoples' property rights in land is States' obligation to demarcate and clearly identify indigenous peoples' territories. In the words of Daes, in her study on land rights: "Demarcation of lands is the formal process of identifying the actual locations and boundaries of indigenous lands or territories and physically marking those boundaries on the ground."[150] As she noted, a purely abstract legal recognition of indigenous peoples' land rights is meaningless unless the physical identity of the land is determined.[151] In addition, she pointed out that "in terms of frequency and scope of complaints, the greatest single problem today for indigenous peoples is the failure of States to demarcate indigenous lands."[152] The ILO Convention 169 refers to an obligation to identify and demarcate indigenous peoples' territories. Article 14.2 of ILO 169 states: "Governments shall take steps as necessary to identify the lands which the peoples concerned traditionally occupy, and to guarantee effective protection of their rights of ownership and possession."[153] Tomei and Swepston have pointed out that "effective" means that there "has to be real and practical protection and not just protection in law."[154] Article 14.3 adds: "Adequate procedures shall be established within the national legal system to resolve land claims by the peoples concerned."[155]

International human rights treaty bodies have also actively promoted the obligation to ensure a proper process of demarcation of indigenous peoples' territories. The Human Rights Committee (HRC) has taken a dynamic approach and interpreted Article 27 of the ICCPR as requiring States to ensure the demarcation of indigenous peoples' territories in order to ensure an effective protection of such territories. For example, the HRC recommended that Brazil ensure the demarcation of indigenous territories. The Committee stated: "in light of article 27 of the Covenant, all necessary measures should be taken to ensure that the process of demarcation of indigenous lands be speedily and justly settled."[156] CERD, in its review of Brazil's report to the

---

150 *See* Erica I. Daes, *Second Progress Report*, U.N. Doc. E/CN.4/Sub.2/1999/18, at 17, para. 47.

151 *Id.*

152 *Id.*

153 Convention Concerning Indigenous and Tribal Peoples in independent Countries (ILO No. 169), 72 ILO Official Bull. 59 (1989), *reprinted in* I.L.M. 1382 (1989), art. 14.2.

154 Manuela Tomei & Lee Swepston, Indigenous and Tribal Peoples: A Guide to ILO Convention No. 169 19 (1996).

155 Convention Concerning Indigenous and Tribal Peoples in independent Countries (ILO No. 169), 72 ILO Official Bull. 59 (1989), *reprinted in* I.L.M. 1382 (1989), art. 14.3.

156 *Concluding Observations of the Human Rights Committee*: Brazil, CCPR/C/79/Add.66; A/51/40, para. 337 (July 24, 1996).

Committee, pointed out that Brazil's objective of completing the demarcation of indigenous lands is an important step towards securing the rights of indigenous peoples. The Committee insisted on the need to ensure such identification as an effective protection of indigenous peoples' access to their lands.[157] CERD also expressed its concerns on the importance of the demarcation indigenous lands in its Concluding Observations on Sweden's report to the Committee. CERD also pointed out that in the light of General Recommendation XXIII "the Committee encourages the state party to ensure that the Boundary Commission fulfils its task within the scheduled time."[158] In general, the Committee has very often highlighted the need for States to ensure that a fair and reliable system of land demarcation is put in place.[159]

At the regional level, the IACHR in its reports has often insisted on States' obligation to demarcate indigenous peoples' territories. The 1999 Report on the Situation of Human Rights in Colombia discusses the progress made in demarcating and titling indigenous lands. The IACHR stated: "[T]he States should take appropriate measures to ensure that the process of legal demarcation, recognition and granting title to land and use of natural resources to indigenous communities is not hindered or delayed by bureaucratic difficulties."[160] Similarly, in its report on the situation in Peru, the IACHR stated: "The recovery, recognition, demarcation, and registration of the lands represent essential rights for cultural survival and for maintaining the community's integrity."[161] The Commission then recommended that Peru "adopt appropriate measures to guarantee the process of legal demarcation, recognition, and issuance to the indigenous communities of land titles, and to ensure that this process does not prejudice the normal development of property and community life."[162] In the *Awas Tingni* case, the Inter-American Court of Human Rights found that Nicaragua had not respected its obligation to demarcate land on the basis of Article 21 of the American Convention. The Court stated: "the State must adopt the legislative, administrative, and any other measures required to create an effective mechanism for delimitation, demarcation, and titling of the

157 CERD, *Concluding Observations*, Brazil, U.N. Doc. CERD/C/64/CO/2, para. 15, (Mar. 12, 2004); *see also* para. 16 in which the Committee expressed its concerns on the identification of indigenous lands in the Quilombo area.

158 CERD, *Concluding Observations*, Sweden, U.N. Doc. CERD/C/64/CO/8, para. 12 (Mar. 12, 2004).

159 *See:* Venezuela, CERD/C/VEN/CO/19-21, 23 September 2013, para. 17.

160 *Third Report on the Human Rights Situation in Colombia*, Ch. X, para. 23.

161 *Second Report on the Situation of Human Rights in Peru*, OEA/Ser.L/V/II.106 Doc.59, para. 16 (June 2, 2000).

162 *Id.*, para. 57.

property of indigenous communities, in accordance with their customary law, values, customs and mores."[163] As noted by the Court in the *Yakye Axa* case: "a strictly juridical or abstract recognition of indigenous lands, territories or resources lacks true meaning where the property has not been physically established and delimited."[164] In its judgment in the *Saramaka* case, the Court ordered Suriname to: "delimit, demarcate, and grant collective title over the territory of the members of the Saramaka people, in accordance with their customary laws, and through previous, effective and fully informed consultations with the Saramaka people, without prejudice to other tribal and indigenous communities"[165] The importance of demarcation was also a central element of the 2014 decision of the Inter-American Court in the case of the Kuna Indigenous Peoples against Panama.[166] In the case of the *Kaliña and Lokono* peoples against Suriname adopted in 2015, the Court has reiterated this approach highlighting that "based on the principle of legal certainty, the land rights of the indigenous peoples must be formalized by the adoption of the administrative and legislative measures required to create an effective mechanism for delimitation, demarcation and the granting of titles that recognizes these rights in the practice."[167] It is also worth noting that OAS Proposed American Declaration enjoins States to "give maximum priority to the demarcation and recognition of properties and areas of indigenous use."[168]

At the local level, the issue of demarcation is increasingly at the center of concerns for indigenous peoples. Often due to the lack of proper national system of land demarcation, indigenous peoples have decided to take themselves the necessary steps for the demarcation of their territories in engaging

163 The Mayagna (Sumo) Awas Tingni Community v. Nicaragua, Inter-Am. Ct. H.R. (ser. C) No. 79 (Aug. 31, 2001). *See also* Moiwana Village v. Suriname, Inter-Am. Ct. HR (ser. C) No. 124, at paras. 209–10 (June 15, 2005); and Yakye Axa Indigenous Community v Paraguay I Inter-Am. Ct. HR (ser. C) No. 125, at para. 121 (June 17, 2005).

164 Case of the Indigenous Community Yakye Axa, Judgment of June 17, 2005 Series C No. 125, para. 143.

165 I/A Court H.R., Case of the Saramaka People v. Suriname. Preliminary Objections, Merits, Reparations and Costs. Judgment of November 28, 2007. Series C No. 172, par. 194(a).

166 I/A Court H.R., *Case of the Kuna Indigenous People of Madungandí and the Emberá Indigenous People of Bayano and their Members v. Panama*. Preliminary objections, merits, reparations and costs. Judgment of October 14, 2014. Series C No. 284.

167 *Case of the Kaliña and Lokono Peoples v. Suriname*, Judgment of November 25, 2015 (Merits, Reparations and Costs), para. 133.

168 OAS Draft Inter-American Declaration on the Rights of Indigenous Peoples, Doc. OEA/Ser/L/V/II.90, doc.9, rev.1 (1995), art. XVIII, para. 8.

in mapping processes of their land.[169] On this issue it is important to highlight that the exercise of indigenous peoples' territorial rights is not conditioned to their express recognition by the State, and the existence of a formal title to property is not a requirement for the existence of the right to indigenous territorial property.[170] Hence, the absence of a formal system of land demarcation and of a titling process does not constrain in itself the right of indigenous peoples over their property rights in land. Consequently, customary possession and use by indigenous peoples must be the guiding principle for the identification and the demarcation of their territories. States have the international legal obligation to define and demarcate the territory of indigenous peoples in accordance with their own traditions and cultures. From that perspective, it is important to recognise the legal value of indigenous peoples' own mapping and demarcation processes.

C Reparation, Remedies and Restitution

There is a clear principle that violations of human rights law give rise to a right of remedies for the victims.[171] The availability of remedies is in itself a right enshrined in several instruments.[172] Remedies refer to "the means by

169 See: M. Chapin, Z. Lamb & B. Threlkeld, *Mapping indigenous lands* Annu. Rev. Anthropol., 34, 619–38 (2005); J. Bryan, *Walking the line: participatory mapping, indigenous rights, and neoliberalism.* Geoforum, 42(1), 40–50; Wainwright & Bryan, *Cartography, territory, property: postcolonial reflections on indigenous counter-mapping in Nicaragua and Belize.* Cultural Geographies, 16(2), 153–78. And also, see the Rainforest UK project on 'Mapping for Rights', at: http://www.mappingforrights.org.

170 *See* I/A Court H.R., Case of the Sawhoyamaxa Indigenous Community v. Paraguay. Merits, Reparations and Costs. Judgment of March 29, 2006. Series C No. 146, par. 128.

171 *See* Dinah Shelton, Remedies in International Human Rights Law (2 ed. 2005); *see also* Velasquez Rodriguez Case. Compensatory Damages, July 21, 1989—IACHR; Reparations for Injuries Suffered in the Service of the United Nations, Advisory Opinion, 1949 I.C.J. 174, 184; Legal Consequences of the Construction of the Wall in the Occupied Palestinian Territory (General List No. 131, Advisory Opinion, July 9, 2004)—I.C.J.

172 Art. 8, Universal Declaration of Human Rights, G.A. Res. 217A(III), U.N. Doc A/810, at 71 (1948); art. 2(3), International Covenant on Civil and Political Rights, U.N. Doc. A/6316 (1966), 999 U.N.T.S. 171; art. 6, International Convention on the Elimination of All Forms of Racial Discrimination, U.N. Doc. A/6014 (1966); art. 13 European Convention for the Protection of Human Rights and Fundamental Freedoms, E.T.S. 5, 213 U.N.T.S. 222; arts. 1, 8 and 25, American Convention on Human Rights, O.A.S. Treaty Series No. 36, 1144 U.N.T.S. 123; art. 7, African Charter on Human and Peoples' Rights, OAU Doc. CAB/LEG/67/3 rev. 5, *reprinted in* 21 I.L.M. 58 (1982).

which a right is enforced or the violation of a right is prevented, redressed or compensated."[173] As Myntti pointed out "the term remedies has two interrelated aspects: *recourse* and *redress*."[174] The following analysis explores the remedies that are available to indigenous peoples when they are losing their right to property in land. To undertake such analysis, it is divided into two different parts. The first looks at the principles put forward by human rights law when it comes to loss of property rights, namely the principles of restitution and compensation. The second part takes a more historical approach to the notion of restitution. As highlighted earlier, indigenous peoples' rights to their lands derive from traditional occupation and use, as well as indigenous laws and customs relating to land ownership. Thus, international law is dealing with arguments of a historical nature. Even though international human rights law is concerned with the present situation facing indigenous peoples, it is certain that when addressing indigenous peoples' land rights the "weight of history" cannot be ignored, and as such the notion of restitution for past violations constitute an important element of the remedies available to indigenous peoples.[175] In many cases the dispossession of indigenous peoples from their territories took place before the contemporary human rights instruments that are invoked were adopted. Accordingly, one lurking question that arises when addressing the issue of restitution is the issue of temporal law, and whether human rights law can serve as a positive force to address past dispossession. Thus, the subsequent discussion examines how human rights law attempts to bridge the gap between past violations and the present situation faced by indigenous peoples.

1 *The Right to Restitution*

Under international law, the term reparation is often used as a generic term to refer to compensation claims. Compensation and restitution are usually the two forms of reparations.[176] Restitution in international law is "aimed at the

173 Black's Law Dictionary 1294 (6th ed. 1990).

174 Myntti Myntti, *The Right to Reparation of Victims of Racial Discrimination in Human Rights Law, in* Reparations: Redressing Past Wrongs 317 (George Ulrich & Louise Krabbe Boserup eds., 2003).

175 As stated by Kreimer: "Indigenous peoples, because of their pre-existence to contemporary States, and because of their cultural and historical continuity, have a special situation, an inherent condition that is juridically a source of rights." Osvaldo Kreimer, *The Future Inter-American Declaration on the Rights of Indigenous Peoples: A Challenge for the Americas, in* Human Rights of Indigenous Peoples 69–70 (Cynthia Price Cohen ed., 1998).

176 *See* Basic Principles and Guidelines on the Right to Reparation for Victims of Gross Violations of Human Rights and Humanitarian Law, U.N. Doc. E/CN.4/Sub.2/1996/17; *see also*

reparation of the effects of a proceeding that was unlawful under International Law."[177] Thus, the first and fundamental principal for restitution of lands supposes that the acquisition of indigenous territories was an unlawful act under international law. It follows that any meaningful consideration on restitution of indigenous peoples' territories should start with an exploration of what are the rules relating to the removal or acquisition of the territories of indigenous peoples. Under international law concerning indigenous peoples' rights, the principle is that of "exceptional" removal. Unless the removal is voluntarily agreed to by indigenous peoples, the two ILO Conventions consider that the removal of indigenous peoples from their lands should take place strictly in "exceptional circumstances." Article 12 of ILO Convention No. 107 provides that governments may remove indigenous populations in respect of national legislation for national security, or in the interest of national economic development or health.[178] This article has been the subject of widespread criticism, as it provides States with almost total freedom to remove indigenous peoples from their lands.[179] The Meeting of Experts for the revision of ILO 107 unanimously concluded that removal should be limited to exceptional circumstances and should take place only with the informed consent of the concerned population.[180] In discussing the nature of "necessary relocation," the Conference resisted specific definition so as not to pre-empt such action.[181] As a result, Article 16 of ILO Convention No. 169 affirms indigenous peoples' right to remain on their land as a principle, which can only be deviated from in specific exceptional circumstances.[182] Article 16 further establishes the "minimum

---

Donna Arzt, *The Right to Compensation: The Right to Compensation Basic Principles under International Law* (July 1999), *at* www.arts.mcgill.ca/mepp/PRRN/arzt.html.

177 Istvan Vásárhelyi, Restitution in International Law 10 (1964).

178 Convention Concerning the Protection and Integration of Indigenous and other Tribal and Semi-tribal Populations in Independent Countries (ILO Convention No. 107), 328 U.N.T.S. 247 (1957), art. 12(1).

179 *See* Russel Lawrence Barsh, *Revision of ILO Convention No. 107*, 81(3) Am. J. Int'lL. 756 (1987).

180 International Labor Conference, *Partial Revision of the Indigenous and Tribal Populations Convention, 1957* (No. 107), ILO Conference, 75th Sess., Report VI(1), at 62–63 (1988).

181 The Office stated that this "would prove both unduly limiting if other imperatives reasons should exist, and unduly permissive by giving explicit authorisation to removal in specified circumstances" International Labor Conference, Report IV(2A), 76th Sess., at 44 (1989).

182 Article 16.1 reads: "Subject to the following paragraphs of this Article, the peoples concerned shall not be removed from the lands which they occupy." Convention Concerning Indigenous and Tribal Peoples in Independent Countries (ILO No. 169) (1989), 72 ILO Official Bull. 59, *reprinted in* 28 I.L.M. 1382 (1989).

requirement" when such relocation is deemed necessary. Article 16.2 states that:

> Where the relocation of these peoples is considered necessary as an exceptional measure, such relocation shall take place only with their free and informed consent. Where their consent cannot be obtained, such relocation shall take place only following appropriate procedures established by national laws and regulations, including public inquiries where appropriate, which provide the opportunity for effective representation of the peoples concerned.[183]

It should be noted that ILO 169 uses the term "relocation" and not the word "removal" that was used in ILO 107. Ferch points out that this change of vocabulary highlights the move from the assimiliationist approach, as the term "relocation" underlines the fact that "temporary interruption of indigenous property rights is preferred to long-term or permanent displacement."[184] Swepston suggests that the ILO has tried to set up "a series of hurdles to be passed, with public hearings as insurance against abuse" in case of relocation. However, he concedes that while this does not always prevent abuse, it marginally diminishes the risk.[185]

While the principle requires the non-removal of indigenous peoples from their lands, only in exceptional circumstances, and then only with their consent, there is no list of what these exceptional measures might be. For example, the notion of national economic development is often used as an excuse for disregarding indigenous peoples' rights. However, there is strong jurisprudence on this issue emerging form regional human rights institutions. The IACHR in its "Report on the Situation of Human Rights of a Segment of the Nicaraguan Population of Miskito Origin" asserted that the relocation of economic development does not meet the criteria of Article 27 of the American Convention, which allows for derogation of rights in time of war, public danger.[186] More specifically, the Inter-American Court has highlighted that, in accordance with Article 21 of the Convention, a State may restrict the use and enjoyment of the

183 *Id.*

184 Michael L. Ferch, *Indian Land Rights: An International Approach to Just Compensation*, 2 Transnat'lL. & Contemp. Prob. 302 (1992).

185 Lee Swepston, *The ILO Indigenous and Tribal Peoples Convention (No. 169): Eight Years after Adoption, in* The Human Rights of Indigenous Peoples 26 (Cynthia Price Cohen ed., 1998).

186 *Report on the Situation of Human Rights of a Segment of the Nicaraguan Population of Miskito Origin*, OEA/Serv.L/V/II.62, doc.26 (1984); *see* Part II, paras. 24 to 35.

right to property where the restrictions are: (a) previously established by law; (b) necessary; (c) proportional, and (d) with the aim of achieving a legitimate objective in a democratic society.[187] Moreover, the Court has added that necessary safeguards need to be put in place when it comes to restriction on property rights of indigenous peoples as these could directly affect their survival. In the case of *Saramaka People v. Suriname*, the Court stated:

> In order to guarantee that restrictions to the property rights of the members of the Saramaka people by the issuance of concessions within their territory does not amount to a denial of their survival as a tribal people, the State must abide by the following three safeguards: First, the State must ensure the effective participation of the members of the Saramaka people, in conformity with their customs and traditions, regarding any development, investment, exploration or extraction plan (hereinafter "development or investment plan") within Saramaka territory. Second, the State must guarantee that the Saramakas will receive a reasonable benefit from any such plan within their territory. Thirdly, the State must ensure that no concession will be issued within Saramaka territory unless and until independent and technically capable entities, with the State's supervision, perform a prior environmental and social impact assessment. These safeguards are intended to preserve, protect and guarantee the special relationship that the members of the Saramaka community have with their territory, which in turn ensures their survival as a tribal people.[188]

According to the Court, these "safeguards are intended to preserve, protect and guarantee the special relationship that the members of the Saramaka community have with their territory, which in turn ensures their survival as a tribal people." The African Commission has adopted a similar approach in highlighting that when it comes to restriction to the property rights to land of indigenous peoples special safeguards need to be in place. In the Endorois decision, the Commission stated that "the 'public interest' test is met with a much higher threshold in the case of encroachment of indigenous land rather than individual private property."[189] On the issue of proportionality of the decision to

187 See: Case of the Indigenous Community Yakye Axa, paras. 144–45; Case of the Indigenous Community Sawhoyamaxa, para. 137.

188 Saramaka People v. Suriname, Preliminary Objections, Merits, Reparations, and Costs, Judgment of November 28, 2007 Series C No. 172 at para 129.

189 African Commisison, Endorois Decision, para. 212.

expropriate the indigenous community, the Commission concluded that the "continued dispossession and alienation from their ancestral land continues to threaten the cultural survival of the Endorois' way of life, a consequence which clearly tips the proportionality argument on the side of indigenous peoples under international law."[190] This evolution of human rights law highlighting that when it comes to property rights in land for indigenous peoples there is a higher threshold to justify the public interest in removing them from their land constitutes an important element of the specificity, or *sui generis* nature of property rights in land for indigenous peoples. Indeed, all rights of tenure in land, including ownership, are subject to the inherent power of the State. This power, often referred to as "eminent domain," gives States the power to expropriate or nationalize lands.[191] Whether it is called eminent domain, compulsory purchase, compulsory acquisition, or expropriation it refers to the overall power of the State to expropriate any private property in land, even if such a right is legally protected. However, in the case of indigenous peoples, as their way of life and survival are deeply embedded in the relationship they have with their lands, the right of the State to expropriate indigenous peoples is submitted to a more stringent test to justify the proportionality of the public interest test, and also submitted to the respect of specific safeguards to ensure the participation of indigenous peoples to the decision making process.[192]

The other distinctive feature of the right to property in land for indigenous peoples relates to the specific forms of remedies available in case of violations. In terms of reparations in case of expropriation, the requirement imposed on States is to compensate the victims of such expropriation. Compensation usually means the payment of money, lands of equal value or other measures agreed upon by the parties. At the national level, under most national legislations, the concept of just compensation refers to the price of the land based on market value.[193] However, in terms of indigenous peoples' land rights, this notion of market value for the allocation of compensation does not take into consideration the non-economic interests of land ownership for indigenous peoples. It seems difficult to evaluate the value of the loss of culture of

---

190 *Id.*, para. 235.

191 On this issue, *see* Richard A. Epstein, Takings: Private Property and the Power of Eminent Domain (1989); *see also* Philip P Frickey, *Domesticating Federal Indian Law*, 81 Minn. L. Rev. 31 (1996); Ellen Frankel Paul, Property Rights and Eminent Domain (2008).

192 This aspect is examined in deeper details in Chapter 5.

193 *See* Andra Eisenberg, *Different Constitutional Formulations of Compensation Clauses*, 9S. Afr. J. Hum. Rts. 412 (1993).

a community resulting from the dispossession of its ancestral lands, based on market prices. U.N. human rights treaty bodies have generally been sensitive to the inadequacy of monetary compensation only as a proper remedy for indigenous peoples' removal from their lands. In its General Recommendation XXIII on indigenous peoples, CERD pointed out that "[O]nly when this is for factual reasons not possible, the right to restitution should be substituted by the right to just, fair and prompt compensation. Such compensation should as far as possible take the form of lands and territories."[194] Similarly, Scheinin highlighted that under Article 27 of the ICCPR, the HRC would not consider the allocation of a monetary compensation *per se* as a remedy for the removal of indigenous peoples from their lands:

> the provision of a lump of money can never, as such, be an effective remedy. The sustainability test requires that the form and modalities of compensation or other remedies for a violation of indigenous rights under Article 27 must be such as to serve the continued viability of the distinctive culture in question.[195]

The criterion that the Committee takes into consideration is how the concerned community will be able to sustain its traditional way of life. The aim of the remedy is to ensure the continued existence of the indigenous specific culture, which, unless the community traditional way of life has already been destroyed, could not take the form of a monetary compensation only.[196]

The notion of providing alternative lands is often viewed as more satisfactory and less ethnocentric. ILO 169 stresses that the granting of comparable lands is to be preferred to compensation. ILO 169 states that when the return of indigenous peoples to their traditional lands is not possible, "these peoples shall be provided in all possible cases with lands of quality and legal status at least equal to that of the lands previously occupied by them, suitable

---

194 CERD, General Recommendation No. 23: *Indigenous Peoples*, U.N. Doc. A/52/18, Annex V, para. 5.

195 Martin Scheinin, *The Right to Enjoy a Distinct Culture: Indigenous and Competing Uses of Land, in* The Jurisprudence of Human Rights: A Comparative Interpretive Approach 159–222. (Theodore Orlin et al. eds., 2000) [hereinafter Scheinin].

196 *Id.*, Scheinin adds that "maybe this part of the test of consultation and sustainability must be understood to rest on a precondition that there exists before the interference in question, a viable economy either judged independently on its own, or viable as a consequence of action taken by the state, e.g. agricultural or fishing policy involving state subsidies."

to provide for their present needs and future development."[197] Thus, the idea is that, in any case, States have to ensure access to land that respects the needs of indigenous peoples. It is only in cases where indigenous peoples express preference for monetary compensation that law ought to accept compensation as an adequate avenue for reparation. This is reflected in the U.N. Declaration on the Rights of Indigenous Peoples, which provides that "unless otherwise freely agreed upon by the peoples concerned, compensation shall take the form of lands, territories and resources equal in quality, size and legal status." However, both compensation and the grant of alternative lands disregard the fact that indigenous peoples' land ownership is not merely a source of individual economic security but the core of indigenous cultures and religions. Thus, such remedies participate in the denial of indigenous peoples' cultural attachment to their lands. The acts of compensation or reparation, by providing alternative lands, are to be considered only if the former legal situation cannot be restored, and should not be the rule as is often the case under national legislation. Indigenous peoples' attachment to their land is specific and therefore requires specific rules, and from this perspective human rights law favors a right to restitution over a right to compensation.

The issue of land restitution has been a central issue of for several of the international human rights bodies. In the case of the dam projects on the Biobio River in Chile, the Human Rights Committee stated: "Relocation and compensation may not be appropriate in order to comply with Article 27 of the Covenant."[198] In the Concluding Observations on Guatemala, the HRC has stated:

> Even though the Committee recognizes that the State party has made efforts to improve the situation of members of indigenous communities, it regrets that it has not been possible to adopt legislation designed to *guarantee the full enjoyment of all their rights under the Covenant, including the restitution of communal lands*, the elimination of discrimination in employment and education and participation in other areas of the life of society.[199]

197 Convention Concerning Indigenous and Tribal Peoples in independent Countries (ILO No. 169), 72 ILO Official Bull. 59 (1989), *reprinted in* I.L.M. 1382 (1989), art. 16, para. 4.

198 U.N. Doc. CCPR/C/79/Add.104, para. 22 (Mar. 30, 1999).

199 Human Rights Committee, *Concluding Observations*, Guatemala, U.N. Doc. CCPR/CO/72/GTM, para. 29 (Aug. 27, 2001) (emphasis added).

Article 6 of ICERD addresses the issue of remedies for violation of the Convention.[200] Myntti has highlighted that "the *travaux préparatoires* of the ICERD imply that Article 6 would not be restricted to the right of victims of racial discrimination to seek financial compensation for damaged suffered as a consequence of racial discrimination, but that it would also establish a right to seek restitution."[201] In General Recommendation XXIII, the Committee has explained further the meaning of remedies in relation to indigenous peoples. Its recommendations invited State parties to:

> Recognise and protect the rights of indigenous peoples to own, develop, control and use their communal land, territories and resources and, where they have been deprived of their lands and territories traditionally owned or otherwise inhabited or used without their free and informed consent, *to take steps to return these lands and territories. Only when this is for factual reasons not possible, the right to restitution should be substituted by the right to just, fair and prompt compensation.* Such compensation should as far as possible take the form of lands and territories.[202]

This focus on restitution as the main form of remedy has been constantly highlighted in CERD Concluding Observations. For example, in its report on the situation in the Philippines, CERD has pointed out that the denial by force of right to return is contrary to ICERD.[203] Likewise, regarding the situation in Chile, the Committee called the government to "expedite the restitution of ancestral lands and furnish effective and sufficient means of protecting indigenous peoples' rights to their ancestral lands and resources in accordance with the Convention, other relevant international instruments and the treaties signed by the State party with indigenous peoples."[204] Regarding the reference to the fact that it is only when factually impossible to return the land that other alternative form of remedies can be envisaged, a ruling form the Inter-American Court of Human Rights of 2014 specifically focused on that issue. The case concerned the Kuna indigenous peoples in Panama. In that case

200 *See* General Recommendation XXVI, art. 6, U.N. Doc. A/55/18, Annex V.

201 Kristian Myntti, *The Right to Reparation of Victims of Racial Discrimination in Human Rights Law, in* Reparations: Redressing Past Wrongs 321 (George Ulrich & Louise Krabbe Boserup eds., 2003).

202 General Recommendation XXIII(51) Concerning Indigenous Peoples, Adopted at the Committee's 1235th meeting on Aug. 18, 1997, U.N. Doc. CERD/C/51/Misc.13/Rev.4, para. 5.

203 A/52/18, para. 425.

204 Chile, CERD/C/CHL/CO/19-21, 23 September 2013, para. 21.

because the territory of the concerned indigenous community was flooded in 1969, it was objectively impossible to return the land to the indigenous communities. As the Court highlighted only because it was physically impossible to return the land, then other forms of compensation could be envisaged.[205]

In terms of the specific treaties regarding indigenous peoples' rights, the question of the restitution of territories was one of the central issues of concern during the revision of ILO 107. The first meeting of experts concluded on the need to re-examine the land rights provisions in relation to the restitution of lands.[206] During the Meeting of Experts, it was pointed out that "although it was acknowledged that there were practical problems in fully implementing such a right, there was support for the inclusion of this principle in the revised Convention."[207] However, the word restitution is not used in the Convention; instead the text refers to the right to return to their lands. The approach being that the removal of indigenous peoples from their lands should be temporary, and thus that they have a right to return to their lands "as soon as the grounds for relocation cease to exist."[208] Regarding remedies for removal of indigenous peoples from their lands, the primary principle is that restitution of lands should be the main form of remedies and that only when it is not factually possible, other forms of redress such as compensation would apply.[209] ILO 169 is clear on this issue: restitution of land is the principle and compensation the exception. Article 16 of ILO 169 reads:

3. Whenever possible, these peoples shall have the right to return to their traditional lands, as soon as the grounds for relocation cease to exist.
4. When such return is not possible, as determined by agreement or, in the absence of such agreement, through appropriate procedures, these peoples shall be provided in all possible cases with lands of quality and legal status at least equal to that of the lands previously occupied by

---

205 I/A Court H.R., Case of the Kuna Indigenous People of Madungandí and the Emberá Indigenous People of Bayano and their Members v. Panama. Preliminary objections, merits, reparations and costs. Judgment of October 14, 2014. Series C No. 284.

206 *Report of the Meeting of Experts*, Geneva, GB.234/5/4 ADD. 234th Sess. (Nov. 17–21, 1986).

207 International Labor Conference, *Partial Revision of the Indigenous and Tribal Populations Convention*, 1957 (No. 107), 75th Sess., at 70 (1988).

208 Convention Concerning Indigenous and Tribal Peoples in independent Countries (ILO No. 169), 72 ILO Official Bull. 59 (1989), *reprinted in* I.L.M. 1382 (1989), art. 16.3; the issue of restitution of lands for past dispossession within the Convention is discussed below.

209 *See Joint submission by indigenous organizations on Indigenous Peoples' Right to Restitution submitted to the WGDD*, U.N. Doc. E/CN.4/2005/WG.15/CRP.4.

> them, suitable to provide for their present needs and future development. Where the peoples concerned express a preference for compensation in money or in kind, they shall be so compensated under appropriate guarantees.
>
> 5. Persons thus relocated shall be fully compensated for any resulting loss or injury.[210]

The UNDRIP takes the same approach where removal remains the exception. In the case of such removal, free and informed consent should be the guiding principle. Article 10 of the Declaration states:

> Indigenous peoples shall not be forcibly removed from their lands or territories. No relocation shall take place without the free, prior and informed consent of the indigenous peoples concerned and after agreement on just and fair compensation and, where possible, with the option of return.

The debates that led to the adoption of the Declaration provide a good insight into the complexity of the right to restitution. The first part of Article 28 reads: "Indigenous peoples have the right to redress, by means that can include restitution or, when this is not possible, of a just, fair and equitable compensation, for the lands, territories and resources which they have traditionally owned or otherwise occupied or used, and which have been confiscated, taken, occupied, used or damaged without their free, prior and informed consent." In the drafting of Articles 25 to 30, one of the central points of governmental concern was the issue of the protection of "third party" rights. State concerns are based on the idea that the recognition of indigenous right of ownership and especially the right to restitution might impede on the right of a third party. For example, during the 2002 meeting of the WGDD, New Zealand pointed out that the failure to explicitly recognize the rights of third parties "would itself create an abuse of human rights."[211] The representative of Guatemala proposed the establishment of a general article on the rights of third parties.[212] Indigenous representatives pointed out that in most of the concerned countries, domestic legislations are framed in a way that already protects third party rights, and

210 Convention Concerning Indigenous and Tribal Peoples in independent Countries (ILO No. 169), 72 ILO Official Bull. 59 (1989), *reprinted in* I.L.M. 1382 (1989), art. 16, paras. 3, 4 and 5.

211 U.N. Doc. E/CN.4/2002/98 (Mar. 6, 2002).

212 *Id.* at para. 20 and Annex V.

thus that there is no need to stress such rights in a declaration on the rights of indigenous peoples.[213] Indigenous representatives added that most often the dispossession of the lands of indigenous peoples "was accomplished by allowing third parties with no pre-existing rights in indigenous territories to steal from, defraud or otherwise illegitimately obtain from, indigenous peoples vast areas of their lands and resources."[214]

This issue of third party's rights over wrongly acquired indigenous peoples' land constitute an important feature of the jurisprudence emerging from the regional human rights institutions. The IACtHR has pointed out, when a State is unable, on objective and reasonable grounds, to adopt measures aimed at returning traditional lands and communal resources to indigenous populations, it must surrender alternative lands of equal extension and quality, which will be chosen by agreement with the members of the indigenous peoples, according to their own consultation and decision procedures.[215] In the *Yakye Axa* and *Sawhoyamaxa* cases, the Court addressed situations where indigenous peoples' traditional lands had been granted by the State to non-indigenous persons. In both cases, the Court highlighted that indigenous peoples have a right to the restitution and restoration of their traditional lands that have been issued to third parties without their consent. In the case of *Sawhoyamaxa*, the Court observed that "the spiritual and material base of the identity of an indigenous people is sustained primarily through its unique relationship with its traditional territory," and held that indigenous peoples "right to restitution continues as long as they maintain some degree of connection with that territory."[216] Evidence of the requisite connection may be found in traditional spiritual or ceremonial use or presence; settlement or sporadic cultivation; seasonal or nomadic hunting, fishing or harvesting; use of natural resources in accordance with customary practices; or any other factor characteristic of the culture of the group. The Court further held that if indigenous peoples are prevented by others from maintaining their traditional relationships with their territories, the right to recovery nonetheless continues "until such impediments disappear."

Overall, regarding reparations, the main principles to bear in mind are that (1) indigenous peoples should not be removed from their lands, only in exceptional circumstances and with their consent (special safeguards);

213 U.N. Doc. E/CN.4/2003/92, para. 35 (Jan. 6, 2003).

214 *Id.*

215 Indigenous Community Yakye Axa, para. 149; and Case of the Kaliña and Lokono Peoples v. Suriname, Judgment of November 25, 2015 (Merits, Reparations and Costs), para. 157.

216 Sawhoyamaxa, para. 131.

(2) restitution of the land should be the main principle; (3) other forms of compensation should only be put in place if it is impossible to return the land and that needs the consent of indigenous peoples. However as highlighted both by the debate that lead to the adoption of UNDRIP and the jurisprudence of the regional human rights bodies, very often the more complex and controversial issue relates to the right of third parties when these lands have been acquired long time ago. The debates on the issue of a right to restitution that took place during the drafting process of the UN Declaration demonstrates that the principal reluctance lies in States' unwillingness to address past dispossession. What is really at stake on the issue of restitution is the problem of restitution for past dispossession.

2 *Addressing Past Dispossession: The Role of Human Rights*

In many ways, the discussion about indigenous peoples' land rights are part of what Barkan has designated as the "new morality of international law," as international law is increasingly used as a tool to address past human rights violations.[217] Indigenous peoples' land rights have entered the contemporary challenge of reparation for historical injustices. At Durban during the U.N. World Conference against Racism, Racial Discrimination, Xenophobia and Related Intolerance (WCAR), indigenous peoples joined their concern with the issues of reparation for slavery and colonialism.[218] However, whereas in the case of reparation for slavery and colonialism the issue of reparation is mainly an issue between States,[219] in the case of indigenous peoples, the principles of responsibility between States would not be applicable. The issue of land restitution has also arisen in post-communist Eastern European States, but remains a different issue, as in such cases individuals are reclaiming the restitution of their lands that were lost during the collectivization era based on their right to private property.[220] Thus, despite the possible analogy with

---

217 Elazar Barkan, The Guilt of Nations, Restitution and Negotiating Historical Injustices 181–87 (2000).

218 On the issue of reparation for Slavery and Colonialism, *see* Marc Bossuyt & Stef Vandeginste, *The Issue of Reparation for Slavery and Colonialism and the Durban World Conference against Racism*, 22 Hum. Rts. L.J. 341 (2001).

219 Max du Plessis, *Historical Injustice and International Law: An Exploratory Discussion of Reparation for Slavery*, 25 Hum. Rts. Q. 624 (2003).

220 Newton has examined such link, as Eastern European countries have aspired to the establishment of property rights based on the U.S. model; thus, the author has examined the value of such model based on U.S. policy towards native rights. *See* Nell Jessup Newton, *Compensation, Reparations, & Restitution: Indian Property Claims in the United States*, 28Ga. L. Rev. 453 (1994).

these other situations, the case of indigenous peoples remains particular. As Falk put it:

> we cannot approach the challenge of the relationship with indigenous peoples as long as it remains an abstraction that can be lumped with other categories of injustice. Instead it has a specific history or series of histories, that is bound up with our modernizing, development civilization. Unless that history is acknowledged and understood, it will be very difficult to make an appropriate response.[221]

One of the crucial issues as regards restitution is how far in history the claim for land restitution can go back. There is a dichotomy, as, *a priori*, international human rights law only addresses the present situation, and, simultaneously, the same law recognizes indigenous peoples' rights as historical rights. Thus, human rights law could be used as a potential bridge between the present situation and past dispossession.

In terms of access to jurisdictions, the principle for admissibility is based on the procedural requirement of *ratione temporis*. Under this principle, human rights institutions consider only human rights violations that have occurred since the relevant treaty entered into force, and violations that continue after a State becomes party to a treaty. This procedural aspect of *rationae temporis* is related to the doctrine of intertemporal law, which in the words of Elias is "one of the most important results of this universalization of international law."[222] The doctrine of intertemporal law has been recognized as part of customary international law and was formulated by Judge Huber as follows: "a juridical fact must be appreciated in the light of the law contemporary with it, and not of the law in force at the time when the dispute in regards to it arises or falls to be settled."[223]

The doctrine of intertemporal law can be viewed as an obstacle to addressing past dispossession of indigenous peoples. While it could be affirmed that contemporary international law has rejected the validity of notions, such as *terra nullius*, as being in violation of the contemporary prohibition of discrimination, it has to be borne in mind that generally the theories of dispossession, which were discussed in the first part of this book, formed the law in the epoch

221 Richard Falk, *The Rights of Peoples, in* The Rights of Peoples (James Crawford ed., 1988).

222 Taslim O. Elias, *The Doctrine of Intertemporal Law*, 74 Am. J. Int'lL. 285 (1980); *see also* Rosalyn Higgins, *Time and the Law: International Perspectives on an Old Problem*, 46 Int'l Comp. L.Q. 501 (1997).

223 Island of Palmas Case (Neth. v. U.S.) 2 R.I.A.A. 831, 845 (1928).

of colonization. Although it has been pointed out that the notion of conquest based on a just war could legally be contested, notions, such as "plenary power" or "domestication," were considered perfectly legal at the time.[224] However, there are two aspects to the rule of intertemporal law. As Huber stated in the Island of Palmas case:

> As regards the question which of different legal systems prevailing at successive periods is to be applied in a particular case (the so-called intertemporal law), a distinction must be made between the creation of rights and the existence of rights. The same principle which subjects the act creative of a right to the law in force at the time the right arises, demands that the existence of the right, in order words its continued manifestation, shall follow the conditions required by the evolution of the law.[225]

These aspects of "continued manifestation" and "evolution of the law" could have far-reaching consequences when applied to indigenous peoples' land rights, as, in many cases, the contemporary situation that indigenous peoples are facing is a direct consequence of the laws of colonization. Because the consequences of such a legacy are still at the center of indigenous peoples' dispossession, it is possible to maintain that such rules of dispossession should be put in perspective with contemporary human rights law in the sense that international law deals with past wrongs, as long as they have current, on-going effects, or as MacKay explains, with "past and on-going wrongs," as "a past violation may have on-going and continuing effects that are presently justiciable."[226]

In its General Comment on Article 2 of the ICCPR, the HRC stated that the "[C]essation of an ongoing violation is an essential element of the right to an effective remedy."[227] In its opinions on individual petitions, the HRC has acknowledged the impact of the continuing effect of past wrongs on indigenous peoples' rights. In the *Lovelace* case, the Committee was asked to adjudicate on a fact that took place in 1970, thus before the ICCPR entered into force. Even though the Committee pointed out that it could not examine

224 *See* Chapters 1 and 2.

225 Island of Palmas Case (Neth. v. U.S.) 2 R.I.A.A. 831, 845 (1928).

226 Fergus MacKay, *Addressing Past Wrongs, Indigenous Peoples and Protected Areas: The Right to Restitution of Land and Resources* (Oct. 2002), *at* www.forestpeoples.org/documents/law_hr/ips_restitution_protected_areas_oct02a_eng.pdf.

227 General Comment on Article 2, U.N. Doc. CCPR/C/74/CRP.4/Rev.6, para. 15 (Mar. 29, 2004).

allegations relating to events that had taken place before the entry into force of the Covenant, it determined its competence in the case based on the notion of "continuing effect." The HRC stated: "[T]his fact persists after the entry into force of the Covenant, and its effects have to be examined without regard to their original cause."[228] More specifically, regarding indigenous peoples' land rights, in the case of *Ominayak v. Canada*, the Committee concluded that the historical inequity of the failure to assure the Lubicon Lake Band land ownership through reservation threatened their way of life and constituted a violation of Article 27. The Committee stated: "[H]istorical inequities to which the State party refers, and certain more recent developments threaten the way of life and culture of the Lubicon Lake Band, and constitute a violation of Article 27 so long as they continue."[229] Thus, in considering whether the economic activities of an indigenous group are being interfered with in such a way as to threaten the way of life and culture of the community, the Committee will take into account historical inequities in consideration. While human rights treaty bodies are not designed to deal with historical dispossession, the HRC has shown that past wrongs could be used as proof of continuous violation of indigenous peoples' land rights.[230]

The ILO Committee has adopted a similar approach. In a case filed by the "Radical Trade Union of Metal and Associated Workers" on behalf of the Chinantec community in Mexico, one of the issues was that the displacement of the concerned indigenous community took place before Mexico's ratification of ILO 169. The government of Mexico challenged the Committee competence in examining events that took place before Mexico's ratification. The Committee stated:

> the effects of the decisions that were taken at that time continue to affect the current situation of the indigenous peoples in question, both in relation to their land claims and to the lack of consultations to resolve those claims. The Committee therefore considers that the Convention

228 Sandra Lovelace v. Canada (Communication No. 24/1977), U.N. Doc. CCPR/C/OP/1 (Aug. 14, 1984), at 10, paras. 10, 11, 12 and 13.

229 Lubicon Lake Band v. Canada (Communication No. 167/1984), U.N. Doc. Supp. No. 40 (A/45/40), at 1, para. 33 (Mar. 26, 1990).

230 *See* Simunek, Hastings, Tuzilova and Prochazka v. The Czech Republic (Communication No. 516/1992), U.N. Doc. CCPR/C/54/D/516/1992 (1995). As Scheinin commented: "One may infer from the case that whenever a state decides to take legislation or other action in relation to earlier dispossession of indigenous lands, these measures will be subject to review despite the rationae temporis rule." *See* Scheinin, *supra* note 194, at 173.

> does currently apply with respect to the consequences of the decisions taken prior to its entry into force.[231]

The Committee adopted a similar position in a decision against Denmark when it stated: "the effects of the 1953 relocation continue today, in that the relocated persons cannot return to the Uummannaq settlement and that legal claims to those lands remain outstanding."[232] Accordingly, the Committee decided:

> that the consequences of the relocation that persist following the entry into force of Convention No. 169 still need to be considered with regard to Article 14(2) and (3), 16(3) and (4) and 17 of the Convention, examined below, despite the fact that the relocation was carried out prior to the entry into force of the Convention.[233]

This position has been affirmed in other cases brought to the ILO Committee.[234] A similar approach has been followed by the Inter-American Commission on Human Rights, which, in the case of Mary and Carrie Dann, affirmed that to the extent that the concerned indigenous peoples remain the victims of "an on-going violation of their rights" then, the State is obliged to resolve the situation in light of its contemporary obligations under international human rights law.[235] A similar approach has been adopted by the Inter-American Court which has also examined land rights violations which resulted from past dispossession. For example in the case of the Kaliña and Lokono peoples against Suriname, one of the issue was to examine the impact of the establishment of nature reserves that had been established long time ago,

231 *Report of the Committee set up to examine the representation alleging non-observance by Mexico of the Indigenous and Tribal Convention, 1989 (No. 169), made under article 24 of the ILO Constitution by the Radical Trade Union of Metal and Associated Workers*, Docs. GB.273/15/6, GB.276/16/3.

232 *Report of the Committee set up to examine the representation alleging non-observance by Denmark of the Indigenous and Tribal Convention, 1989 (No. 169), made under article 24 of the ILO Constitution by the Sulinermik Inuussutissarsiuteqartut Kattuffiat (SIK)*, Docs. GB.277/18/3, GB.280/18/5, submitted 1999.

233 *Id.*

234 *Report of the Committee set up to examine the representation alleging non-observance by Ecuador of the Indigenous and Tribal Convention, 1989 (No. 169), made under article 24 of the ILO Constitution by the Confederación Ecuatoriana de Organizaciones Sindicales Libres (CEOSL)*, Docs. GB.277/18/4, GB.282/14/2, submitted 2000.

235 Mary and Carrie Dann v. United States, Case 11.140, Report No. 75/02, Doc. 5 rev. 1, at 860 (2002); *see* para. 167—IACHR.

before the American Convention and the jurisdiction of the Court were in force in Suriname.[236] The Court ruled that since there were still negative impacts on the right of indigenous peoples to land in the current situation, the State had an obligation to ensure the restitution of these lands. Likewise as stated by the Court in the case of the Xákmok Kásek Indigenous Community: "[…] the State must adopt the necessary measures to ensure that [its domestic laws concerning the protected area] do not represent an obstacle to the return of traditional lands to the members of the Community."[237] This approach based on analysing the impact of past dispossession in the light of the contemporary impact on indigenous peoples is extremely important as in many situations, and not only on the American continent, indigenous peoples are the victims of forced displacement that took place long time ago but which has still a dramatic effects on their current situation. Thus, even though international human rights bodies, such as the HRC or the Inter-American Commission/Court, as well as the ILO Committee, would not directly address past dispossession, they would take into consideration the historical inequities that led to the situation facing indigenous peoples. The rationale is based on a link between historical dispossession and the present situation; therefore, it could deduce that human rights bodies and courts would not address past dispossession unless it is linked with a present violation.

This restriction is reflected by national practices, as at the national level, this notion of "continuous past violations" is also the basis of indigenous peoples' right to land restitution. The Australian High Court in *Mabo* based its decision on two constraints: the indigenous community must have continuously occupied the land since before annexation, and also it must have maintained its connection and traditional usage of the land. Thus, the notion of the effects of past violations remains limited, for indigenous peoples have to be presently living on the land. This notion of continuous violation does not address the situation of lands that were taken a long time ago, and offers no remedy where the colonial annexation totally annihilated indigenous communities from a given part of territory. Further, as Barkan pointed out "the test of continuous usage could not apply to land previously confiscated by whites in acts that are viewed as irreversible."[238] This is generally the rule under human rights law. The factor to be taken into consideration is continuous possession, which is the basis for the recognition of indigenous peoples' rights. Therefore, without

236 Case of the Kaliña and Lokono Peoples v. Suriname, Judgment of November 25, 2015 (Merits, Reparations and Costs).

237 Case of the Xákmok Kásek Indigenous Community, para. 313.

238 Barkan, *supra* note 216, at 240.

possession, indigenous peoples cannot claim for restitution, because the "violation" is "total" and so "past" not "continuous."

This issue of restitution for historical dispossession was a central issue of discussion during the revision of ILO 107. During the drafting of ILO 169, one of the issues of debate was the reference in Article 14 to land that indigenous peoples traditionally occupy. The United States stated that the Convention should be limited to lands that tribes currently occupy, not lands that have been historically occupied.[239] States strongly resist any address of the notion of past dispossession. For example, as regards the discussion leading to the adoption of Article 14 of ILO 169, Canada insisted that the word "traditionally" should not be used, as this was addressing the question of land ownership of territories that are no longer occupied by indigenous peoples.[240] On the same issue, the U.S. delegates stated that "the term 'traditionally occupy' (present tense) may not apply to situations where members of the populations concerned have been removed from their traditional lands."[241] The answer of the Committee of Experts was that: "the use of the term 'traditionally' refers to the manner of, and criteria for, land occupation, rather than giving rise to a detailed inquiry into past history, though it is also consistent with claims for restitution."[242] The ILO Guide makes clear that the phrase "traditionally occupy" does not imply that there must be continued occupation but rather that "there should be some connection with the present, such as relatively recent expulsion from these lands, for example, or a recent loss of title."[243]

Thus, ILO 169 tries to establish a balance between historical wrongs and the present situation; however, it is clear that the Convention would not cover lands from which indigenous peoples have been expelled a long time ago.[244] There should be a connection between historical occupation and the present situation. Thus, even though the Convention does not stipulate that indigenous peoples occupy the land at present, there should be a close link between historical occupation and the current situation. Similarly, in relation to ILO

239 International Labor Conference, *Partial Revision of the Indigenous and Tribal Populations Convention*, 1957 (No. 107), 76th Sess., Report IV(2A), at 35.

240 International Labor Conference, *Partial Revision of the Indigenous and Tribal Populations Convention*, 1957 (No. 107), 75th Sess., Report VI(2), at 47; it has to be noted that Canada was in favor of a specific article to deal with the resolution of claims to traditional lands.

241 *Id.*

242 *Id.*, 48.

243 Manuela Tomei & Lee Swepston, Indigenous and Tribal Peoples: A Guide to ILO Convention No. 169 18 (1996).

244 In such cases, the Convention provides for the establishment of national mechanisms to determine land claims arising from past dispossession.

107, the ILO Committee of Experts held that the rights attached to Article 11 of ILO 107 apply to lands that indigenous peoples presently occupy irrespective of immemorial possession, and stated: "that the fact that the people in question has some form of relationship with the land presently occupied, even if only for a short time, was sufficient to form interest and, therefore, rights to that land and the attendant resources."[245] As Thornberry puts it: "[I]f a right is to mean anything, it should mean the right to claim back when expelled from traditional territories; international law should at least have the capacity to address cases of historically recent grievance."[246]

The issue of restitution for past dispossession was an important source of debates during the drafting of the UNDRIP. As noted earlier, article 26 of the Declaration makes a distinction between rights to lands 'presently' occupied by indigenous peoples and rights to land 'traditionally' occupied by indigenous peoples. This distinction is the result of intense negotiation in which some States were reluctant to recognise indigenous peoples' land rights to traditionally owned territories that are now out of indigenous peoples' control. Australia for example underlined that it only could support the text of article 26 if it applied to lands that indigenous peoples currently owned or exclusively used.[247] As a result Article 26 makes a distinction between traditional territories and land now in possession of indigenous peoples and those that are not. Under paragraph 1 indigenous peoples have, "the right to the lands, territories and resources which they have traditionally owned, occupied or otherwise used or acquired"; while under paragraph 2 they have, "the right to own, use, develop and control the lands, territories and resources that they possess by reason of traditional ownership or other traditional occupation or use, as well as those which they have otherwise acquired." The content of the 'right' in paragraph 1 remains very ambiguous as it mentions a 'right' to the lands but does not qualify whether it is a right to own, use, control or develop. The non-qualification of such right to land traditionally owned but lost in the present day could be seen as 'ambiguous compromise.' It could be termed as ambiguous as it will be up to national jurisdictions to interpret what rights indigenous peoples have to the lands that they have traditionally owned, occupied or used in the past. Likewise, by recognising a right for indigenous peoples over their traditional territories, it could also be seen as a compromise as it does not adopt the

245 International Labor Conference, *Report of the Committee of Experts on the Application of Conventions and Recommendations*, 75th Sess., Report III(4A), at 287 (1988).

246 Patrick Thornberry, Indigenous Peoples and Human Rights 354 (2002).

247 Report of the Working Group established in accordance with Commission on Human Rights Resolution 1995/32, UN Doc. E/CN.4/2003/92 (6 January 2003), p. 8 para 32.

position of those States which wanted to make sure that land rights were only recognised to land presently occupied. Such 'ambiguous compromise' is not surprising as the issue of land rights over historical and traditional territories touches on the contentious issue of restitution. In many ways this relates to the issue of reparations for past wrongs, an issue with which, traditionally, international law has not been at ease.[248]

More specifically, Article 28 of Declaration states that indigenous peoples have the right to redress for "the lands, territories and resources which they have traditionally owned or otherwise occupied or used, and which have been confiscated, taken, occupied, used or damaged without their free, prior and informed consent." During some of the meetings of the Working Group established to draft the Declaration (WGDD), Canada, the United States and Australia have opposed the use of the past tense and expressed their concern about the retrospective nature of the draft.[249] It is worth noting that in a initial draft the word restitution was clearly indicated, but New Zealand had proposed changing the word "restitution" to "redress" in order to leave it to the national legislation or jurisdiction to decide which form the remedies should take.[250] Finally, during the final meetings of the WGDD, the discussions centered on the question of whether there was a need to introduce a provision for the protection of lands currently owned by indigenous peoples but not traditionally occupied by them.[251] As indicated in the preamble of the Declaration, there was a consensus on the need to address past dispossession within the text of the declaration; however States had been reluctant to recognize a right to restitution and have pushed for the introduction of notions of redress and compensation. This was translated in the text of the declaration as article 28 refers to a right to redress rather than a right to restitution.

Such a debate on restitution for past dispossession also constitutes an important bone of contention within the negotiations that might lead to the adoption of an American Declaration of the Rights of Indigenous Peoples. The proposed text addresses the issue of restitution in its Article XVIII which states:

---

248 See generally: G Ulrich and K Boserup, (eds.), *Reparations: Redressing Past Wrongs* (Oslo: Kluwer Law International, Human Rights in Development Yearbook, 2003); and E Barkan, *The Guilt of Nations, Restitution and Negotiating Historical Injustices* (Baltimore: The Johns Hopkins University Press, 2000).

249 U.N. Doc. E/CN.4/2003/92, at 8.

250 *Id.* at 9.

251 U.N. Doc. E/CN.4/2004/81, at 17, para. 117.

> Indigenous peoples have the right to the restitution of the lands, territories and resources which they have traditionally owned or otherwise occupied or used, and which have been confiscated, occupied, used or damaged, or when restitution is not possible, the right to compensation on a basis not less favorable than the standard of international law.[252]

However, at a later stage this paragraph had been removed from the consolidated text. Nonetheless, both texts, the IACHR proposed declaration and the consolidated text, refer to the States' obligation to recognized indigenous peoples' rights over the territories they have historically owned. Article XVIII, paragraph 3 of the Proposed Declaration reads: "where property and user rights of indigenous peoples arise from rights existing prior to the creation of those States, the States shall recognize the titles of indigenous peoples relative thereto as permanent, exclusive, inalienable, imprescriptible and indefeasible."[253] Overall, what is emerging from both the UN Declaration and the proposed OAS declaration, as well as ILO 169, is a call on States to establish at the national level processes to address past dispossession, under the more generic term of redress rather than restitution. ILO 169 insists on the need for States to establish such national institutions, Article 14(3) of the Convention states that "[A]dequate procedures shall be established within the national legal system to resolve land claims by the peoples concerned."[254] However, it is fair to say that despite such call to establish processes for addressing past dispossession, very little engagement have materialised at the national levels.[255]

Conclusion

This chapter has delved into the theories on proprietary rights to examine whether international human rights law could offer a proper legal avenue to indigenous peoples in their territorial claims. As this chapter has demonstrated, the answer is not straightforward. On the one hand, international law

252 OAS Draft Inter-American Declaration on the Rights of Indigenous Peoples, Doc. OEA/Ser/L/V/II.90, doc.9, rev.1 (1995).

253 In the Chair' consolidated text these paragraphs are introduced in art. XXIV, paras. 3, 4 and 5.

254 Convention Concerning Indigenous and Tribal Peoples in independent Countries (ILO No. 169), 72 ILO Official Bull. 59 (1989), *reprinted in* I.L.M. 1382 (1989), art. 14.3.

255 *See* Federico Lenzerini (ed.), Reparations for Indigenous Peoples: International and Comparative Perspectives (2008).

remains entrenched in its Western and individualistic approach to proprietary rights, which, in the context of land rights, sees property as meaning individual ownership of a land. As examined earlier on, the main international human rights treaties do not integrate a specific mention of property rights in land, the right to property was not included in the two international Covenants. And when property rights have been integrated, it is mainly in the context of non-discrimination and equality (ICERD and CEDAW). Ultimately property rights are only strongly affirmed in the UDHR, and the connection to land rights in this context remains tenuous since it was not even originally envisaged.

On the other hand, the more recent jurisprudence, notably form regional human rights institutions, are pointing towards the development of a specific approach to property rights to land for indigenous peoples encapsulating a more collective approach to the meaning of property rights. Regarding the recognition of indigenous peoples' customary systems of land rights, especially in their collective form, the recent legal developments show that despite States usually obstructing the recognition of collective rights at the international level, there is strong jurisprudential evolution recognizing the collective nature of indigenous peoples' land rights. What this chapter has analysed is that regional human rights institutions and specialised instruments have been at the forefront of a new approach to property rights which have totally challenged the western and individualistic approach to property rights making space for an indigenous approach to the meaning and content of property rights in land. One of the outcomes of such approach is the gradual recognition of a collective form of land ownership for indigenous peoples. By demanding the recognition of their collective right to land ownership, indigenous peoples have challenged the traditional individualistic approach to property right. As such, indigenous peoples' land claims breathe new life to the issue of property rights within the human rights discourse, through the emerging recognition of a collective right of land ownership.

One of the important contributions of this jurisprudence emerging from the regional human rights institutions but also the international human rights monitoring bodies is that for indigenous peoples possession means property. As highlighted in the first part of this book, for centuries States, and international law, have rejected indigenous peoples' own systems of land tenures. The more contemporary approach to property rights shows that this approach is in violation of the fundamental principle of non-discrimination. Hence, an important aspect of a human rights approach to property rights is to affirm that States have to recognise indigenous peoples' property rights based on their own system of land tenure, and not necessarily under the formal legal systems. As analysed in this chapter, when it comes to property rights in land there is a positive duty for States to recognise indigenous peoples' land rights as property right and a corollary duty of providing remedies in case of forced displacement. The right to restitution constitutes an important pillar of the right to property for indigenous peoples. This process of restitution must also answer the fear that the word restitution usually evokes, as many people see a claim for restitution as a return to *status quo ante*. In the general public sphere, but also in the diplomatic arena, restitution is often understood as meaning that indigenous peoples will tomorrow reclaim New York City or Sydney harbour. By building concrete legal mechanisms for restitution, human rights law seeks to address this unfounded fear[256] in developing a theory of restitution based on fair dialogue between indigenous peoples and the rest of the population. This dialogue involves a rethinking of the relations between States and indigenous populations. With the development of a theory on land restitution, human rights law could greatly participate to the fostering of a new relationship between indigenous peoples and States by imposing a fairer and more effective legal framework to support such dialogue.

After centuries of rejection of indigenous peoples' approaches to land tenure systems, the recent developments that have taken place under human rights law offer great promises. The emerging human rights discourse on collective land ownership integrates the social, cultural and spiritual facets of indigenous peoples' relationship with their territories. The recognition of indigenous peoples' own form of territorial right makes the whole human rights system more universal by affirming that all cultures are equal and should be treated equally. By recognising indigenous peoples' cultural approach to land ownership, human rights law reflects the idea that different cultural systems of laws could co-exist in the same territory and that there should not be any antagonism between such culturally diverse approaches to land usage. This evolution towards the recognition of collective and cultural form of land ownership certainly opens the door to the emergence of what Daes has called the "different conceptual framework," which recognizes "the cultural differences that exist because of the profound relationship that indigenous peoples have to their lands, territories and resources."[257] The next chapter focuses on this cultural approach to land rights.

---

256 Hill described the overreaction that followed the *Mabo* decision in Australia as an unfounded fear of Aborigines claiming your backyard as traditional lands. *See* Ronald Paul Hill, *Blackfellas and Whitefellas: Aboriginal Land Rights, The Mabo decision, and the Meaning of Land*, 17(2) Hum. Rts. Q. 303 (1995).

257 *Preliminary working paper prepared by the Special Rapporteur on Indigenous People and their Relationship to Land*, U.N. Doc. E/CN.4/Sub.2/1997/17, para. 5.

CHAPTER 4

Land Rights as Cultural Rights

> Next to shooting indigenous peoples, the surest way to kill us is to separate us from our part of the earth.
>
> POKA LAENUI (HAYDEN BURGESS)[1]

"Without the land and the knowledge that comes mainly from use of the land, we as indigenous peoples cannot survive."[2] This statement from Lars Anders Baer, a well renowned indigenous activist, is representative of many other similar statements made by indigenous peoples highlighting how land is central to their culture. For many indigenous peoples across the globe, territories and lands are not only an issue of property but also the source of spiritual, cultural and social identity. While indigenous communities certainly represent the world's most diverse population, most indigenous cultures worldwide share a similar deep-rooted relationship between cultural identity and their ancestral territories. Even though indigenous land tenure systems vary significantly across the world, human rights law has begun to recognise that landholding systems constitute a central aspect of indigenous peoples' cultures, and thus represent a crucial criteria of "indigenousness."[3] The approach is that where land is of central significance to the sustenance of a culture, the right to enjoy one's culture requires the protection of land. In this context the right to territory is understood as requiring sufficient habitat and space to reproduce culturally as a people. The argument in the following analysis is that human rights law has been developed in a manner that favours a right for indigenous peoples to use their lands as part of the fundamental right of everyone to enjoy their own culture.

Generally speaking, the word "culture" is a word that carries lot of meanings: (a) a style of social and artistic expression; (b) the totality of social transmitted behaviour patterns, arts, beliefs, characteristic of a community or population; (c) the customary beliefs, social forms, and material trait of a racial, religious, or social group.[4] Hence, law has to deal with a notion which is usually discussed

---

1 Declaration made at a meeting of the UN Working Group on Indigenous Populations, reprinted in World Council of Indigenous Peoples, Right of the Indigenous Peoples to the Earth, U.N. Doc.E/CN.4.Sub.2/AC.4/1985/WP.4, at 5.

2 L-A Baer, *Protection of Rights of Holders of Traditional Knowledge, Indigenous and Local Communities*, World Libraries 12:1 (2002).

3 *See* the discussion on definition in the introduction of the book.

4 Oxford Dictionary of English (2d ed. 2002).

 | DOI 10.1163/9789004323254_008

more by anthropologists, sociologist and historians.[5] In terms of international law, it is generally admitted that there is a dual nature to cultural rights. Cultural rights are considered in the sense of arts and sciences but also in the sense of respect for cultural differences.[6] Thus, there are some debates on the notion, but it is admitted that from a legal perspective, culture is a way of talking about collective identities.[7] Concretely, human rights law has developed an approach putting forward everyone's right to enjoy their own culture.[8] In terms of indigenous peoples' land rights, this results in the legal recognition of indigenous peoples' specific cultural attachment to their traditional territories.

The subsequent analysis explores how human rights law acknowledges the importance of recognising land rights as an essential element of indigenous peoples' cultural rights. Under the heading of cultural rights, there is a reference to protection of a way of life, access to the means of livelihood and protection of cultural heritage. When addressing indigenous peoples' cultural right to own and use their lands, there is an issue of survival for the group that includes reference to civil and political rights (as ultimately the issue is to protect the right of a group to survival, and thus the right to life), but also to economic, social and cultural rights (as it is through the use of their lands that indigenous peoples' economic, social and cultural rights will be guaranteed). Thus, the following analysis intends to explore how human rights law has developed a strong recognition of indigenous peoples' right to use their land as part of this wide approach to cultural rights. In this context, land rights are an essential element to support the geographical space necessary for the cultural expression and social reproduction indigenous peoples.[9] Consequently,

---

5 *See* Richard A. Wilson, Human Rights, Culture and Context: Anthropological Perspectives (1997); *see also* Claude Lévi-Strauss, Race et histoire (1952); Norbert Rouland, L'anthropologie Juridique (1990).

6 *See* UNESCO, Projet relatif à une déclaration des droits culturels (1993); Roger O'Keefe, *The 'right to take part in cultural life' under Article 15 of the ICESCR*, 47 Int'l Comp. L.Q. 904 (1998); Asbjørn Eide, *Cultural Rights and Minorities: Essay in Honour of Erica-Irene Daes, in* Justice Pending: Indigenous Peoples and Other Good Causes, Essays in Honour of Erica-Irene A. Daes 85 (Gudmundur Alfredsson & Maria Stavropoulou eds., 2002).

7 Adam Kuper, Culture: The Anthropologists' Account (2000).

8 Rodolfo Stavenhagen, *Cultural Rights: A Social Science Perspective, in* Economic, Social and Cultural Rights—A Textbook 85–109 (Asbjørn Eide, Catarina Krause & Allan Rosas eds., 2d ed. 2005); *see* UNDP, Human Development Report 2004 88–90 (2004).

9 *See* IACHR, *Report on the situation of human rights in Ecuador*, OAS/Ser.L/II.96. Doc.10, rev.1, at 115 (APR. 24, 1997); The Commission stated: "Control over the land refers to both its capacity for providing the resources which sustain life and the geographic space necessary for the cultural and social reproduction of the group."

different approaches to cultural rights will be explored. The first section focuses on the notion of land rights as essential elements of indigenous peoples survival, it explores how land rights are connected to the group existence, and how this relates to an enlarged approach to the right to life and access livelihoods. The second section examines the connection between land rights and the protection of a particular way of life, looking how cultural and spiritual traditions connected to a territory are protected under human rights law. The third section takes a critical approach to the legal framework governing the protection of cultural heritage with the aim of analysing to what extent indigenous peoples could find protection for the territorial aspect of their heritage. As such it offers an analysis of the relevance of the notion of a "right to cultural integrity" to guarantee a more comprehensive approach to indigenous peoples' cultural rights.[10]

A *Land is Life*: Land Rights as Subsistence Rights

There is an obvious connection between indigenous peoples' right to use their land and their survival, as without access to their land, indigenous communities would not access their means of livelihood. Many indigenous peoples across the globe have put forward the fact that for them "land is life".[11] The IACHR has observed that control over their lands by indigenous peoples is essential for their survival, as a necessary way to provide them with the resources that sustain life and to "the geographic space necessary for the cultural and social reproduction of the group."[12] This statement highlights two important aspects of the essential connection between land rights and indigenous peoples' survival:

(1) a right to a collective existence, as territories are essential for the continuation and perpetuation of the existence of the group, and
(2) a right to subsistence, as access to land guarantees indigenous communities access to resources for their livelihood.

10 See: James Anaya, Indigenous Peoples in International Law 134–141 (2004).

11 See the coalition of indigenous peoples, 'Land is Life' at: http://landislife.org; see also: Marcus Colchester, *Land is life: Land rights and oil palm development in Sarawak* (Forest Peoples Programme, 2007); Richard Baker and Richard Munro Baker, Land is Life: From Bush to Town-the Story of the Yanyuwa People (1999).

12 IACHR, *Report on the Situation of Human Rights in Ecuador*, OAS. Ser.L/V/II.96. Doc.10 Rev 1, at 115 (Apr. 24, 1997).

1 *Land Rights as a Means to a Collective Existence*

Article II of the Genocide Convention and Article 6 of the Rome Statute for the International Criminal Court (ICC) both recognise that deliberately inflicting conditions of life calculated to cause the physical destruction of a specific ethnic group is an act that constitutes genocide.[13] Article 6 of the ICC highlights the fact that the destruction of the conditions of life of a group, in order to physically destroy it, is an act of genocide. The Text of the Elements of Crimes states that: "[T]he term 'conditions of life' may include, but are not necessarily restricted to, deliberate deprivation of resources indispensable for survival, such as food or medical services, or systematic expulsions from homes."[14] In terms of indigenous peoples' rights, this part of the text could be crucial, as in most of the cases that lead to the physical destruction of indigenous communities those notions of access to food or systematic expulsion are the facts that give rise to the destruction of physical life.[15] For example, 25 percent of the Brazilian Xingu Indians who were relocated died from diseases and homesickness, as their natural environment was part of their conditions of life.[16] Therefore, one of the questions that arise is whether the removal of indigenous communities from their land could be regarded as a means of destruction to ensure the disappearance of the group.

On the relevance of the protection of groups under the prohibition of genocide, it has to be emphasized that, ultimately, the test will be based on the notion of "specific intent." This notion of "specific intent" is a central component of the crime of genocide, which requires that the criminal has to have the "specific intent" to destroy a group as such.[17] Regarding indigenous peoples' land rights, this would mean proving that by removing indigenous communities

---

13 Convention on the Prevention and Punishment of the Crime of Genocide (1948), 78 U.N.T.S. 277, art. II(c), and Rome Statute of the International Criminal Court, U.N. Doc. A/CONF.138/9, art. 6.

14 *See* Assembly of States Parties to the Rome Statute of the International Criminal Court, First Sess., September 2002 ICC-ASP/1/3, at 114, n.4; *see also* Report of the Preparatory Commission for the International Criminal Court, *Finalized Draft Text of the Elements of Crimes*, PCNI.C.C./2000/INF/3/Add.2, at 7 (July 6, 2000).

15 *See* Amnesty International and the Sierra Club, Defending Those Who Give the Earth a Voice (2000). Note that CERD in its 2005 Declaration on the Prevention of Genocide mentions the adverse effect of economic globalization; CERD, *Declaration on the Prevention of Genocide*, U.N. Doc. CERD/C/66/1 (Oct. 17, 2005).

16 Independent Commission on International Humanitarian Issues, Indigenous Peoples, A Global Quest for Justice 85 (1987).

17 On this issue, *see* William Schabas, Genocide in International Law 217–21 (2000) [hereinafter Schabas].

from their lands, the intent was to place the survival of the group in jeopardy with the effect of destroying the group. The situation in Paraguay has shown the difficulty in proving the specific intent to support a claim of genocide.[18] In Paraguay, the Aché, who are now considered as an extinct cultural group, were the victims of acts of the government that were seeking to promote transnational corporations' oil exploration on ancestral lands.[19] In this case it was not possible to prove the intent to destroy the group, even if notions of planned and voluntary destruction were factually real, for the government argued that it was in the name of development. In Guatemala, the Commission for Historical Clarification concluded that genocide had been committed against the Mayan population during the civil war.[20] In its finding, the Commission highlighted that the destruction of property and the burning of the harvest, as well as the practice of so-called scorched earth operations, amounted to genocide.[21] The Commission concluded "that the reiteration of destructive acts, directed systematically against groups of the Mayan population, within which can be mentioned the elimination of leaders and criminal acts against minors who could not possibly have been military targets, demonstrates that the only common denominator for all the victims was the fact that they belonged to a specific ethnic group and makes it evident that these acts were committed 'with intent to destroy, in whole or in part' these groups."[22] Thus, in the case of Guatemala, it is the combination of massive killings and land destruction that amounted to genocide.[23] This case shows that when there is a plan or policy to drag indigenous peoples out of their lands by terrorising the population, by

18 Aché Indian in Paraguay, Case No. 1802 (Paraguay), Annual Report 1977, at 36–37, OAS Doc. OEA/Ser.L/V/II.43 Doc.21 (1978)—IACHR.

19 In 1983, the Sub-Commission appointed a Special Rapporteur on Genocide that widely studied the systematic massacre against Indigenous Achẹ́ of Paraguay, but its mandate was not renewed. *See generally* Genocide in Paraguay (Richard Arens ed., 1976); on the situation in Brazil, *see* Martin Geer, *Foreigners in their Own Land: Cultural Land and Transnational Corporations—Emergent International Rights and Wrongs*, 38 Va. J. Int'l L. 331 (1998).

20 Eighty-three percent of fully identified victims were Mayan; *see* Report of the Commission for Historical Clarification, *Guatemala: Memory of Silence* (1999).

21 *Id.*

22 *Id.*, para. 111; on this issue, *see also* Plan de Sánchez Massacre, Guatemala, Case 11.763, Report No. 31/99 (Mar. 11, 1999)—IACHR.

23 On this issue, *see also* the situation in Brazil in March 2001, where following the killing of 14 Indian Tucuna, a Brazilian federal tribunal condemned the perpetrators for genocide. The Indians were killed during a meeting for organizing land distribution as part of the national plan organized by the Fundação Nacional do Indio (FUNAI). *See* Amnesty International, *Justice pour les Tucuna*, 31(5) Le Fil D'ai 7 (Juillet 2001).

killing some its members and destroying their natural resources, there might be a connection between the crime of genocide and the policy of land dispossession.[24] Thus, on the question of the possible applicability of the crime of genocide in cases of land dispossession, it is certain that if the land destruction can be associated with the intent to destroy, the definition of genocide may apply. Without the proof that the genocide was based on the specific intent of the destruction of the group as such, the crime of genocide would not be applicable.[25] Genocide may be recognised if it is proven that the destruction of the conditions of life was one of the principal mechanisms used to destroy the group.

One of the difficulties resides in the fact that the actual definition of the crime of genocide does not refer to the notions of "cultural genocide" and "ethnocide";[26] notions that are based on the idea that a group can be destroyed by attacks on its capacity to preserve and transmit its own specific culture, which would then disappear.[27] During the debates leading to the adoption of the 1948 Genocide Convention, the notion of cultural genocide was discarded.[28] The main reason for this rejection, invoked by some of the States involved

---

24 In Australia, it was alleged in two cases that the government had committed genocide through its formulation of the Native Title Amendment Act 1998; however, the judges were of the view that either genocide had no status in Australian law, or there was no foundation to the charge of genocide. *See* Nulyarimma v. Thompson and Buzzacott v. Minister for the Environment (1999) F.C.A. 1192, 165 A.L.R. 621—Federal Court of Australia.

25 For an overview on the application of the crime of genocide in an indigenous peoples context, *see* Chris Tennant & Mary Ellen Turpel Turpel, *A Case Study of Indigenous Peoples: Genocide, Ethnocide and Self-determination*, 59–60 Nordic J. Int'l L. 287 (1990–91); R.K. Hitchcock, *Genocide of Indigenous Populations, in* Encyclopedia of Genocide 349–54 (Israel W. Charny ed., 1999); and William Schabas, *Cultural Genocide and the Protection of the Right of Existence of Aboriginal and Indigenous Groups, in* International Law and Indigenous Peoples 117–29 (Joshua Castellino & Niamh Walsh eds., 2005).

26 According to the UNESCO Declaration of San Jose: "Ethnocide means that an ethnic group is denied the right to enjoy, develop and transmit its own culture and its own language, whether individually or collectively." UNESCO Latin-American Conference, Declaration of San Jose (Dec. 11, 1981) UNESCO Doc. FS 82/WF.32 (1982), *reprinted in* The Rights of Peoples (James Crawford ed., 1988); for a discussion on the two terms, *see* U.N. Doc. E/CN.4/Sub.2/1993/29, para. 48.

27 The 1948 Convention in Article II(e) refers to "Forcibly transferring children of the group to another group"; but does not fully incorporate the broader concept of "cultural" genocide. *See* Convention on the Prevention and Punishment of the Crime of Genocide (1948), 78 U.N.T.S. 277.

28 For a discussion on the drafting process, *see* Johannes Morsink, *Cultural Genocide, the Universal Declaration, and Minority Rights*, 21 Hum. Rts. Q. 1009 (1999); *see also* Schabas, *supra*

in the drafting process, was that such protection was an issue of human rights, which was to be covered under the rubric of minority rights, and that some States feared that their action towards the indigenous populations living in their territories might fall under the category of genocide.[29]

On this debate on cultural genocide and ethnocide, it is worth noting that earlier draft of the UN Declaration on the Rights of Indigenous Peoples (UNDRIP), and notably an earlier draft adopted by the former Sub-Commission used the term "ethnocide" and "cultural genocide." The draft text established a clear link between so-called "cultural genocide" and "any action which has the aim or effect of dispossessing" indigenous peoples of their lands.[30] The use of the term "aim or effect," which suggests that the perpetrator would have to be found to have acted with the knowledge that his act will cause a prohibited destruction of life, a requirement that is less onerous than the "specific intent" threshold. However, the text adopted by the General Assembly in 2007 does not mention cultural genocide or ethnocide. The newly adopted text affirms that indigenous peoples should not be subjected to any act of genocide, forced assimilation or destruction of their culture but does not specifically mention cultural genocide.[31]

More generally, on the correlation between territorial destruction or forced removal and the crime of genocide, it has to borne in mind that international criminal law is a rapidly expanding area of international law, and, in the near future, there may be some links between land destruction or dispossession and criminal prosecution. For example, the Rome Statute classifies forcible transfer of population as part of a widespread or systematic attack, as a crime against humanity.[32] Thus, it could be argued that the forced removal of indigenous peoples from their land, with the intended aim being the destruction of the community, could be regarded as a crime against humanity. Yet, this has never been tested, as the ICC is still in its preliminary stages, but this could well

note 17, at 179–89, the only exception being Article 2(e), which defines as act of genocide "Forcibly transferring children of the group to another group."

29 Schabas, *supra* note 17, at 184.

30 *See* U.N. Doc. E/CN.4/Sub.2/1994/56, U.N. Draft Declaration, art. 7 which stated: "indigenous peoples have the collective and individual right not to be subject to ethnocide and cultural genocide."

31 UN Declaration on the Rights of Indigenous Peoples, Article 8, paragraph 1. For more analysis, see: Bartolomé Clavero Salvador, 'Study on international criminal law and the judicial defence of indigenous peoples' rights', UN Doc. E/C.19/2011/4. See also the Proposed American Declaration does not mention genocide, OAS Draft Inter-American Declaration on the Rights of Indigenous Peoples, Doc. OEA/Ser/L/V/II.90, doc.9, rev.1 (1995).

32 Rome Statute of the International Criminal Court, U.N. Doc. A/CONF.138/9, art. 7.

transpire in a near future. Article 10 of the Rome Statute affirms that "nothing in this part shall be interpreted as limiting or prejudicing in any way existing or developing rules of international law for purposes other than this Statute."[33] From this perspective, the development of international criminal law and the jurisprudence of the Court could potentially have some impacts on indigenous peoples' land rights.

2 *Right to Subsistence, Access to Livelihood and the Right to Life*

For most indigenous peoples access to their lands and territories constitute an essential element to ensure their livelihoods. As such access to sources of livelihoods that are inherently attached to land rights form part of the right to life. The right to life constitute the most fundamental of all the rights, it follows that the right to life expansively interpreted, can give an effective content to all guaranteed rights – economic, civil, political, social and cultural. This approach on the right to life has far reaching consequences, one of them being that States have to make sure that indigenous peoples have access to natural resources produced within their traditional lands.[34] This approach to the protection of the right to life is to be understood as a right of access to livelihood, as in this context indigenous peoples' right to use their lands is part of the larger right to life in which land is referred to in its capacity for providing the resources that sustain life. As highlighted by Ramcharan, the fundamental character of the right to life renders inadequate narrow approaches to it, the question being: "[T]o what extent does the right to life contain a component with regard to the satisfaction of requirements necessary for sustaining life, e.g. food, water and health protection?"[35] As noted by the Human Rights Committee in its General Comment on the right to life has noted that the right to life has been interpreted narrowly too often:

> The expression "inherent right to life" cannot properly be understood in a restrictive manner, and the protection of this right requires that States adopt positives measures. In this connection, the Committee considers that it would be desirable for States parties to take all possible measures

33 *Id.*, art. 10.

34 There is a distinction to be made between the issue of access to natural resources, which sustain life, and other natural resources, which are linked with the larger issue of economic development; whereas this part deals with the first issue, the latter will be addressed later in Chapters 5 and 6.

35 Bertrand G. Ramcharan, *The Concept and Dimensions of the Right to Life, in* The Right to Life in International Law 17 (Bertrand G. Ramcharan ed., 1985).

> to reduce infant mortality and to increase life expectancy, especially in adopting measures to eliminate malnutrition and epidemics.[36]

In this regard, the right to life, in its modern sense, is not only a protection against any arbitrary deprivation of life, but rather creates specific State obligations to take all possible measures to prevent its violation.[37] Thus, the issue is to appreciate whether ensuring that indigenous peoples have access to the natural resources, which are contained in their traditional land, is part of this larger obligation.

One of the first connections between land rights and livelihood is the right to food.[38] Eide pointed out that indigenous peoples' right to food has been especially affected by the dispossession of their lands.[39] The U.N. study on the "Right to Food as a Human Right" stressed that the realisation of the right to food implies the recognition of indigenous peoples' customary land rights.[40] The CESCR, in its General Comment on the Right to Adequate Food, has placed special emphasis on the fact that Article 11 encompasses both economic and physical accessibility of access to food. The Committee pointed out that: "[A] particular vulnerability is that of many indigenous population groups whose access to their ancestral lands may be threatened."[41] This approach has also been part of the Committee's reports. For example, in its observation in relation to Paraguay, the Committee noted that: "the main reason for hunger and malnutrition among the indigenous population and the deprivation of their right is linked to the severe problem of obtaining access to traditional and ancestral lands."[42] The former UN Special Rapporteur on the Right to Food,

36 Human Rights Committee, General Comments, U.N. Doc. CCPR/C/21/Rev 1, at 5.

37 *See* Essays on the Concept of a 'Right to Live' in Memory of Yougindra Khushalani (Daniel Prémont ed., 1988).

38 *See*, for example, *Report of the World Food Conference*, Rome, Nov. 5–16, 1974 (U.N. publication, Sales No. E.75.II.A.3), which stressed the link between land ownership and the right to food.

39 Asbjørn Eide, *The Right to an Adequate Standard of Living including the Right to Food, in* Economic, Social and Cultural Rights—A Textbook 142–43 (Asbjørn Eide et al. eds., 2d ed. 2005).

40 *Right to adequate food as human rights*, Study Series No. 1, U.N., New-York, 1989 (U.N. Sales No. 89.XIV.2).

41 CESCR, General Comment 12, *Right to Adequate Food (Art. 11)*, U.N. Doc. E/C.12/1999/5, para. 13 (1999).

42 *Report of Fourteenth and Fifteenth Sessions*, para. 83, U.N. Doc. E/C.12/1996/6; *see also Conclusions and Recommendations of the Committee on Economic, Social and Cultural Rights*, Russian Federation, U.N. Doc. E/C.12/1/Add.13 (1997).

Olivier de Schutter, has directly connected the right to food with the question of large-scale land acquisitions, notably on indigenous people's territories.[43] The connection between the realisation of the right to food and land rights has also received attention from the European Parliament which, in its 2003 resolution on Guatemala, stated that the human right to food as recognised in Article 11 of ICESCR "implies the obligation to guarantee the access of vulnerable groups to the resources needed to feed themselves, in particular access to land."[44] Likewise, based on Article 30 of the Convention on the Rights of the Child, which specifically mentions the rights of indigenous children, the Committee on the Rights of the Child has recommended that States pay special attention to the inter-communal distribution of wealth. In the case of Ecuador, the Committee pointed out that "uneven distribution of land" was one of the factors that affected indigenous children.[45] Thus, access to land rights has been recognised as necessary to ensure access to means of subsistence, and this notion of access to livelihood has also been interpreted in relation to the right to food.

Another consequence of this enlarged approach to the right to life is linked with the right to health. This connection between life and health has been particularly highlighted in the case of indigenous peoples.[46] In its General Comment on "the right to the highest attainable standard of health," the CESCR has pointed out:

> that development-related activities that lead to the displacement of indigenous peoples against their will from their traditional territories and environment, denying them their sources of nutrition and breaking their symbiotic relationship with their lands, has a deleterious effect on their health.[47]

---

43 Report of the Special Rapporteur on the Right to Food, Olivier de Schutter, 'Large-scale Land Acquisitions and Leases: A Set of Minimum Principles and Measures to Address the Human Rights Challenge', UN Doc. A/HRC/33/13/Add.2., para. 4.

44 European Parliament, Resolution on Guatemala, P5_TA-PROV (2003) 0190 (96/PE 330.845).

45 *Concluding Observations on the Initial Report*, Ecuador, A/55/41, para. 280.

46 See Stephens, Carolyn, et al., *Disappearing, displaced, and undervalued: a call to action for Indigenous health worldwide*, THE LANCET 367.9527 (2006): 2019–2028; Townsend, Mardie, Rebecca Phillips, and David Aldous, *"If the land is healthy... it makes the people healthy": The relationship between caring for Country and health for the Yorta Yorta Nation, Boonwurrung and Bangerang Tribes.* HEALTH & PLACE 15.1 (2009): 291–99.

47 CESCR, General Comment 14, *The right to the highest attainable standard of health*, U.N. Doc. E/C.12/2000/4, para. 27 (2000).

Similarly, in an individual observation to Brazil in 1996, the ILO Conference Committee on the Application of Standards stated that: "[T]he Committee is bound to deplore the fact that the invasion of indigenous lands, and particularly the lands of the Yanomamis continues year after year, with the serious consequences that such invasions have on the health and survival of these peoples."[48] This connection between the right to life, the right to health and indigenous peoples' territories has also been examined by regional human rights institutions. In a case, submitted on behalf of the Yanomani Indians of Brazil to the IACHR, it was alleged that the Brazilian government had violated their right to life by constructing a highway through their territory and by authorizing the exploitation of their territory resources and therefore the intrusion of outsiders carrying various contagious diseases into their territory.[49] The Commission found that because the government permitted this intrusion without providing the essential medical care, there was a breach of their right to life.[50] This case suggests an obligation of States to act to deflect the physical impacts of the exploitation of natural resources within indigenous territories. In another case, the Inter-American Court has recalled that indigenous and tribal peoples have the right to access their territory and the natural resources necessary "to practice traditional medicine to prevent and cure illnesses."[51]

Another issue relevant in this context is the obligation to protect an environment that allows indigenous peoples to live on their lands. In this sense, indigenous peoples' land rights are part of the wider connection between environmental protection and human rights law.[52] As pronounced by the International Court of Justice (ICJ) "the environment is not an abstraction but represents the living space, the quality of life and the very health of human beings, including generations unborn."[53] This holistic approach to the protection of the environment is reflected in the UNDRIP. The Declaration underlines

48 International Labor Conference Committee, *Individual Observation*, Brazil, para. 6 (1996).

49 Yanoamami Decision, Res. No. 12/85, Case No. 7615, *Annual Report of the Inter-American Commission on Human Rights 1984–85*, OEA/Ser.L/V/11.66, doc. 10 rev.1 (1985).

50 *Id.*

51 I/A Court H.R., *Case of the Yakye Axa Indigenous Community v. Paraguay. Merits, Reparations and Costs.* Judgment of June 17, 2005. Series C No. 125, par. 168.

52 *See* U.N. Commission on Human Rights, Sub-Commission on the Prevention of Discrimination and Protection of Minorities, *Human Rights and the Environment*, Final Report of the Special Rapporteur, U.N. Doc. E/CN.4/Sub.2/1994/9 (July 6, 1994); *see also* Laura Westra, Environmental Justice and the Rights of Indigenous Peoples: International and Domestic Legal Perspectives (2012).

53 Legality of the Threat or Use of Nuclear Weapons (Request by the United Nations General Assembly for an Advisory Opinion), 1996 I.C.J. 226, at para. 29.

this connection between environmental protection and land rights, stating in Article 29: "Indigenous peoples have the right to the conservation and protection of the environment and the productive capacity of their lands or territories and resources. States shall establish and implement assistance programmes for indigenous peoples for such conservation and protection, without discrimination." Similarly Article 7.4 of ILO 169 states that "Governments shall take measures, in co-operation with the peoples concerned, to protect and preserve the environment of the territories they inhabit." Indigenous peoples' right to use their natural resources also implicates a right to their traditional practices for using, managing and conserving these resources. Article 10(c) of the Convention on Biological Diversity protects the "customary use of biological resources in accordance with traditional cultural practices,"[54] and this article has been interpreted to require the recognition of indigenous peoples' control over natural resources that lie on their lands.[55] The connection between environmental degradation and land rights has also been drawn by international human rights monitoring bodies. For example, the CESCR observations to the Russian Federation stated:

> The Committee expresses its concern at the situation of the indigenous peoples of the Russian Federation, many of whom live in poverty and have inadequate access to food ... The Committee is particularly concerned for those whose food supply is based on fishing and an adequate stock of reindeer, and who are witnessing the destruction of their environment by widespread pollution.[56]

At the regional level, in the *Awas Tingni* case the IACtHR has argued that "land and resources are protected by other rights set forth in the American Convention, such as the right to life."[57] The Court has also highlighted the link between environmental degradation of indigenous territories and violations of the right to life. As noted in the case of the Yakye Axa community: "the State, by not ensuring the right of the Community to its ancestral territory, has failed to comply with its duty to guarantee the life of its members, as it has deprived

---

54 Convention on Biological Diversity, *reprinted in* 31 I.L.M. 818 (1992).

55 *See Traditional Knowledge and Biological Diversity*, UNEP/CBD/TKBD/1/2, Oct. 18, 1997; the connection between biological diversity and land rights for indigenous peoples is examined in details in Chapter 6.

56 *Concluding Observations*, Russian Federation, U.N. Doc. E/1998/22.

57 *The Mayagna (Sumo) Awas Tingni Community v. Nicaragua*, Inter-Am. Ct. H.R. (ser. C) No. 79, (Aug. 31, 2001), at para. 140(f).

the Community of its traditional means of subsistence, forcing it to survive under appalling conditions and leaving it at the mercy of State assistance."[58] Likewise in the case of Xákmok Kásek, the Inter-American Court found a violation of the right to life in relation to the living conditions of the Xákmok Kásek, including the lack of water, food and medical treatment, linking this situation to the community's lack of access to lands and inability to provide for and support themselves, according to their ancestral traditions and cultural patterns.[59] This approach is not limited to the Inter-American system as the African Commission on Human and Peoples' Rights has also highlighted the direct connection between land rights and the right to life in its decision regarding the Endorois community in Kenya. The Commission made direct reference to the approach developed by the Inter-American Court, noting that: "the Court found that the fallout from forcibly dispossessing indigenous peoples from their ancestral land could amount to an Article 4 violation (right to life) if the living conditions of the community are incompatible with the principles of human dignity"[60] In a previous decision, the African Commission had also focused its attention on the connection between the right to life and land rights in the context of the rights of the Ogoni in Nigeria. In that decision the Commission had highlighted that by not preventing the destruction of the Ogoni land by the Shell Oil Company, the Federal Republic of Nigeria had violated, among others, the right to life of Ogoni as articulated by Article 4 of the African Charter on Human and Peoples' Rights.[61] The Commission noted: "the State is obliged to respect the free use of resources owned or at the disposal of the individual alone or in any form of association with others … for the purpose of rights-related needs. And with regard to a collective group, the resources belonging to it should be respected, as it has to use the same resources to satisfy its needs."[62] On the duty to protect life, the Commission observed that State protection must include an effective interplay of laws and

58 IACHR, Arguments before the Inter-American Court of Human Rights in the case of Yakye Axa v. Paraguay. Cited in: I/A Court H.R., *Case of the Yakye Axa Indigenous Community v. Paraguay. Merits, Reparations and Costs.* Judgment of June 17, 2005. Series C No. 125, par. 157(b).

59 Inter-American Court of Human Rights, Merits and reparations. Judgment of August 24, 2010. Series C No. 214, at paras 202–17.

60 African Commission on Human and Peoples' Rights, *Centre for Minority Rights Development (Kenya) and Minority Rights Group International on behalf of Endorois Welfare Council v Kenya,* Communication 276/2003 (2010), at para 216.

61 Communication 155/96 (*Ogoni* Case), ACHPR/COMM/A044/1 (May 27, 2002).

62 *Id.*, para. 45.

regulations that allow individuals to fully realise their rights and freedoms.[63] Overall, all these decisions from the regional human rights institutions are based on an enlarged comprehension of the right to life, encompassing access to livelihood and the right to live in an environment that does not threaten life. In this regard, the connection between land rights and the right to life has farther-reaching meanings, as access to livelihood implies rights such as the right to food, health or natural environment, which allow for human development. All these decisions are based on the fact that indigenous peoples' rights to land, not as a proprietary right only but as a right to subsistence, and thus encompass indigenous perspectives that view land as a central element for their survival.

Thus, to conclude, it has to be underlined that emerging standards indicate that the right to life includes an obligation on States to prevent foreseeable harm to life including activities that might threaten life, such as environmental degradations.[64] This raises the possibility for arguing that indigenous peoples' right to access their traditional territory is part of the protection of the right to life. This argument rests on two pillars: the notion of access to subsistence and right to livelihood, and through States' obligations to ensure the protection of an environment that allows for safe conditions of life. The CESCR has been especially proactive in addressing the issue of indigenous peoples' land rights through the different rights protected under the Covenant. This suggests that the Committee has recognised that access to their land for indigenous peoples is at the heart of the realisation of other economic, social and cultural rights of indigenous peoples. The approach of the Committee highlights the fact that the realisation of rights, such as the right to health, food, and water is deeply embedded in the recognition of indigenous peoples' right to access and use their lands. An overview of some of the recent decisions from the regional human rights bodies also shows that without the recognition of indigenous peoples' right to use their lands, States would fail to protect indigenous peoples' right to food, health, housing and a safe environment, and ultimately violate the right to life. Thus, the recognition of indigenous peoples' land rights has wide implications, and, from this perspective, the right of indigenous peoples to use their lands highlights the indivisibility and interdependence with other rights, and importantly the right to life.

---

63 On this issue, *see* Dinah Shelton, *Decision Regarding Communication 155/96 (Social and Economic Rights Action Center/Center for Economic and Social Rights v. Nigeria). Case No. ACHPR/COMM/A044/1*, 96 Am. J. Int'l L. 937 (2002).

64 *See* Jérémie Gilbert, *Environmental Degradation as a Threat to Life: A Question of Justice?*, 16 Trinity Coll. L. Rev. 81 (2002).

B Land Rights as a Way of Life: Traditions and Spirituality

Indigenous peoples' claims to their ancestral lands are manifold and are based on a social, religious, and cultural approach to their relationship with their territories. In this regard, indigenous peoples' claims to the preservation and the right to use their territories, enshrines social and cultural significance of their lands to their cultural survival. This has to be put in the perspective that indigenous peoples usually live in countries where they are in a non-dominant position, the consequence being that their cultures are often disregarded and oppressed. With the emergence of the State-centred system, the ideal of the modern state was often based on the notion of a culturally homogenous people constituting a State.[65] The general view was that people that are not sharing such a common culture should be gradually assimilated within the dominant society. Most of the political philosophers of the 18th century viewed a people and a nation as a community bound together by an implicit common good and sharing of common institutions and traditions that form a dominant culture.[66] As Kuper pointed out: "[I]n the Enlightenment view, civilization was engaged in a great struggle to overcome resistance of traditional cultures, with their superstitions, irrational prejudices, and fearful loyalties to cynical rulers."[67] International law was used as a tool to impose the culture of the "civilised" nations on the so-called "savages." Law has for a long time used words such as "savages" and "civilization," and in this regard international law has also been a vehicle for the idea that "culture" was the part of the civilised peoples as opposed to the so-called "savages."[68] Yet, with decolonisation, international law has taken another direction, and the contemporary movement is towards the affirmation and protection of cultural diversity.[69] It is especially through the development of human rights discourse that international law has gradually recognised the need to protect minority cultures, as one of the central angles of human rights law is the cultural protection of minorities or indigenous peoples within

65 *See* Walker Connor, *Nation-building or Nation Destroying*, 24(3) World Pol. 319 (1972).

66 On this issue, *see* John Hutchinson & Anthony Smith, Nationalism (1994).

67 Adam Kuper, Culture: The Anthropologists' Account (2000).

68 *See* Charles H. Alexandrowicz, *The Juridical Expression of the Sacred Trust of Civilization*, 65(1) Am. J. Int'l L. 149 (1971).

69 For example, the 1975 Intergovernmental Conference on Cultural Policies in Africa stated: "Affirmation of cultural identity was considered as an act of liberation, a tool in the struggle for effective independence and the best way for the complete realization of the individual and the harmonious development of society." *See* Intergovernmental Conference on Cultural Policies in Africa (UNESCO-OAU, 1975).

a society.[70] In terms of indigenous peoples' rights, the human rights discourse has profound implications for their cultural approach to territory.

1 *The Minority Rights Approach: Land Rights as Tradition*

Cultural rights constitute an essential element of the right of minorities. While indigenous peoples' rights are specific and differ from the rights of the minorities, there are nonetheless some very strong synergies between the two specific regimes of protection of both minorities and indigenous peoples.[71] As such indigenous peoples have found some form of protection under the legal regime dedicated to minorities, notably under article 27 of the I.C.C.P.R. which states: "In those States in which ethnic, religious or linguistic minorities exist, persons belonging to such minorities shall not be denied the right, in community with the other members of their group, to enjoy their own culture, to profess and practise their own religion, or to use their own language." Based on this article, the Human Rights Committee (HRC) has developed a very rich jurisprudence connecting cultural rights for minorities with a specific entitlement to land rights for indigenous peoples. Its jurisprudence has been progressive regarding indigenous peoples' right to enjoy their own way of life. The Committee established a link between culture and traditional forms of livelihood in the *Kitok* decision in 1988, when it highlighted that the Saami lifestyle was linked to reindeer culture, and Sweden ought to respect this part of the Saami culture.[72] In a second important decision, the Committee found that Canada violated indigenous peoples' rights by allowing the exploitation of natural resources in a territory used by indigenous peoples.[73] The Committee stated: "that the rights protected by article 27 includes the right of persons, in community with others, to engage in economic and social activities which are part of the culture of the community to which they belong."[74] As Kingsbury pointed out, this decision from the Committee implies that where indigenous peoples "are not

---

70 On this issue, *see* Patrick Thornberry, International Law and the Rights of Minorities (1991).

71 See Erika-Irene Daes and Asbjørn Eide, *Working paper on the relationship and distinction between the rights of persons belonging to minorities and those of indigenous peoples*, UN Doc. E/CN.4/Sub.2/2000/10 (2000); Asbjørn Eide, *International Cooperation for Group Accommodation through Minority Protection: A Review of Standard Setting and Institution Building at Regional and Global Levels*, Int'l J. on Minority & Group Rts. 13 (2006): 153.

72 Kitok v. Sweden (Communication No. 197/1985), Official Records of the Human Rights Committee 1987/88, vol. II, 442 (1995).

73 Bernard Ominayak, Chief of the Lubicon Lake Band v. Canada (Communication No. 167/1984), U.N. Doc. Supp. No. 40 (A/45/40), at 1 (1990).

74 *Id.*, para. 32.2.

allocated the land and control of resource development necessary to pursue economic activities of central importance to their culture," States are violating Article 27, which protects the group's cohesiveness through the possession of their lands.[75] In 1994, the Committee adopted General Comment regarding article 27 of the Covenant which specifically mention the connection between cultural rights and land rights stating:

> With regard to the exercise of the cultural rights protected under article 27, the Committee observes that *culture manifests itself in many forms, including a particular way of life associated with the use of land resources, especially in the case of indigenous peoples. That right may include such traditional activities as fishing or hunting and the right to live in reserves protected by law.* The enjoyment of those rights may require positive legal measures of protection and measures to ensure the effective participation of members of minority communities in decisions which affect them.[76]

This affirmation by the HRC of the cultural importance of land rights for indigenous peoples has been a crucial starting point in terms of access to human rights law for many indigenous peoples. In several decisions involving individual complaints from members of indigenous communities the HRC has established a link between culture and traditional forms of livelihood. One of the difficulties for the HRC was to establish what constituted an activity forming an essential element of indigenous peoples' culture. For example in the case of reindeer herding for the Sami populations, one of the arguments developed by the government of Sweden was that reindeer herding was more an economic, rather than a purely cultural, activity. On this point the HRC concluded that: "the regulation of an economic activity is normally a matter for the State alone. However, where that activity is an essential element in the culture of an ethnic community, its application to an individual may fall under article 27 of the Covenant."[77] This was later confirmed in other decisions in which the HRC re-affirmed that economic activities may come within the ambit of article 27, if they are an essential element of the culture of an ethnic community. On that issue, an interesting decision was made by the Committee regarding the

75 Benedict Kingsbury, *Claims by Non-State Groups in International Law*, 25 Cornell Int'l L.J. 481 (1992).

76 General Comment No. 23: The Rights of Minorities (art. 27), U.N. Doc. CCPR/C/21/Rev.1/Add.5 (emphasis added).

77 Ivan Kitok v. Sweden, Communication No. 197/1985, CCPR/C/33/D/197/1985 (1988), at 9.2.

situation of the Rehoboth Community in Namibia as it established a distinction between economic activity and traditional activity that form part of an indigenous community way of life.[78] The Committee affirmed that a purely economic activity would not be regarded as an "activity forming an essential part of an indigenous culture." This decision was based on the fact that "although the link of the Rehoboth community to the lands in question dates back some 125 years, it is not the result of a relationship that would have given rise to a distinctive culture."[79] The Committee affirmed that in terms of land rights forming part of cultural rights covered under Article 27, it would take into consideration the fact that in order to be considered as an essential element of an indigenous community, this relationship to land should be historical and part of the traditional way of life of the indigenous community, not simply an economic activity. Even though there is no specific time-frame mentioned, the Committee seems to have adopted the view that to be recognised as an activity that constitutes an essential element of an indigenous population, such cultural practice needs to be 'traditional' and historical, and cultural rather than purely economical. This decision also highlights that the Committee would recognise that an economic activity would not be protected under Article 27. As pointed out by two members of the Committee in their individual opinions, there is a difference between indigenous peoples "which can very often show that their particular way of life or culture is, and has for long been closely bound up with particular land in regard to both economic and other cultural and spiritual activities" and other minority groups which cannot "show that they enjoy a distinct culture which is intimately bound up with or dependent on the use of these particular lands."[80] This decision highlights that the Committee establishes a distinction between purely economic activity and economic activities that are part of an indigenous culture. This position might be problematic when there is a clash between indigenous peoples' way of life and economic development within their territories. As pointed out by Hannum: "[I]n the case of mineral or other underground resources which need to be extracted before they can be used, it is difficult to concede the existence of a cultural attachment to such resources."[81]

---

78 J.G.A. Diergaardt (late Captain of the Rehoboth Baster Community) et al. v. Namibia, Communication No. 760/1997, U.N. Doc. CCPR/C/69/D/760/1997 (Sept. 6, 2000).

79 *Id.*, para. 10.6.

80 *Id.*, Individual Opinion of Elizabeth Evatt and Cecilia Medina Quiroga (concurring).

81 Husrt Hannum, Autonomy, Sovereignty, and Self-Determination: The Accommodation of Conflicting Rights 465 (1990).

One of the issues that the Committee has carefully dealt with when balancing economic interests is that when there is a clash between traditional indigenous economy and national development, the HRC has strongly rejected recourse to the notion of "margin of appreciation."[82] In the first *Länsman* case the Committee stated that:

> A State may understandably wish to encourage development or allow economic activity by enterprises. The scope of its freedom to do so is not to be assessed by reference to a margin of appreciation, but by reference to the obligations it has undertaken in article 27. Article 27 requires that a member of a minority shall not be denied his right to enjoy his own culture. Thus, measures whose impact amounts to a denial of the right will not be compatible with the obligations under article 27. However, measures that have a certain limited impact on the way of life of persons belonging to a minority will not necessarily amount to a denial of the right under article 27.[83]

The approach of the Committee is that the infringement shall not deny indigenous peoples their essential needs; the limitation shall be acceptable, i.e., reasonable limitation not denial, based on the concept of reasonableness in the hands of States themselves.[84] The Committee insisted that obligations under Article 27 impose constraints on government's economic development policies. Before entering into developmental projects within indigenous territories, States have a duty to take into consideration the eventual impact of such projects on indigenous culture. The "acceptability" of the developmental project will depend on whether the members of the concerned indigenous community have had the opportunity to participate in the decision making and whether they would benefit from it. The Committee insisted that: "[W]hen planning actions that affect members of indigenous communities, the State party must pay primary attention to the sustainability of the indigenous culture and way of life and to the participation of members of indigenous

---

82 Unlike the HRC, the European Court of Human Rights (ECoHR) when dealing with issues of competing land usage has adopted an approach based on the "margin of appreciation." On margin of appreciation, *see* Yourow Howard Charles, The Margin of Appreciation Doctrine in the Dynamics of the European Court of Human Rights Jurisprudence (1996).

83 Länsman et al. v. Finland, (Communication No. 511/1992), U.N. Doc. CCPR/C/52/D/511/1992, para. 9.4 (1994).

84 On this issue, *see* Anni Äärelä and Jouni Näkkäläjärvi v. Finland (Communication No. 779/1997), Views adopted Oct. 24, 2001, Report of the Human Rights Committee, Vol. II, U.N. Doc. A/57/40 (Vol. II), at 117–30.

communities in decisions that affect them."[85] The Committee has also set up a two-part "test"; or in the words of Scheinin a "cultural test,"[86] when there is a conflict between indigenous peoples and States relating to land use. First, it would ensure that there has been a proper consultation with the concerned indigenous communities. Secondly, the Committee would evaluate economic sustainability, i.e., the development project should not affect the economic sustainability of "an activity forming an essential element of the indigenous peoples culture."[87]

Another important element of the HRC approach in linking cultural way of life and traditional practices was to define what constitute a 'traditional' cultural activity. Indeed only 'traditional' cultural activities are protected under this minority rights approach. Indeed very early on, in some of the individual complaints made to the Committee some States have raised the issue of the use of modern technology as being antonymic to 'traditional' activities. For example, some States have raised the issue that the use of a helicopter to practice traditional reindeer herding, or the use of modern technology fishing nets, could not be regarded as activities constituting an essential element of indigenous peoples' culture. On this issue, in a case concerning Sami communities in Finland, the HRC highlighted: "that the authors may have adapted their methods of reindeer herding over the years and practice it with the help of modern technology does not prevent them from invoking article 27 of the Covenant."[88] Likewise in a case concerning fisheries in New Zealand, the HRC re-affirmed "that article 27 does not only protect traditional means of livelihood of minorities, but allows also for adaptation of those means to the modern way of life and ensuing technology."[89] The approach is that notion of culture in article 27 is not static; it can be invoked in support of the indigenous way of life, with historical links to traditional life which may have nevertheless changed over the centuries. The view is that this provision can be invoked to support indigenous traditional cultural way of life while having evolved over the centuries. Human rights law is not advocating keeping indigenous cultures 'frozen in

---

85 *Concluding Observations of the Human Rights Committee*, Chile, U.N. Doc. CCPR/C/79/Add.104, para. 22 (1999).

86 Martin Scheinin, *The Right to Enjoy a Distinct Culture: Indigenous and Competing Uses of Land, in* The Jurisprudence of Human Rights: A Comparative Interpretive Approach (Theodore S. Orlin & Martin Scheinin eds., 2000).

87 *Id.*

88 I. Länsman et al. v. Finland (Communication No. 511/1992), U.N. Doc. CCPR/C/52/D/511/1992, para. 9.3.

89 Apirana Mahuika et al. v. New Zealand, Communication No. 547/1993, U.N. Doc. CCPR/C/70/D/547/1993 (2000), at 9.4.

time', but allows indigenous peoples to develop in their own way and offers protection for their right to enjoy their own traditional culture. This approach, based on a dynamic approach to cultural rights, has not been developed in a vacuum, as there are strong echoes of such approach in some domestic jurisprudence.[90] As described by the Aboriginal and Torres Strait Islanders Social Justice Commissioner: "[T]he right to enjoy a culture is not 'frozen' at some point in time when culture was supposedly 'pure' or 'traditional.' The enjoyment of culture should not be falsely restricted as a result of anachronistic notions of the 'authenticity' of the culture."[91]

There are echoes of such approach linking minority rights and land rights for indigenous peoples at the regional level. In *G & E v. Norway*, the European Commission on Human Rights stated that the right to private life as enshrined in Article 8 of the ECHR extended to the protection of a person's way of life.[92] Even though the Commission found the case to be inadmissible, it acknowledged the link between land rights and the Saami way of life. The Commission stated that "under article 8, a minority group is, in principle, entitled to claim the right to respect for the particular life-style it may lead as being 'private life,' 'family life' or 'home'."[93] The Advisory Committee on the Framework Convention for the Protection of National Minorities (Advisory Committee) has taken a dynamic approach to Article 5 of the Framework Convention for the Protection of National Minorities as regards indigenous peoples' rights to enjoy their own culture.[94] For example, in one of its opinion regarding the situation in the

90 *See* Delgamuukw v. British Columbia, (1997) 3 S.C.R. 1010—Supreme Court of Canada; *see also* John Borrows, *Frozen Rights in Canada: Constitutional Interpretation and the Trickster* 22 Am. Indian L. Rev. 37 (1997).

91 Aboriginal and Torres Strait Islander Social Justice Commissioner, *Native Title Report 2000* (Report of the Aboriginal and Torres Strait Islanders Social Justice Commissioner to the Attorney General).

92 App. No. 9278/81 35 DR 30 (Council of Europe).

93 *Id.*, at 35. *See* Jérémie Gilbert, *Still no Place to Go: Nomadic Peoples' Territorial Rights in Europe*, 4 Eur. Y.B. Minority Issues 141–59 (2006). *See also* Buckley v. the United Kingdom, App. No. 20348/92, 1996-IV Eur. Ct. H.R. 1271 (Sept. 25); Carol and Steven Smith v. the United Kingdom, Application No. 22902/93 (Jan. 21, 1997); Chapman v. the United Kingdom, Application No. 00027238/95; Jane Smith v. the United Kingdom, Application No. 25154/94; Lee v. the United Kingdom, Application No. 25289/94; Coster v. the United Kingdom, Application No. 24876/94; Bear v. the United Kingdom, Application No. 24882/94.

94 Article 5 states: "The Parties undertake to promote the conditions necessary for persons belonging to national minorities to maintain and develop their culture, and to preserve the essential elements of their identity, namely their religion, language, traditions and cultural heritage." Framework Convention for the Protection of National Minorities (ETS No. 157).

Russian Federation, the Advisory Committee warned that small indigenous groups' specific cultures could be on the verge of extinction, highlighting the fact that such cultural extinction is directly connected to the lost of access to their lands and territories. The Committee points out:

> This is partially due to the fact that many features of their traditional culture, such as reindeer herding, fishing and hunting, are closely linked to the use of their territories and that many of these territories are simultaneously subject to competing interests and exploitation by gas, oil and other industries, which in practice frequently prevail and contribute also to the large-scale environmental problems threatening many of the territories concerned.[95]

Overall, both at the international and regional level, there is a significant jurisprudence regarding the connection between the cultural rights of minorities and land rights for indigenous peoples. Under such development, human rights law goes at the heart of indigenous peoples' claims under international law, as this demand is based on the protection of indigenous culture, with this culture being generally defined on a territorial basis.

2 *Religion, Spirituality and Land Rights*

For many indigenous communities, another important element of their cultural connection to their lands relates to the religious and spiritual aspects of such attachment. The spiritual connection to land and territories forms an important element of the protection of land rights under international human rights law. The UNDRIP affirms the right for indigenous peoples "to maintain, protect and have access in privacy to their religious and cultural sites…" and adds that "States shall take effective measures, in conjunction with the indigenous peoples concerned, to ensure that indigenous sacred places, including burial sites, be preserved, respected and protected".[96] More specifically regarding land rights, article 25 states:

---

95 Advisory Committee on the Framework Convention on National Minorities, *Opinion on the Russian Federation*, ACFC/INF/OP/I(2003)005, para. 49 (Sept. 13, 2002); *see also Opinion on Sweden*, ACFC/INF/OP/I(2003)006 (Aug. 25, 2002); *Opinion on Finland*, ACFC/INF/OP/I(2001)002 (Sept. 22, 2000). *See* Dieter Kugelmann, *The protection of minorities and indigenous peoples respecting cultural diversity*, Max Planck Yearbook of United Nations Law 11 (2007): 233–263.

96 Declaration on the Rights of Indigenous Peoples, Article 12.

> Indigenous peoples have the right to maintain and strengthen their distinctive spiritual relationship with their traditionally owned or otherwise occupied and used lands, territories, waters and coastal seas and other resources and to uphold their responsibilities to future generations in this regard.

In a similar vein, Article 13 of ILO 169 affirms: "governments shall respect the special importance for the cultures and spiritual values of the peoples concerned of their relationship with the lands or territories (...)." The main international human rights treaties do not put such a direct emphasis son the spiritual value of the land, but contain important norms to protect and guarantee freedom of religion. Freedom of religion and belief is affirmed in Article 18 of the ICCPR. As noted by the HRC, this article:

> (...) protects theistic, non-theistic and atheistic beliefs, as well as the right not to profess any religion or belief. The terms 'belief' and 'religion' are to be broadly construed. Article 18 is not limited in its application to traditional religions or to religions and beliefs with institutional characteristics or practices analogous to those of traditional religions.[97]

This affirmation constitutes an important statement, as often States deny that a spiritual attachment could constitute a religion as such. Many of indigenous peoples have highlighted that spiritual life is "different from that of monotheistic faiths in that they are 'geosophical' or earth-centred, rather than 'theosophical' or god-centred."[98] Spirituality is a broader term than religion, understood as more diffuse and less institutionalised than religion. Hence, it was important for the Committee to highlight the fact that freedom of religion is not restricted to 'classical' forms of religion but covers other form of spirituality. In terms of its practice, the HRC has indirectly addressed expulsion from sacred grounds as violation of a group's right to religious freedom.[99] In a case concerning the construction of a hotel in Tahiti on the site of a pre-European occupation burial ground, the authors of the submission did not raise an

97 Human Rights Committee, General Comment 22, Article 18, U.N. Doc. HRI\ GEN\1\ Rev.1 (1994), 35.

98 *See* Katja Mikhailovich and Alexandra Pavli, Freedom of Religion, *Belief, and Indigenous Spirituality, Practice and Cultural Rights* (Australian Institute of Aboriginal and Torres Strait Islanders Studies, 2011).

99 Francis Hopu and Tepoaitu Bessert v. France, Human Rights Committee, Communication No. 549/1993, U.N. Doc. CCPR/C/60/D/549/1993/Rev.1 (1997).

Article 18 claim due to admissibility complications. However, dissenting judges recognised that the permanent denial of access to ancestral burial grounds may involve "denial of the right of religious or ethnic minorities, in Community with other members of their group, to enjoy their own culture or to practise their own religion".[100]

This interpretation of freedom of religion as including and protecting a spiritual connection to a land has been at the centre of several of the landmark cases at the regional level. The Inter-American Court has put a great emphasis on the connection between land rights and religion. In the *Mayagna (Sumo) Awas Tingni* case, the Court directly identified the religious element of land for indigenous peoples, stating:

> (...) the close ties of indigenous people with the land must be recognized and understood as the fundamental basis of... their spiritual life.... For indigenous communities, relations to the land are not merely a matter of possession and production but a material and spiritual element which they must fully enjoy.[101]

The same approach has been repeatedly adopted by both the Inter-American Commission and the Court and in subsequent jurisprudence.[102] The African Commission on Human and Peoples' Rights has adopted a similar approach highlighting that indigenous peoples' spiritual connection to their ancestral lands and territories should be protected under the banner of freedom of religion protected under the African Charter. In the *Endorois* decision, the African Commission highlighted that "religion is often linked to land, cultural beliefs

---

100 Ibid. See dissent by David Kretzmer and Thomas Buergenthal with Nisuke Ando and Lord Coville, para. 3.

101 *The Awas Tingni Case* (2001), *supra* note 57, para. 149.

102 See *Maya indigenous community of the Toledo District v. Belize* Case 12.053, Report No. 40/04, Inter-Am. C.H.R., OEA/Ser.L/V/II.122 Doc. 5 rev. 1 at 727 (2004) at para 155; *Moiwana Community v. Suriname*, Preliminary Objections, Merits, Reparations and Costs. Judgment of June 15, 2005. Series C No. 124 at paras 101 and 103; *Yakye Axa Indigenous Community v. Paraguay*, Merits, Reparations and Costs Judgment of June 17, 2005. Series C No. 125 at para 131, *Sawhoyamaxa Indigenous Community v. Paraguay*, Merits, Reparations and Costs Judgment of March 29, 2006. Series C No. 146 at para 119; *Saramaka People v. Suriname*, Preliminary Objections, Merits, Reparations, and Costs, Judgment of November 28, 2007 Series C No. 172 at para 90; *Xákmok Kásek Indigenous Community v Paraguay* Merits and reparations. Judgment of August 24, 2010. Series C No. 214, at para 86; *Kichwa People of Sarayaku v Ecuador* Merits and reparations Judgment of June 27, 2012. Series C No. 245 at para 149.

and practices, and... freedom to worship and engage in such ceremonial acts is at the centre of the freedom of religion."[103] In this case, the Endorois argued that the decision to remove them from their traditional territories was directly affecting their right to religious freedom as access to Lake Borogia plays an important role in the religious tradition of the Endorois, as it is a place of an annual religious ritual and at the centre of other important places of worship for the community. The Endorois contended that their dispossession amounted to a violation of Article 8 of the African Charter which states: "[F]reedom of conscience, the profession and free practice of religion shall be guaranteed. No one may, subject to law and order, be submitted to measures restricting the exercise of these freedoms." They claimed that their spiritual beliefs and ceremonial practices attached to the land constitute a religion. In their complaint, the Endorois highlighted that an indigenous group whose spiritual belief is intimately tied to the land requires special protection that should fall under the protection of freedom to practice a religion. By not allowing them to access their ancestral spiritual sites, the Government had violated their right to practice their religion.

The African Commission recognised that the concerned territory was a significant spiritual place for the community, on the basis that the Endorois regularly hold religious ceremonies at several spiritual sites situated around Lake Bogoria, and that their ancestors are buried near the Lake. In this context, the Commission acknowledged that: "religion is often linked to land, cultural beliefs and practices, and that freedom to worship and engage in such ceremonial acts is at the centre of the freedom of religion."[104] The Commission found that the restriction imposed on the Endorois to practice their religion was a significant restriction to their freedom of religion that was not justified by any significant public security interest or other justification. The Commission concluded that Kenya had violated Article 8 of the African Charter since the forced eviction of the Endorois from their ancestral land "interfered with the Endorois' right to religious freedom and removed them from the sacred grounds essential to the practice of their religion, and rendered it virtually impossible for the Community to maintain religious practices central to their culture and religion."[105] This recognition that access to a territory is part of the freedom to practice their religion for indigenous peoples is an important statement not only within the context of this particular case but more generally under international law. It is worth highlighting that in reaching such conclusion, the Commission took had into consideration the Human Rights Committee's

103 The *Endorois* decision, *supra* note 60, para. 166.

104 Id, para. 166.

105 Id, para. 173.

General Comments on religion,[106] as well as its own jurisprudence.[107] These decisions merging from the regional human rights bodies are important as they clearly ascertain that a spiritual connection to land can constitute and be part of a religion, as protected under the right to freedom of religion. This is an important legal development knowing that very often the national legal systems do not recognise such connection.

Indeed at the national levels many communities' spiritual connection to their ancestral territories are still be ignored and disagreed. For example, the Kumargank, or Hindmarsh Island, dispute in South Australia has been at the centre of such tension. This case concerned the building of a bridge over the traditional territory of the Ngarrindjeri people; this case is often referred to as the "Ngarrindjeri women's secret business," as the concerned land was sacred to Aboriginal women, and that such business was not to be divulged outside women's circles.[108] The Aboriginal community challenged the building of such bridge by applying to the then Federal Minister for Aboriginal and Torres Strait Islander Affairs for a declaration under the Aboriginal and Torres Strait Islander Heritage Protection Act 1984 (Cth).[109] However, to get protection of their cultural attachment to their land, the Aboriginal community had to reveal "the secret women's business" in front of the Royal Commission, the body appointed by the government of South Australia to investigate the claims.[110] At the end, the project went ahead and the bridge was built, as the Aboriginal women's business was regarded as being "fabricated."[111] This case illustrates how indigenous peoples' spiritual practices could easily be disregarded, as

106 Human Rights Committee, General Comment 22, Article 18 (Forty-eighth session, 1993), Compilation of General Comments and General Recommendations Adopted by Human Rights Treaty Bodies, U.N. Doc. HRI\ GEN\1\ Rev.1 (1994).

107 See *Free Legal Assistance Group v. Zaire, African Commission on Human and Peoples Rights*, Comm. No. 25/89, 47/90, 56/91, 100/93 (1995).

108 *See* Diane Bell, Narrindjeri Wurruwarrin: A World That Is, Was, and Will Be (1998).

109 *See* Wilson v. Minister for Aboriginal and Torres Strait Islander Affairs (1996) 189 C.L.R. 1—High Court of Australia.

110 *See* the cases from the Supreme Court of South Australia: Aboriginal Legal Rights Movement v. South Australia (July 26, 1995); Aboriginal Legal Rights v. South Australia [No 1] (1995) 64 S.A.S.R. 551; Aboriginal Legal Rights v. South Australia [No 2] (1995) 64 S.A.S.R. 558; Aboriginal Legal Rights v. South Australia [No 3] (1995) 64 S.A.S.R. 566.

111 *See* Report of the Hindmarsh Island Bridge Royal Commission (1995); Greg Mead, A Royal Omission. A Critical Summary of the Evidence Given in the Hindmarsh Island Bridge Royal Commission with an Alternative Report (1995); Hindmarsh Island Bridge Bill 1996—Bills Digest 50 1996–97; Mark Harris, *The Narrative of Law in the Hindmarsh Island Royal Commission*, 14(2) L. in Context 115(1996). *See also* Kartinyeri v. The Commonwealth (1998) H.C.A. 22—High Court of Australia.

in this case the cultural tradition of the concerned community was regarded as "fabricated."[112] These difficulties regarding the disclosure of indigenous peoples' cultural practices, and especially spiritual practices relating to their lands, is not limited to Australia. For example, the U.S. Supreme Court in *Lyng v. Northwest Indian Cemetery Protective Association* refused to recognize the specific religious relationship between an indigenous group and their land.[113] In this case a road was being built on public land that had specific religious significance for the Indian plaintiffs who argued that the road would destroy the tranquility necessary for the religion that had been practiced on the land for generations. As pointed out by Kinsgbury, in this case the judge did not take into consideration such historical and cultural issues and decided that the Indian had the same religious right as any other citizen that would not extend to controlling the use of public lands.[114] These are only two illustrations of the lack of recognition, or the 'seriousness', of indigenous peoples' spiritual attachment to their ancestral territories, as across the globe most legislations still do not acknowledge such important aspect of land rights for indigenous peoples. Overall the jurisprudence linking freedom of religion and land rights represents an important steps towards the recognition of the spiritual and cultural elements of indigenous peoples' connection with their ancestral territories, a connection which is often subsumed within the broader concepts of property rights. It also shows the universality of human rights law which has managed to include and recognise the boarder notion of religion to include a deeper spiritual collective connection to a territory as constituting religion.

C Land Rights as Cultural Heritage: Towards a Right to Cultural Integrity

As highlighted throughout this chapter, indigenous peoples' land rights are deeply connected to specific world perspectives, knowledge, cultures,

---

112 James Weiner, *Religion, belief and action: The case of Ngarrindjeri 'women's business' on Hindmarsh Island, South Australia, 1994–1996*, 13 Australian J. Anthropology 51 (April, 2002), and Mark Harris, *'... another box of tjuringas under the bed': The Appropriation of Aboriginal Cultural Property to Benefit Non-Indigenous Interests, in* International Law and Indigenous Peoples 133 (Joshua Castellino & Niamh Walsh eds., 2005).

113 Lyng v. Northwest Indian Cemetery Protective Association, 485 U.S. 439 (1988).

114 Benedict Kingsbury, *Reconciling Five Competing Conceptual Structures of Indigenous Peoples' Claims in International and Comparative Law, in* Peoples' Rights 74 (Philip Alston ed., 2001). *See also* Kristen Carpenter, *A Property Rights Approach to Sacred Sites Cases: Asserting a Place for Indians as Nonowners*, 52 UCLA L. Rev. 1061 (2005).

traditions, customs, and spiritual practices, as such land rights constitute an essential element of their cultural heritage. Hence, another important legal approach regarding cultural rights and land rights comes under the banner of the legal framework governing cultural heritage protection. The field of cultural heritage protection constitutes in itself a very complex, rich and specialised body of international law.[115] This body of international law has not always been concerned with the rights of indigenous peoples to cultural heritage, as for a long time the emphasis has been on States' cultural heritage. However as it is examined below, this State-centric approach has been challenged by indigenous peoples to make space for an approach which includes and respect their cultural heritage, notably putting forward the importance of land rights. The other limitation regarding the relevance of the international legal framework governing cultural heritage relates to its fragmentation in several different regimes which are notably dividing cultural heritage and natural heritage. As analysed in the second section, this division between different 'types' of heritage does not capture the holistic approach that indigenous peoples have with their territories. It then examines how the emergence of a right to cultural integrity offers a much more comprehensive and holistic approach to cultural heritage.

1 *The Cultural Heritage Approach: The Danger of Compartmentalisation*

In general, the notion of cultural heritage is often associated with physical artefacts such as museums, libraries and other institutional aspects of culture. However, more recently the concept has been broadened to refer also to intangible and ethnographic heritage.[116] The term 'cultural heritage' has changed content considerably in recent decades, having at one time referred exclusively to the monumental remains of cultures, cultural heritage as a concept has gradually come to include new categories, notably putting more emphasis on intangible heritage.[117] Standards relating to cultural heritage are dispersed in

115 *See* Janet Blake, International Cultural Heritage Law (2015).

116 See: UNESCO Convention concerning the Protection of the World Cultural and Natural Heritage (1972), art. 1, Convention for the Safeguarding of the Intangible Cultural Heritage (2003), art. 2; Council of Europe Framework Convention on the Value of Cultural Heritage for Society (Faro Convention) (2005), art. 2 (a); ASEAN Declaration On Cultural Heritage (2000), art. 1.

117 See: UNESCO Convention for the Safeguarding of the Intangible Cultural Heritage which defines intangible cultural heritage as "the practices, representations, expressions, knowledge, skills – as well as the instruments, objects, artefacts and cultural spaces associated therewith – that communities, groups and, in some cases, individuals recognize as part of their cultural heritage."

several international regimes, in particular instruments developed under the UNESCO, but also intellectual property treaties, and the international environmental law and policy regime.[118] Various instruments, as well as U.N. agencies, such as UNESCO, aim at the preservation and strengthening of cultural heritage have highlighted the importance of the interaction between heritage protection and land rights for indigenous people.[119] However, indigenous peoples' land rights are not always properly protected under these treaties, and to the opposite have sometimes been victims of such approach to cultural heritage. A large number of World Heritage Sites that have been established under Convention concerning the Protection of the World Cultural and Natural Heritage are directly infringing on indigenous peoples' territories.[120] For example, in 2011, the African Commission on Human and Peoples' Rights took the decision to adopt a specific resolution condemning the inscription of Lake Bogoria National Reserve in Kenya on the World Heritage List. The Commission noted its concerned about the classification of the lake as a world heritage site without respecting the human rights of the Endorois community living on the concerned land.[121] Outside the specific case of lake Bogria, the resolution highlights a general common lack of integration and respect for the human rights of indigenous peoples when it comes to the inscription of their ancestral territories on list of World Heritage Sites. The resolution makes general comments about cultural heritage in the context of indigenous peoples' human rights notably "noting with concern that there are numerous World Heritage sites in Africa that have been inscribed without the free, prior and informed consent of the indigenous peoples in whose territories they are located and whose management frameworks are not consistent with the principles of the UN Declaration on the Rights of Indigenous Peoples." The fact that the African Commission had to resort to the adoption of such a resolution is indicative

118 For a review on how these instruments relate to indigenous peoples, see: Study by the Expert Mechanism on the Rights of Indigenous Peoples, *The promotion and protection of the rights of indigenous peoples with respect to their cultural heritage*, UN Doc. A/HRC/EMRIP/2015/2 (2015).

119 *See*, for example, Convention for the Safeguarding of the Intangible Cultural Heritage (2003); On UNESCO and indigenous peoples, *see* http://www.unesco.org/new/en/indigenous-peoples/. *See also* Commission on Human Rights Resolution 2005/20, Apr. 14, 2005, entitled *Promotion of the enjoyment of the cultural rights of everyone and respect for different cultural identities*.

120 *See* World Heritage Sites and Indigenous Peoples' Rights (Disko & Tugendhat (eds.), 2015).

121 Resolution on the Protection of Indigenous Peoples' Rights in the Context of the World Heritage Convention and the Designation of Lake Bogoria as a World Heritage site, Adopted at the 50th Ordinary Session held from 24th October to 5th November 2011, available at: http://www.achpr.org/sessions/50th/resolutions/197/.

of a lack of respect of the right of indigenous peoples in the context of World Heritage Site. The resolution is also an indication of the general lack of integration and understanding on the rights of indigenous peoples in the context of cultural heritage protection, and the need to integrate a human rights-based approach to cultural heritage protection.

While cultural heritage is not directly mentioned in the core human rights treaties, cultural rights form an important and overarching right proclaimed in most human rights instruments. As such a number of human rights provisions constitute a legal basis of a right of access to and enjoyment of cultural heritage.[122] The UNDRIP makes several references to indigenous peoples cultural heritage. Articles 11–13 distinguish between indigenous tangible heritage, indigenous traditions and customs (art. 11); the spiritual and religious aspects of indigenous cultures (art. 12); indigenous intangible heritage (art. 13). More specifically regarding cultural heritage, Article 31 highlights that "indigenous peoples have the right to maintain, control protect and develop their cultural heritage, traditional knowledge and traditional cultural expressions," which notably include genetic resources, seeds, knowledge of the properties of fauna and flora. The ILO Convention 169 requires protection of indigenous cultural heritage through special safeguarding measures,[123] and the recognition and protection of cultural practices.[124] Many human rights institutions have highlighted how the recognition of indigenous peoples' rights to own, control and manage their ancestral territories constitutes an essential element of their cultural heritage.[125] As noted by the CESCR in its general comment No. 21, States parties must "respect the rights of indigenous peoples to their culture and heritage and to maintain and strengthen their spiritual relationship with their ancestral lands and other natural resources traditionally owned, occupied or used by them, and indispensable to their cultural life."[126] Given the importance of cultural heritage for indigenous peoples, the former UN Sub-Commission on Prevention of Discrimination and Protection of Minorities requested Erica-Irene Daes to conduct a study on the issue at the start of the 1990's. The study considered measures to strengthen respect for the cultural and intellectual

122 *See* Report of the independent expert in the field of cultural rights, Farida Shaheed, UN Doc. A/HRC/17/38 (2011).

123 Convention (No. 169) Concerning Indigenous and Tribal Peoples in Independent Countries 1650 UNTS 383: arts 2(2)(b); 4(1); 5 (1).

124 ILO Convention 169, Art 5(1).

125 See: Jérémie Gilbert, *Indigenous Peoples' Heritage and Human Rights*, in Indigenous Peoples and the World Heritage Convention (Disko & Tugendhat (eds.), 2015).

126 General comment No. 21 (2009), para. 49 (d).

property of indigenous peoples, including the development of draft Principles and Guidelines on the Heritage of Indigenous Peoples.[127] Crucially, the study highlighted that when indigenous peoples are dispossessed of the lands, they are in succession despoiled of their sciences, arts and cultures.[128] It also pointed out that land represents a strong component of indigenous peoples' identity, notably due to the inter-generational aspect of indigenous attachment to their territories.[129] In this context, heritage has been defined as "all objects, sites and knowledge including languages, the nature or use of which has been transmitted from generation to generation, and which is regarded as pertaining to a particular people or its territory of traditional natural use."[130] Consequently, the Draft Guideline affirmed: "indigenous peoples' cultural heritage is intrinsically linked and connected to their traditional territories, lands, waters and natural resources."[131] An important emphasis of the Draft Guideline is that indigenous peoples' control over their lands should be at the heart of the protection of their cultural heritage. However, so far these guidelines have not yet been approved.[132]

Another problematic issue regarding the cultural heritage approach towards indigenous peoples' land rights is the lack of participation of indigenous peoples in many of the decisions that relates to cultural heritage. In general, there has been a lack of proper procedures to ensure that indigenous peoples can participate in the nomination and management of World Heritage Sites when these sites are located on indigenous territories.[133] In most situations, indigenous peoples themselves are only subjects to these decisions; they have a very limited role to play between the cultural heritage, archaeological or anthropological experts that are called to provide evidence of the "cultural value" of a particular site. Likewise, when cultural heritage sites are established indigenous peoples usually end up with a very limited role in the management

127 E/CN.4/Sub.2/1995/26.

128 Erica I. Daes, *Protection of Heritage of Indigenous Peoples*, para. 18 (Geneva: United Nations Publications, 1997).

129 U.N. Doc. E/CN.4/Sub.2/1999/18 (June 3, 1999).

130 *Report of the Seminar on the Draft Principles and Guidelines for the Protection of the Heritage of Indigenous Peoples*, U.N. Doc. E/CN.4/Sub.2/2000/26, annex 1.

131 *Draft Guideline on the Protection of the Cultural heritage of Indigenous Peoples*, U.N. Doc. E/CN.4/Sub.2/AC.4/2005/3, at 4, para. g.

132 In 2006, the former Working Group on Indigenous Populations was invited to review the draft principles and guidelines on the heritage of indigenous peoples, see: E/CN.4/Sub.2/AC.4/2005/3, para. 14.

133 Call to Action, International Expert Workshop on the World Heritage Convention and Indigenous Peoples, Copenhagen, 20–21 September 2012.

of these sites, and their land rights are very often restricted and submitted to external controls. Thus, even though, through the protection of their cultural heritage, indigenous peoples have gained the recognition of some of their rights to use their lands, this approach remains restricted and should be embarked upon with great caution. The development of cultural heritage protection under international law should be based on the recognition of indigenous peoples' crucial role in such heritage protection, as indigenous peoples should have control over their own traditional cultural sites.[134]

The other limitation of the cultural heritage approach towards indigenous peoples' land rights relates to the fragmentation and compartmentalisation of the legal regimes governing cultural heritage protection. Under these regimes, there is still a strong distinction made between cultural and natural heritage; tangible and intangible heritage; and traditional knowledge and intellectual property. All these distinctions, and compartmentalisation, of the cultural heritage contained within indigenous territories does not accommodate and consider the holistic approach that most indigenous communities have with their territorial heritage. Indigenous peoples have highlighted how their cultural heritage needs to be apprehended in a holistic and inter-generational manner based on common material and spiritual values influenced by their environment.[135] The existence of such complex and parallel systems of protection of cultural heritage leads to the compartmentalisation of their cultural heritage within a multitude of legal frameworks, which ultimately do not adequately protect indigenous peoples' cultural heritage. This fragmentation fails to recognise that, for indigenous peoples, cultural heritage is holistic and includes their spiritual, economic and social connection to their lands and territories.

2 *The Holistic Approach: Land Rights as Cultural Integrity*

Indigenous peoples have often highlighted that their cultural connection to their lands and territories should be approached in a 'holistic' and inter-generational manner, meaning that it encompasses cultural but also spiritual values, including for example language, art, music, dance, song, and spiritual sites, but also relates to future generations. The IACtHR has recognised that indigenous peoples' relationship with land ownership is not merely a question

134 On the development of international law as regards this cultural heritage approach, *see Working Paper submitted by Yozo Yokota and the Saami Council*, U.N. Doc. E/CN.4/Sub.2/AC.4/2004/5.

135 *See* Karolina Kuprecht, Indigenous Peoples' Cultural Property Claims: Repatriation and Beyond (2013); Brendan Tobin, Indigenous peoples, Customary Law and Human Rights – Why Living Law Matters (2014).

of possession and production but also an essential element of indigenous peoples' way of life.[136] As noted by the Court in its decision in the case of Yakye Axa community:

> The culture of the members of the indigenous communities directly relates to a specific way of being, seeing, and acting in the world, developed on the basis of their close relationship with their traditional territories and the resources therein, not only because they are their main means of subsistence, but also because they are part of their worldview, their religiosity, and therefore, of their cultural identity.[137]

To capture the specific holistic and inter-generational aspect of land rights, and their importance for the cultural life of indigenous peoples, there has been an increased reference made to the need to respect the right to cultural integrity of indigenous peoples.[138] The right to cultural integrity supports a much more holistic approach to the importance of land rights by amalgamating some of the relevant rights such as the right to culture, religion, cultural heritage and natural resources. Legally speaking, references to the need to respect the integrity of indigenous peoples are made in article 8 (2) of the UNDRIP which prohibits any action "which has the aim or effect of depriving them of their integrity as distinct peoples, or of their cultural values or ethnic identities." Likewise, Article 2 of the ILO Convention 169 states: "Governments shall have the responsibility for developing, with the participation of the peoples concerned, coordinated and systematic action to protect the rights of these peoples and to guarantee respect for their integrity." The Committee on Economic, Social and Cultural Rights has also alluded to the need to protect the cultural integrity of indigenous peoples.[139] The Special Rapporteur on the rights of indigenous peoples, former and present, have often made specific references to the need

136 *Awas Tingni* case, *supra* note 57, at para. 149.

137 *Yakye Axa Indigenous Community*, *supra* note 51, para 135.

138 *See* James Anaya, Indigenous Peoples in International Law 134–141 (2004), pp. 134–41; Fergus MacKay, *Universal Rights or a Universe unto Itself – Indigenous Peoples' Human Rights and the World Bank's Draft Operational Policy 4.10 on Indigenous Peoples*, 17 Am. U. Int'l L. Rev. 527 (2001–2002); James Anaya, *International Human Rights and Indigenous Peoples: The Move toward the Multicultural State*, 21 Ariz. J. Int'l & Comp. L. 13 (2004); Asia Pacific Forum of National Human Rights Institutions and the Office of the United Nations High Commissioner for Human Rights, The United Nations Declaration on the Rights of Indigenous Peoples: A Manual for National Human Rights Institutions (United Nations, August 2013).

139 See: Concluding Observations: Guatemala, UN Doc. E/C.12/GTM/CO/3, at para. 7.

to protect the cultural integrity of indigenous peoples.[140] The Special Rapporteur on the right to food has also mentioned the need to respect the cultural integrity of indigenous.[141] It is also worth noting that one of the main objectives of the Second Decade of the World's Indigenous Peoples is to promote the full and effective participation of indigenous peoples in "decisions which directly or indirectly affect their cultural integrity."[142] However, the clearer expression of the importance of the right to cultural integrity in the context of land rights comes from the regional human rights institutions.

The Inter-American Commission, and the Court, have both made several references to the need to respect the right to the cultural integrity of indigenous peoples, highlighting how land rights have to be placed within such framework. For example, the Inter-American Commission on Human Rights has examined a case submitted by two members of the Western Shoshone who alleged that the U.S. government had violated their right to cultural integrity by not respecting their right to live on their traditional lands.[143] The petitioners pointed out that the government, by not respecting their enjoyment of their lands, was threatening their cultural integrity and thus violating Article XXII (right to property), Article III (right to religious freedom), Article VI (right to family) and Article XIV (right to take part in the cultural life of the community) of the American Declaration of the Rights and Duties of Man. In other situations, the Commission has also referred to the need to protect and respect the 'socio-cultural integrity' of indigenous peoples.[144] For example, the Commission has noted that: "extractive concessions in indigenous territories, in having the potential of causing ecological damage, endanger the economic interests,

140 See for examples: Report of the Special Rapporteur of the Human Rights Council on the rights of indigenous peoples, Victoria Tauli-Corpuz, UN Doc. A/69/267 (2014), para. 16, 18 and 29; Report of the Special Rapporteur on the situation of human rights and fundamental freedoms of indigenous people, S. James Anaya, UN Doc. A/HRC/9/9 (2008), para. 22; Report by the Special Rapporteur on the situation of human rights and fundamental freedoms of indigenous people, James Anaya, Situation of indigenous peoples in Australia, UN Doc. A/HRC/15/37/Add.4 (2010), para. 4, 13, 16, 28, 44, 65, 72.

141 Special Rapporteur on the Right to Food, Visit to Canada, UN Doc. A/HRC/22/50/Add.1, 25 December 2012, para. 62.

142 Second International Decade of the World's Indigenous People, UN Doc. A/RES/59/174; and Report of the Secretary-General, Mid-term Assessment, UN Doc. A/65/166.

143 Mary and Carrie Dann v. United States, Case No. 11.140 (Oct. 15, 2001)—IACHR.

144 IACHR, Third Report on the Human Rights Situation in Colombia. Doc. OEA/Ser.L/V/II.102, Doc. 9 rev. 1, 26 February 1999, Chapter IX, par. 37. IACHR, Report on the Situation of Human Rights in Brazil, Doc. OEA/Ser.L/V/II.97, Doc. 29 rev. 1, September 29, 1997, par. 47.

survival, and cultural integrity of the indigenous communities and their members (...)."[145] The notion of cultural integrity represents an important aspect of the jurisprudence of the Inter-American Court which has underlined that the close relationship between indigenous peoples and their lands must be recognized and understood as the fundamental base of their culture, spiritual life, *integrity*, economic survival and cultural preservation.[146] Based on such holistic approach to indigenous peoples' relationship with their lands and territories, the Court has made several references to the need to protect the cultural integrity of indigenous peoples.[147] For example, in a case against Suriname, an indigenous community had specifically made the claim that the government had violated their right to cultural integrity. The Court received the argument highlighting that "in order for the culture to preserve its very identity and integrity, [indigenous peoples] ... must maintain a fluid and multidimensional relationship with their ancestral lands."[148] The approach of the Court being that it is important to consider the integrity of indigenous peoples' cultures, which includes a strong connection with their lands, territories, and their natural resources. Overall, both the Inter-American Court and Commission have made several references to the need to protect the integrity of indigenous peoples' cultures, highlighting how this concept of a right to cultural integrity is relevant in ensuring a holistic approach to indigenous peoples' rights.

One the clearest judicial expression of the right to cultural integrity, and its content, probably comes from the 2010 decision of the African Commission in the Endorois.[149] In this case, the Endorois claimed that access to their ancestral territory "in addition to securing subsistence and livelihood, is seen as sacred, being inextricably linked to the *cultural integrity* of the community and its traditional way of life."[150] As the Endorois highlighted, access to their

145 IACHR, 'Indigenous and Tribal Peoples' Rights over Their Ancestral Lands and Natural Resources: Norms and Jurisprudence of the Inter-American Human Rights System' (2009) OEA/Ser.L/V/II. Doc. 56/09 at para 206.

146 I/A Court H.R., Yakye Axa Indigenous Community v. Paraguay, judgement of 17 June 2005 (Series C, No. 125) para. 51.

147 See: I/A Court H.R., Case of the Yakye Axa Indigenous Community v. Paraguay (Merits, Reparations and Costs) Judgment of June 17, 2005. Series C No. 125, par. 147 and 203; Kuna Indigenous People of Madungandí and the Emberá Indigenous People of Bayano v. Panama, Ser. C No. 284, para. 143.

148 I/A Court H.R., Moiwana Village Case, at para. 101, 102–03.

149 African Commission on Human and Peoples' Rights, *Centre for Minority Rights Development (Kenya) and Minority Rights Group International on behalf of Endorois Welfare Council v Kenya*, Communication 276/2003 (2010).

150 Ibid., para. 16, emphasis added.

traditional lands relates to "health, livelihood, religion and culture", as they "are all intimately connected with their traditional land, as grazing lands, sacred religious sites and plants used for traditional medicine are all situated around the shores of Lake Bogoria."[151] The Endorois argued that by removing them from their land, and not allowing access to this important site, the government had violated their fundamental right to cultural integrity. There is no specific provision in the African Charter on Human and Peoples' Rights referring to a 'right to cultural integrity'. Instead the Endorois claimed that their removal meant a violation of their right to practice their own religion (Article 8), their right to culture (Article 17) and their right to access natural resources (Article 21). They nonetheless put forward the argument that all these rights were to be regarded as part of their right to cultural integrity. The community contended that their eviction from their ancestral lands was a violation of their right to enjoy their own culture, but also their right to religion and access to their natural resources. The Commission found that the Government had violated the Endorois' right to take part in the cultural life of their community, notably highlighting that the Government had "denied the community access to an integrated system of beliefs, values, norms, mores, traditions and artefacts closely linked to access to the Lake."[152] This broader approach to cultural rights integrates indigenous peoples' claim that land rights ought to be integrated in the protection of their cultural heritage. As noted earlier an important aspect of the decision relates to the connection made between the right to freedom of religion and land rights. But as highlighted by this decision this is only one aspect of the larger right to cultural integrity of the community. Indeed what comes out clearly from that decsio is the need to take a holistic approach to land rights which relate directly to the right to freedom of religion, cultural rights, property rights and rights over natural resources. An important aspect of this decision was on the connection between cultural rights and access to natural resources. The land around Lake Bogoria is a fertile soil and rich in salt licks providing great support to the cattle, which represent an important aspect of the pastoralist way of life of the community. The lack of access to these specific lands, the water and the salt licks resulted in serious loss of cattle for the Endorois. Outside the economic aspect of the restriction,[153] one of the arguments put forward by the community was that such infringement was disrupting their pastoralist way of life and therefore encroaching on their right to cultural integrity. In the view of the Commission this restriction constituted a

151 Id., para. 16.

152 Ibid., para. 250.

153 This aspect is examined in further details in Chapter 6.

violation of the community's cultural rights since "by forcing the community to live on semi-arid lands without access to medicinal salt licks and other vital resources for the health of their livestock, the Respondent State have created a major threat to the Endorois pastoralist way of life."[154] Relying on this approach, the African Commission adopted a holistic approach by highlighting that access to natural resources does constitute an essential element of the cultural integrity of the concerned indigenous community. The decision indicates how important it is to take a comprehensive approach to the cultural heritage of indigenous peoples, and how the right to cultural integrity, which integrates all these different facets of a territorially based culture, constitutes an important tool to capture the holistic and fundamental aspect of land rights. This decision from the African Commission, but also the decisions and rulings emerging from the Inter-American system of human rights, show how the different rights that are relevant to indigenous peoples' cultural heritage, including religion, culture, property, and natural resources, should be considered under the same umbrella of cultural integrity rather than divided and clustered into different rights. The right to cultural integrity fully integrates the holistic approach that indigenous peoples have with their lands and territories, which is rooted in their spiritual, cultural, economic and social norms, and which is central to the integrity and survival of their culture. This marks an important evolution towards the recognition of the need to adopt a holistic approach to the importance of land rights for indigenous peoples.

Conclusion

As demonstrated by the present chapter, under the heading of cultural rights, international law offers a variety of approaches that are recognising and protecting the connection between land and cultural rights. This includes the 'worst-case scenario', when violations of land rights result in a direct loss of life, by losing access to fundamental sources of livelihoods, but also via the physical destruction of the group cultural identity. In this context land rights have to be understood as forming part of a larger approach to the right to life. The cultural rights approach also includes a minority rights approach protection which is concerned with the rights of non-dominant group to enjoy and maintain their own way of life. As noted this include the right to practice traditional activities related to the use of a land and its resources. It also embraces the larger issue of cultural heritage with its complex and rich international legal framework

154 Endorois Decision, *supra* note 142, para. 251.

on cultural heritage protection. This variety of approaches, namely (1) life and livelihood, (2) way of life, traditions and spirituality, (3) cultural heritage and cultural integrity, means that indigenous peoples might find different legal frameworks to seek protection for their rights to land. It also implies a very complex, scattered and fragmented approach to land rights. In capturing the spiritual, cultural, inter-generational and holistic approach to land rights, but also in integrating it fundamental connection with cultural survival and livelihood, the emergence of a right to cultural integrity appears as a potential bridge been these different approaches to land rights. Hence, this is an encouraging development, however as noted it is still an emerging approach which has been mainly adopted by the regional human rights bodies in Africa and the Americas. It remains to gain a more systematic and universal application.

More generally, there are two other interrelated issues that seems to be emerging from the review of the cultural approach to land rights. First, it appears that in many situations the cultural approach is relying on experts (cultural, anthropological, legal, or sociological) rather than indigenous peoples themselves to evaluate, assess and classify the cultural attachment of indigenous peoples to their lands and territories. This is one of the potential dangers of the cultural rights approach which could result in approaching indigenous peoples as passive subjects of protection rather than owners and principal actors of their cultural rights. This clearly comes out of the cultural heritage approach which relies heavily on experts of cultural heritage, often to the detriment of indigenous peoples. This point about lack of direct and primary participation by indigenous peoples relates to another potential drawback of the cultural approach to land rights which intrinsically relies on a predetermined vision of the connection between cultural rights and land rights. In many ways, the legal categorisation of indigenous peoples' connection with their lands and territories forces them to fit within pre-established legal categories. As captured by Antkowiak this approach might limit the autonomy of indigenous peoples and their capacity for change as "indigenous peoples are expected to follow an uncompromising 'cultural script' with numerous parts: strict observer of customary practices, guardian of nature, and even steward of non-capitalist economies."[155] Moreover, as noted in the previous chapter on property rights, the protection of land rights are also embedded into the international legal language on property rights, which has been largely developed under a dominant individualistic and market oriented approach to the

155 Thomas Antkowiak, *Rights, Resources and Rhetoric: Indigenous Peoples and The Inter-American Court*, Vol. 35, No. 1 of University of Pennsylvania Journal of International Law (2013).

meaning of property in land. From this perspective, to get protection for their fundamental rights to lands and territories indigenous peoples have to adjust to these pre-determined legal narratives. Indigenous peoples have to adjust, follow, and integrate legal norms that might not always fit and represent their own approach to land rights.

On a more positive note, it was also noted throughout these two chapters that in recent years international human rights has managed to offer a more flexible approach to these legal concepts, notably giving space for collective notions of custodianship and by recognising the holistic cultural importance of land rights. Hence taking an overall approach to the legal approaches examined in these two chapters, it is certain that a strong doctrine and jurisprudence acknowledging the fundamental importance of land rights for indigenous peoples both in term of property and cultural rights has emerged, and that such jurisprudence has gradually provided more space for indigenous peoples themselves to influence the normative framework of international law. As noted in the previous chapter, the recognition of collective possession as a source of property rights is an important milestone. Likewise the affirmation of a non-frozen approach to traditional practices and the recognition of spiritual attachments to a land are all important indicators showing that international law, particularly under the human rights agenda, is able to change and challenge its individualistic western origins. Comparing to the legal international theories which victimised indigenous peoples that were examined in the first part of the book, such developments are extremely significant. Nonetheless, these two principal legal approaches to land rights on property and cultural rights are still fundamentally founded on the notion that indigenous peoples are subjects of protection rather than direct actors of international law. Indigenous peoples' land rights still remain fundamentally defined, protected, and guaranteed by the State. The whole legal approach to property and cultural rights still relies on the State being the main dominant actor which guarantees, protects and recognises land rights to indigenous peoples. This leaves little space for indigenous peoples to be the actor of their own future and to control their lands on their own terms. The next part of the book examines how international law is addressing this point by offering an approach where indigenous peoples could play a more direct role by being actors rather than subjects of international law.

PART 3

Indigenous Peoples as Actors: Negotiating Land Rights

From a historical perspective, it could be said that after the age of dispossession, the age of forced integration and assimilation, and the age of rights,[1] we are currently entering an age of negotiation. This movement is part of the larger development of international human rights law that has increasingly addressed the issue of political participation and, more generally, the democratic entitlements of indigenous peoples.[2] One of the strong trends within human rights law is the increasing recognition that indigenous peoples should have more control in the conduct of their own affairs. In terms of land rights, this is reflected in the rights of indigenous peoples to participate, to be consulted, and to consent to decisions affecting their territories and natural resources. All these rights relating to participation, consent, and consultation are pointing towards a new approach under which States, and other actors,[3] have to negotiate with indigenous peoples regarding the use of their lands and resources. Legally, an important catalysis for such development emanates from the right to self-determination which plays a central role to support the right of indigenous peoples to determine their own future, including the use of the lands and resources.

This third part of the book focuses on the rights of indigenous peoples to directly participate and decide the future of their own lands and territories. It scrutinises the latest development in the negotiations between indigenous peoples and States, but also private actors, and the role of international human rights law within these negotiations. It is divided in two chapters. Chapter 5 evaluates the relevance of the discourse of self-determination on indigenous peoples' territorial entitlements under international law. Indeed as noted above, the right to self-determination represents an extremely important legal anchor to support indigenous peoples' territorial entitlements under international law. Based on such analysis, Chapter 6 examines the role of human rights in supporting indigenous peoples' rights to manage and benefit from the exploitation of the natural resources found on their lands. In doing so it focuses on the right to development and its correlation with land rights. This third part of the book aims at analysing how human rights law though its discourse on participation, consent and development supports the rights of indigenous

1 *See* Patrick Thornberry, Indigenous Peoples and Human Rights (2002).

2 James Anaya, Indigenous Peoples in International Law 151–56 (2d ed. 2004); Will Kymlicka, Multicultural Odysseys: Navigating the New International Politics of Diversity (2007); *see also* Thomas Franck, *The Emerging Right to Democratic Governance*, 86 Am. J. Int'l L. 46 (1992).

3 Including international development agencies but also private actors such as corporations and investors. This examined in details in Chapter 6.

 | DOI 10.1163/9789004323254_009

peoples to finally become the main actors when it comes to their rights to lands and natural resources. It elaborates on how the human rights discourse is supporting the development of a new phase in the relationship between States and indigenous peoples in which the latter will finally be recognised as actors playing a part in their own future.

CHAPTER 5

Self-determination, Territoriality and Consent

> Self-determination may make some people think of the right to vote, or the right to belong to political parties or the right to self-government. (…) But when I think of self-determination I think also of hunting, fishing, and trapping. I think of the land, of the water, the trees, and the animals.
>
> TED MOSES[1]

This chapter examines the territorial implications of the right to self-determination for indigenous peoples. Regarding indigenous peoples' land rights, the extent to which the discourse on self-determination can provide indigenous peoples with control over their own destiny remains a critical issue. Even though there is a large body of literature available on the subject, there is still great uncertainty regarding the precise substantive content of self-determination.[2] Self-determination refers to political aspirations but also to territorial aspirations.[3] In terms of land rights, the right to self-determination certainly contains many promises, as ultimately it concerns the issue of territorial control of a people over a specific territory. However, as under international law, the issue of territoriality is one of the main focuses of States' concerns, and as many governments fear that any recognition of such rights might impair their territorial integrity, indigenous peoples' right to self-determination remains a controversial issue. Hence, the purpose of this chapter is to explore how, despite the theoretical and practical challenges, self-determination has proven to be efficient platforms for indigenous peoples to claim their rights to land and territories.

1 Ted Moses, *Self-Determination and the Survival of Indigenous Peoples, in* Operationalizing the Right of Indigenous Peoples to Self-Determination 162 (Pekka Aikio & Martin Scheinin ed., 2001).

2 *See*, for examples, Maivân Clech Lâm, At the Edge of the State: Indigenous Peoples and Self-Determination (2000); Operationalizing the Right of Indigenous Peoples to Self-Determination (Pekka Aikio & Martin Scheinin ed., 2001); Karen Knop, Diversity and Self-Determination in International Law (2002); James Anaya, Indigenous Peoples in International Law (2d ed. 2004); Alexandra Xanthaki, Indigenous rights and United Nations standards: self-determination, culture and land (2007).

3 *See* Lea Brilmayer, *Secession and Self-determination: A Territorial Interpretation*, 16 Yale J. Int'l L. 177 (1991).

 | DOI 10.1163/9789004323254_010

Self-determination encompasses the aspirations of freedom and represents the ideal of a people entitled to pursue its own destiny.[4] Regarding territorial rights, because indigenous peoples' land rights are often understood as collective aspiration, there is a clear link between land rights and the right of peoples to self-determination.[5] For many indigenous representatives, self-determination appears as the best vehicle to embark upon the recognition of their right to live on their lands. As pointed out by Daes: "[A] fundamental aspect of the true spirit of self-determination is respect for the *land* without which indigenous peoples cannot fully enjoy their cultural integrity."[6] However, self-determination also remains one of the most controversial and complex rights under international law. The reluctance of States to recognise indigenous peoples' right to self-determination during the long process that finally led to the adoption of the UNDRIP is a vivid illustration of such specific place of self-determination.[7] On many occasions, representatives of indigenous peoples have affirmed: "the right of self-determination is the heart and soul of the declaration. We will not consent to any language which limits or curtails the right of self-determination."[8]

It is beyond the remit of the following chapter to address the larger question of whether and to what degree indigenous peoples are beneficiaries of self-determination.[9] The issue in the context of indigenous peoples' land rights is

---

4 For an overview of the evolution of self-determination, *see* Antonio Cassese, Self-Determination of Peoples, A Legal Reappraisal (1995) [hereinafter Cassese]; Hurst Hannum, Autonomy, Sovereignty, and Self-Determination: The Accommodation of Conflicting Rights (1990); The Modern Law of Self-Determination (Christian Tomuschat ed., 1993) [hereinafter Tomuschat]; Martti Koskenniemi, *National Self-Determination Today: Problems of Legal Theory and Practice*, 43 Int'l Comp. L.Q. 241 (1994).

5 *See* Allen Buchana, *The Role of Collective Rights in the Theory of Indigenous Peoples' Rights*, 3 Transnat'l L. & Contemp. Probs. 89 (1993).

6 Erica I. Daes, *The Spirit and Letter of the Right to Self-Determination of Indigenous Peoples: Reflections on Making of the United Nations Draft Declaration, in* Aikio & Scheinin, *supra* note 2, at 81.

7 *See* discussion on art. 3, U.N. Doc. E/CN.4/2004/81; and for an analysis of the discussion on the issue, *see* Karen Knop, Diversity and Self-Determination in International Law (2002)—especially Ch. 5.

8 *Quoted in* Indigenous Peoples, the United Nations, and Human Rights 46 (Sarah Pritchard ed., 1998).

9 On this issue, *see* notably Benedict Kingsbury, *Reconciling Five Competing Conceptual Structures of Indigenous Peoples' Claims in International and Comparative Law, in* Peoples' Rights (Philip Alston ed., 2001) [hereinafter Kingsbury]; Timo Makkonen, Identity, Difference and Otherness, The Concepts of 'Peoples,' 'Indigenous People' and 'Minority' in International Law (2000); Craig Scott, *Indigenous Self-Determination and Decolonization of the International Imagination: A Plea*, 18 Hum. Rts. Q. 814–20 (1996).

to appreciate the extent to which self-determination entails territorial rights for indigenous peoples. The following analysis first examines the territorial implications of the right to self-determination, and secondly it explores how self-determination invites States and indigenous peoples to enter territorial negotiations, notably when it comes to the use of the natural resources found on their lands. Ultimately, the purpose of this analysis is to appreciate to what extent self-determination could serve as a positive force in indigenous peoples' quest to territorial rights and how indigenous peoples' territorial claims remain significant in altering the classical approach to the right to self-determination.

A The Self-determination and Land Rights Nexus

Self-determination is an evolving right under international law, the content and understanding of which is not fixed and has proved to be developing over time.[10] Accordingly, regarding territorial rights, self-determination has had several different consequences. As a driving force of the decolonisation movement, self-determination was often understood as a right for the colonised peoples to break away from the colonial States and to establish their own entity.[11] In a post-colonial context, there is an increasing movement towards the recognition of self-determination as comprising a right to effective political participation within States' borders.[12] These different understandings of a right to self-determination have some important consequences regarding indigenous peoples' land rights, which will be examine in the following discussion. The subsequent analysis first explores how self-determination has been framed as a right that "shall not be constructed as authorizing or encouraging any action that would impair States' territorial integrity,"[13] and how such reference to States' territorial integrity might affect indigenous peoples' land rights. Based on such overview, it then explores how self-determination has been gradually interpreted as a right for indigenous peoples to participate in decisions affecting their territories.

10 Cassese, *supra* note 4; Surya Prakash Sinha, *Is Self-Determination Passé?*, 12 Colum. J. Transnat'l L. 260 (1973).

11 Rigo Sureda, The Evolution of the Right to Self-Determination: A Study of the United Nations Practice (1973); *see also* Helen Quane, *The United Nations and the Evolving Right to Self-Determination*, 47 Int'l Comp. L.Q. 537 (1998); Gerry J. Simpson, *The Diffusion of Sovereignty: Self-Determination in the Post-Colonial Age*, 32 Stan. J. Int'l L. 255 (1996).

12 *See* Tomuschat, *supra* note 4.

13 Declaration on Principles of International Law concerning Friendly Relations and Co-operation among states in accordance with the Charter of the United Nations, G.A. Res. 2625(XXV), 25 U.N. GAOR, Supp. (No. 28), U.N. Doc. A/8028 (Oct. 24, 1970).

1 *The Caveat of Self-determination: States' Territorial Integrity*

In all the U.N. instruments mentioning self-determination, very few mention the territorial implications of such a principle. Generally, in most of the U.N. documents, the main allusion to the territorial aspect of self-determination is the reference to States' territorial integrity. Even though Article 1(2) of the U.N. Charter refers to self-determination as one of the fundamental purposes of the United Nations, its Article 2(4) also makes States' territorial sovereignty one of its keys principles.[14] Resolution 1514 condemns any attempt aimed at partial or total disruption of the national unity and the territorial integrity of a country.[15] Similarly, the Declaration on Principles of International Law concerning Friendly Relations and Cooperation among States in accordance with the Charter of the United Nations affirms that it should not be constructed as authorizing an action that would impair, totally or in part, the territorial integrity of a State.[16] The instruments relating to minority rights carefully indicate that, in any case, minority rights should not impair States' territorial integrity.[17]

Regarding indigenous peoples' rights, Article 3 of the UNDRIP, which affirms indigenous peoples' rights to self-determination, has been one of the most significant stumbling blocks to the adoption of the text. During the negotiations, one of the amendments proposed to the right to self-determination included reference to the principle of territorial integrity.[18] Ultimately, the negotiations led to the inclusion of a new article 4 which puts specific conditions on the exercise of self-determination within the respect of the territorial integrity of the State.[19] In a similar vein, the Proposed American Declaration on the Rights

14 U.N. Charter, *reprinted in* 1 U.N.T.S. xvi, U.K.T.S. 67 (1946).

15 Declaration on the Granting of Independence to Colonial Countries and Peoples, G.A. Res. 1514(XV), 15 U.N. GAOR, Supp. (No. 16), U.N. Doc. A/4684 (1960).

16 Declaration on Principles of International Law concerning Friendly Relations and Cooperation among states in accordance with the Charter of the United Nations, G.A. Res. 2625(XXV), 25 U.N. GAOR, Supp. (No. 28), U.N. Doc. A/8028 (Oct. 24, 1970).

17 *See* art. 8(4) of the U.N. Declaration on the Rights of Minorities and Preamble of the Framework Convention for the Protection of National Minorities; *see also* Patrick Thornberry, *Self-determination, Minorities, Human Rights: A Review of International Instruments*, 38 Int'l Comp. L.Q. 872 (1989), in which the author pointed out that "a territorial concept of self-determination appears to rule out minorities without a specific territorial base."

18 *See* proposal by Norway, U.N. Doc. E/CN.4/2003/92; *See also* Joint statement by Australia, New Zealand and the United States of America on the Chair's Text on the Declaration on the Rights of Indigenous Peoples, Human Rights Council, June 2006. This was included in article 46 of the text.

19 Article 4 of the UNDRIP states: "Indigenous peoples, in exercising their right to self-determination, have the right to autonomy or self-government in matters relating to

of Indigenous Peoples states that: "[N]othing in this Declaration may be construed as permitting any activity contrary to the purposes and principles of the OAS, including sovereign equality, territorial integrity."[20] Likewise, the contribution of ILO Convention 169 to indigenous aspirations for self-determination is minimal, given that the Convention states that, "the use of the term 'peoples' in this Convention shall not be constructed as having any implications as regards the rights which may attach to the term under international law."[21] The drafting of this article was notably guided by States' concern that indigenous peoples' rights might alter the principle of States' territorial integrity.[22] Overall, all the instruments referring to self-determination indicate that any elaboration on the nexus between land rights and self-determination has to start with a discussion of the notion of States' territorial integrity, which constitutes the inherent impasse in the quest for the recognition of indigenous peoples' territorial rights.

As Cassese pointed out, the first connection between territorial claims and self-determination comes through the fact that self-determination "eroded one of the basic postulates of the traditional international community: territorial sovereignty."[23] This was particularly true during decolonisation. Under the U.N. regime, it is admitted that self-determination as part of the decolonisation process offers three options: (1) emergence as a sovereign independent state; (2) free association with an independent state; (3) integration with an independent state on the basis of equality.[24] Hence, self-determination was more about gaining statehood (and related choices) than about land and territorial control, management and ownership.[25] In this post-colonial context,

their internal and local affairs, as well as ways and means for financing their autonomous functions."

20 Proposed American Declaration on the Rights of Indigenous Peoples, approved by the Inter-American Commission on Human Rights at its 1333d Sess., 95th Regular Sess. (Feb. 26, 1997), OEA/Ser.L/V/II.95, Doc.7, rev.1997, art. XXVI [hereinafter Proposed American Declaration].

21 Convention Concerning Indigenous and Tribal Peoples in Independent Countries (ILO No. 169), 72 ILO Official Bull. 59 (1989), *reprinted in* 28 I.L.M. 1382 (1989) (entered into force Sept. 5, 1991). *See* Karen Knop, Diversity and Self-Determination in International Law Ch. 5 (2002).

22 On this issue, *see* International Labor Conference, *Partial Revision of the Indigenous and Tribal Populations Convention*, 1957 (No. 107), 76th Sess., Report IV(2A), at 8–13 (1989).

23 Antonio Cassese, International Law 105 (2001).

24 *See* Res. 1541(XV), Principle VI (Dec. 15, 1960).

25 For considerations on the post-colonial aspects of self-determination, *see* Joshua Castellino, International Law and Self-Determination (2000); Siegfried Wiessner, *Indigenous*

one of the first impediments to indigenous peoples' right to self-determination came through the answer to the Belgian proposal to recognise that colonisation should not only be seen as an overseas expansion, and, thus that Article 73 of the U.N. Charter should apply to all non-self-governing territories.[26] In answer to this proposal, several countries, notably led by Latin America, advanced the so-called "salt-water" or "blue water" principle, recognising the right to self-determination only to territories colonised by invaders from abroad.[27] Thus, even though it might well be argued that indigenous peoples' history is another account of colonialism; during the decolonisation process indigenous peoples were largely excluded from the benefice of Chapter XI of the U.N. Charter, which was regarded as applying to peoples under foreign colonial (i.e., European powers) domination only.[28] This rejection of indigenous peoples as peoples living under colonial rules ensured that the boundaries drawn by the ex-colonial powers were to be preserved with total disregard to indigenous peoples' claims, as the colonial powers handed on the torch of territorial integrity to the emerging post-colonial States to the detriment of indigenous peoples.[29] Under this discourse, indigenous peoples could not claim

---

Sovereignty: A Reassessment in Light of the UN Declaration on the Rights of Indigenous People Vand. J. Transnat'l L. 41 (2008): 1141.

26 *See* Fernand van Langenhove, *Le problème de la protection des aborigènes aux Nations Unies*, 89 Receuil Des Cours 321 (1956); keeping in mind that Belgium did so for political reasons, as behind the proposal was a challenge to "the growing anti-colonial movement by pointing out that anti-colonial states would ultimately suffer from the identification of self-determination with secession and independence." *See* Patrick Thornberry, *Self-Determination and Indigenous Peoples: Objections and Responses, in* Aikio & Scheinin, *supra* note 2, at 54.

27 The so-called "Belgian Thesis" could have had far-reaching consequences in terms of indigenous peoples' territorial rights. *See* Gordon Bennett, Aboriginal Rights in International Law (1978); *see also* Patrick Thornberry, International Law and the Rights of Minorities 16–17 (1991).

28 In this regard, New Caledonia remains one of the few territories with a significant indigenous population (42.5 percent) that is still regarded as a territory under colonial power. The Western-Sahara is still in the process of decolonisation; however, Spain has informed the Secretary-General that it had terminated its presence in the Territory of the Sahara. *See* General Assembly, A/AC.109/2003/23 (June 13, 2003). With the exception of the Kanaks in New Caledonia and the Saharawis in Western Sahara, the situation of Guam and West Papua are also relevant to indigenous peoples; *see also* Mililani Trask, *Historical and Contemporary Hawaiian Self-Determination*, 9 Ariz. J. Int'l & Comp. L. 77 (1991). Generally, on the link between decolonisation and indigenous peoples, *see* Lâm, *supra* note 2.

29 It is certainly possible to argue that many indigenous peoples are still living under colonial rules, especially communities that found themselves in states as a consequence of

control of their lands and territories as this was seen as falling outside the remit of the post-colonial interpretation of self-determination. Yet, notwithstanding the reference to the "salt-water" principle, the issue of indigenous peoples' entitlement to self-determination is far from being resolved.[30] Despite the rejection of indigenous peoples as potential beneficiaries of decolonisation under this particular discourse, the quest for the recognition of their right to self-determination, and its link with control of their lands and territories did not stop for indigenous peoples.[31] Indeed many indigenous communities are still claiming their right to decolonisation.[32]

Outside the post-colonial interpretation of self-determination, an important discussion regarding the meaning of self-determination relates to the introduction of the notion of "internal self-determination." The development of such a concept of internal self-determination reflects the obsession with protecting States' territorial integrity. Indeed the principle of territorial integrity of the States is reflected in the debates concerning the introduction of "internal" self-determination, with "external self-determination" implying the possibility of secession and "internal self-determination" referring to "separateness within the state structure."[33] To some extent, this notion of "internal self-determination" is merely another 'technique' to ensure respect for State's territorial integrity, as, ultimately, "internal" self-determination is a truncated version of self-determination (self-determination with no threat to States' territorial integrity). Regarding the substantive aspect of "internal" self-determination, CERD in its General Recommendation XXI described the

uti possidetis, as they did not have any aspiration to be part of such a country, but rather became part of such countries as a consequence of the colonial drawing of boundaries. On this issue, *see* discussion on the doctrine of *uti possidetis* in Chapter 1.

30 For example, Anaya has highlighted three categories of peoples that are entitled to self-determination: peoples living under colonisation, peoples facing apartheid and indigenous peoples. James Anaya, *Self-Determination as a Collective Human Right under Contemporary International Law, in* Aikio & Scheinin, *supra* note 2, at 6.

31 The Human Rights Committee has affirmed that self-determination is not limited to decolonisation and also applies to peoples living in independent states; *see* General Comment 12(21) on art. 1, U.N. Doc. A/39/40, at 142–43.

32 *See* J. Zalcberg and D. French, *The Kanak indigenous peoples of New Caledonia: decolonisation and self-determination in practice*, International Law Association; Statehood and self-determination; reconciling tradition and modernity in international law (2011); Irene Watson, Aboriginal Peoples, Colonialism and International Law: Raw Law (2015).

33 On the notion of "internal" self-determination, *see* Allan Rosas, *Internal Self-Determination in Modern Law of Self-Determination, in* Tomuschat, *supra* note 13; *see also* Cassese, *supra* note 4.

internal aspect of self-determination as incorporating "the right of every citizen to take part in the conduct of public affairs at any level."[34] From this perspective, internal self-determination is about political participation. What is really at stake here is that the move towards internal self-determination may cast away the issue of territoriality. The focus of the internal aspect of self-determination is on peoples' right to a representative government rather than a right to a territory, as ultimately internal self-determination is a right to determine their own future within the physical limits of State territory. Hence, one of the dangers could be that the move to a limited internal form of self-determination might disregard the fundamental connection between indigenous peoples and their territory.

This movement towards separating an "external" and "internal" aspect of self-determination is also reflected through the reference to self-determination as a "remedial right."[35] In this debate on the limitation to self-determination posed by the principle of State territorial integrity, it has often been argued that peoples would have a right to break away from a State if it did not respect the existence of a peoples living on its territory.[36] The so-called "safeguard" or non-discrimination clause in U.N. Resolution 2625 affirms that States' territorial integrity might be questioned if a government is not "representing the whole people belonging to the territory without distinction as to race, creed or colour."[37] Such a requirement means that States have to ensure that particular groups (based on race, creed or colour) should be guaranteed a right to participate in the political process. As an illustration, this approach was affirmed by the Supreme Court of Canada which stated: "[A] right of secession only arises (...) where a people is subject to alien subjugation, domination or exploitation; and possibly where a people is denied any meaningful exercise of its right to self-determination within the state of which it forms a part."[38]

---

34 CERD, General Recommendation XXI(48) on Self-Determination, U.N. Doc. CERD/48/Misc. 7/Rev. 3, para. 4 (1996).

35 Hurst Hannum, *Self-Determination in the Post-Colonial Era, in* Self-Determination: International Perspectives 12–44 (Donald Clark & Robert Williamson eds., 1996).

36 *See* Patrick Thornberry, *The Democratic or Internal Aspect of Self-determination with some Remarks on Federalism, in* Tomuschat, *supra* note 4, at 101–38.

37 Resolution 2625(XXV), Declaration on Principles of International Law concerning Friendly Relations and Co-operation among states in accordance with the Charter of the United Nations; this was re-affirmed by the Vienna Declaration and Programme of Action, June 1993, [ST/]DPI/1394, para. 2 (The Vienna Declaration states "without distinction of any kind.").

38 Reference *re* Secession of Québec [1998] 2 S.C.R. 217, 161 D.L.R.(4th) 385, 228 N.R. 203, *reprinted in* 37 I.L.M. 1340 (1998), para. 154; *see also* Theodore Christakis, Le droit a l'autodetermination en dehors des situations de decolonisation (1999).

In the same fashion, the African Commission in *Katangese People's Congress v. Zaire* stated that "[I]n the absence of concrete evidence of violations of human rights" the people of Katanga should exercise a "variant of self-determination."[39] This decision confirms the view that as long as massive human rights violations are not proven, a people cannot exercise external self-determination, and that, *a contrario*, in cases of gross human rights violations, a right to external self-determination could be exercised. Based on this case, Pitayana argued: "The Commission clearly pronounced that autonomy, as a variant of self-determination, could be recognised to be exercised within the territorial borders of the country in which the group is claiming it. This may be extended to indigenous communities and ... interpreted to suit their situation."[40] On this case, Thornberry concluded: "in the absence of grave human rights denial, internal self-determination is the 'normal' manner of exercising the right."[41] Applied to indigenous peoples, this would mean that indigenous peoples have access to "external" self-determination as a remedial tool against serious human rights violations; such a remedial regime would entail secession only in cases of very serious human rights violations.[42] Thus, indigenous peoples' self-determination would amount to a right to secede in situations in which the existence of the group is in jeopardy. In terms of indigenous peoples' land rights, only in extremely limited situations the non-respect of indigenous peoples' land rights would amount to a gross violation of human rights allowing for secession.[43] Thus, in this debate on the remedial value of self-determination, one of the outcomes is that secession is considered the exception; the normal way of exercising self-determination is within States' territorial framework, through the so-called "internal aspect" of self-determination.

It is crucial to bear in mind that for indigenous peoples to be meaningful, participation implies the exercise of some degree of territorial rights

39 Communication No. 75/92, Compilation, at 50–51.

40 Nyameko Barney Pityana, *Situation of Indigenous Peoples in Africa*, DOC/OS(XXVI)/130, para. 11.

41 Patrick Thornberry, Indigenous Peoples and Human Rights 257 (2002) [hereinafter Thornberry].

42 In practice, this remedial aspect of self-determination remains limited. *See* Joshua Castellino, *The Secession of Bangladesh in International Law: Setting New Standard?*, 7 Asian Y.B. Int'l L. 83 (2000).

43 It is generally admitted that the notion of gross violations of human rights would include: genocide, slavery and slavery-like practices, summary or arbitrary executions, torture, disappearances, arbitrary and prolonged detention and systematic discrimination. *See* Kristian Myntti, *The Right to Reparation of Victims of Racial Discrimination in Human Rights Law, in* Reparations: Redressing Past Wrongs 315 (George Ulrich & Louise Krabbe Boserup eds., 2003); Dinah Shelton, Remedies in International Human Rights Law 320–57 (1999).

over their traditional territories. Thus, by insisting on the rights of peoples to take part in the conduct of public affairs, the so-called internal aspect of self-determination supports the idea that indigenous peoples should take part in decisions affecting their lands. Hence, self-determination, even in its internal form, still has some territorial consequences especially for indigenous peoples. Thus, even though there is a gradual development towards an internal form of self-determination,[44] this movement is not antonymic with self-determination being a central right in ensuring indigenous peoples' land rights, albeit within State exiting boundaries, in respect of the principle of State territorial integrity.

From this perspective there has been some emphasis put on the fact that autonomy and self-government could act as specific forms of self-determination. Autonomy is usually presented in the shadow of self-determination as a form of so-called "internal" application of self-determination. There is often confusion as regards the meaning and content of autonomy and self-government. Based on its Greek origins, the notion of autonomy, *auto* (self) and *nomos* (rule/law), has generally been interpreted as meaning self-government.[45] One of the difficulties is that there is no reliable theory of autonomy, and its legal basis remains unclear.[46] Autonomy is often viewed as the exercise of a right to internal self-determination. Hannum asserted that autonomy is the logical evolution of indigenous peoples' claim for more control over their own life in a manner that is not ultimately inconsistent with state sovereignty.[47] There is a clear evolution towards linking the notions of self-determination, autonomy and self-government when discussing self-determination within the indigenous peoples' context. For example, the *Nuuk Conclusions and Recommendations on Indigenous Autonomy and Self-Government* declare that indigenous peoples have the right to autonomy and self-government as an integral part of their right to self-determination.[48] The UNDRIP explicitly links self-determination and autonomy, autonomy being a specific form of self-determination. Article 4 of the Declaration states:

44 For example, *see* Reference re Secession of Québec [1998] 2 S.C.R. 217, 161 D.L.R.(4th) 385, 228 N.R. 203, *reprinted in* 37 I.L.M. 1340 (1998). *See also* Patrick Thornberry, *The Democratic or Internal Aspect of Self-Determination in* Tomuschat, *supra* note 4.

45 Yoram Dinstein, *Autonomy, in* Models of Autonomy 291 (Yoram Dinstein ed., 1981).

46 *See* Allen Buchanan, Justice, Legitimacy, and Self-Determination: Moral Foundations for International Law: Moral Foundations for International Law (2003); Geoff Gilbert, *Autonomy and minority groups: A right in international law*, Cornell Int'l LJ 35 (2001): 307.

47 Husrt Hannum, Autonomy, Sovereignty, and Self-Determination: The Accommodation of Conflicting Rights (1990) [hereinafter Hannum].

48 United Nations Meeting of Experts, U.N. Doc. E/CN.4/1992/42 (Nuuk, Greenland, 1991).

> Indigenous peoples, in exercising their right to self-determination, have the right to autonomy or self-government in matters relating to their internal and local affairs, as well as ways and means for financing their autonomous functions.

Even though this article does not expressly connect autonomy with a land base, there is a clear reference to the fact that autonomy includes land and resources management. Article 4 has to be read in conjunction with Article 26, which affirms that indigenous peoples' right to own their lands includes the right to the full recognition of their laws, traditions and customs, land-tenure systems and institutions. Within the Declaration it is clear that the part relating to land and territorial rights (Articles 25–30) considers indigenous peoples' land rights as rights to be exercised within the State based on the recognition of indigenous institutions and customs relating to the management of their territories; thus, they could be considered a form of autonomous management. As noted earlier while the ILO Convention 169 puts restriction on self-determination, it nonetheless puts a great emphasis on the right for indigenous peoples to establish their own institutions.[49] Article XV(2) of the Proposed American Declaration also refer to the right of indigenous peoples to set up their own institutions.[50] Hence, there is a clear evolution in increasingly linking autonomy and self-government as a way to operationalize the right to self-determination whilst respecting the principle of territorial integrity of the State.

Overall, in all the instruments, whether especially addressing indigenous peoples' rights, or more generally dealing with self-determination under international law, the doctrine of State territorial sovereignty acts as a limiting factor to indigenous peoples' territorial claims. As examined above, this reference to State territorial sovereignty is expressed either directly in the documents relating to self-determination or indirectly via the reference to internal and/or remedial self-determination. Yet, despite putting an inherent limitation to indigenous peoples' territorial aspirations, the principle of States' territorial integrity still leaves some room for indigenous peoples to claim their rights to lands using the language of self-determination. Brilmayer has pointed out that territorial integrity is not opposed to peoples' right to determine their own future. She stated:

> The apparent inconsistency arises because two competing versions of the principle of territoriality can be discerned. Territoriality might be

49 ILO 169, *supra* note 21, art. 6.1.

50 Proposed American Declaration, *supra* note 20.

> understood to require protection of the existing territorial status quo. However, it might also include territorial arguments about why existing national boundaries should be redrawn.[51]

From this perspective, the rule of State territorial integrity does not preclude indigenous peoples from entering into discussion about territory. Regarding the interaction between the principle of States' territorial integrity and indigenous peoples' territorial entitlements through their right to self-determination, one of the central issues is to appreciate to what extent the discourse of self-determination allows indigenous peoples to enter into territorial negotiations with States.[52] With regard to international legal theory, indigenous peoples' claim to self-determination is very challenging, as most indigenous peoples have never effectively consented to extension of state territorial sovereignty over their territories.[53]

2 *The Relational and Interpretative Values of Self-determination*

As it was highlighted earlier, when it comes to discussion on indigenous peoples' right to self-determination, States often base their approach on the equation that sees self-determination as amounting to secession.[54] This persistent view, which posits indigenous peoples' claim to self-determination as an inevitable threat to State territorial integrity, ignores the fact that most indigenous peoples do not claim independent Statehood.[55] Lâm has highlighted that a large

51 Brilmayer, *supra* note 3.

52 National illustrations include the territorial negotiations taking place across Canada, see Royal Commission on Aboriginal Peoples, *Treaty Making in the Spirit of Coexistence: An Alternative to Extinguishment*, at 70 (Ottawa: Minister of Supply and Services Canada, 1995); Marcia Langton (ed.), *Settling with Indigenous People: Modern Treaty and Agreement-making* (2006); Michael Asch, On Being Here to Stay: Treaties and Aboriginal Rights in Canada (2014).

53 *See* discussion in Chapters 1 and 2.

54 As Lâm put its: "the persistence of the assumption [that the right to self-determination means secession] demonstrates how the modernistically totalizing approach that 'a rose is a rose is a rose' compels us to find a thorn even when alchemical circumstances of the late, and interdependent, twentieth century have already transformed the defiant rose into an accommodating, if enigmatic, violet." Maivân Clech Lâm, *Making Room for Peoples at the United Nations: Thoughts Provoked by Indigenous Claims to Self-Determination*, 25 Cornell Int'l L.J. 609 (1992).

55 *See*, for example, Lars-Anders Baer from the Saami Council: "[T]he aim of our advocacy for our right of self-determination has nothing to do with the creation of western style nation-states. (…) We are only trying to get greater control over our lives and future." Lars-Anders Baer, *The Right of Self-Determination and the Case of the Sami*, *in* Aikio &

majority of the indigenous peoples seek a specific form of self-determination, and the overwhelming majority of indigenous peoples do not plan to exercise the right to secede, but rather seek the protection of their traditional territories from further encroachment.[56] On several occasions, indigenous peoples' representatives have supported the view that for them self-determination perceived to be automatically leading to secession. For example, a declaration made by a representative of the Dene nation is illustrative:

> What we Dene are struggling for is the recognition of the Dene Nation by the governments and peoples of the world. And while there are realities we are forced to submit to such as the existence of a country called Canada, we insist on the right to self-determination as a distinct people and the recognition of the Dene Nation… What we seek then is independence and self-determination within the country of Canada. This is what we mean when we call for a just land settlement of the Dene Nation.[57]

As pointed out by Heintze, this statement underlines the clear need to demystify the concept of self-determination in connection with indigenous peoples, as in this case "it does not mean statehood or independence or any sort of secession but rather self-development."[58] But what is also crucial in this statement is the call for a just land settlement. What self-determination should be about is the right for indigenous peoples to enter into territorial negotiations.

While debates on self-determination tend to focus on the issue of an eventual right to secession, there is the emergence of another view that sees self-determination as a "relational principle." As advocated by Kingsbury, based on the emerging practice of self-determination between States and indigenous peoples, there is a need to reconstruct the concept of self-determination

---

Scheinin, *supra* note 2, at 230. As stated by Anaya: "[T]he notion, that self-determination necessarily means a right to choose independent statehood, ultimately rests on a narrow state-centred vision of humanity and the world." James Anaya, *The Contours of Self-Determination and its Implementation: Implications of Developments Concerning Indigenous Peoples, in* Justice Pending: Indigenous People and Other Good Causes, Essays in Honor of Erica-Irene A. Daes 11 (G. Alfredsson & M. Stavropoulou eds., 2003).

56 *See* Lâm, *supra* note 2.

57 *Quoted in* Maureen Davies, *Protection of the Identity of Aboriginal Peoples with Particular Reference to Canada*, 54 Nordisk Tidsskrift for Int'l Ret 25 (1985).

58 Hans-Joachim Heintze, *The Protection of Indigenous Peoples under the ILO Convention, in* Legal Aspects of the Preservation of the Environment and Development in the Last Open Spaces (Michael Bothe et al. eds., 1993).

"from an end-state approach to a relational approach to self-determination."[59] Under this "relational approach" self-determination is about organising the relationship between States and peoples through negotiations.[60] Likewise, Daes has described the requirements of self-determination as entailing a form of "belated state-building" through negotiation. She asserts that self-determination entails a process:

> through which indigenous peoples are able to join with all the other peoples that make up the state on mutually-agreed upon and just terms, after many years of isolation and exclusion. This process does not require the assimilation of individuals as citizens like all others, but the recognition and incorporation of distinct peoples in the fabric of the state, on agreed terms.[61]

It is worth noting that in the 1993 version of the U.N. Draft Declaration, Article 3 affirmed indigenous peoples' right to self-determination but added that "by virtue of this, they have the right, *inter alia*, to negotiate and agree upon their role in the conduct of public affairs, their distinct responsibilities and the means by which they manage their own interests."[62] Even though this version was later rejected, this approach to self-determination as a negotiation tool has been part of the discussion between States and indigenous observers within the WGDD. Canada put some emphasis on the role of negotiations as the best way to allow indigenous peoples to enjoy their own destiny. An indigenous representative also pointed out: "harmonisation would be sought by viewing the right of self-determination as containing a procedural right that could be exercised through negotiations between indigenous peoples and Government."[63] From this perspective, self-determination is seen as a "procedural right" that invites indigenous peoples and States to enter into negotiations. In a similar vein, Henriksen stated that:

---

59 Benedict Kingsbury, *Reconstructing Self-determination: A Relational Approach, in* Aikio & Scheinin, *supra* note 2, at 22.

60 *See* reference to the notion of "shared sovereignty," *in* Report of the Royal Commission on Aboriginal People (1996), especially Volume II. *See also* references to the concept of "earned sovereignty," Paul R. Williams & Francesca Jannotti Pecci, *Earned Sovereignty: Bridging the Gap between Sovereignty and Self-Determination*, 40 Stan. J. Int'l L. 1 (2004).

61 Erica I. Daes, *Discrimination Against Indigenous Peoples—Explanatory Note Concerning the Draft Declaration on the Rights of Indigenous Peoples*, U.N. Doc. E/CN.4/Sub.2/1993/26/Add.1, 19, para. 26 (July 1993).

62 U.N. Doc. E/CN.4/Sub.2/1993/26, *see also* U.N. Doc. E/CN.4/1996/84.

63 U.N. Doc. E/CN.4/1996/84.

> The right of self-determination should be regarded as a 'process right' rather then a right to a pre-defined outcome. In other words, the outcome of any exercise of the right of self-determination must be individually defined, through a process of dialogue in which all peoples and nations concerned are participating on equal terms.[64]

In the debates relating to the right of self-determination, it is often forgotten that for many indigenous peoples, self-determination appears as a mechanism to enable them to negotiate their political status and to consent to the terms of their future relationships with States. Such approach was echoed during some of the negotiations of the OAS Working Group on the elaboration of the Proposed American Declaration which has labelled echo self-determination as a "relational principle." As noted by the Rapporteur of the working group:

> It was agreed that the concept of self-determination is no longer an object of *opposition*, but that now it is a matter of establishing a new *relationship* between indigenous peoples and their states, with a view to releasing potential energy to ensure more equitable and genuine development to improve governance and strengthen democracy in states.[65]

The relational approach of self-determination is also visible within the jurisprudence emerging from some of the international human rights monitoring bodies. Some States have already made reference to indigenous peoples' right to self-determination in their report to the HRC as a right that can be exercised within the State structure. For example, in its initial report to the Committee, the United States pointed out that: "tribal self-determination meant that tribes had the right to operate under their own governmental systems within the American framework."[66] The dialogue between the HRC and Canada is also extremely enlightening. Following Canada's Fifth Periodic Report to the HRC in 2005, the Committee raised several issues regarding "the concept of self-determination as it is applied to Aboriginal peoples in Canada."[67] In its

64 John B. Henriksen, *Implementation of the Right of Self-Determination of Indigenous Peoples within the Framework of Human Security* (International Conference on Indigenous Peoples' Self-Determination and the Nation states in Asia, Baguio, Philippines, Apr. 18–21, 1999).

65 Special Meeting of the Working Group, Report of the Rapporteur, OAS/Ser.K/XVI; GT/DADIN/doc.83/02, at 15 (June 26, 2002).

66 U.N. Doc. CCPR/C/81, Add.4, paras. 9–76 (Aug. 14, 1994).

67 List of issues to be taken up in connection with the consideration of the Fifth Periodic Report of Canada, CCPR/C/CAN/2004/5, U.N. Doc. CCPR/C/85/L/CAN, at paras. 1 to 3.

written response to the issues raised by the HRC regarding indigenous peoples' right to self-determination, Canada highlighted that the "exercise of the right involves negotiations between States and the various indigenous peoples within those States, to determine the political status of the indigenous peoples involved, and the means of pursuing their economic, social and cultural development."[68] Similarly, during the oral questions that preceded the *Concluding Observations*, one of the delegates for Canada pointed out that in the view of the government, the exercise of the right to self-determination "depended on negotiations between the Aboriginal members and the Government."[69] In result, in its *Concluding Observations*, the Committee refers to Article 1 as supporting the current territorial negotiations between the government and indigenous nations.[70] The monitoring exercised by the Committee in this case shows that under Article 1 of the Covenant, one of the ways to implement the right to self-determination for indigenous peoples is through the establishment of territorial negotiations between States and indigenous peoples.

Regarding its individual opinions, for a long time the position of the Committee was based on the fact that self-determination was not a valid ground for individual complaints under the mechanism of the Optional Protocol.[71] Nonetheless, the Committee has cautiously broadened its interpretation of the content of Article 1, and has recognised that the content of Article 1 should be used as a way to interpret the content of other individual rights in the Covenant. This approach is clearly discernible in the *Mahuika* decision, where the Committee affirmed that "the provisions of article 1 may be relevant in the interpretation of other rights protected by the Covenant, in particular article 27."[72] Similarly in the case of *Diergaardt*, the Committee stressed that "the provisions of article 1 may be relevant to the interpretation of other rights protected by the Covenant, in particular article 25, 26 and 27."[73] Likewise, on many

68 *Canada's Responses to the List of Issues, Presentation of the Fifth Report on the International Covenant on Civil and Political Rights*, Human Rights Committee, at para. 21 (Oct. 2005).

69 *Human Rights Committee considers Report of Canada*, U.N. Press Release, Oct. 18, 2005.

70 *Concluding Observations*, Canada, U.N. Doc. CCPR/C/CAN/CO/5, at paras. 8.

71 Bernard Ominayak, Chief of the Lubicon Lake Band v. Canada (Communication 167/1984), Views adopted Mar. 26, 1990, Report of the Human Rights Committee, GAOR, 38th Sess., Supp. No. 40 (A/38/40), at 1–30; MikMaq Tribal v. Canada (Communication No. 78/1980), 39th Sess., Supp. No. 40, 200, U.N. Doc. A/39/40 (1984).

72 Apirana Mahuika et al. v. New Zealand (Communication No. 547/1993), Views adopted Oct. 27, 2000, Report of the Human Rights Committee, U.N. Doc. A/56/40 (Vol. II), at 11–29, *see*, in particular, para. 9.2.

73 J.G.A. Diergaardt (late Captain of the Rehoboth Baster Community) et al. v. Namibia (Communication No. 760/1997), para. 10.3, U.N. Doc. CCPR/C/69/D/760/1997 (2000).

occasions, the Committee has found in favour of indigenous peoples in relation to their right to self-determination in the context of "subsistence."[74] Scheinin has described such an approach as a recognition of indirect "interpretative" effect of Article 1 in the application of other provisions of the Covenant.[75] Regarding the interrelationship between Article 27 and Article 1, Scheinin has argued that indigenous representatives should explore such a correlation as a way of pushing for the recognition of their right to self-determination. As he states, "for most indigenous peoples what self-determination is *really* about is their right to 'freely dispose of their natural wealth and resources' and a negative guarantee not to 'be deprived of its own means of subsistence.'"[76]

The HRC has increasingly tackled the link between self-determination and land rights resulting in the recognition of indigenous peoples' rights to be notified and consulted before any exploitation of natural resources contained within their traditional territories, as part of their right to self-determination.[77] For example, in its concluding observations to the report submitted by Australia, the Committee highlighted that, based on Article 1, paragraph 2, the "state party should take the necessary steps in order to secure for the indigenous inhabitants, a stronger role in decision-making over their traditional lands and natural resources."[78] Similarly, in its *Concluding Observations* on Mexico, the Committee placed an emphasis on the link between control of land and resources and self-determination. The HRC pointed out that "[A]ppropriate measures should also be taken to increase their participation in the country's institutions and the exercise of the right to self-determination."[79] It is worth

---

74 Bernard Ominayak, Chief of the Lubicon Lake Band v. Canada (Communication 167/1984), Views adopted Mar. 26, 1990, *Report of the Human Rights Committee*, GAOR, 38th Sess., Supp. No. 40 (A/38/40), at 1–30; Kitok v. Sweden (Communication No. 197/1985), Official Records of the Human Rights Committee at 442–45 (New York: United Nations, 1995); I. Länsman et al. v. Finland (Communication No. 511/1992), U.N. Doc. CCPR/C/57/1; J. Länsman et al. v. Finland (Communication No. 671/1995), U.N. Doc. CCPR/C/58/D/671/1995.

75 *See* Martin Scheinin, *The Right to Self-Determination under the Covenant on Civil and Political Rights, in* Aikio & Scheinin, *supra* note 2, at 179–99.

76 Martin Scheinin, *The Right to Enjoy a Distinct Culture: Indigenous and Competing Uses of Land, in* The Jurisprudence of Human Rights: A Comparative Interpretive Approach (Theodore S. Orlin & Martin Scheinin eds., 2000).

77 *See*, for example, *Concluding Observations*, Venezuela, U.N. Doc. CCPR/CO/71/VEN para. 28 (Apr. 26, 2001).

78 *Concluding Observations of the Human Rights Committee*, Australia, GA 55th Sess., Supp. 40, U.N. Doc. A/55/40 vol. I (July 24, 2000).

79 *Concluding Observations*, Mexico, U.N. Doc. CCPR/C/79/Add. 109, para. 19 (1999); *Comments by the Government of Mexico on the Concluding Observations of the Human Rights Committee*, UN. Doc. CCPR/C/Add. 123.

noting that the government of Mexico in its Comments on the *Concluding Observations* of the Committee reported that national legislation had subsequently been developed to provide for the participation of indigenous peoples in decisions affecting the use of their natural resources.[80] This illustrates the adequacy of the Committee approach based on the interrelation between self-determination and participation in decisions affecting indigenous peoples' territories.

As noted earlier, the right to self-determination also constitutes article 1 of the International Covenant on Economic and Social Rights (ICESCR), as such the Committee on Economic, Social and Cultural Rights (CESCR) has also acknowledged the strong connection between self-determination and land rights for indigenous peoples. For example, in its Concluding Observations to a report submitted by the Russian Federation, the Committee has expressed its concerns on the non-implementation of a national law that provides for the demarcation of indigenous territories and the protection of indigenous land rights as affecting indigenous peoples' right to self-determination. The Committee implicitly established a connection between indigenous peoples' land rights and their right to self-determination, as, for the Committee, the non-demarcation as well as the non-protection of indigenous peoples land rights affect their right to self-determination.[81]

CERD has also highlighted the importance of the right to self-determination regarding indigenous peoples' land rights. In its General Recommendation XXI on the right to self-determination, CERD pointed out that the right to self-determination implies an obligation for States to act in order to preserve the culture of ethnic groups within their territory. The Committee found that such an obligation arises as a consequence of the right of self-determination and stated that such a right gives persons belonging to ethnic groups "the right to engage in activities which are particularly relevant to the preservation of the identity of such persons or groups."[82] Based on such wording, and, knowing that access to their territories is essential for indigenous peoples for the preservation of their culture, it could be argued that, in such a context, self-determination would include a right for indigenous peoples to participate in

80 *Comments by the Government of Mexico on the Concluding Observations of the Human Rights Committee*, U.N. Doc. CCPR/C/Add. 123.

81 U.N. Doc. E/C.12/1/Add.94, para. 11 (Nov. 28, 2003). The national law in question is the Law 2001 On Territories of Traditional Nature Use of Indigenous Numerically Small Peoples of the North, Siberia and the Far East of the Russian Federation.

82 CERD, General Recommendation XXI(48) on Self-Determination, U.N. Doc. CERD/48/Misc. 7/Rev. 3, para. 5 (1996).

decisions affecting the use of their territories.[83] As an illustration, in its concluding observations regarding the situation in Russia, the Committee expressed concern for the "precarious situation of indigenous communities in the State party, affecting their right to self-determination under article 1 of the Covenant."[84]

Overall, there is an evolution towards self-determination seen as a 'relational principle,' but also as an essential right which should serve as the basis to interpret other rights, including land right. Under such approach, self-determination is perceived as a procedural right allowing indigenous peoples to enter negotiations with States and not as a right with any predefined outcomes. This is evolution is utterly consistent with the historical development of the norm of self-determination, as, for example, during decolonisation self-determination, was seen as a right for colonised peoples to enter negotiations allowing for their freedom rather than a right with a pre-defined outcomes.[85] Self-determination does not evolve in vacuum but is part of the larger development of international human rights law that favours a dialogue between indigenous peoples and States, particularly when it comes to land rights. From this perspective, self-determination is about free control, choice and way of life, and not only about secession. Importantly, self-determination is about the right of indigenous peoples to freely determine the use, control and management of their lands and territories.

B Self-determination, Natural Resources and Consent

As examined above, self-determination understood as a 'relational' principle appears as an efficient vehicle for ensuring indigenous peoples' participation in decisions affecting their lands. From this perspective, self-determination can be seen as a "democratic" standard supporting the participation of indigenous peoples to decisions affecting them within the overall framework of

83 General Recommendation XXIII(51) on Indigenous Peoples calls upon states parties to ensure indigenous peoples effective participation but makes no mention of self-determination per se, U.N. Doc. CERD/C/365, in A/52/18, Annex V (1997).

84 U.N. Doc. E/C.12/1/Add.94, December 12, 2003, para. 11.

85 *See* the three options mentioned above in Resolution 1541(XV), Principle VI (Dec. 15, 1960). As Foster pointed out: "a wealth of state practice can be canvassed in the context of decolonization demonstrating that the exercise of self-determination has in practice nearly always taken place through agreement with the parent state." Caroline E. Foster, *Articulating Self-Determination in the Draft Declaration on the Rights of Indigenous Peoples*, 12 Eur. J. Int'l L. 141 (2001).

the State authorities (and in respect to the principle of territorial integrity). Hence, in this context self-determination seems to mean a right for indigenous peoples to be integrated in the political decision-making process, not a right to choose their own destiny. This approach remains limited, as self-determination is seen as a right for indigenous peoples to participate in decisions affecting their lands, not as a right to freely pursue their economic, social and cultural development by controlling their territories without external interferences. One can wonder what has happened to the other aspect of self-determination, the right to "freely determine their political status and freely pursue their economic, social and cultural development" as contained in Article 1(1) of the two International Covenants (ICCPR and ICESCR). Yet, as it was also highlighted, self-determination is a right which understanding has evolved across the centuries. An important evolution of the right to self-determination relates to its connection with the natural resources contained on indigenous territories. The following discussion examines the emerging doctrine and jurisprudence supporting indigenous peoples' fundamental right to self-determination over the natural resources located on their territories. Based on such analysis, it then focuses on the emergent correlation between self-determination and indigenous peoples' right to consent to the exploitation of the natural resources located on their territories—notably through the emergence of the right to free, prior and informed consent as an expression of indigenous peoples' right to self-determination.

1 *Self-determination, Land Rights and Natural Resources*

An important aspect of self-determination relates to its relationship with control over natural resources, or what is often been termed as the "economic aspect of self-determination."[86] The right of peoples to freely dispose of their natural wealth and resources has been one of the main claims of post-colonial countries. This right, first mentioned by the U.N. General Assembly in 1952,[87] was strongly affirmed by Resolution 1803(XVII).[88] In terms of human rights law, the right of peoples to freely dispose of their natural resources was incorporated in the two Covenants under the heading of self-determination, as is reflected in Article 1(2) of the Covenants. It states:

> All peoples may, for their own ends, freely dispose of their natural wealth and resources without prejudice to any obligations arising out of

86 *See* Antonio Cassese, Self-Determination of Peoples: A Legal Reappraisal (1995).

87 *Right to Exploit Freely Natural Wealth and Resources*, G.A. Res. 626(VII) (Dec. 21, 1952).

88 *Permanent Sovereignty over Natural Resources*, G.A. Res. 1803(XVII) (Dec. 14, 1962). *See also* East Timor (Portugal v. Australia) (1991–1995), 1995 I.C.J. 90.

> international economic co-operation, based upon the principle of mutual benefit, and international law. In no case may a people be deprived of its own means of subsistence.[89]

This right is clearly granted to "peoples."[90] Hence, classically the question remains who the peoples are. It is often argued that this right means that every nation has the right to exercise full sovereignty over its national wealth, the State being the legal expression of the peoples, for ultimately it is the State that is entrusted with the exercise of this right. The view is that governments are in charge of ensuring the "best" utilisation of the natural resources that represent the "common heritage of the nation."[91] For example, Article 21(1) of the African Charter speaks of the "interest of the people" and not of the peoples of a country.[92] In this context the word "people" is seen as synonymous with the State.[93] This limitation has been clearly put into perspective in the *Ogoni* decision in which the African Commission,[94] as Appiagyei-Atua argued, had too narrow an approach, which saw such a right to natural resources as a State right, and thus failed to recognise it as a right of peoples to economic self-determination.[95] It is important to keep in mind that indigenous peoples, as a non-dominant component of society, would often see their fundamental right

89 Joint Art. 1, International Covenant for Civil and Political Rights and International Covenant for Economic, Social and Cultural Rights (1966).

90 *See also* art. 21 of the African Charter on Human and Peoples' Rights, OUA Doc. CAB/LEG/67/3 Re. 5, *reprinted in* 21 I.L.M. 58 (1982).

91 On this issue, *see* Nicolaas Schrijver, Sovereignty over Natural Resources, Balancing Rights and Duties (2008); the common heritage terminology has been especially developed through the Law of the Sea, *see* Convention on the Law of the Sea, U.N. Doc.A/CONF. 62/122 (1982), *reprinted in* 21 I.L.M. 1261, art. 136; on the issue of the common heritage of mankind, *see* Sylvie Paquerot, Le statut des ressources vitales en droit international, Essai sur le concept de patrimoine commun de l'humanité (2002).

92 However, there is a contradiction between the French version, which uses the term "des populations"; on this issue *see* Fatsah Ouguergouz, The African Charter on Human and People's Rights: A Comprehensive Agenda for Human Dignity and Sustainable Development in Africa 287 (2003).

93 Richard Kiwanuka, *The Meaning of 'People' in the African Charter on Human and Peoples' Rights* 82(1) Am. J. Int'l L. 80 (1988).

94 The Social and Economic Rights Action Center and the Center for Economic and Social Rights v. Nigeria, Communication 155/96.

95 Kwadwo Appiagyei-Atua, *Self-Determination v. State Sovereignty: A Critique of the African Commission' Decision in the Ogoni Case, in* International Law & Indigenous Peoples 303 (Joshua Castellino and Niamh Walsh eds., 2005); *see also* Nsongurua Udombana, *The Third World and the Rights to Development: Agenda for the Next Millennium*, 22(3) Hum. Rts. Q. 753 (2000).

to freely dispose of their natural resources running in opposition to the national interest.[96] In many instances, States have relied on the well-established principle of State sovereignty over natural resources to justify encroachment of indigenous territories to access the natural resources located in indigenous peoples' territories.[97] Thus, for indigenous peoples the right of peoples to freely dispose of their natural resources leads to a legal impasse, as ultimately it is States themselves who control the exercise of such a right. On this issue Ouguergouz has concluded that: "[C]onsequently, apart from the case of a successful secession, it is hard to conceive that an ethnic group could freely dispose of—and therefore exclusively enjoy—natural resources situated in the territory in which it is attached."[98]

One of the difficulties with the economical aspect of self-determination is that such a right could be seen from two different perspectives, either as a right of the State or as a right of the peoples.[99] The dominant vision has often been in favour of the States as under most national legal systems control over natural resources is traditionally one of the attributes of State sovereignty. However, more recently there is been an increasing recognition of the importance of the right of peoples to freely dispose of their natural resources, notably in the context of indigenous peoples' rights. The development of the legal framework on indigenous peoples' human rights, and notably its focus on self-determination, has challenged such a State centric approach to control over the use of natural resources.

As highlighted earlier, in terms of human rights law, there are different dimensions to the right to self-determination within Article 1 of the ICCPR, however it is mostly through the resources part (i.e., paragraph 2) that the HRC has addressed indigenous peoples' right to self-determination. For example, in its *Concluding Observations* on Canada, the HRC emphasised that "the right to self-determination requires, *inter alia*, that all peoples must be able to freely dispose of their natural resources and that they may not be deprived of their

96 On this issue, *see* the jurisprudence from the IACHR (Yanomami Decision, Report 12/85, Annual Report of the IACHR 1984–85), the HRC (Länsman et al. v. Finland, U.N. Doc. CCPR/C/52/D/511/1992). *See also* Emeka Duruigbo, *Permanent Sovereignty and Peoples' Ownership of natural Resources in International Law*, 38 Geo. Wash. Int'l L. Rev. 33 (2006).

97 *See* Erica I. Daes, *Indigenous peoples' permanent sovereignty over natural resources*, U.N. Doc. E/CN.4/Sub.2/2004/30 and Add.1.

98 Fatsah Ouguergouz, The African Charter on Human and People's Rights: A Comprehensive Agenda for Human Dignity and Sustainable Development in Africa 288 (2003).

99 See Jérémie Gilbert, *The Right to Freely Dispose of Natural Resources: Utopia or Forgotten Right?*, Netherlands Quarterly of Human Rights Vol. 31/3, 295–322 (2013).

own means of subsistence (art. 1, para. 2)."[100] Likewise, the Committee has invited Norway to report "on the Saami peoples' right to self-determination under article 1 of the Covenant, including paragraph 2 of that article."[101] References to indigenous peoples' right to self-determination were also made in the *Concluding Observations* on Mexico, Australia, Denmark and Sweden. This approach fleshes out the evolution of human rights law towards a specific form of indigenous peoples' right to self-determination based on control over natural resources. In this context, self-determination does not only ensure a right of access to subsistence (as examined in Chapter 4) but also the right to freely dispose of their natural wealth and resources "for their own ends" as Article 1(2) of the two Covenants seeks to guarantee.

This second aspect of control over the natural resources contained in indigenous territories is crucial, as the "subsistence" aspect of self-determination is limited to an obligation for States to ensure that indigenous peoples are not deprived of their means of subsistence—an approach that remains entrenched in a rather paternalistic view of society. From a contemporary perspective, in which self-determination as a principle should bring freedom of choice to oppressed peoples, self-determination ought to be more than a right not to be deprived of one's own means of subsistence. Hence, the development of an interpretation, which sees self-determination as meaning the free control over natural resources, represents an important step.

This approach to self-determination is not only doctrinal, or limited to international human rights treaty bodies, as there are some echoes of this approach within the jurisprudence of the regional human rights institutions. For example, the Inter-American Court of Human Rights has made direct reference to the importance of the right to self-determination of indigenous peoples in relations to their right to freely determine the way the natural resources located on their lands are used. In the case of the *Saramaka People*, the Court explained that indigenous peoples "property rights must be interpreted so as not to restrict their right to self-determination, by virtue of which indigenous peoples may 'freely pursue their economic, social and cultural development' and may 'freely dispose of their natural wealth and resources.'"[102] The African Commission on Human and Peoples' Rights has also highlighted the connection between the right to self-determination, control of natural

100 *Concluding Observations*, Canada, U.N. Doc. CCPR/C/79/Add.105 (Apr. 7, 1999).

101 *Concluding Observations*, Norway, U.N. Doc. CCPR/C/79/Add.112 (1999).

102 *Saramaka People v. Suriname*, para. 93.

resources and land rights. In the Endorois decision, the Commission found that the non-respect of the right to land of the indigenous community a violation of Article 21 of the African Charter which states that "all peoples shall freely dispose of their wealth and natural resources." In finding a violation of Article 21, the Commission did acknowledge that the right to freely dispose of natural resources is of crucial importance to indigenous peoples and their way of life.[103] A similar approach was adopted in the case of Kaliña and Lokono peoples against Suriname.[104] The Court stated: "the right to property protected by Article 21 of the American Convention, and interpreted in light of the rights recognized in Article 1 common to the two Covenants, and Article 27 of the ICCPR which cannot be restricted when interpreting the American Convention in this case, confer on the members of the Kaliña and Lokono peoples the right to the enjoyment of their property in keeping with their community-based tradition."[105] This emerging jurisprudence linking self-determination, control over natural resources and land rights certainly represents an important development knowing that for most indigenous communities the notion of territory includes a collective rights-based approach to the access, disposal and use of the natural resources.

From this perspective, the right to self-determination represents an important legal platform to ensure that land rights are guaranteed and protected when natural resources exploitation is taking place on indigenous territories. The importance of linking control of natural resources and land rights was also put forward as an important element in the UN study on indigenous peoples' permanent sovereignty over natural resources.[106] The study notably highlighted that for indigenous peoples, territorial claim implies the direct enjoyment of their right to self-determination over their natural resources, including the right to freely dispose of these resources. As examined below, one of the practical applications of this correlation between self-determination, land rights and control over natural resources has emerged under the banner of a right to consent to natural resources exploitation.

---

103 On the correlation between cultural rights and access to natural resources, see also: *Social and Economic Rights Action Center and the Center for Economic, and Social Rights/Nigeria*, Communication No. 155/96.

104 *Case of the Kaliña and Lokono Peoples v. Suriname*, Judgment of November 25, 2015 (Merits, Reparations and Costs).

105 Ibid, at para. 124. Interestingly the Court has also included an examination of Article 23 of the American Convention relating to the right to participate in government (para. 126).

106 *Indigenous peoples' permanent sovereignty over natural resources*, UN Doc. E/CN.4/Sub.2/2004/30 and Add.1.

2 *Self-determination and Free, Prior, and Informed Consent*

A major limitation to the interpretation of the right to self-determination as meaning participation is that such an approach is about the right to engage with the national governmental structures, an approach that may not accommodate indigenous peoples' aspirations and cultures. For indigenous peoples, self-determination contains the promise of granting them the right to determine the ownership of their territories based on their own traditions. The view of self-determination as a right to participate relies on indigenous peoples' acceptance of territorial rights as established by States in which indigenous peoples' views are often scorned or not recognised, whereas self-determination should be about special accommodation for indigenous peoples' approaches to territorial rights. In this context, political participation is a step towards self-determination, as Turpel puts it: "participation rights may be useful or, more likely, essential on the road to the recognition of self-determination."[107] However, it is important to keep in mind that, ultimately, self-determination is about the right of a people to freely determine their political status and freely pursue their economic, social and cultural development. Knowing that land rights are a fundamental element of indigenous peoples' political, economic, social and cultural development, it is certain that self-determination should grant them the right to freely determine the use of their territories that are so central to their cultures.

The recent developments of indigenous peoples' land rights as part of the "democratic" entitlement contained in the norm of self-determination are undoubtedly significant, as such evolution guarantees indigenous peoples with a right to participate in decisions that directly affect their territories; however, this does not provide indigenous peoples the right to freely decide on developments that would affect their rights over their territories. At this stage, it is crucial to bear in mind that indigenous peoples are, by definition, in a non-dominant situation in the society in which they live.[108] Thus, even though a right for indigenous peoples to participate in decisions affecting their lands is promising, this approach remains entrenched within a sense of dependency,

107 Mary Ellen Turpel, *Indigenous Peoples' Rights of Political Participation and Self-Determination: Recent International Legal Developments and the Continuing Struggle for Recognition*, 25 Cornell Int'l L.J. 593 (1992).

108 The different definitions on who indigenous peoples are all concur on the fact that indigenous peoples form a non-dominant sector of the population. For references, *see* Timo Makkonen, Identity, Difference and Otherness, The Concepts of 'Peoples,' 'Indigenous People' and 'Minority' in International Law (2000); Benedict Kingsbury, *Indigenous Peoples' in International Law: A Constructivist Approach to the Asian Controversy*, 92 Am. J. Int'l L. 414 (1998).

as, ultimately, indigenous peoples might participate, but their views might not be heard. In this scenario indigenous peoples can participate in a choice that would be imposed by the majority of the State in which they live. What self-determination is really about in this context is what Steiner has qualified as the "take part clause" of the right to political participation.[109] In this approach, indigenous peoples have no right to determine their own destiny, but only a right to agree or not to a destiny imposed by the "other people" forming the State in which they live.

Based on the central importance of the relationship to their territories for indigenous peoples, the right to freely determine their political status and freely pursue their economic, social and cultural development should undoubtedly embrace their right to freely determine the use and ownership of their territories. Thus, in terms of land rights, self-determination ought to be about the right of indigenous peoples to freely decide on development programs affecting their territories, not only the right to participate in the decisions that would affect them. It is based on that perspective that the notion of consent has been emerging, notably as an expression of the right to self-determination. For example, the CESCR in its *Concluding Observations* on Colombia urged the State party to consult and seek the consent of the indigenous peoples concerned by the implementation of timber, soil or sub-soil mining projects affecting them.[110] To arrive to such statement, the Committee referred to the notion of consent as contained in ILO 169 to which Colombia is a State party, and thus highlighted the interdependence of self-determination as contained in Article 1 of the Covenant and the obligations of prior consent contained in ILO 169.[111] What emerges from this approach is that the concrete application of the right to self-determination leads to the notion of consent.

In terms of international instruments, the UNDRIP makes clear that indigenous peoples should consent to decisions affecting their lands and resources.[112] This is the angle that is developed in Article 32 of the Declaration, which reads:

> Indigenous peoples have the right to determine and develop priorities and strategies for the development or use of their lands or territories and

109 *See* Henry Steiner, *Political Participation as a Human Right*, 1 Harv. Y.B. Int'l L. 77 (1988).

110 CESCR, *Concluding Observations*, Colombia, U.N. Doc. E/C.12/1/Add.74, paras. 12 and 33 (Nov. 30, 2001); *see also Concluding Observations*, Brazil, U.N. Doc. E/C.12/1/Add.87, para. 58 (May 23, 2003).

111 Article 6(2) of ILO 169 states: "the consultations carried out in application of this Convention shall be undertaken, in good faith and in a form appropriate to the circumstances, with the objective of achieving agreement or consent to the proposed measures."

112 See U.N. Declaration on the Rights of Indigenous Peoples at arts. 10, 11, 18, 32.

> other resources. States shall consult and cooperate in good faith with the indigenous peoples concerned through their own representative institutions in order to obtain their free and informed consent prior to the approval of any project affecting their lands or territories and other resources, particularly in connection with the development, utilization or exploitation of their mineral, water or other resources.

This article refers to the right of indigenous peoples to determine the use of their lands, vocabulary that reflects upon the content of self-determination. While this article does not mention self-determination, the debates that lead to the adoption of such article relied heavily on the language of self-determination. For example, during one of the discussions of the WGDD, Norway proposed that this article be divided into two different parts and removed from the cluster on land rights, to be re-clustered in the discussion on self-determination.[113] Other documents also illustrate how the right to self-determination was instrumental in pushing for the adoption of a right to free, prior and informed consent.[114] As a working paper from the WGIP on the issue of free, prior and informed consent highlighted "the universal and continuing applicability of the fundamental right of peoples to self-determination is the general principle underlying free, prior and informed consent."[115] Regarding land rights, the working paper concluded that "self-determination of peoples and the corollary right of free, prior informed consent, is integral to indigenous peoples' control over their lands and territories, to the enjoyment and practice of their cultures, and to make choices over their own economic, cultural and social development."[116] As highlighted earlier, self-determination refers to the right for peoples to freely determine their political status, to freely determine pursue their economic, social and cultural development and freely dispose of their natural wealth and resources. Thus, knowing that control over their territories is inextricably related to their political, economic, social and cultural developments, any meaningful application of self-determination ought to provide indigenous peoples with a right to consent to decisions that are affecting their territories. The notion of consent is pivotal to the idea of a right for

113 *See* U.N. Doc. E/CN.4/2003/92.

114 For an in depth and rich analysis, see Cathal Doyle, Indigenous Peoples, Title to Territory, Rights and Resources: The Transformative Role of Free Prior and Informed Consent (2015).

115 *Expanded working paper submitted by Mrs. Antoanella-Iulia Motoc and the Tebtebba Foundation offering guidelines to govern the practice of Implementation of the principle of free, prior and informed consent of indigenous peoples in relation to development affecting their lands and natural resources*, U.N. Doc. E/CN.4/Sub.2/AC.4/2005/WP.1, at 33.

116 *Id.* at 45.

peoples to freely dispose of their natural resources. From this perspective, the affirmation of the right to free, prior and informed consent before the exploitation of any natural resources contained on indigenous territory constitutes a concrete application of the right to self-determination.[117]

The interconnection between control over natural resources, land rights and consent is also reflected within the jurisprudence of the regional human rights institutions. In a case concerning a Mayan community in Belize, the Inter-American Commission has recognised that the authorities had violated the rights of the community to property by allowing the exploitation of timber and oil on their ancestral lands.[118] The Commission highlighted that the exploitation of the resources contain on the land of the indigenous community would require the fully informed consent of the community, which requires "at a minimum, that all of the members of the community are fully and accurately informed of the nature and consequences of the process and provided with an effective opportunity to participate individually or as collectives."[119] The Commission held that the obligation to obtain indigenous peoples "consent applies to all State decisions, including the granting of natural resource exploitation concessions, that may have an impact upon indigenous lands and communities." This approach was echoed in the African Commission on Human and Peoples' Rights decision in the case of the Endorois community of Kenya.[120] In this case the African Commission found Kenya in violation of article 21 of the African Charter affirming peoples' right to freely dispose of their natural resources for not having undertaken proper consultation with the concerned indigenous community and not having obtained their consent.[121] These situations are all pointing towards the importance of ensuring that indigenous peoples' right to freely determine the use of the natural resources located on their lands is respected. In that context the right to FPIC is a direct application

117 See: Cathal Doyle & Jeremie Gilbert, "Indigenous Peoples and Globalization: From 'Development Aggression' to 'Self-Determined Development'", European Yearbook of Minority Issues, Volume 8 (2009), 219–62.

118 Maya Indigenous Community of the Toledo District v. Belize, Case 12.053, Report No. 40/04, Inter-Am. C.H.R., OEA/Ser.L/V/II.122 Doc. 5, rev. 1, para. 117 (2004).

119 Ibid, para. 142.

120 African Commission on Human and Peoples' Rights, Centre for Minority Rights Development (Kenya) and Minority Rights Group International on behalf of Endorois Welfare Council v Kenya, Communication 276/2003 (hereinafter: Endorois Case). The decision was adopted by the African Commission in May 2009 and approved by the African Union at its January 2010 meeting.

121 See: Jérémie Gilbert, *Indigenous Peoples' Human Rights in Africa: the Pragmatic Revolution of the African Commission on Human and Peoples' Rights*, International & Comparative Law Quarterly, vol 60, (January 2011), pp. 37–62.

of the right to self-determination as it implies the possibility for indigenous peoples to decide, and eventually withhold consent, to development projects that would affect their territories.

However, whilst undeniably the emergence of the right to FPIC as a concrete application of the right to self-determination is an important and welcomed step, it is important to highlight that it is only one limited and specific application of the right to self-determination. Indeed consent is certainly offering a much more active and free role for indigenous peoples than mere participation,[122] however it still remains a limited and truncated version of self-determination. As highlighted in this chapter, the right to self-determination reflects deeper aspirations to freedom for many indigenous peoples; it implies an act of free will on behalf of the indigenous party, which is not entirely reflected in the consent approach to self-determination. As pointed out by Brilmayer, even though consent is about making choices, these choices are limited to a set of choices that the State would impose based on the amount of its sovereign power.[123] From this perspective, self-determination should reflect deeper aspirations to a right to freely determine one's own destiny, not only a right to rely on prior assignment of entitlements that are made available by the State.

Conclusion

As examined in this chapter, indigenous peoples have clearly played an important role in pushing for a new contemporary interpretation of the right to self-determination. This evolution is notably based on insisting on the potential of the right to self-determination to encompass claims to territorial resources as an essential element of international human rights law. In this context, self-determination appears as a valuable mechanism to address controversial territorial claims being one of only legal principles that create a links between historical claims to sovereignty, control of natural resources and the contemporary relationships between States and indigenous peoples. It is also one of the very few legal rights which include both the civil and political aspects of land rights and its economic, social and cultural elements. From an indigenous perspective, it is heartening to see that the issue of control over territory has finally been linked to the principle of self-determination in its totality including its economic, social and cultural aspects, as well as the civil and political ones. It is an important evolution as for too long self-determination

122 This is discussed into more details in Chapter 6.

123 Lea Brilmayer, *Consent, Contract, and Territory*, 74 Minn. L. Rev. 1 (1989–1990).

has been narrowly interpreted as mainly a political right. Self-determination has been the guiding spirit of both American and French revolutions, one of the leading principles of post-First World War Europe and, finally, a right for peoples under the yoke of colonisation.[124] So historically, self-determination is an evolving force. Thus, even though in many respects the debates relating to self-determination remain entrenched in the post-colonial perspective, indigenous peoples' claim to self-determination is another central development in the history of self-determination. Indigenous peoples' "appropriation" of self-determination brings together notions of ethnicity and territoriality. It is clear that the issue of indigenous peoples' land rights has played a tremendous role in this maturation of indigenous claims to self-determination.

Overall, while indigenous peoples' claim to self-determination attracts a lot of controversy, they have succeeded in proving that self-determination is a living and evolving principle of human rights law, which plays an increasing role in the development of their land rights. In this regard, self-determination for indigenous peoples should be seen as an interesting new chapter in the on-going development of self-determination. Based on this approach, self-determination should be a guiding principle for territorial negotiations between States and indigenous peoples based on equal rights. In the contemporary evolution towards a strong corpus of indigenous peoples' land rights under international law, self-determination could prove to be an efficient platform for territorial negotiations between States and indigenous peoples.

As noted in this chapter an important aspect of this new evolution of the right to self-determination concerns its relationship with indigenous peoples' land rights. On the interaction between self-determination and land rights for indigenous peoples, the overall evolution towards a 'relational' approach to self-determination is built on the cultural and livelihood connections to natural resources, as well as the right of indigenous peoples to participate in decisions affecting their territories. In examining the different interpretations of the right to self-determination when it comes to land rights, two main aspects and consequences of self-determination seem to be emerging. First self-determination implies the right of indigenous peoples to participate in the decisions that affect their territories. Second, it refers to a right to access natural resources as part of indigenous peoples' right to economic development and means of subsistence, or what has often been described as the "economic" aspect of self-determination.

With limitations (see discussions above) these two aspects of the right to self-determination are parts of an evolving understanding of self-determination regarding indigenous peoples. What has also been highlighted is that under

124 *See* Cassese, *supra* note 4.

international law, self-determination is a right in constant evolution, and thus should not be set rigidly in a precise narrow 'internal' interpretation. Approaching self-determination as a 'relational' principle inviting for territorial negotiations would positively impact the imbalance of power created by the dispossession of indigenous peoples' land that were imposed through the establishment of state territorial sovereignty.[125] This notion of a 'relational' approach to self-determination corresponds with the mutual respect that Daes mentioned when she described the "true spirit" of self-determination for indigenous peoples.[126] In this regard, the mix of democratic rights and territorial issues embedded in the right to self-determination could certainly play an increasingly important role in the future. It invites a new approach as ultimately it is framed within the context of a dialogue between States and indigenous peoples to negotiate some territorial arrangement. In this dialogue it is important that the right to self-determination is given a prominent place as ultimately it is the legal principle which should support the fundamental right of indigenous peoples to freely determine decisions regarding their territories. It certain the self-determination has greatly evolved from a concept which was understood as meaning Statehood in the immediate post-colonial era to become now connected with decision regarding the use, management, and control of lands and natural resources. This new and more comprehensive understanding of self-determination invites for new challenges as indeed it puts forward the notion that States are not anymore the only actors of decisions regarding on how lands and natural resources should be used. This refocus on the fundamental right to self-determination of indigenous peoples over their own natural resources undoubtedly constitutes an important development at a time of scarcity and increased marketization and exploitation of natural resources. It puts indigenous peoples at the frontline as its supports the fundamental principle that they have the right to freely determine the way their lands, and the natural resources should be used, protected, and respected based on their own terms. This evolution puts indigenous peoples at the frontline of issues related to development, conservation and more generally economic globalisation. It is towards those issues that the book is now turning its attention as in many ways the doctrinal and fundamental debate that is based on the right to self-determination needs to be evaluated in the context of development and economic globalisation to judge on its relevance and efficiency.

125 *See* Chapters 1 and 2.

126 Erica I. Daes, *The Spirit and the Letter of the Right to Self-determination of Indigenous Peoples: Reflections on the Making of the United Nations Draft Declaration, in* Aikio & Scheinin, *supra* note 2, at 74.

CHAPTER 6

Development, Globalisation and Land Rights

> We are not against the developments, but our way of living has to be taken into account.
>
> CARLO LEWIS, Village Chief of Apura, Lokono Indigenous Community, Suriname[1]

The constant and ever-increasing demand for primary natural resources necessary to the global economy is having a particularly negative impact on the livelihood of many indigenous peoples across the globe. Usually living in areas rich in natural wealth, indigenous peoples' lives are deeply affected by the exploitation of natural resources as well as by development projects which are affecting their rights lands and natural resources. The large-scale exploitation of natural resources, including subsoil resources often entails the development of considerable infrastructures for transportation and exploitation of these resources. In many situations this has a direct impact on indigenous peoples' land rights as they see their lands degraded but also their rights to use these territories obfuscated. In many ways such phenomenon is not recent as indigenous peoples have historically experienced many waves of globalisation, with colonisation being an important one.[2] However it seems that the more recent tide of economic globalisation is pushing the quest for natural resources to new levels under which no indigenous community remains immune. This chapter focuses on the impact that globalisation has on indigenous peoples' land rights.

There are as many definitions of globalisation as disagreements regarding its meanings, but in this context globalisation refers to a process by which the world is becoming increasingly interconnected as a result of increased trade and cultural exchange.[3] It is also not entirely sure whether globalisation is a

---

1 'Implementation of the Kabalebo Project: Land Rights Capture the attention of Indigenous Peoples in Southern Suriname', *De Ware Tijd*, 05 May 2005 (Original in Dutch), as quoted in *Indigenous Peoples' Rights, Extractive Industries and Transnational and Other Business Enterprises: A Submission to the Special Representative of the Secretary-General on human rights and transnational corporations and other business enterprises* (Forest Peoples Programme and Tebtebba Foundation, 2006).

2 See: K.S. Coates, A Global History of Indigenous Peoples: Struggle and Survival (2004).

3 For a discussion on the concept of globalization see Thomas Hylland Eriksen, Globalization (2007); Jurgen Osterhammel and Niels P. Petersson, Globalization: A Short History (2009); and David Kinley, Civilising Globalisation Human Rights and the Global Economy (2009).

distinctive new phenomenon, rather than the continuation of the global history of mankind.[4] However, the current wave of economic globalisation possesses distinctive features. Broadly speaking, economic globalisation, in its current manifestation, refers to the emergence of a globalized commercial market premised on the free movement of capital and increasing levels of consumerism with reductions on controls in relation to the movement of goods. An important aspect of such globalisation is the central role played by global private actors, notably transnational corporations and investors.[5]

Another specific aspect of the current and on-going wave of globalisation relates to its drivers which seem to be particularly affecting indigenous peoples. In the last few years, the very large increase in land investments, mainly in developing countries, has been labelled a 'land grab', a term which has now entered the international lexicon. This 'land grab' is driven by the increased marketization of land and its potential production. This is the result of many related phenomenon including the globalisation of agricultural production, the quest for food security by countries lacking arable lands, the strive for investment in energy and biofuel security ventures and other climate change mitigation strategies, and recent demands for resources from newer hubs of global capital. This 'global land rush' is very often negatively impacting indigenous peoples who due to discrimination, lack of recognition of land tenure and extreme marginalisation are seeing a drastic loss of access to their own lands and territories.[6] Another factor of the globalisation of the economy that has a significant impact is the considerable rise of tourism taking place on indigenous peoples' territories. Tourism has had a significant impact on indigenous peoples' land rights. While there are a few positive situations where tourism has supported the rights of indigenous peoples, in general across the globe tourism has been synonymous with more land destitution for indigenous peoples.[7]

Closely related to the development of large-scale tourism on indigenous territories is the increasing establishment of wildlife and natural reserves across the globe. The conservation effort and the establishment of natural and wildlife reserves is not a new phenomenon, but over the last decades the

4 See Robert O. Keohane and Joseph S. Nye Jr., *Globalization: What's New? What's Not? (And So What?)*, 118 Foreign Policy (2000), 104–19.

5 See: Francis Snyder, *Economic globalisation and the law in the 21st century*, in Sarat, Austin, (ed.) The Blackwell Companion to Law and Society (2004).

6 See: Jérémie Gilbert, *Land Grabbing, Investors, and Indigenous Peoples: New legal strategies for an old practice?* Community Development Journal 2015.

7 See: Alison M. Johnston, Is the Sacred For Sale? Tourism and Indigenous Peoples (2005).

numbers of lands that have been transformed into nature reserves has been largely expanding. Whilst undoubtedly this is a positive evolution which supports a more sustainable and environmental use of the planet, for many indigenous peoples this has often resulted in serious violations of their land rights. It is not possible to list all the different aspects, both positive and negative, that the increased globalisation of the economy is having on indigenous peoples, but some of these drivers that are based on notions of development and the protection of the environment deserve specific attention as they put in the balance contradictory rights and discourse. Contradictory as it seems that on the one hand governments, international developmental agencies, conservation societies and corporations are using the larger umbrella of development and conservation of natural resources to justify the encroachment on indigenous peoples' territories, whilst on the other hand indigenous peoples are claiming that such encroachments are in violation of the fundamental human rights, notably their right to development. By focusing on the connection between development, globalisation and land rights, the aim of the chapter is to analyse the relevance of the human rights-based approach to indigenous peoples' land rights in this context.

To undertake such a journey the chapter is divided into three main sections. The first section focuses on the notion of development with the aim of analysing how the right to development could play an important role in protecting indigenous peoples' land rights. The second section focuses on natural resources management and its impact on indigenous peoples' land rights.[8] The management of natural resources located on indigenous peoples territories has often been dominated by misappropriation of land, environmental degradation coupled with a denial of human rights and prevailing insecurities, including in some situations conflicts and violence. This section examines the issue of ownership, control and management of natural resources which is increasingly becoming a central battleground to define land rights. Based on this analysis, the third section focuses on the principal actors and industries that are affecting indigenous territories, namely conservation, tourism and extractive industries. An important legal development that this chapter wishes to examine relates to the increased focus on the role and place of non-state actors when it comes to human rights law, and notably their impact on the rights of indigenous peoples to land and natural resources. This relates to the increased focus on the role of transnational corporations, and notably the extractive industries, when it comes to their impact on indigenous peoples' land rights.

8 Natural Resources Management (NRM) refers to the sustainable utilization of major natural resources, such as land, water, air, minerals, forests, fisheries, and wild flora and fauna.

A Development, Participation and Land Rights

This section focuses on the relevance of the human rights approach to development since a strong link can be made between the right to development and security of land tenure, access and management of natural resources, for indigenous peoples. First it examines the content of the right to development and how it relates to land rights. In doing so it explores how development, and notably large-scale developmental projects can negatively impact indigenous peoples' rights to their lands and territories, and how in this context development has often been termed as 'an aggression.' This context of 'development aggression' is put into perspective regarding the right to development and its jurisprudential analysis. Based on this overview on the right to development, the second sub-section focuses on notions of consultation, effective participation and consent as practical and procedural ways to implement the right to development. The aim of the section is to analyse how the right to development, with its procedural aspects relating to participation and consultation, could support indigenous peoples' land rights.

1 *'Development Aggression', the Right to Development and Land Rights*

States often justify the removal of indigenous peoples from their lands as a necessity for national development. As described by Ngugi in the African context, in State rhetoric the issue of indigenous peoples' rights is often classified as a "development problem."[9] Based on this "developmental" perspective, States often argue that they have a duty to support the "development" and "modernisation" of indigenous peoples; thus, States intervene in indigenous peoples' territories to ensure a "modern" use of natural resources to support development. This rhetoric is not limited to Africa, as across the globe governments have also reverted to the notion of development to justify their encroachment on indigenous peoples' territories.[10] In this context, States raise the banner of economic development to justify the removal of indigenous peoples from

9 Joel Ngugi, *The Decolonization-Modernization Interface and the Plight of Indigenous Peoples in Post-Colonial Development Discourse in Africa*, 20 Wis. Int'l L.J. 297 (2002); *see also* Nsongurua Udombana, *How Should We Then Live? Globalization and the New Partnership for Africa's Development*, 20 B.U. Int'l L.J. 1 (2002).

10 Development or Domestication?: Indigenous Peoples of Southeast Asia (Don McCaskill & Ken Kampe eds., 1997); Jenny R. Culler, *The U'wa Struggle to Protect their Cultural Land: A Framework for Reviewing Questions of Sovereignty and the Right to Environmental Integrity for Indigenous Peoples*, 29 Ga. J. Int'l & Comp. L. 335 (2001); Karen Bravo, *Balancing Indigenous Rights to Land and the Demand of Economic Development: Lessons from the United states and Australia*, 30 Colum. J.L. & Soc. Probs. 529 (1997).

their lands based on the precept that development could be undermined by granting indigenous peoples a right to control the use of natural resources contained in their lands.[11] The other rhetorical element used by States to justify such encroachment is that development needs to be 'brought' to indigenous peoples. This approach to development, which is based on a very State-centric vision, reposes on what Nader refereed to the "theory of lack" under which less "developed" segments of the society, mainly the marginalised cultures, are seen as lacking proper development which then needs to be imposed on them.[12] In many ways this top-down approach to development is not entirely different to previous waves of colonisation. As Daes has observed:

> The legacy of colonialism is probably most acute in the area of expropriation of indigenous lands, territories and resources for national economic and development interests. In every part of the globe, indigenous peoples are being impeded from proceeding with their own forms of development consistent with their own values, perspectives and interests.[13]

The UN Special Rapporteurs on indigenous peoples' rights, past and present, have all highlighted the largely negative impact that large-scale developmental projects have on indigenous peoples' land rights. For example, in its thematic report to the Commission on Human Rights in 2003, the former UN Special Rapporteur on the Rights of Indigenous Peoples, Stavenhagen, focused his attention on the impact of large-scale development projects on the human rights of indigenous peoples, highlighting that in most of the situations governments do not take into consideration the rights and interests of indigenous peoples when making plans for major development projects.[14] He reported that usually

11 On this issue, *see* the minority rights and development program of Minority Rights Group, *see* especially Gerardo Gobrin & Almira Andin, *Development Conflict: The Philippine Experience; available at* www.minorityrights.org; *see also Indigenous Peoples and their Right to Development*, U.N. Doc. E/CN.4/Sub.2/AC.4/2001/2.

12 Nadia Nader, *Promise or Plunder? A Past and Future Look at Law and Development,* Global Jurist 7(2), (2007).

13 Daes, 2001 at 21.

14 Report of the Special Rapporteur, UN Doc.E/CN.4/2003/90, the Special Rapporteur pointed out that by "major development project" should be understood a process of investment of public and/or private, national or international capital for the purpose of building or improving the physical infrastructure of a specified region, the transformation over the long run of productive activities involving changes in the use and property rights to land, the large-scale exploitation of natural resources including subsoil resources, the building of urban centres, manufacturing and/or mining and extraction plants, tourist developments, port facilities, military bases and similar undertakings.", p. 2.

"the concerns of indigenous peoples who are seldom consulted on the matter, take a back seat to an overriding 'national interest', or to market-driven business objectives aimed at developing new economic activities, and maximizing productivity and profits."[15] In reaction indigenous peoples have used the term "development aggression" to describe these situations.[16] These types of aggressive developments can take many forms, including the development of large-scale infrastructures on indigenous territories, such as dams or major roads, or the inevitable degradation of the environment which goes with the exploitation of natural resources, such as mining or logging.

In many situations aggressive forms of development also arise as a result of activities related to the tourism industry and conservation. Many indigenous communities, especially in Africa, have suffered from the establishment of wildlife and tourism reserves on their lands, which has resulted in their forced removal or serious limitations to their rights of access to their territories. All these developments usually take place under the banner of national development. As aptly captured by Saugestad in the case of Botswana, such national policies are usually based on "authoritarian and patronising model for development, elevating the preferred lifestyle of the majority to the national norm."[17] To resist such rhetoric on national development, indigenous peoples often put forward the counter argument of their right to development as a fundamental human right. Under international law, the right to development is a complex and controversial right.[18] One of the controversies relates to the notion of duty bearers of the right to development notably between 'developed' and 'developing' States and its lack of possible legal enforcement mechanisms. There is a very large literature regarding the complexity and controversies related to the right to development.[19] The focus in this book is not on these aspects but

15 *Ibid* at para. 8, p. 5.

16 *See* Cathal Doyle and Jérémie Gilbert, *Indigenous Peoples and Globalization: From 'Development Aggression' to 'Self-Determined Development'* 8 European Yearbook on Minority Issues 219 (2011).

17 S. Saugestad, *Impact of International Mechanisms on Indigenous Rights in Botswana*, 15 (1) The International Journal of Human Rights 37–61 (2011), at 54.

18 For a review and references, see: Philip Alston, *Making Space for New Human Rights: The Case of the Right to Development*, 1 Harvard Human Rights Yearbook (1988), 3; Daniel Aguirre, The Human Right to Development in A Globalized World (2008); and Koen De Feyter, World Development Law (2001); Margot Salomon, Global Responsibility for Human Rights: World Poverty and the Development of International Law (2007).

19 See references in previous footnote as well as: Olajumoke O. Oduwole, International Law and the Right to Development: A Pragmatic Approach for Africa (2014); S Marks (Ed), Implementing the Right to Development – The Role of International Law (2008).

on whether the right to development as expressed under international human rights law can support indigenous peoples' land rights.

The right to development can be rooted in the provisions of the Charter of the United Nations, the Universal Declaration on Human Rights, the two International Covenants and the African Charter on Human and Peoples' Rights. In terms of human rights law, while common Article 1 on the right to self-determination of the two Covenants (Covenant on Civil and Political Rights and the Covenant on Economic Social and Cultural Rights) establishes the right of all peoples "to freely pursue their economic, social and cultural development" it was not until 1986, when the UN Declaration on the Right to Development was adopted, that the relationship between development and human rights was given serious and focused consideration by States. Crucially, its article 1 affirms that "the right to development is an inalienable human right by virtue of which every human person and all peoples are entitled to participate in, contribute to, and enjoy economic, social, cultural and political development, in which all human rights and fundamental freedoms can be fully realized." It also adds that the right to development "implies the full realization of the right of peoples to self-determination which includes…the exercise of their inalienable right to full sovereignty over all their natural wealth and resources." However, the Declaration does not make any specific reference to the rights of indigenous peoples. The content of the right was further elaborated by the former UN Independent Expert on the Right to Development, Sengupta, who made specific reference to States' obligations to ensure that indigenous peoples "have access to productive assets such as land, credit and means of self-employment."[20]

Regarding the legal framework on the right to development, the specific international instruments dedicated to the rights of indigenous peoples put more specific emphasis on the right to development and its connection to land rights. Several provisions of the ILO Convention 169 relate to indigenous peoples' right to development and its relationship with land rights. The Convention puts a great emphasis on the need to ensure the direct participation of indigenous peoples in development polices. Article 7 states:

> The peoples concerned shall have the right to decide their own priorities for the process of development as it affects their lives, beliefs, institutions

20 The Right to Development Report of the Independent Expert on the Right to Development, Dr. Arjun Sengupta, pursuant to General Assembly Resolution 54/175 and Commission on Human Rights Resolution E/CN.4/RES/2000/5, 11 September 2000, UN Doc. E/CN.4/2000/WG.18/CRP 1, para. 67.

> and spiritual well-being and the lands they occupy or otherwise use, and to exercise control, to the extent possible, over their own economic, social and cultural development. In addition, they shall participate in the formulation, implementation and evaluation of plans and programmes for national and regional development which may affect them directly.[21]

Likewise the UNDRIP includes several references to the right to development. The Preamble of the Declaration specifically links development and land rights in affirming: "that control by indigenous peoples over developments affecting them and their lands, territories and resources will enable them to maintain and strengthen their institutions."[22] The Preamble also highlights that indigenous peoples' current lack of enjoyment of their right to development, in accordance with their "own needs and interests", is a result of the dispossession of their lands, territories and resources. The enjoyment of land rights is therefore seen as a prerequisite for the realization of their right to development. The right to development is central to many of the articles of the Declaration, including Articles 3, 5, 18, 20, 23 and 34 which are all putting forward the right of indigenous peoples to participate and decide on their own development. More specifically regarding land rights, Article 32 stipulates: "Indigenous peoples have the right to determine and develop priorities and strategies for the development or use of their lands or territories and other resources." It adds that any project affecting their lands or territories and other resources, particularly in connection with the development, should be submitted to their free, prior and informed consent. Overall, the UNDRIP clearly puts forward the right to development as essential rights for indigenous peoples which needs to be connected with their rights to lands and natural resources, and that no developmental project should take place on their territories without their consent.

The best way to judge the relevance of the right to development in the context of land rights for indigenous peoples is to examine its impact in the jurisprudence. There are not many decisions, or rulings, that are addressing the right to development and its consequence in terms of land rights. Under international human rights there has been debate on the theoretical implications of the right to development but very rare instances of legal adjudication. From that perspective the 2010 decision from the African Commission on Human and Peoples' Rights in the case of the Endorois community against Kenya constitutes an important milestone as it focused on the practical implementation of the right to development. In this case a central argument put forward by the

21 ILO 169, art. 7.1; *see also* art. 6.

22 U.N. Declaration, arts. 18, 20, 23 and 36.

government of Kenya to justify the removal of the indigenous community from its territory was the need to support national development as the land was to be used for both tourism and mining purposes. The government argued that tourism and the exploitation of natural resources (notably the mining of ruby) would bring significant resources to the region and the country. The government highlighted the fact that the project for tourism around Lake Borogia was seen as a potential positive development and all the revenues raised by the Game Reserves were re-used to support development projects carried out by the County Council for the area. One of the arguments put forward by the government was that the establishment "of a Game Reserve under the Wildlife laws of Kenya is with the objective of ensuring that wildlife is managed and conserved to yield to the nation in general and to individual areas in particular optimum returns in terms of cultural, aesthetic and scientific gains as well as economic gains as are incidental to proper wildlife management and conservation."[23] The government highlighted that other communities, and the country as a whole, was to benefit from these developments. They also added that the community itself knew about the mining concession and would benefit from its exploitation. The government concluded "the task of communities within a participatory democracy is to contribute to the well-being of society at large and not only to care selfishly for one's own community at the risk of others."[24] It is worth noting that such argument put forward by the government of Kenya is not unusual. Indeed when it comes to development and exploitation of natural resources States often put forward the argument that they cannot stop such large-scale developments that will bring significant wealth to the whole country to protect just a few 'marginalised' indigenous peoples.[25]

By contrast, the advocate for the Endorois argued that such developmental projects were taking place in violation of their right to development protected under Article 22 of the African Charter, since they were not involved in the development process and were not benefiting from it. Article 22 of the African Charter states: "All peoples shall have the right to their economic, social and cultural development with due regard to their freedom and identity and in the equal enjoyment of the common heritage of mankind." The Endorois contended that regarding the development taking place on their lands, their

23 African Commission on Human and Peoples' Rights, *Centre for Minority Rights Development (Kenya) and Minority Rights Group International on behalf of Endorois Welfare Council v Kenya*, Communication 276/2003 (2010), para. 178.

24 Id., para. 270.

25 See: In the Way of Development: Indigenous Peoples, Life Projects and Globalization (Mario Blaser, Harvey A. Feit, and Glenn McRae, 2004).

only choice was to actually leave the lake; they argued that this lack of choice was a violation of their right to development which should be equitable, non-discriminatory, participatory, accountable and transparent. The indigenous community contended that Kenya had violated their right to development by its failure to adequately involve them in the development process taking place on their customary lands as well as its failure to ensure the continued improvement of the community's well-being. Finally, the Endorois highlighted that the government "did not embrace a rights-based approach to economic growth, which insists on development in a manner consistent with, and instrumental to, the realisation of human rights and the right to development through adequate and prior consultation."[26] It is not so much the legitimacy of the decision of the government in turning the land into a tourism and wildlife reserve that the community was contesting but rather the way such decisions were made and notably the lack of consideration to their culture and survival. They believed that the Game Reserve and their pastoralist way of life should not be mutually exclusive. An important point put forward by the community was that "self-determination also include the ability to dispose of natural resources as a community wishes, thereby requiring a measure of control over the land."[27] Linking self-determination and development, they highlighted that they had "suffered a loss of well-being through the limitations on their choice and capacities, including effective and meaningful participation in projects that will affect them."[28]

Hence, the African Commission was asked to balance the two competing claims on the scope of the right to development. Adopting a pragmatic focus, the Commission concentrated on two principal issues: (1) to what extent was the community consulted prior to the establishment of the wildlife reserve on their lands and (2) whether such development provides benefit to the concerned community. Regarding the scope of the right to development, the Commission highlighted that "the right to development is a two-pronged test, that it is both constitutive and instrumental, or useful as both a means and an end. A violation of either the procedural or substantive element constitutes a violation of the right to development."[29] Regarding the procedural aspect of the right to development, the Commission found that the consultations undertaken with the community were inadequate and could not be considered to constitute effective participation. The Commission observed that the

26 Endorois Case, *supra* note 23, para. 135.

27 Id., para. 129.

28 Id., para. 129.

29 Id., para. 277.

"community members were informed of the impending project as a fait accompli, and not given an opportunity to shape the policies or their role in the Game Reserve."[30] Moreover the forced eviction of the community from its land took away any possible form of participation to the project. Importantly, regarding the content of such participation, the Commission stated: "(...) even though the Respondent State says that it has consulted with the Endorois community, the African Commission is of the view that this consultation was not sufficient. It is convinced that the Respondent State did not obtain the prior, informed consent of all the Endorois before designating their land as a Game Reserve and commencing their eviction."[31] On the second aspect, the substantive element of the right to development, the Commission put the emphasis on the fact that the result of development should be empowerment of the Endorois community. In this case the Commission found a violation of the State's obligation to ensure and support such process of empowerment. The failure to provide adequate compensation and benefits emerging from these development meant that the indigenous community was left out of the development process. The Commission added that it supported the view that "the Endorois, as beneficiaries of the development process, were entitled to an equitable distribution of the benefits derived from the Game Reserve."[32]

From a global legal perspective, this aspect of the decision from the African Commission is significant since there are few cases that have specifically focused on the right to development in the context of large-scale developmental projects taking place on indigenous peoples' territories.[33] The decision from the African Commission put forward two interrelated, and essential, elements of the right to development when connected with land rights. First it is a process right which should be operationalized though an effective process of participation rooted into the right to free, prior and informed consent (FPIC). Second, it should translate into direct and tangible compensation and benefits for the concerned communities. Indigenous peoples should benefit from development projects taking place on their territories, an approach which goes against the dominant history of the development aggression faced by most indigenous communities across the globe. It is worth noting that the decision of the African Commission relied on the evolution of the right to development

30 Id., para. 281.

31 Ibid, at 290.

32 Ibid, at para. 297.

33 See: Margot Salomon and Arjun Sengupta, *The right to development: obligations of states and the rights of minorities and indigenous peoples* (Minority Rights Group International, 2003).

under international law and notably its interpretation by the Inter-American Court of Human Rights as well as international human rights treaty bodies.[34] The decision of the African Commission represents an important landmark regarding the practical interpretation of the right to development in connection to land rights. Overall, what comes out strongly from the legal instruments, the doctrinal debates, and the jurisprudence on the right to development is the fundamental importance of ensuring the right of indigenous peoples to effectively participate and provide their informed consent to any development taking place on their territories.

2 *Development, Effective Participation and Consent*

Since the 1993 Vienna Declaration and Program of Action, which "urges states to ensure the full and free participation of indigenous peoples in all aspects of society, in particular in matters of concern to them,"[35] there have been some important developments regarding indigenous peoples' right to participation. In terms of international treaties, the ILO Convention 169 clearly puts a great emphasis on the rights to consultation, participation and consent. The spirit of ILO 169 is based on the notion of participation and consultation.[36] Article 6(2) of ILO 169 states: "the consultations carried out in application of this Convention shall be undertaken, in good faith and in a form appropriate to the circumstances, with the objective of achieving agreement or consent to the proposed measures." The ILO Committee of Experts has emphasized that the spirit of consultation and participation constitutes the essence of Convention 169, which "requires that the parties involved seek to establish a dialogue allowing them to find appropriate solutions in an atmosphere of mutual respect and full participation."[37] The manual on the application of ILO 169 states:

34 See: Serges Alain Djoyou Kamga *The right to development in the African human rights system: The Endorois case* 2 De Jure 381 (2011); and Serges Alain Djoyou Kamga and Charles Manga Fombad, *A Critical Review of the Jurisprudence of the African Commission on the Right to Development*, 57 (2) Journal of African Law 196 (2013).

35 U.N. Doc. A/CONF.157/23, para. 31 (June 25, 1993).

36 *See* arts. 6, 7, 15(2), 17, 22, 27 and 28, Convention Concerning Indigenous and Tribal Peoples in Independent Countries (I.L.O. No. 169), 72 ILO Official Bull. 59, *reprinted in* 28 I.L.M. 1382 (1989), and on these issues, *see* International Labour Organization, ILO Convention on Indigenous and Tribal Peoples, 1989 (No. 169): A Manual 15–20 (2000).

37 *Report of the Committee of Experts set up to examine the representation alleging non-observance by Ecuador of the Indigenous and Tribal Peoples Convention, 1989 (No. 169), made under article 24 of the ILO Constitution by the Confederación Ecuatoriana de Organizaciones Sindicales Libres* (*CEOSL*). Docs. GB.277/18/4, GB.282/14/2, submitted 2000.

> Convention No. 169 gives indigenous and tribal peoples the right to be consulted, and to express their views. It offers them the opportunity to participate in decision-making processes and to influence their outcomes. It provides the space for indigenous and tribal peoples to negotiate to protect their right.[38]

The ILO 169 provides indigenous peoples with bargaining power. This bargaining power is especially relevant in matters concerning indigenous peoples' territorial rights: Article 15 affirms that indigenous peoples have the right to participate in the use, management and conservation of the natural resources pertaining to their lands, and that indigenous peoples should be consulted over decisions relating to mineral or sub-surface resources.

On several occasions the ILO Committee of Experts has pointed out that Articles 13, 14 and 15 of ILO 169 must be read in conjunction with Articles 2(1) and 6, "which require, respectively, that the state develop, with the participation of the affected Indigenous peoples, coordinated and systematic action to respect their rights and guarantee their integrity and; that Indigenous peoples must be consulted with and participate in decisions that affect them."[39] Article 6.1 states that in applying the provisions of this Convention, governments shall:

> consult the peoples concerned, through appropriate procedures and in particular through their representative institutions, whenever consideration is being given to legislative or administrative measures which may affect them directly. (…) Establish means for the full development of these peoples' own institutions and initiatives, and in appropriate cases provide the resources necessary for this purpose.

Thus, there are two aspects to this article: a right for indigenous peoples to participate and be consulted in decisions affecting their natural resources, and a right to self-control in matters concerning their lands through the establishment of their own institutions.

---

38 International Labour Organization, ILO Convention on Indigenous and Tribal Peoples, 1989, No. 169, A Manual 17 (2000).

39 *Report of the Committee set up to examine the representation alleging non-observance by Mexico of the Indigenous and Tribal Peoples Convention, 1989 (No. 169), made under article 24 of the ILO Constitution by the Trade Union Delegation, D-III-57, Section XI of the National Trade Union of Education Workers* (SNTE), *Radio Education*, Docs. GB 270/16/3, GB 272/7/2 (1998).

Similarly, the UNDRIP strongly insists on the duty of States to consult indigenous peoples in any decision that may affect them, and on the duty to ensure indigenous peoples' participation in decision-making. The duty to consult indigenous peoples is reflected in several provisions of the Declaration.[40] More specifically articles 19 and 32(2) require States to consult indigenous peoples in good faith, through appropriate procedures, with the objective of obtaining their agreement or consent when measures that may affect indigenous peoples are considered. Regarding the content of consultation in the context of development, article 32 affirms:

> States shall consult and cooperate in good faith with the indigenous peoples concerned through their own representative institutions in order to obtain their free and informed consent prior to the approval of any project affecting their lands or territories and other resources, particularly in connection with the development, utilization or exploitation of their mineral, water or other resources.

In doing so the UNDRIP highlights the indivisibility of the concepts of development, consultation and FPIC. From this perspective, the right to development embodies the right of indigenous peoples to decide their own development priorities and to participate in any decision relating to developmental projects affecting their lands and resources. Practically, this right is operationalized through the right to FPIC as the aim of any consultation on developmental project taking place on indigenous territories should be to obtain indigenous peoples' consent. As such the right to development, as operationalized via the right to FPIC, should ensure that indigenous territories are included in developmental projects only with their consent. This article on development needs to be read in conjunction with article 10 of the Declaration which relates to situations where indigenous peoples might be removed from their lands or territories. In these situations, their consent is an absolute prerequisite. In the same vein, the Proposed American Declaration refers several times to the right of indigenous peoples to participate in decisions affecting them and regarding the management of their territories.[41]

Indigenous peoples' entitlement to participation, consultation and consent to decisions affecting them is not limited to the instruments especially dedicated to indigenous peoples' rights but is also emerging from the more general international human rights instruments. The central importance of the right

40 Arts. 10, 11, 15, 17, 19, 28, 29, 30, 32, 36, 37 and 38.

41 *See* especially arts. XV(2) and XVIII(5).

to consultation, effective participation and consent is reflected in the practice of the international human rights monitoring bodies. In its General Comment 23, the HRC pointed out that, as part of State obligations under Article 27 of the ICCPR, "Indigenous communities must have effective participation in decisions that affect the community." The Committee has also affirmed that when taking action that might infringe indigenous peoples' rights, states have a duty to consult indigenous peoples.[42] In a 2009 individual opinion concerning an indigenous community in Peru, the Committee explained in details the meaning of effective application in the context of land rights. It stated:

> The Committee considers that participation in the decision-making process must be effective, which requires not mere consultation but the free, prior and informed consent of the members of the community. In addition, the measures must respect the principle of proportionality so as not to endanger the very survival of the community and its members.[43]

This constitutes an important clarification from the Committee, joining the content of indigenous rights defined in both the ILO 169 and the UNDRIP, highlighting that ultimately free, prior, and informed consent constitutes the practical way to put in place a process of effective participation in decisions affecting indigenous peoples' land rights. As noted in both Chapters 4 and 5, the CESCR has also embraced the notion that effective participation in decisions affecting indigenous peoples means that a process of FPIC needs to be in place when such decisions will affect their economic, social and cultural rights.[44]

CERD has also engaged with the connection between the right to consultation, effective participation, development and land rights. In its General Recommendation 23 on indigenous peoples, the Committee pointed out that States have to "ensure that members of indigenous peoples have equal rights in respect of effective participation in public life and that no decisions directly relating to their rights and interests are taken without their informed

42 *Länsman et al. v. Finland* (Communication No. 511/1992), U.N. Doc. CCPR/C/52/D/511/1992, at 9.5.

43 *Ángela Poma Poma v. Peru*, Communication No. 1457/2006. UN Doc. CCPR/C/95/D/1457/2006, 24 April 2009, at para. 7.6.

44 See for examples the general recommendations: Ecuador, UN Doc. E/C.12/1/Add.100 (2004), paras. 12 & 35; Brazil, UN Doc. E/C.12/1/Add.87 (2003), para. 58; Nicaragua, UN Doc. E/C.12/NIC/CO/4 (2008), para. 11; Colombia, UN Doc. E/C.12/COL/CO/5 (2010), para. 9; Russian Federation, UN Doc. E/C.12/RUS/CO/5 (2011), para. 7; see also General comment No. 21: Right of everyone to take part in cultural life, UN Doc. E/C.12/GC/21 (2009), and see Chapters 4 and 5.

consent."[45] Thus, there is clearly a principle of participation and consultation in matters affecting indigenous peoples, and it is certain that decisions affecting indigenous peoples' territories fall into this category of matters that especially affect indigenous peoples. These principles of participation and consultation are reflected through different angles of the human rights law discourse. CERD has also made reference to indigenous peoples' right to consent to decisions directly affecting them. CERD urged States to make sure "that no decisions directly relating to [indigenous] rights and interests are taken without their informed consent."[46] Thus, the Committee made a distinction between a right to effective participation in public life and a right to consent in decisions that directly affect indigenous peoples.[47] From this perspective, as decisions affecting indigenous peoples' territories directly affect them, indigenous peoples ought to have a right to consent to these decisions.

The debate within the Committee, which eventually led to the adoption of the general recommendation, is extremely relevant as an important discussion on the connection between participation and consent took place. Indeed in drafting the General Recommendation, the point about "consent" occasioned considerable discussion within the CERD.[48] Difficulties arose on the use of the terms "participation," "consultation" and "consent." CERD member Diaconu highlighted that one of the dangers was to give indigenous peoples a right of veto as "there were many cases ... where a small community could hinder the taking of decisions that would be of benefit to citizens."[49] Garvalov stated that "the two terms 'consent' and 'participation' meant entirely different things. If indigenous peoples were to give their 'consent,' they must agree to the proposal; they could 'participate' and express their approval or disapproval, without having any power over the final decision." Thornberry explained that finally: "[T]he consensus formula distinguishes between the general right of effective participation in public life, and the narrower issue of decisions directly affecting those indigenous groups. In the latter case, the sense of the Committee's deliberations appears to be that peoples do have a right of veto."[50] Indeed, it is worth highlighting that consent means the right of indigenous peoples

---

45 CERD, General Comment XXIII (51st Sess.), para. 4(d) (1997).

46 General Recommendation XXIII(51), U.N. Doc. CERD/C/365, in A/52/18, Annex V, para. 3 (1997).

47 On this issue, Patrick Thornberry, Indigenous Peoples and Human Rights (2002), at 43; *see also* discussion in Chapter 2 and 6.

48 U.N. Doc. CERD/C/SR.1235; on this issue, *see* Patrick Thornberry, Indigenous Peoples and Human Rights 217 (2002).

49 Id.

50 Id.

to agree or not. Thus, consent provides indigenous peoples with much more power in decisions affecting their territories than a simple right to participate in such decisions. This approach has been reflected in many of the Committee's concluding observations, notably when decisions taken in the name of development or conservation have been imposed on indigenous peoples. For example, in 2002, the Committee held that "no decisions directly relating to the rights and interests of members of indigenous peoples be taken without their informed consent" in connection with a game reserve in Botswana.[51] This approach has been re-emphasised in several other recommendations of the Committee which has consistently highlighted that States have an obligation to put in place processes to seek the informed consent of indigenous peoples before adopting any decisions relating to the use of natural resources located on their lands.[52]

Regional human rights institutions have also engaged with the issue of consultation, participation and consent. As noted in Chapter 3, the Inter-American Court (IACtHR) has highlighted that effective participation is an essential element of the safeguards necessary to ensure that the survival of indigenous peoples is protected in case of expropriation from their territories. In the *Saramaka* case, the IACtHR explained that effective participation includes a duty to actively consult with affected communities, "according to their customs and traditions," in relation to any proposed development or investment project. The ruling of the court in this case provides a very detailed analysis of the meaning of effective participation. In the words of the Court, effective participation means the carrying out of "good faith" consultations "with the objective of reaching an agreement." Getting into the details on the process that is necessary to ensure such effective participation, the Court highlighted several obligations for the State, including:

(1) actively consult with said community according to their customs and traditions and guarantee that consultations "should take account of the [indigenous]…people's traditional methods of decision-making";
(2) conduct consultations in "in good faith" and commence consultations at the "the early stages of a development or investment plan, not only when the need arises to obtain approval from the community;"

---

51 Concluding observations of the Committee on the Elimination of Racial Discrimination: Botswana, UN Doc. A/57/18 (2002), see paras. 292–314, at 304.

52 For a compilation of these recommendations, see: *Legal Companion to the UN-REDD Programme Guidelines on Free, Prior and Informed Consent (FPIC): International Law and Jurisprudence Affirming the Requirement of FPIC* (2013).

(3) disseminate proper and relevant information to ensure that consultations make communities "aware of possible risks, including environmental and health risks";

(4) carry out consultations "with the objective of reaching an agreement" to guarantee that "proposed development or investment plan" must be "accepted knowingly and voluntarily."[53]

Crucially, the Court added that States have a duty to obtain FPIC where "large-scale development or investment projects (....) would have a major impact within [indigenous peoples] territory."[54] This requirement to obtain consent is based on the fact that the exploitation of natural resources would deprive indigenous peoples of the capacity to use and enjoy their lands and other natural resources necessary for their subsistence. It means that there is a duty to consult with indigenous peoples to reach an informed agreement for any developmental project which might affect them, and that there is a requirement to obtain their FPIC when such developmental projects will affect the resources located on their territories. In the case of the Garífuna Community of Punta Piedra in Honduras, the Court also indicated that the process of consultation must take place beforehand, and must be carried out starting in the initial stages of the development plan so that the indigenous peoples may truly participate and influence the decision-making process.[55] The Court stated that:

> (...) in the case of any development, investment, exploration or extraction project in traditional territories of indigenous or tribal communities, the State must comply with the following safeguards: (i) conduct an appropriate and participatory process that guarantees their right to consultation; (ii) make a prior social and environmental impact assessment, and (iii) as appropriate, reasonably share the benefits produced by the exploitation of the natural resources.[56]

---

53 IACtHR, *Case of the Saramaka People v Suriname*, Judgment of November 28, 2007 (Preliminary Objections, Merits, Reparations, and Costs) Inter-Am. Ct. H.R., (Ser. C) No. 172 (2007), at para. 133.

54 Ibid, at para. 134.

55 IACtHR, *Case of the Garífuna Community of Punta Piedra and its members v. Honduras* (Preliminary Objections, Merits, Reparations and Costs) Judgment of October 8, 2015. Series C No. 304, paras. 217 and 223.

56 Ibid, para. 215.

This approach has been affirmed in a several other cases examined by the Court as well as decisions of the Commission.[57] For example, in the *Maya Indigenous Communities Case*, the Inter-American Commission held that the obligation to obtain indigenous peoples "consent applies to all State decisions, including the granting of natural resource exploitation concessions, that may have an impact upon indigenous lands and communities."[58]

The connection between participation, development and land rights was also at the heart of the decision of the African Commission on Human and Peoples' Rights in the *Endorois* case. Regarding participation, the government of Kenya had put forward the argument that the community had been involved in the process since the community's mining committee had entered into an agreement with the Kenyan company prospecting for minerals, and that the decision was taken by the Country Council. The Endorois counter-argued that the government had refused to include their own representative leaders in the decision-making process. Traditionally the Endorois community's leadership is based on elders. However, more recently, and due to external pressure on the survival of the community, they have established the Endorois Welfare Committee (EWC) to represent their interests. The local authorities have refused to register the EWC despite two separate efforts to do so since its creation in 1996. In their complaint the Endorois highlighted that "this failure to register the Endorois Welfare Committee (…) has often led to illegitimate consultations taking place, with the authorities selecting particular individuals to lend their consent 'on behalf' of the community."[59] This is an important point since many indigenous communities find themselves in similar situations where States are conducting consultation with selected members of indigenous communities rather than customary leaders.[60] On this point, the Commission drew on a previous decision from the IACtHR in the *Saramaka* case, where the court highlighted that the government has a duty to actively consult with the community according to their customs and traditions and such consultations must be in

57 See for example, *Case of the Kaliña and Lokono Peoples v. Suriname*, Judgment of November 25, 2015 (Merits, Reparations and Costs); for references to other cases, see IACHR, *Indigenous and Tribal Peoples' Rights over their Ancestral Lands and natural Resources: Norms and Jurisprudence of the Inter-American Human Rights System*, OEA/Ser.L/V/II. Doc. 56/09 (2010), Section IX.

58 IACHR, Report No. 40/04, Case 12.053, *Maya Indigenous Communities of the Toledo District* (Belize), October 12, 2004, at para. 142.

59 Id., para. 20.

60 See: Marcus Colchester and Fergus MacKay, *In search of Middle Ground: Indigenous Peoples, Collective Representation and the Right to Free, Prior and Informed Consent* (Forest Peoples Programme, 2004).

good faith, through culturally appropriate procedures and with the objective of reaching an agreement.[61] Building on this case, the Commission highlighted that to protect indigenous peoples' special relationship with their ancestral territories, States have to put in place three safeguards. First, the government has to ensure the effective participation of the members of the community in conformity with their customs and traditions, regarding any development, investment, exploration or extraction plan that will take place on their lands. Second, there should be a guarantee that the concerned community will receive a reasonable benefit from any such plan within their territory. Third, the government should ensure that no concession will be issued unless and until independent and technically capable entities, with the State's supervision, perform a prior environmental and social impact assessment.[62]

This jurisprudence coupled with the guidance emerging from international human rights treaty monitoring bodies clearly indicate a legal right for indigenous peoples to effectively participate, to be consulted, and to consent to any developmental project which would affect their territories and the resources located on these territories. What is coming out strongly from both international human rights instruments and the jurisprudence is that a process of consultation to seek indigenous peoples' FPIC before the exploitation of natural resources is a prerequisite to any developmental project which will potentially affect the resources located on indigenous peoples' territories. If such process leads to an eventual relocation then consent is mandatory. In order to ensure that consultations are 'meaningful', certain procedural rights have also evolved. Consultations must be free from manipulations and coercion, respect traditional decision-making processes, be held in sufficient time in advance of project execution with adequate information provided to enable informed decisions to be taken. Based on its central importance in both the instruments and the jurisprudence, Anaya, a former UN Special Rapporteur, has highlighted that the requirement to conduct "meaningful consultation" should be regarded as representing a norm of customary international law.[63] Another point put forward by Anaya relates to the fact that such obligation to ensure the effective participation and seek the consent of indigenous peoples is a duty of the

61 Inter-American Court of Human Rights, *Case of the Saramaka People v Suriname* Inter-Am. Ct. H.R., (Ser. C) No. 172 (2007).

62 Endorois Case, *supra* note 23, para. 227.

63 James Anaya, *Indigenous Peoples' Participatory Rights in Relation to Decisions about Natural Resource Extraction: The More Fundamental Issues of What Rights Indigenous Peoples Have in Lands and Resources*, 22(8) Arizona Journal of International and Comparative Law (2005), 7–17.

State. As he highlighted, it is important that States exercise this process, as private actors, corporation or investors who might be involved in the exploitation natural resources are not a neutral party having a direct interest in the developmental project.[64] From that perspective, whilst recent developments which are pushing private actors to engage and respect international human rights and the rights of indigenous peoples are certainly critical,[65] it is important to bear in mind that States have the ultimate obligation to ensure that the right of indigenous peoples to land are protected and guaranteed.

Nonetheless it is relevant to note that increasingly the private sector is also engaging with the rights of indigenous peoples and notably the right to FPIC. For example, in 2012, the International Finance Corporation (IFC), part of the World Bank, adopted a new lending policy requiring the negotiation of mutual agreements with indigenous peoples whose use of the land may be affected by development and to obtain their FPIC, where serious, unavoidable impacts are identified. Likewise, the International Council on Mining and Metals has similarly endorsed the right to FPIC in a position statement issued in May 2013.[66] These examples are a good indication on the increased inclusion of land rights and FPIC by the private sector.[67]

Taking a look back at the centuries of imposed aggressive developmental policies and practices which have resulted in the encroachment of indigenous territories and their loss of land rights, the evolution of international law putting forward the right to effective participation, consultation and consent undoubtedly constitutes a significant and positive development. Whilst in most situations it still remains to be seen how such processes will be implemented at the local levels, in terms of international legal development it is a very significant evolution which gives a much more articulated and practical meaning to the right to development, notably in the context of land rights. However one point that still remains to be explored relates to the legal nature of the rights that indigenous peoples have over the natural resources located on their

---

64 Report of the Special Rapporteur on the situation of human rights and fundamental freedoms of indigenous people, James Anaya. UN Doc. A/HRC/12/34, 15 July 2009, paras. 54, 55, 70.

65 See for examples: OECD Due Diligence Guidance for Meaningful Stakeholder Engagement in the Extractives Sector (2015); International Council on Mining and Metals: Indigenous Peoples and Mining Position Statement (2013); International Finance Corporation: Performance Standard 7 Indigenous Peoples (2012), see also section on private actors below.

66 International Council on Mining and Metals. Indigenous Peoples and Mining Position Statement. May 2013.

67 This aspect is examined in greater details in Section 2 of this chapter.

territories. Indeed, so far what has been put forward is a right to effectively participate, to be consulted, and ultimately to consent to the exploitation of natural resources. But this does not provide a right of ownership and control of these resources. As noted in the introduction to this book, for indigenous peoples, land rights include rights over the natural resources located on their ancestral lands. As such land rights are connected to their right to own, control and manage the natural resources. It is towards this particular issue of natural resources and their connection to land rights that the next section is focusing on.

B Management of Natural Resources: From Subsistence to Benefit-Sharing

As noted earlier, indigenous peoples' territories are usually situated in regions of the globe where natural wealth is concentrated, their territories and the natural resources they contain are often at the centre of mining, logging and other forms of natural resources extraction. In this context of natural resources exploitation, an important issue relates to the legal status of these resources. The following discussion examines to what extent the rights that indigenous peoples have over their lands and territories integrate, or not, some ownership and control rights over the natural resources. The other important issue that this section focus on is the issue of benefits. Indeed, the exploitation of natural resources usually creates important sources of revenues and benefits, since these resources are extracted or exploited on indigenous territories, an important issue is to define to what extent their rights to land provide them with a right to benefit-sharing over these resources.

1 *Ownership and Control of Natural Resources: A Right to Subsistence?*

In terms of classical land law concepts, the owner of the land is usually assumed as also owning the natural resources of the land, as per the Latin phrase: "*cuius est solum eius est usque ad coelum et usque ad inferos*" – the owner of the soil owns up to the heavens and down to the depths.[68] However natural resources, and especially sub-soil resources are usually seen to be part of the sovereign power of the State. Traditionally under public international law, the issue of control over natural resources falls under the category of sovereignty rights.[69]

68 *See* Robert Pearce & John Mee, Land Law 31 (2d ed. 2000).

69 See: Nico Schrijver, Sovereignty over Natural Resources: Balancing Rights and Duties (2008).

More precisely, territorial sovereignty conventionally includes the ownership and control of the natural resources located within the territory of a State.[70] Likewise, a large majority of the national legal systems guarantee States with ownership and sovereignty over these natural resources. This is especially the case when it comes to sub-soil resources. However, as examined in Chapter 5, under international human rights law peoples have the right to "freely dispose of their natural resources" as affirmed in article 1 of the two International Covenants. Hence under human rights law peoples have a right over these resources, whereas under classical tenets of public international law on sovereignty it is deemed to be an asset of the State. In this contradictory approach to natural resources, it is worth highlighting that indigenous peoples are indeed peoples, so they should be entitled to 'freely dispose of their natural resources.' The issue in this chapter is not to focus on the issue of sovereignty and self-determination over natural resources as this has been examined in Chapter 5, but to analyse the language of international law when it comes to indigenous peoples' rights to own the natural resources located on their territories.

In terms of international legal standards on indigenous peoples' rights, the issue of control over natural resources, and specifically sub-soil resources, formed an important element of the debates that led to the adoption of the ILO Convention 169. One of the only previous approaches to the issue was made under the ILO Recommendation 104 adopted in 1957 which undertook a non-discriminatory approach to the issue and recommends that indigenous populations "receive the same treatment as other members of the national population in relation to the ownership of underground wealth."[71] The issue of ownership was then left untouched. It came back during the process of revision of the ILO Convention 107 as the issue of control over natural resources became the subject of wide-ranging debates. The Meeting of Experts noted that when States retained total control of the rights to subsoil minerals and other natural resources, this caused serious damage to indigenous lifestyle.[72] During the debates a number of States insisted that the ownership of natural resources was exclusively for the States and that in most national legislations such resources could be granted to private individuals on a concessionary basis only.[73] Despite long debates that finally led to the adoption

70 See: Antonio Cassese, International Law in A Divided World 376–90 (1986).

71 ILO Recommendation 104, 40th Sess., June 5, 1957.

72 International Labor Conference, *Partial Revision of the Indigenous and Tribal Populations Convention*, 1957 (No. 107), Report VI(1), 75th Sess., at 58.

73 *See*, especially, the debates of the Working Party: International Labor Conference, *Partial Revision of the Indigenous and Tribal Populations Convention*, 1957 (No. 107), Provisional Record 25, 76th Sess.

of the Convention, the ILO rejected the full recognition of property rights to include natural resources, flora, fauna, freshwater areas, sea ice areas, minerals and other underground raw material that are part of indigenous peoples' territories. The Convention distinguishes between the right of ownership of the lands (art. 14) and the right to use natural resources (art. 15). It is worth noting that "ownership" as defined in Article 14 concerns only lands, whereas the right to use lands in Articles 15 and 16 includes the concept of territories, which covers the total environment of the areas that the peoples concerned occupy or otherwise use. Hence, there is no right of ownership but instead, a right of use which is connected to a right to participate in the management of the natural resources. Article 15 affirms:

> The rights of the peoples concerned to the natural resources pertaining to their lands shall be specially safeguarded. These rights include the right of these peoples to participate in the use, management and conservation of these resources. In cases in which the State retains the ownership of mineral or sub-surface resources or rights to other resources pertaining to lands, governments shall establish or maintain procedures through which they shall consult these peoples, with a view to ascertaining whether and to what degree their interests would be prejudiced, before undertaking or permitting any programmes for the exploration or exploitation of such resources pertaining to their lands.

An examination of the debates surrounding the drafting of ILO 169 sheds some light on the background to this conservative and, from the perspective of the many impacted indigenous peoples, increasingly inadequate, position of the convention regarding their rights to natural resources. During the debates, the Employer's group expressed its concerns over the eventual recognition of indigenous peoples' rights to subsoil resources fearing that this could lead to a right of veto over exploration and exploitation of those resources, and thus affect the national interest.[74] The response of the representative of the Indian Council of South America was that: "[W]ith regard to natural resources, we believe that it is essential to include explicit reference in the revised Convention to both surface and subsurface resources. The claims of States to exclusive ownership of these resources have often been based on premises that ignored the pre-existing rights of indigenous peoples."[75] Ultimately the text of

74 *See* International Labor Conference, *Partial Revision of the Indigenous and Tribal Populations Convention*, 1957 (No. 107), Provisional Record 36, 75th Sess., at 19.

75 *See* International Labor Conference, *Partial Revision of the Indigenous and Tribal Populations Convention*, 1957 (No. 107), Provisional Record 36, 75th Sess., at 19.

the Convention takes a mid-way approach by not affirming ownership rights but protecting participation and management rights. On a more positive note, it means that one of the differences between ILO 107 and 169 resides in the fact that Convention 169 has a specific provision on sub-surface resources.

The issue of ownership and control over natural resources came back as a major issue during the negotiations that led to the adoption of the UNDRIP. Article 26 of the Declaration proclaims indigenous peoples' rights to their lands and resources "which they have traditionally owned, occupied or otherwise used or acquired". Hence resources are included in the same category as lands. The Declaration clearly put together the rights to lands, territories and resources under the same heading, not making any distinctions between the legal rights of indigenous peoples over lands, territories and resources. This represents a significant evolution from the right to resources recognized under ILO Convention 169 as it affirms a direct connection between property rights to land and natural resources. It is worth noting that this follows the approach put forward by the CERD Committee in its General Recommendation on indigenous peoples which also invited States to "recognize and protect the rights of indigenous peoples to own, develop, control and use their communal lands, territories and resources."[76] This approach, which integrates lands, territories and resources under the same heading, corresponds more to indigenous peoples' holistic approach to their territorial rights which usually do not make a distinction between lands and resources. On that front, Article 25 of UNDRIP also recognizes the special spiritual and intergenerational aspects of the relationship indigenous peoples have with their resources. Their right to resources is implicit in article 20 when it recognizes indigenous peoples' rights to "traditional and other economic activities" and their entitlement to "just and fair redress" where they are deprived of "their means of subsistence and development". Article 32(3) also addresses the need for redress in the event of indigenous peoples' resources being exploited in the context of development projects. Combined, the aforementioned articles of the Declaration recognize the need to protect indigenous peoples' means of subsistence and the fact that their lands and resources are fundamental elements of such subsistence.

This focus on subsistence and participation is reflected in the jurisprudence of international and regional institutions. Many of the cases that have been examined by the IACtHR concern the rights of indigenous peoples over their natural resources. In its jurisprudence the Court has highlighted that land rights are intrinsically connected to resource rights. For example, in the *Yakye Axa*

76 CERD, General Recommendation 23 on indigenous peoples, UN Doc. A/52/18, Annex 8 (1997), para. 5

and *Sawhoyamaxa* cases, the Court highlighted that members of tribal and indigenous communities have rights to the natural resources they have traditionally used within their territory as it is a right attached to their right to own the land they have traditionally used and occupied for centuries.[77] This constitutes an important recognition that land rights ought to include resource rights. The precise content of indigenous peoples' land rights and its connection to natural resources was a central element of the *Saramaka* case against Suriname. In this case both the government and the members of the Saramaka people were claiming their right over the natural resources contained on the indigenous territory. On the one hand, the Saramaka highlighted that their right to use and enjoy their natural resources was a necessary condition for the enjoyment of their right to property to land. On the other hand, the government was arguing that all the rights to the natural resources, particularly the subsoil resources, are vested in the State, which can freely dispose of these resources through concessions to third parties. Hence the Court was stuck between the traditional sovereign discourse which equates State power with ownership rights over natural resources, and the land rights claim to natural resources made by the indigenous community. Referring to its own previous jurisprudence, the Court highlighted that: "members of tribal and indigenous communities have the right to own the natural resources they have traditionally used within their territory for the same reasons that they have a right to own the land they have traditionally used and occupied for centuries."[78] It is important to highlight the reference to a 'right to own' the natural resources, and not a right to use only. In a statement, which has since become an important reference under international law, the Court stated:

> (...) due to the inextricable connection members of indigenous and tribal peoples have with their territory, the protection of their right to property over such territory (...) is necessary to guarantee their very survival. Accordingly, the right to use and enjoy their territory would be meaningless in the context of indigenous and tribal communities if said right were not connected to the natural resources that lie on and within the land.[79]

77 Case of the Yakye Axa Indigenous Community v. Paraguay. Merits, Reparations and Costs. Judgment of June 17, 2005. Series C No. 125, pars. 124, 137; Case of the Sawhoyamaxa Indigenous Community v. Paraguay. Merits, Reparations and Costs. Judgment of March 29th, 2006. Series C No. 146, pars. 118, 121.

78 IACtHR, *Saramaka People v. Suriname*, 2007 Inter-Am. Ct. H.R. (ser. C) No. 172, (Nov. 28, 2007), para. 121.

79 Ibid, para. 122.

However as noted by the Court the natural resources which falls under the protection of the right to property to land "are those natural resources traditionally used and necessary for the very survival, development and continuation of such people's way of life."[80] In terms of international legal development, this represents an important statement as it limits the rights over natural resources to resources that are traditionally used by indigenous peoples. It also limits the potential infringement on these rights to activities which could affect the traditional use of the resources that are essential to the survival of indigenous peoples.

It was based on this test of 'traditional use' and 'survival' that the court defined which natural resources were the subject of protection. The Court got into a deep analysis on the impact of logging and mining activities undertaken on the indigenous territory in judging to what extent these extractive activities were affecting the traditional use of natural resources essential to the survival of the concerned community. For example, regarding the gold mining taking place on the territory of the Saramaka, the Court highlighted that "the members of the Saramaka people have not traditionally used gold as part of their cultural identity or economic system. Despite possible individual exceptions, members of the Saramaka people do not identify themselves with gold nor have demonstrated a particular relationship with this natural resource (...)."[81] More generally, it will be an arduous task to demonstrate a cultural attachment with sub-soil resources, notably primary resources exploited by the mining industry.[82] But the Court recognised that such mining activities affected the usage of other natural resources which are essential to the survival of indigenous peoples. The Court highlighted that since gold mining activities within Saramaka territory will inevitably affect other natural resources necessary for the survival of the Saramakas, such as waterways, the State had a duty to consult with them, in conformity with their traditions and customs, regarding any proposed mining concession within their territory. The Court added that the government should also allow the members of the community to reasonably participate in the benefits derived from any such possible concession, and perform or supervise an assessment on the environmental and social impact prior to the commencement of the project.

80 Ibid.

81 Ibid, at para. 155.

82 However see the Constitutional Court of South Africa: *Alexkor v Richtersveld Community*, 2003 (12) BCLR 1301: in this case the community managed to prove a traditional usage of copper (see para. 61 and ss).

Overall, this case put forward some important elements regarding the connection between land rights and natural resources by ruling that (1) indigenous peoples have a right to use and enjoy the natural resources that lie within their traditionally owned territory that are necessary for their survival; and (2) that the State may restrict these rights by granting concessions for the exploration and extraction of natural resources found on and within indigenous peoples' territories only if the three necessary safeguards have been strictly followed (effective participation, benefit sharing, prior environmental and social impact assessments).[83] On the first point, it is relevant to go back to the earlier statement made by the Court which stated that "members of tribal and indigenous communities have the right to own the natural resources they have traditionally used"; it seems that the Court has gone away from this approach to embrace a more 'traditional' and positivist reading of international law which goes back to the principle of State sovereignty over natural resources. It is indeed a disappointing reading of international law from the Court knowing that international human rights law supports and proclaims the rights of peoples to freely dispose of their natural resources.[84] Ultimately, the Court adopted a pragmatic attitude in pushing for a midway approach which puts forward the fact that indigenous peoples have rights over their natural resources if these resources are traditionally being used and form an important element of their survival. It is a pragmatic approach in the sense that it does not fundamentally challenge the principle of State sovereignty and ownership over natural resources, but it does nonetheless impose a duty on States to put in place certain safeguards when it comes to the use of the resources that are located on indigenous territories. As noted earlier these are the need to ensure: (1) effective participation; (2) access and guarantee of benefits; and (3) prior environmental and social impact assessments.

The jurisprudence of the Inter-American Court on this issue is extremely significant as it had a direct impact on the jurisprudence of the African Commission in its decision regarding the Endorois community against Kenya. Indeed the African Commission relied heavily on the *Saramaka* case to examine the connection between natural resources and land rights. The references to traditional use of resources, survival and the need for safeguards to ensure

83 This approach is also confirmed in other cases: *Case of the Yakye Axa Indigenous Community*, , paras. 135 and 137, and *Case of the Garífuna Community of Punta Piedra and its members*, paras. 165 to 167 and 172.

84 See: Jérémie Gilbert, *The Right to Freely Dispose of natural Resources: Utopia or Forgotten Right?*, Netherlands Quarterly of Human Rights 31 (3):314–41 (2013).

such survival are also present in the decision of the African Commission. The only major difference relates to the fact that unlike the American Convention on Human Rights which does not specifically include an article on natural resources, the African Charter in its Article 21 states that "all peoples shall freely dispose of their wealth and natural resources." The Commission highlighted that in an earlier decision regarding the Ogoni of Nigeria, it had ruled that the right to natural resources contained within their traditional lands is also vested in the right of the indigenous community, making it clear that a people inhabiting a specific region within a State could also claim their rights under Article 21 of the African Charter.[85] Ultimately the Commission highlighted that the Endorois had "the right to freely dispose of their wealth and natural resources in consultation with the government."[86] The Commission found a violation of Article 21 based on the lack of proper restitution and compensation for the violation of the community's rights to land. However the Commission remained very vague on the exact meaning of consultation in the context of article 21. But it gave a clearer meaning on the notion of consultation and control over the natural resources under its examination of the complaint under the right to development (article 22). Under this article on the right to development, the Commission made a clear connection between the use of natural resources and the need to obtain the free, prior and informed consent (FPIC) of the community.

This connection between FPIC, land rights and natural resources is confirmed by the approach adopted by international human rights treaty monitoring bodies.[87] For example, the CESCR committee has focused on this connection in its recommendations to New Zealand in 2012. It stated:

> The Committee is concerned that the State party does not give sufficient protection of the inalienable rights of indigenous people to their lands, territories, waters and maritime areas, and other resources, as manifested by the fact that Maori free, prior and informed consent on the use and exploitation of these resources has not always been respected (arts. 1, para. 2; and 15).[88]

85 *The Social and Economic Rights Action Center and the Center for Economic and Social Rights v. Nigeria* (Communication 155/96), paras 56–58.

86 Endorois decision, *supra* note 23, para. 268.

87 See earlier discussion on consent and natural resources above

88 New Zealand, UN Doc. E/C.12/NZL/CO/3, 31 May 2012, para. 11.

Here it is worth noting that whilst undeniably the recognition of the need to obtain the FPIC of the concerned indigenous peoples before allowing exploitation of resources located on their lands is important, it falls short of recognising their right of ownership over these resources. As noted in Chapter 5, an important development of the right to self-determination relates to its connection with control of natural resources, which has notably been interpreted as meaning a right to consent to natural resources exploitation located on indigenous territories. Likewise as examined earlier, the right to FPIC extends to natural resources located on indigenous territories. This certainly constitutes a significant and meaningful development of international law when it comes of control over natural resources, however regarding the issue of ownership of these resources the right to FPIC does not fully challenge the assumption of States ownership of the resources. As noted by Doyle on this issue: "[To a certain extent, FPIC represents a compromise on behalf of indigenous peoples in so far as it falls short of fully challenging the predominant claims asserted by States, under doctrines such as *jura regalia*, to exclusive ownership over resources located in indigenous territories."[89] Hence FPIC appears as a compromise which does not directly challenge the issue of ownership of natural resources, but instead offers a platform for indigenous peoples to be directly integrated into the management of these resources.

Overall, going back to the main issue of ownership and control over natural resources what is emerging from the international instruments and the jurisprudence is a somewhat fuzzy approach. On the one hand there is no doubt that land rights include the right to use natural resources. This is clear in both the instruments (the ILO 169 and the UNDRIP) and the jurisprudence which have put forward the connection between land rights and natural resources as fundamental. What is also strongly emerging is the obligation for States to ensure that the exploitation of the natural resources located on indigenous peoples' territories will not affect their survival, and that indigenous peoples should be consulted and participate in the decisions leading to the exploitation of the resources. On the other hand, what is less clear is the exact status of the right over these resources. As noted earlier the Inter-American Court had initially referred to a right to own these resources, but then limited it to natural resources traditionally used by indigenous peoples. This means that most sub-soil resources would not usually be included as these do not qualify

89 Cathal Doyle, Indigenous Peoples, Title to Territory, Rights and Resources: The Transformative Role of Free Prior and Informed Consent (2015), p. 4.

"traditionally" used by indigenous peoples.[90] Hence what seems to be emerging is a right to own the "traditionally used resources" and a more general right to use natural resources located on their lands. However this would need to be more precisely examined, as so far the approach has been quite hesitant. It would also need to be put into context with the approach of the UNDRIP which does not make such a distinction between resources "traditionally" used or not. On a more positive side, the jurisprudence clearly indicates that when it comes to natural resources located on indigenous territories, States have certain obligations including to put in place specific safeguards when allowing exploitation of resources, which are to ensure consultation (and consent in case of removal) and that indigenous peoples will participate and benefit from this exploitation. The next section focuses on these aspects of benefits and participation in the management of natural resources.

2 *Towards a Right to Benefit-Sharing?*

The exploitation of natural resources, either for purposes of mining or other forms extractive activities such as logging, or for the purpose of conservation or tourism, often generates important revenues. Despite the fact that these revenues are generated from the use of the resources located on indigenous territories, in most situations indigenous peoples do not get any benefits from these revenues which go to States authorities and private actors involved in the exploitation of these resources. Whilst exploitation of natural resources generates risk of environmental and social harm, it can also potentially generate substantial revenues for indigenous peoples. In this context it is worth bearing in mind that indigenous peoples often represent the most deprived and impoverished segments of society. Hence the significant revenues created by the exploitation of natural resources located on their territories could represent important incomes to support indigenous peoples' right to development. As noted earlier, usually this is not the case as in most situations exploitation of resources located on indigenous lands has been synonymous with forced relocation, land degradation, and loss of access to essential sources of livelihoods. International law is increasingly putting emphasis on a right for indigenous peoples to benefit from the exploitation of the resources located on their territories. The Declaration on the Right to Development highlights that States should "formulate appropriate national development policies that aim at the

---

90 This is confirmed by several cases at the national level, see the analysis of Stefania Errico, *The Controversial Issue of Natural Resources: Balancing States' Sovereignty with Indigenous Peoples' Rights*, in Stephen Allen and Alexandra Xanthaki (eds.) Reflections on the UN Declaration on the Rights of Indigenous Peoples (2011).

constant improvement of the well-being of the entire population and of all individuals, on the basis of their active, free and meaningful participation in development and in the fair distribution of the benefits resulting therefrom." It adds that development should be seen as a process which should benefit "the entire population and … all individuals on the basis of their active, free and meaningful participation in development and in the fair distribution of benefits resulting therefrom." More specifically for indigenous peoples, the ILO Convention 169 in its article 15 states: "The peoples concerned shall wherever possible participate in the benefits of such activities, and shall receive fair compensation for any damages which they may sustain as a result of such activities."

International human rights treaty bodies have also engaged with the right of indigenous peoples to benefit from the exploitation of natural resources located on their lands. For example, in *Apirana Mahuika et al. v. New Zealand*, the Human Rights Committee highlighted that the right to culture of an indigenous population, as protected under Article 27 of the ICCPR, means that the community should participate and benefit from activities taking place on their lands. The Committee stated that "the acceptability of measures that affect or interfere with the culturally significant economic activities of a minority depends on whether the members of the minority in question have had the opportunity to participate in the decision-making process in relation to these measures and whether they will continue to benefit from their traditional economy".[91] This approach was also put forward by the CESCR Committee which has referred to the right of the indigenous communities to "enjoy tangible benefits from the exploitation of their resources."[92] Likewise, in the context of logging activities taking place on indigenous territories in the Democratic Republic of Congo, the Committee has highlighted that the government should "(…) ensure that future forest concessions do not deprive the indigenous peoples of the full enjoyment of their rights to their ancestral lands and natural resources, and that the benefits thereof contribute to their poverty alleviation."[93] The CERD Committee has also highlighted the right of indigenous peoples to an equitable sharing of benefits for the exploitation of natural resources. In a 2002 report on the situation in Ecuador, the Committee has specifically mentioned the need to ensure the equitable sharing of benefits. It stated:

91 *Apirana Mahuika et al. v. New Zealand*, UN Doc. CCPR/C/70/D/547/1993 (2000), para. 9.5.

92 New Zealand, UN Doc. E/C.12/NZL/CO/3 (2012), para. 11.

93 Democratic Republic of Congo, UN Doc. E/C.12/COD/CO/4 (2009), para. 14.

> As to the exploitation of the subsoil resources of the traditional lands of indigenous communities, the Committee observes that merely consulting these communities prior to exploiting the resources falls short of meeting the requirements set out in the Committee's general recommendation XXIII on the rights of indigenous peoples. The Committee therefore recommends that the prior informed consent of these communities be sought, and that the *equitable sharing of benefits* to be derived from such exploitation be ensured.[94]

In 2011, the Committee has positively noted the fact that the government of Bolivia had put in place processes to ensure "[p]rofit-sharing when natural resources are extracted from the territories of [indigenous peoples]."[95] These are only illustrations as increasingly international human rights monitoring bodies are including references to the fact that indigenous peoples have a right to benefit from the exploitation of resources located in their territories.

The notion of benefit sharing is also appearing as an important issue in the jurisprudence of the regional human rights institutions. As noted by the African Commission in the case of the Endorois community against Kenya: "the failure to guarantee effective participation and to guarantee a reasonable share in the profits of the Game Reserve (or other adequate forms of compensation) also extends to a violation of the right to development."[96] Specifically connecting the right to property and benefit-sharing the African Commission noted "that the concept of benefit-sharing also serves as an important indicator of compliance for property rights; failure to duly compensate (even if the other criteria of legitimate aim and proportionality are satisfied) result in a violation of the right to property."[97] In this context, the Commission highlighted that the right to benefit from the exploitation of their lands emerges form the right to obtain "just compensation" resulting from the deprivation of their right to the use and enjoy their traditional lands and of those natural resources necessary for their survival. In its recommendations, the Commission not only invited the government to recognise the rights to land of the Endorois, but also "pay royalties to the Endorois from existing economic activities and ensure that they benefit from employment possibilities within the Reserve." The right to benefit sharing has also appeared in the jurisprudence of the Inter-American system. In the cases of the Kichwa Indigenous People of Sarayaku, and

94 Ecuador, UN Doc. CERD/C/62/CO/2 (2003), para. 16 (emphasis added).

95 Bolivia, UN Doc. CERD/C/BOL/CO/17-20 (2011), para. 7 (f).

96 ACHPR: *Endorois Decision, supra* note 23, para. 228.

97 Ibid, at para. 294.

subsequently in the case of the Garífuna Community of Triunfo de la Cruz, the Court specified that:

> (...) to ensure that the exploration for, or extraction of, natural resources in ancestral territories does not entail a negation of the survival of the indigenous people as such, the State must comply with the following safeguards: (i) conduct an appropriate and participatory process that guarantees the right to consultation, particularly with regard to large-scale development or investment projects; (ii) make an environmental impact assessment, and (iii) as appropriate, reasonably share the benefits produced by the exploitation of natural resources (as a form of just compensation required by Article 21 of the Convention), with the community itself determining and deciding who the beneficiaries of this compensation should be, according to its customs and traditions.[98]

The Court adopted a similar approach in the case of the Kaliña and Lokono communities in reiterating its prior jurisprudence highlighting that when States are "considering development plans within the territories of indigenous and tribal peoples, [they] should, within reason, share the benefits of the project in question, as appropriate."[99]

Regarding the legal grounding of this approach, the Court spent more time getting into the detail on the meaning of benefit sharing in the case of the Saramaka peoples. In this case, the IACtHR stated "(...) in the event that development or investment plans are carried out within indigenous territories, the benefits arising from those plans must be reasonably shared with the indigenous communities concerned."[100] In this context, the Court put forward the idea that the benefits are part of the process of reparations and compensation for loss of lands and territories. The notion of benefit was addressed under the heading of a right to compensation as guaranteed under article 21 of the American Convention. This is a worrying approach, as benefit sharing, and a right to benefit, should not be confused with compensation.

---

98 *Case of the Kichwa Indigenous People of Sarayaku v. Ecuador* (Merits and Reparations) Judgment of June 27, 2012. Series C No. 245, para. 157; and *Case of the Garífuna Community of Triunfo de la Cruz and its members v. Honduras* (Merits, Reparations and Costs) Judgment of October 8, 2015. Series C No. 305, para. 156.

99 *Case of the Kaliña and Peoples v. Suriname*, Judgment of November 25, 2015 (Merits, Reparations and Costs), para. 227.

100 *Case of the Saramaka People v. Suriname*, Series C No. 172, Judgment of 28 November 2007, para. 138ff.

Indeed benefit-sharing should not be confused with compensation schemes sometimes paid by governments or corporations. These compensations concern reparations for forced resettlement, or for damages directly faced by the local communities due to damage directly caused by the extractive activities taking place on indigenous territories. Benefit sharing refers to a right to participate in the benefits of the project. Compensation is an absolutely different issue relating to damages. The IACtHR, but also the African Commission, seemed to have confused the two issues by encapsulating benefit sharing within the issue of compensation and reparation.

International human rights law could learn from other areas of international law where the right to benefit sharing has been more developed. The notion of benefit sharing regarding the use of natural resources was first formalised in international law in 1992 through the Convention on Biological Diversity (CBD). As articulated in article 1, one of the objectives of the convention is to ensure "the fair and equitable sharing of the benefits arising out of the utilization of genetic resources (…)." The preamble recognises "the close and traditional dependence of many indigenous and local communities embodying traditional lifestyles on biological resources, and the desirability of sharing equitably benefits arising from the use of traditional knowledge, innovations and practices relevant to the conservation of biological diversity and the sustainable use of its components." More specifically, the CBD requires State Parties to ensure "the equitable sharing of the benefits" that are arising from the utilization of indigenous and local communities' traditional knowledge (Article 8(j)). The Nagoya Protocol on Access to Genetic Resources and the Fair and Equitable Sharing of Benefits Arising from their Utilization to the Convention on Biological Diversity (Nagoya Protocol), which was adopted in 2010 to complement the text of the convention, puts more flesh to the notion of benefit sharing. It notably affirms the rights of indigenous peoples and local communities to fair and equitable sharing of benefits arising from the utilization of their genetic resources and traditional knowledge by third parties (art. 12). The main thrust of the protocol is that, at national levels, States should provide for the fair and equitable sharing of benefits arising from the utilization of genetic resources located on indigenous territories. This approach based on equitable sharing of the benefits arising from the use of resources located on indigenous territories should serve as a platform to push international human rights law to fully embrace the concept.

There is also the emergence of an important body of States' practice regarding benefit sharing arrangements. In Canada several 'Impact and Benefit Agreements' (IBA) have been established between the federal, or provincial governments, and extractive industries. More and more of these agreements are directly negotiated between indigenous peoples and corporations.[101] As such IBAs signal a new era in which it is no longer acceptable to exploit natural resources without previously entering directly within a process of negotiations and agreement making with Aboriginal peoples in Canada.[102] The legal obligation to develop such IBAs stems from two sources. IBAs are explicitly required under the Nunavut Land Claims Agreements, concerning all of Nunavut, and the Inuvialuit Final Agreement which concerns the northern coast of the Northwest Territories. For the rest of Canada, the legal requirement stems from the decisions of the Supreme Court and its affirmation of a duty to consult with Aboriginals who may be affected by projects occurring on or near their traditional land.[103] Likewise, in Australia several indigenous communities have entered into "Indigenous Land Use Agreements" (ILUAs) which are agreements passed between a Native title group and other peoples who wish to gain interests over the use and management of land and waters of a determined area. ILUAs concern activities, such as mining developments, gas pipelines, national parks, marina developments or any other activity involving the use of natural resources. Typically, these agreements provide indigenous peoples with sharing of project revenues, and preferential indigenous access to employment and business development opportunities.[104] The development of these agreements is not limited to Canada and Australia as many other indigenous communities across the globe have entered a process of land negotiation based on the development of agreements which include specific focus on benefit sharing.[105] In terms of land rights, rather than addressing the

101 See: Ciaran O'Faircheallaigh, *Aboriginal-mining company contractual agreements in Australia and Canada: Implications for political autonomy and community development*" Canadian Journal of Development Studies/Revue Canadienne D'études Du Développement 30.1–2 (2010): 69–86.

102 There are some limitations to such process, see: Courtney Fidler and Michael Hitch, *Impact and benefit agreements: A contentious issue for environmental and aboriginal justice*, Environments 35.2 (2007): 49;; Ken J., Caine and Naomi Krogman, *Powerful or just plain power-full? A power analysis of impact and benefit agreements in Canada's north*, Organization & Environment 23.1 (2010): 76–98.

103 See: T Isaac and A. Knox, *Canadian Aboriginal Law: Creating certainty in resource development*, University of New Brunswick Law Journal (2004) 53, 3–41; Deborah McGregor, *Aboriginal/non-Aboriginal relations and sustainable forest management in Canada: The influence of the Royal Commission on Aboriginal Peoples*, Journal of environmental management 92.2 (2011): 300–10.

104 See: Ciaran O'Faircheallaigh, *Negotiating cultural heritage? Aboriginal–mining company agreements in Australia*, Development and Change 39.1 (2008): 25–51.

105 See Ciaran O'faircheallaigh, Negotiations in the Indigenous World: Aboriginal Peoples and Extractive Industry in Australia and Canada (2016).

issue of ownership of the natural resources, these agreements regulate land uses, and, more specifically, the use of natural resources based on a notion of co-management and benefit sharing. This is part of a larger trend as the notion of benefit-sharing agreements is increasingly put forward in the guidance documents published by international private actors. For example, in 2013 the mining industry body, the industry-wide International Council on Mining and Metals (ICMM) published its new position statement on indigenous peoples, with a crucial focus on FPIC. It also produced a "Good Practice Guide" which puts great emphasis on the notion of benefit.[106]

These practices on benefit sharing emerging from the national and local levels as well as the international guidance from the industries could support a better articulation of a right to benefit sharing under international human rights law. International human rights law is increasingly putting forward a right to benefit from the exploitation of natural resources located on indigenous territories, and the practice at the national levels is indicating an increased direct relationship between indigenous peoples and corporate actors to developed agreements regarding benefit-sharing. This indicates a new direction in terms of international law under which a triangular relationship is being developed between indigenous peoples, States and corporations.[107] It is towards this triangular relationship that the chapter is now turning its attention.

C Nature Conservation, Exploitation of Natural Resources, and Private Actors

The following section focuses on the role played by some of the largest 'industries' operating on indigenous territories with the aim of examining to what extent international law is developing tools to address the rights of indigenous peoples' land rights in this context. Two main types of 'industries' seem to have particularly negatively impacted on indigenous peoples' land rights, namely the 'conservation industry' and the extractive industries. The first sub-section examines the relationship between the efforts to protect nature, notably through the establishment of nature reserves, and indigenous peoples' land

106 International Council on Mining and Metals (ICMM), Good Practice Guide: Indigenous Peoples and Mining (2013).

107 See: Jérémie Gilbert and Nadia Bernaz, "Resources Grabbing and Human Rights: Building a Triangular Relationship between States, Indigenous Peoples and Corporations", in Angelica Bonfanti, Francesca Romanin Jacur and Francesco Seatzu (Eds), Natural Resources Grabbing: Natural Resources Grabbing: An International Law Perspective (2016).

rights. The second sub-section focuses on the extractive industries and the legal obligations of corporations to respect indigenous peoples' land rights.

1 *Nature Conservation, Tourism & Indigenous Peoples' Land Rights: Towards Co-management?*

The establishment of specifically dedicated protected areas for the protection of nature and its wildlife has often had some very negative consequences on the rights of indigenous peoples. In many situations across the globe the establishment of protected areas for conservation of nature has resulted in the forced displacement of indigenous communities from their ancestral lands, in most situation with no consultations, or compensations.[108] Under what has been labelled 'fortress conservation', nature and wildlife reserves have been established based on the precept that humans, including indigenous peoples, needed to be removed from the reserves in the name of nature conservation.[109] Under this approach States and international agencies working on nature conservation often use the issue of nature protection to remove indigenous peoples from their lands, ignoring that, for centuries, indigenous communities have inhabited these areas in harmony with their natural environment. Despite this adverse relationship between conservation of nature and indigenous peoples' rights, in recent years, international standards relating to the conservation of nature have increasingly paid attention to the protection of indigenous peoples within protected areas.[110] In terms of international guidance on protected areas an important U-turn took place during the 2003 World Parks Congress. During the Congress, organized by the International Union for Conservation of Nature (IUCN) and the World Commission on Protected Areas, a 'new protected area paradigm' was adopted that superseded the consideration of a nature reserve as a mere national conservation space and introduced scientific, economic and cultural claims and implemented management and funding policies involving different stakeholders, including

108 See: Marcus Colchester, *Salvaging nature: indigenous peoples, protected areas and biodiversity conservation* (Diane Publishing, 1994); Dawn Chatty and Marcus Colchester (Eds.), Conservation and Mobile Indigenous Peoples: Displacement, Forced Settlement, and Sustainable Development (2002).

109 See Amity A. Doolittle, "Fortress Conservation", in Paul Robbins, ed., *Encyclopedia of Environment and Society* (Sage Press, 2007).

110 *See* Agenda 21, U.N. Doc. A/CONF.151/26, (Ch. 26), arts. 8 and 10(c) of the Convention on Biological Diversity, *reprinted in* 31 I.L.M. (1992); *see* Forest Peoples Programme, *Indigenous Peoples' Rights, State Sovereignty and the Convention on Biological Diversity* (Forest Peoples Programme, 2004).

indigenous peoples.[111] More generally, since then there has been an increased recognition on the part of many international actors involved in the protection of nature that indigenous peoples may play an important role in nature conservation.[112] The World Wildlife Fund, for instance, has acknowledged that, "without recognition of the rights of indigenous peoples, no constructive agreements can be drawn up between conservation organizations and indigenous peoples groups."[113] Nonetheless, despite the changes of approach from agencies involved in the conservation of nature, across the globe many indigenous communities are still the victims of forced eviction from their ancestral territories following the establishment of nature and wildlife reserves on their territories. Knowing that the number of national parks, nature and wildlife reserves is expanding in recent years, the numbers of indigenous peoples who are negatively affected has also dramatically increased.

In terms of international legal instruments, the approach connecting the protection of the environment and indigenous peoples' rights is clearly expressed in the text of the Convention on Biological Diversity. In its Article 8(j) the Convention indicates that each State shall "respect, preserve and maintain [...] practices of indigenous and local communities embodying traditional lifestyles relevant for the conservation and sustainable use of biological diversity and promote their wider application with the approval and involvement of the holders of such knowledge (...)." Article 10(c) indicates that the State shall "[p]rotect and encourage customary use of biological resources in accordance with traditional cultural practices that are compatible with conservation or sustainable use requirements." Based on such articles, the Conference of the Parties to the Convention, the governing body of the Convention, has established "the obligations of Parties towards indigenous and local communities in accordance with Article 8(j) and related provisions [for] the establishment,

111 See: Durban Accord and Action Plan adopted at the Vth World Parks Congress, Durban, South Africa, 2003, p. 25; see also: Marcus Colchester, Maurizio Farhan Ferrari, John Nelson, Chris Kidd, Peninnah Zaninka, Messe Venant, Len Regpala, Grace T. Balawag, Borromeo Motin, and Banie Lasimbang, *Conservation and Indigenous Peoples: assessing the progress since Durban* (Forest Peoples Programme, 2009).

112 See: Secretariat of the Convention on Biological Diversity: Principles and Guidelines for the Sustainable Use of Biological Diversity (CBD Guidelines, 2004); International Union for Conservation of Nature and WWF-International, Indigenous and Traditional Peoples and Protected Areas: Principles, Guidelines and Cases Studies; WWF International, Indigenous Peoples and Conservation: WWF Statement of Principles (2008).

113 *WWF Statement of Principles: Indigenous Peoples and Conservation* (Gland, World Wide Fund for Nature International, 1996); *see also* Indigenous and Traditional Peoples and Protected Areas: Principles, Guidelines and Case Studies (Javier Beltran ed., 2000).

management and monitoring of protected areas [that] should take place with the full and effective participation of, and full respect for the rights of, indigenous and local communities consistent with national law and applicable international obligations."[114] The connection between nature conservation and indigenous peoples' rights was also affirmed in the Rio Declaration on Environment and Development which stated that: "[i]ndigenous people and their communities [...] have a vital role in environmental management and development because of their knowledge and traditional practices. States should recognize and duly support their identity, culture and interests and enable their effective participation in the achievement of sustainable development."[115] In terms of human rights law, this approach is reflected in the text of the UNDRIP as Article 29 affirms that indigenous peoples "have the right to the conservation and protection of the environment and the productive capacity of their lands or territories and resources. States shall establish and implement assistance programmes for indigenous peoples for such conservation and protection, without discrimination." In its preamble, the Declaration highlights that "respect for indigenous knowledge, cultures and traditional practices contributes to sustainable and equitable development and proper management of the environment." The ILO Convention 169 affirms that "[G]overnments shall take measures, in co-operation with the peoples concerned, to protect and preserve the environment of the territories they inhabit."[116] Article 15 of the Convention states: "The rights of the peoples concerned to the natural resources pertaining to their lands shall be specially safeguarded. These rights include the right of these peoples to participate in the use, management and conservation of these resources." Participation to the management and the conservation of the natural resources is then specifically put forward by the convention.

In terms of the jurisprudence, the relationship between the protection of the environment and indigenous peoples' land rights has been examined in detail by the IACtHR in several of its cases. The issue of conservation of nature and indigenous peoples' land rights was at the heart of the 2015 decision form the Inter-American Court in the case of Kaliña and Lokono peoples against Suriname.[117] The concerned indigenous communities had lost access to their

114 Decisions adopted by the Conference of the Parties to the Convention on Biological Diversity at its seventh meeting, Decision VII/28, Protected Areas (Articles 8 (a) to (e), para. 22.

115 Rio Declaration on Environment and Development, Principle 22.

116 ILO Convention 169, article 7 (4).

117 IACtHR, *Case of the Kaliña and Lokono Peoples v. Suriname*, Judgment of November 25, 2015 (Merits, Reparations and Costs).

territories following the establishment of three different nature reserves on some parts of the ancestral territories. In this process their rights to lands and resources were not recognised, and hunting and fishing were forbidden in the reserves. Hence the concerned indigenous communities lost access to their lands as well as to essential natural resources necessary to their livelihood. Before the Court, the representatives of the government had argued that the nature reserves had been established to "advance nature conservation efforts and that they responded to a higher interest that prevailed over the property rights of the Kaliña and Lokono peoples."[118] In addressing this claim the Court highlighted that the protection of nature and the establishment of nature reserves should be compatible and respect the rights of indigenous peoples. The court stated:

> (…) the protection of natural areas and the right of the indigenous and tribal peoples to the protection of the natural resources in their territories are compatible, and it emphasizes that, owing to their interrelationship with nature and their ways of life, the indigenous and tribal peoples can make an important contribution to such conservation.

Based on this approach the Court put forward three essential elements that need to be put in place to ensure such correlation between environmental aims and the rights of indigenous peoples, namely: (1) effective participation; (2) a right to access and use of traditional territories; and (3) the possibility of receiving benefits from conservation.

In this case, the Court ruled that the lack of explicit mechanisms to ensure the access, use and effective participation of the Kaliña and Lokono indigenous peoples in the conservation of the concerned nature reserves violated the rights to collective property, cultural identity, and participation in public affairs. The Court ordered the State to guarantee their effective participation by means of a consultation process, the execution of social and environmental impact assessments, and the sharing of benefits. In reaching its decision the Court took great efforts to highlight that when it comes to the management of natural resources (in this case for environmental purposes), the State "retain the supervision, access and management of areas of general and strategic interest, and for safety reasons, that allow it to exercise its sovereignty, and/ or protect the borders of its territory." The approach is based on the need to ensure co-management between public authorities and indigenous peoples in the management of the nature reserves. Legally the Court relied on the right

118 Ibid, at para. 120.

"to take part in the conduct of public affairs", stating that "in this sense, the participation of the indigenous communities in the conservation of the environment is not only a matter of public interest, but also part of the exercise of their right as indigenous peoples." An important aspect of the ruling is to put forward the right of indigenous peoples to monitor and manage the nature reserves.

There are strong echoes of this approach based on co-management over natural resources in many of the emerging international policy documents relating to the conservation of nature, but also more generally regarding the management of resources located on indigenous territories.[119] Policy makers, international organisations and practitioners are increasingly using terms such as management, co-management, and participatory management. In practice several States and nature conservation agencies have entered into co-management agreements with indigenous peoples. For example, in South Africa some indigenous communities have entered into a negotiation over agreements regarding land use and co-management in conservation areas.[120] One of the first indigenous peoples' claims filed under post-apartheid legislation was filed by the ‡Khomani San.[121] The community claimed ownership over their traditional territory before the Land Claim Court, but one of the difficulties was that most of the indigenous community's land was placed within the Kalahari Transfrontier Park, a natural reserve.[122] In 2001, the South African government concluded a settlement with the ‡Khomani San people providing for the recognition of their land rights over a large area of the Kalahari Transfrontier Park.[123] There was another co-management signed by the government

119 See: Alfonso Peter Castro and Erik Nielsen, *Indigenous people and co-management: implications for conflict management*, Environmental Science & Policy 4.4 (2001): 229–39; Grazia Borrini and Hanna Jaireth, Sharing Power: Learning-by-Doing in Co-management of Natural Resources Throughout the World (2007); Helen Ross et al, *Co-management and Indigenous protected areas in Australia: achievements and ways forward*, Australasian Journal of Environmental Management *16*.4 (2009): 242–52.

120 See: Rachel Wynberg, Doris Schroeder, and Roger Chennells. Indigenous Peoples, Consent and Benefit Sharing: Lessons from the San-Hoodia Case (2009).

121 Nigel Crawhall, *Still Invisible: San and Khoi in the New South Africa* (Southern Africa Report, May 26–30, 1998).

122 Steven Robins, *Whose 'culture,' whose 'survival'? The Khomani San Land Claim and the Cultural Politics of 'Community,' and 'Development' in the Kalahari, in* Africa's Indigenous Peoples: 'First Peoples' or 'Marginalised Minorities'? 229–53 (Alan Barnard & Justin Kenrick eds., 2001).

123 Roger Chennells, *The Khomani San Land Claim*, 26(1) Cultural Survival Q. 51 (2002).

(through the South African National Parks) and the Makuleke community.[124] Several Aboriginal communities across Australia have also entered into "Indigenous Protected Area Programs."[125] As part of the National Strategy for the Conservation of Australia's Biological Diversity, adopted following Australia's ratification of the Convention on Biological Diversity, an increasing number of collaborative agreements recognizing Aboriginal peoples' rights over their traditional natural resources have been passed. These are only illustrations as across the globe more and more co-management agreements are being developed.[126] These agreements, which recognise the need to ensure the integration of indigenous peoples into the conservation effort, are part of the larger legal framework recognising a right for indigenous peoples to directly participate and benefit from the use of resources located on their territories. However, as highlighted earlier there is still a long road ahead to fundamentally challenge the forced removal of indigenous peoples from their lands in the name of nature conservation. The ruling of the IACtHR in the case against Suriname in 2015 is putting forward some important statements regarding the need to ensure the compatibility of nature conservation and the rights of indigenous peoples over their lands and territories.

However in practice many communities are still suffering from the exclusion from their lands in the name of conservation. Moreover, despite the recent changes in the approach of some of the international agencies that are involved in nature conservation, many indigenous communities are still suffering from forced expulsion that took place under the previous precept of fortress conservation. As such an important issue to be tackled concerns the restitution of these lands that were wrongly acquired.[127] The other emerging factor to be included in this discussion on the relationship between nature conservation and indigenous peoples' land rights relates to the role played by

---

124 The agreement will run for 50 years; and is subject to review after 25 years, it was endorsed by the Land Claims Court, which made the order that the land should be resituated to the community. See Land Claims Court, Judgement on Case Number 90/98 (Pretoria, Dec. 15, 1998).

125 "An Indigenous Protected Area is an area of land or sea over which the Traditional Indigenous Owners have entered into a voluntary agreement for the purposes of promoting biodiversity and cultural resource conservation." *See* www.deh.gov.au/indigenous/ipa/.

126 See: Stan Stevens (Eds), Indigenous Peoples, National Parks, and Protected Areas A New Paradigm Linking Conservation, Culture, and Rights (2014); Thora Martina Herrmann, Thibault Martin, Indigenous PEOPLES' Governance of Land and Protected Territories in the Arctic (2016).

127 *See* Fergus MacKay, *Addressing Past Wrongs, Indigenous Peoples and Protected Areas: The Right to Restitution of Lands and Resources* (Forest Peoples Programme, October 2002).

private actors, and notably corporations involved in tourism which is taking place on indigenous territories. Nature reserves and wildlife-protected areas are increasingly attracting mass tourism, and many of the actors involved in pushing indigenous peoples out of their lands are part of the tourism industry. There is a plethora of illustrations of cases across the globe of wrongdoing from the tourism industry when it comes to indigenous peoples' rights.[128] It is toward this relationship between corporations and indigenous peoples' land rights that the next section is focusing on.

2 *Corporations, Human Rights Law and Land Rights*

The relationship between private actors, and in particular corporations, with human rights law has been the subject of intense debates over the last two decades. Traditionally human rights law is not seen as addressing private actors as it relates to the relationship between States and their citizens. However the obligation of non-state actors to respect human rights law is increasingly been recognised.[129] This includes corporations.[130] Since the 1970s, the UN has sought to establish international standards for the conduct of transnational corporations. After decades of debates on a Draft Code of Conduct on Transnational Corporations that was proposed in the 1990/2000, no agreement could be reached regarding the content of the responsibilities of corporations.[131] In 2005, to revive the issue, the UN Secretary General nominated a Special Representative on the issue of human rights and transnational corporations and other business enterprises. The Special Representative developed a set of guidelines on the relationship between businesses and human rights. In 2011,

128 See: Tourism and Indigenous Peoples: Issues and Implications (Richard Butler and Thomas Hinch, eds., 2007); Fred Nelson, *Community rights, conservation and contested land: The politics of natural resource governance in Africa* (2012); Jessica Coria and Enrique Calfucura, *Ecotourism and the development of indigenous communities: The good, the bad, and the ugly*, Ecological Economics 73 (2012): 47–55.

129 See Andrew Clapham, Human Rights Obligations of Non-state Actors (2006); John H Knox, *Horizontal human rights law*, American Journal of International Law (2008): 1–47.

130 See Steven Ratner, *Corporations and human rights: a theory of legal responsibility*, The Yale Law Journal 111.3 (2001): 443–545; David Weissbrodt and Muria Kruger, *Norms on the responsibilities of transnational corporations and other business enterprises with regard to human rights*, The American Journal of International Law 97.4 (2003): 901–22; David Weissbordt, *Human Rights Standards Concerning Transnational Corporations and other Business Entities, Minn.* J. Int'l L. 23 (2014): 135.

131 See: P. Muchlinski, "Attempts to extend the Accountability of Transnational Corporations: The Role of UNCTAD", Menno Kamminga and Saman Zia-Zarifi (eds.), Liability of Multinational Corporations under International Law (2000), 101.

the UN Human Rights Council unanimously endorsed the UN Guiding Principles on Business and Human Rights.[132] The Guiding Principles rest on three pillars, the State duty to protect human rights, the corporate responsibility to respect human rights and access to remedies for victims of corporate human rights abuse. The "Protect, Respect and Remedy" framework is now widely used as the basis to approach the issue of corporations and human rights. The Guiding Principles do not specifically refer to indigenous peoples' land rights, nor do they acknowledge the central importance of land rights for indigenous peoples. However in general terms the Guidelines stipulate that business enterprises have a responsibility to respect internationally recognized human rights, and that this responsibility is independent of State obligations. This includes respect for the international human rights of indigenous peoples.[133] The Guiding Principles also affirm that corporations have a responsibility to respect human rights independently of the State compliance with its duty to protect those rights.

Whilst these guidelines are significant as they serve as a benchmark in terms of the relationship between corporations and human rights law, these are not binding and are only 'guidelines'. One of the values of these guidelines is to invite States to develop national plans on business and human rights. Some of these national plans have started to specifically mention indigenous peoples' rights. For example the United Kingdom national plan invites UK companies to "consult people who may potentially be affected at all stages of project design and implementation, in a manner that ensures free and informed participation and takes into account language and other potential barriers to effective engagement, paying particular attention to indigenous peoples and other groups, including women and girls."[134] However in general it remains to be seen to what extent this voluntary approach will have practical impact to protect indigenous peoples' land rights.

In terms of the jurisprudence, the IACtHR has made specific reference to the Guiding Principles in its 2015 ruling regarding the Kaliña and Lokono communities against Suriname. Referring to the Guiding Principles, the Court highlighted that "States must protect against human rights abuse within their territory and/or jurisdiction by third parties, including business enterprises. This requires taking appropriate steps to prevent, investigate, punish

132 UN Doc. A/HRC/17/31, annex.

133 For analysis, see: Johannes Rohr and José Aylwin, *Business and Human Rights: Interpreting the UN Guiding Principles for Indigenous Peoples* (IWGIA, 2014).

134 Good Business: Implementing the UN Guiding Principles on Business and Human Rights (United Kingdom, 2013).

and redress such abuse through effective policies, legislation, regulations and adjudication."[135] One of the issues in this case related to the negative impact that mining for bauxite had on indigenous territories. The Court observed that "the adverse impact on the environment and, consequently, on the rights of the indigenous peoples, were carried out by private agents; first by Suralco alone, and then by the joint venture, BHP Billiton-Suralco." The Court noted that the concerned corporations did not conduct any proper social and environmental impact assessments before undertaking their mining activities on indigenous territories. However the approach of the Court was still focused on the obligations of the State to protect the rights to land of the indigenous communities rather than the violations committed by the corporations. This approach is symptomatic of the international human rights approach to accountability and the responsibilities of corporations for violations of indigenous people' land rights. Behind the debates that led to the adoption of the Guiding Principles, one of the major issues was to determine to what extent corporations could be held accountable for violations of international human rights obligations. In general, under international human rights law, there are very little mechanisms for accountability. As summarized by Miranda: "corporate accountability available to indigenous peoples are often ineffective where state and corporate interest are aligned in the execution of large-scale land development projects, particularly projects involving natural resources extraction."[136] On the issue of accountability, the main approach of the Guiding Principles is to put forward the fact that remedies should be available for violations of human rights by corporations.

When it comes to land rights for indigenous peoples, an important aspect of the accessibility of a forum for remedies relates to the issue of extraterritoriality. The principle of extraterritoriality refers to the obligation of States to ensure that corporations registered in their country are not violating human rights abroad. The issue has been seen as controversial as many States have highlighted that they can only control human rights violations in their

135 IACtHR, *Case of the Kaliña and Lokono Peoples v. Suriname, supra* note 98, at para. 224 citing Guiding Principles on Business and Human Rights, Principle 1.

136 Lillian Aponte Miranda, "The U'Wa and Occidental Petroleum: Searching for Corporate Accountability in Violations of Indigenous Land Rights", 31 Am. Indian L. Rev. 651 (2006–2007). See also: Forest People Programme & Tebtebba Foundation, *Indigenous Peoples' Rights, Extractive Industries and Transnational and Other Business Enterprises, A Submission to the SRSG* (Forest People Programme & Tebtebba Foundation pub, 2006); Andy Whitmore (ed.), Pitfalls and pipelines: indigenous peoples and extractive industries (IWGIA and Tebtebba Foundation, 2012).

territory.[137] For many indigenous communities, extraterritoriality is a fundamental issue as corporations operating on their lands are very often transnational extractives corporations registered in other countries. The CERD Committee has addressed the issue of extraterritoriality in highlighting that States have an obligation to ensure that corporations acting abroad do not violate indigenous peoples' land rights. In its 2007 report on the situation in Canada, the Committee noted "with concern the reports of adverse effects of economic activities connected with the exploitation of natural resources in countries outside Canada by transnational corporations registered in Canada on the right to land, health, living environment and the way of life of indigenous peoples living in these regions (arts 2. 1(d)d), 4 (a) and 5(e))."[138] The Committee invited the government of Canada to "take appropriate legislative or administrative measures to prevent acts of transnational corporations registered in Canada which negatively impact on the enjoyment of rights of indigenous peoples in territories outside Canada." The Committee has made similar statements regarding the obligations of the governments of Australia, Norway, the USA and the UK regarding the action of corporations acting aboard.[139] It is an important approach as in many situations indigenous peoples' land rights are violated by corporations having headquarters in these countries. Moreover this approach based on exterritorial application of human rights is essential as in many situations the local legal settings in which the companies are operating do not allow indigenous peoples to have access to any form of remedies in case of violations. As noted by Anaya, the former UN Special Rapporteur on the rights of indigenous peoples, "in many cases in which extractive companies have been identified as responsible for, or at least associated with, violations of the rights of indigenous peoples, those violations occur in countries with weak

137 On this issue, see: ETo Consortium "Maastricht principles on extraterritorial obligations of states in the area of economic, social and cultural rights" (2012); Margot Salomon and Ian Seiderman, *Human Rights Norms for a Globalized World: The Maastricht Principles on Extraterritorial Obligations of States in the area of Economic, Social and Cultural Rights*, Global Policy (2012), 3: 458–62.

138 Concluding observations of the Committee on the Elimination of Racial Discrimination: Canada, UN Doc. CERD/C/CAN/CO/18 (2007), para. 17.

139 Concluding observations of the Committee on the Elimination of Racial Discrimination: Australia, UN Doc. CERD/C/AUS/CO/15-17 (2010), para. 13; Concluding observations of the Committee on the Elimination of Racial Discrimination: United States of America, UN Doc. CERD/C/USA/CO/7-9 (2014), para. 10.; Norway: UN Doc. CERD/C/NOR/CO/19-20; Concluding observations of the Committee on the Elimination of Racial Discrimination: United Kingdom of Great Britain and Northern Ireland, UN Doc. CERD/C/GBR/CO/18-20 (2011), para. 29.

regulatory regimes, and the responsible companies are domiciled in other, typically much more developed, countries."[140] From this perspective, and despite the debates regarding the principle of extraterritoriality of human rights obligations, the principle of extraterritorial application of human rights put forward by CERD is an important element to ensure that violations of indigenous peoples' land rights are covered.

Other significant developments regarding the relationship between corporations, indigenous peoples and human rights law are emerging from initiatives launched by international developmental and financial institutions. These institutions are increasingly developing some oversight mechanisms which are relevant to indigenous peoples' land rights. One of the most developed oversight mechanisms comes from the Organization for Economic Cooperation and Development (OECD) which has adopted a set of voluntary Guidelines on Multinational Enterprises. The Guidelines, which have been first adopted in 1976, have been amended on several occasions, notably to include more references to human rights law. More specifically regarding indigenous peoples, one paragraph of the revised OECD Guidelines makes mention of indigenous peoples' rights noting that the activities of companies could have adverse impacts on the international human rights of indigenous peoples.[141] Whilst in itself the Guidelines are voluntary and lack any form of binding obligations, the OECD has established National Contact Points (NCPs) which are national platforms for resolving practical issues that may arise with the implementation of the Guidelines. Under this mechanism, some indigenous communities have been able to engage with the impact that corporations have had on their rights to lands and natural resources. For example, the UK NCP has received a claim regarding the impact of a bauxite mine in the Niyamgiri Hills in the State of Orissa in India. The mine was developed by Vedanta Resources plc (Vedanta) on the territory of the Dongria Kondh, an indigenous community. The UK NCP highlighted that in this case the mining company had not complied with the OECD Guidelines in falling to put in place an adequate and timely consultation mechanisms to engage with the Dongria Kondh.[142] In reaching its decision the NCP notably found that the company had failed to respect the

140 Report of the Special Rapporteur on the rights of indigenous peoples, James Anaya: Extractive industries and indigenous peoples, UN Doc A/HRC/24/41, 1 July 2013, para. 47.

141 OECD (2011), OECD Guidelines for Multinational Enterprises, OECD Publishing. http://dx.doi.org/10.1787/9789264115415-en, para. 40.

142 Final Statement by the UK National Contact Point for the OECD Guidelines for Multinational Enterprises: Complaint from Survival International against Vedanta Resources plc (2009).

human rights obligations that are both applicable in India and the UK regarding indigenous peoples' rights. It concluded: "Vedanta failed to put in place any general human rights or indigenous rights policies or a mechanism, such as an indigenous (or human) rights impact assessment, to assess the impact of the construction of the mine on the Dongria Kondh." The NCP added: "the company has so far failed to develop and apply an effective self-regulatory practice to foster a relationship of confidence and mutual trust between the company and the Dongria Kondh, a constituent of the society in which it is operating."[143] Another illustration on the interaction between the OECD NCP and the relevance of international law comes from Norway. In a situation which related to mining in the Philippines, the Norwegian NCP has examined the rights of the concerned indigenous communities notably in referring to international human rights law and their rights to land. In its final statement, the NCP provided detailed guidance in relation to FPIC and noted the need for due diligence to address the "entire project impact area, including associated infrastructure."[144] These are only illustrations, as many more indigenous communities, and their supportive organisations, have recourse to the NCP process. These processes undoubtedly represent a relevant avenue for communities, however it is important to bear in mind that it relies on a purely voluntary approach based on mediation rather than adjudication. There are other types of non-judicial grievance mechanisms to address human rights violations by corporations, but none of these is as yet proven to offer a reliable and effective platform for redress.[145] Overall as noted by Doyle: "One of the purported potential strengths of these mechanisms is their capacity to function as early warning systems which serve to prevent human rights harms by identifying low-level complaints or concerns before they escalate into more serious disputes and human rights abuses."[146]

The other notable evolution regarding corporations and indigenous peoples' land rights comes from the increased reference made to indigenous peoples' rights within the voluntary codes of conduct and other related corporate social responsibilities plans. These voluntary codes of commitment are developed

143 Ibid, para. 66.

144 The Norwegian National Contact Point for the OECD Guidelines for Multinational Enterprises: "Final Statement Complaint from the Future In Our Hands (FIOH) against Intex Resources ASA and the Mindoro Nickel Project", (Oslo, OECD, 2011), at 10.

145 For analysis, see: Cathal Dolyle (Ed), Business and Human Rights: Indigenous PEOPLES' Experiences with Access to Remedy: Case Studies from Africa, Asia and Latin America (2015).

146 Cathal Dolyle, "Operational-Level Grievance Mechanisms and Indigenous Peoples' Access to Remedy", Ibid, p. 30.

either at the level of the corporations or at the larger industry levels. As noted earlier the mining industry body, the industry-wide International Council on Mining and Metals (ICMM) has published a position statement on indigenous peoples, with a crucial focus on FPIC. Other initiatives include the Initiative on Responsible Mining Assurance (IRMA), the Forest Stewardship Council (FSC) and the Roundtable on Sustainable Palm Oil (RSPO) also include the right to FPIC as a necessary safeguard to avoid corporate violations of indigenous peoples' land rights.[147] The Aluminium Stewardship Initiative (ASI) performance standard has specifically identified the potential impacts that aluminium industry could have on indigenous peoples' rights to lands, territories and resources.[148] Corporations have also adopted their own internal processes of safeguards and corporate policies which include references to the rights of the local communities.[149] All these initiatives are mainly driven by the notion of risk management, corporate reputation and a will to maximize long-term financial returns. Most of these policies are putting forward the importance of focusing on the decision-making process in relation to access to and use of lands and resources.

As noted earlier, there has been an increased level of direct negotiations and agreement making between corporations and indigenous peoples. This includes the multiplication of Impact and Benefit Agreements (IBA) in Canada, Indigenous Land Use Agreements (ILUAs) in Australia, and other forms of agreement making across the globe. However, there is an inherent danger of a fundamental imbalance of powers in these negotiations between corporations and indigenous peoples. Arguably these agreements are inscribed within the larger international legal agenda which is recognising the need to provide more direct participatory rights for indigenous peoples. In this context the rights to land and natural resources that have been examined throughout this book should serve as minimum standard for negotiations. As noted by Anaya: "Agreements with indigenous peoples allowing for extractive projects within their territories must be crafted on the basis of full respect for their rights in relation to the affected lands and resources and, in particular, should include

147 For more analysis, see: J. Carino and C. Doyle, *Making Free, Prior & Informed Consent a Reality, Indigenous Peoples and the Extractive Sector* (London, Middlesex University, Indigenous Peoples Links, Ecumenical Council for Corporate Responsibility, 2013).

148 ASI Performance Standard: Principles and Criteria (2014), see criterion 9.

149 For an analysis of some of these mechanism and notably their grievances mechanisms, see Cathal Doyle, "Operational-Level Grievance Mechanisms and Indigenous Peoples' Access to Remedy", in Cathal Dolyle (Ed), Business and Human Rights: Indigenous Peoples' Experiences with Access to Remedy: Case Studies from Africa, Asia and Latin America (2015).

provisions providing for impact mitigation, for equitable distribution of the benefits of the projects within a framework of genuine partnership, and grievance mechanisms."[150]

Overall, international human rights law is pushing for a triangular relationship between States, indigenous peoples and corporations. There are certainly some values to this approach which is based on the fundamental right of indigenous peoples to direct participation, development and self-determination. However there are some dangers with not pushing and ensuring proper accountability of private actors for violations of indigenous peoples land rights, which can hide behind the veil of State responsibilities. As noted by Macklem: "(….) the triangular relationship of the actors involved in each case reveals the fragility of the efforts to establish a bright line between public and private action in the context of multinational corporate activities that threaten indigenous interests."[151] This danger was also highlighted in a study conducted by Sawyer and Gomez which highlighted that "public-private partnerships studied here eventually led to institutional capture, undermining the neutrality of the state and its capacity to protect indigenous communities."[152] The dominant focus of international human rights law on the responsibilities of the States could contribute to supporting the "elusive" charter of the corporations' actions. Allowing corporations to hide behind the responsibility of the State is even more troublesome in situations of weak and corrupted States whose acts are dictated by the corporations. The issue of corporate accountability is not totally gone from the international agenda. In 2014, the Human Rights Council gave the mandate to an intergovernmental working group on transnational corporations and other business enterprises "to elaborate an international legally binding instrument to regulate, in international human rights law, the activities of transnational corporations and other business enterprises."[153] It is not possible to indicate whether this will lead to the adoption of a legally binding treaty which would impose direct responsibilities and accountability on corporations for human rights violations. Nonetheless, the move towards

150 Report of the Special Rapporteur on the rights of indigenous peoples, James Anaya, Extractive industries and indigenous peoples, UN Doc. A/HRC/24/41 (2013), at para. 92.

151 Patrick Macklem, *Indigenous Rights and Multinational Corporations at International Law*, 24 Hastings Int'l & Comp. L. Rev. 475, at 483 (2001), at 477.

152 Suzana Sawyer and Edmund Terence Gomez, *Transnational Governmentality and Resource Extraction: Indigenous Peoples, Multinational Corporations, Multilateral Institutions and the State* (United Nations Research Institute for Social Development, 2008), at 5.

153 Human Rights Council, *Elaboration of an international legally binding instrument on transnational corporations and other business enterprises with respect to human rights*, UN Doc. A/HRC/RES/26/9 (2014).

the development of a binding treaty provides a positive indication on the necessity to ensure that human rights are legally protected rather than submitted to voluntary principles dominated by market values. It will be important that if adopted, this new treaty clearly integrates and stipulates the obligation to respect and protect indigenous peoples' land rights.

Conclusion

By focusing on the issues of development and globalisation, this chapter has covered a lot of ground. To be able to capture some of the essential points that have been highlighted it is worth going back to the main frame that this part of the book wishes to enquire about: namely to what extent are indigenous peoples becoming direct actors in their own future rather than victims and subjects of international law? As examined the reference to development should be used with great caution. Potentially it is both a negative and positive notion. Negative as many States and international agencies have referred to development as a way to impose top-down visions of what development should mean. This is often translated into forced relocation, removal and loss of lands for indigenous peoples. On a more positive side there is the emergence of a stronger corpus of international human rights pushing for a much more inclusive and respectful approach to development. This will mean affirming indigenous peoples as the main actors of their development, though processes of effective participation, consent and benefit-sharing.

Regional human rights institutions such as the IACtHR/IACHR and the African Commission have put forward the fact that three essential safeguards are necessary to ensure that the rights to lands and natural resources are respected in the context of developmental projects taking place on their lands. First, governments have to ensure the effective participation of the members of the community in conformity with their customs and traditions, regarding any development, investment, exploration or extraction plan that will take place on their lands. If there is danger that a developmental project could eventually lead to the relocation of indigenous peoples, their consent is necessary. Second, there should be a guarantee that the concerned community will receive a reasonable benefit from these developments. Third, the government should ensure that no concession is issued until independent and technically capable entities perform a prior environmental and social impact assessment. These three safeguards which are based on a composite of fundamental rights including the right to development, property rights, self-determination and political participation represent an important legal framework to ensure a future based on a much more inclusive and participatory approach to development. Overall international law is putting forward the right to effective participation by means of a consultation process, the execution of social and environmental impact assessments, and the sharing of benefits as essential ingredients to ensure respect for indigenous peoples' land rights.

One of the limitations, and uncertainty, of international law relates to the exact nature of the rights of indigenous peoples over their natural resources. A right to ownership seems to be limited to natural resources traditionally used by indigenous peoples. As examined what is emerging is a right to participation and benefits from the use of these resources. However as highlighted the jurisprudence of the regional human rights bodies is still unclear on the legal foundation of such a right, linking it to compensation and reparation. As highlighted in Chapter 3, reparation and compensation for loss of land rights are certainly important aspects of property rights, but these should not be confused with a right to benefit from the exploitation of natural resources. It is true that in practice when indigenous peoples are facing forced relocation and loss of territories the two issues of compensation and benefits might be interlinked. Benefit sharing should not be confused with compensation or damages, and other forms of packages offered by States and corporations. Indigenous peoples have a fundamental right to benefit from any exploitation of resources located on their lands which is independent from their right to compensation. Their right to compensation is part of their right to property, whilst their right to benefit sharing is part of their right to development and their right to self-determination.

The other relevant issue that is emerging as good practice is the notion of co-management. As noted in this chapter, the principle of co-management of natural resources has increasingly been put forward by international organisations as a positive way forward to ensure that developmental projects respect the rights of indigenous peoples. This is often translated in direct negotiations between indigenous peoples and corporations. In many ways the increased use of direct negotiations and agreement making are emerging as solutions to fill the gaps in the protection offered by international law when it comes to the accountability of private actors. In this "treaty renewal", it is worth bearing in mind the past history of betrayal that has marked previous waves of treaty making between indigenous peoples and private corporations in the past. As examined in Chapter 2, indigenous peoples have been there before. They had signed treaties in good faith, which were not respected and were then unilaterally extinguished. There is also a rich historical account of unfair and coerced negotiations. Hence, whilst the move towards direct negotiations on land use and co-management of resources between indigenous peoples, States and corporations provides more space for indigenous peoples to be direct actors of their own future, there is a need for more developed and efficient safeguards to be developed. To be successful, an agreement must entail the establishment of independent judicial or quasi-judicial bodies facilitating the negotiation process and ensuring the implementation of the agreements.[154] Despite the clear needs for such independent and reliable institutions, international law remains underdeveloped in monitoring these agreements.[155] However, the overall conclusion on the impact of agreements between indigenous peoples, States and corporations should be positive. These modern treaties should be encouraged, as such treaties either allow indigenous peoples to gain a definite recognition of their rights over some of their lands, or represent the only way to put a halt to violent conflict over indigenous territorial rights. By entering into treaty negotiations over land ownership and use, governments and corporations acknowledge the existence of indigenous peoples' land rights. But above all, by entering into negotiation with indigenous peoples on the issue of land ownership and land use, States and other private actors finally put a halt to centuries of total disregard for indigenous peoples. From this perspective, these developments can be said to be part of the larger human rights discourse against racial discrimination: by entering into negotiation, States and corporations finally recognize indigenous peoples as partners. This new dialogue is not merely a renewal of treaty making. Rather, it seems to herald the initiation of a new era in the relationship between States, corporations and indigenous peoples, who, for the first time, are regarded as actors of their own future. But this new chapter needs to be written with great caution.

---

154 See Elifuraha I. Laltaika, *Proposing an Oversight Mechanism to Bolster Implementation of the United Nations Declaration on the Rights of Indigenous Peoples*, Expert Group Meeting Dialogue on an optional protocol to the United Nations Declaration on the Rights of Indigenous Peoples, January 2015, UN Doc. PFII/2015/EGM (2015).

155 See *Conclusions and Recommendations of the Seminar on Treaties, Agreements and Other Constructive Arrangements between States and Indigenous Peoples*, U.N. Doc. E/CN.4/2004/111, para. 9.

Conclusion

After centuries of colonization and dispossession, indigenous peoples have finally begun to gain a degree of recognition of the right to live on their lands. One of the threads of the book has been to demonstrate that indigenous peoples have been victims, then subjects, and finally actors of international law. While there remain some grey areas, such as the practice of extinguishment, the lack of accountability for private actors, and uncertainty regarding the legal status of natural resources, overall, the rights of indigenous peoples over their lands and territories are now strongly imbedded in the international legal architecture. The book has explored different angles of the international legal discourse and its relationship with indigenous peoples' land rights. The review of this discourse offers mixed results. There are two perspectives on the development of indigenous peoples' land rights. The first is to adopt a pessimistic approach, as reports coming from indigenous peoples across the globe still reveal a predominant story of dispossession and land encroachment, rather than recognition, respect and protection of their rights to lands and territories. From this perspective, the recent developments of international law seem relatively minimal. The second way is to adopt an optimistic view based on the fact that for centuries indigenous peoples' territorial rights have been ignored and discarded under discriminatory and racist theories and practices. From this standpoint, the recent, albeit gradual, steps towards the recognition of indigenous peoples' land rights appears as a light at the end of the tunnel. This book has proposed to adopt the middle ground between these two views, as ultimately it suggests that international human rights law potentially provides a beneficial platform for the recognition of indigenous peoples' land rights. This has to be qualified keeping in mind some States' refusal to adopt a forward-looking approach and instead to maintain the same discriminatory attitude towards indigenous peoples.

There are positives developments emerging from the recognition of indigenous peoples' attachment to their lands as a human rights issue, a recognition that demonstrates the ability of human rights law to acknowledge the different facets of indigenous peoples' attachment to their lands. Based on the indivisibility and interdependence of human rights, international treaty-monitoring bodies have engaged in the discussion of indigenous peoples' land rights relying variously on civil and political rights, and economic, social and cultural rights. This suggests the capacity of human rights law to engage with most of the different aspects of indigenous peoples' attachment to their territories. This regime has many facets. Chapter 3 showed how it encompasses a revised approach to the language of property rights to encapsulate the collective and non-exclusive nature of land rights for many indigenous communities. Chapter 4 has highlighted that the approach based on cultural rights also offers an important and complementary approach to integrate indigenous peoples' holistic, spiritual and cultural attachments to their territories. As shown in Chapters 5 and 6, this regime is also materializing through the international legal discourse on indigenous peoples' rights to participate in decisions affecting their lands and their rights over their natural resources. However, as highlighted throughout the book, one of the major challenges for international law is the recognition of a right to collective ownership, and its fundamental connection to the right to self-determination. This represents an inherent difficulty, for, in terms of territorial rights under international law, only States have traditionally exercised a collective form of territorial control. Several States are still reluctant to recognize indigenous peoples' collective form of land ownership.[1] From this perspective, the recognition of a collective right to land ownership involves a new relationship between States and indigenous peoples.

One of the recurring themes of friction between States and indigenous peoples relates to the issue of restitution. In Chapter 3 we saw that human rights law is starting to develop a theory on land restitution. One of the most positive outcomes is that such a discourse has opened up a dialogue between the different actors on restitution and reduced the "myths" that usually go come with restitution. Nonetheless, in order to be effective, the discourse on restitution remains dependent on the political will of States. It has been highlighted that the notion of reparation for past dispossession is crucial. Thus, the developing human rights discourse on land restitution, the emerging discourse on collective land ownership, and the gradual recognition of indigenous peoples' customary laws should be seen as stepping-stones on the way towards making the human rights discourse itself more universal. These evolutions open the door to the acceptance of indigenous peoples as actors guiding their own future, by recognizing their past and their history.

One of the main elaborations of the book was to examine how international human rights law is supporting the development of a new phase in the relationship between States and indigenous peoples in which the latter will finally

---

1 *See*, for example, the U.S. government statement following the decision of the Inter-American Commission on Human Rights in the *Danns*' case which stated: "[T]he Danns' claim is, fundamentally, not a human rights claim, but an attempt by two individual Indians to reopen the question of collective Western Shoshone tribal property rights to land." United States Government, "Response of the Government of the United States to October 10, 2002 Report No. 53/02, Case No. 11.140 (Mary and Carrie Dann)."

be recognized as actors playing a part in their own future. As noted in Part II, there are some positive signs that confirm that human rights law is moving towards such recognition by increased reference to indigenous customary laws. Also, the development of a strong human rights obligation on States to demarcate indigenous territories implies positive duties that are proactive and encourage participation from affected parties.[2] These developments, in turn, have had the effect of inviting collaboration between State organs and indigenous peoples themselves, resulting in indigenous peoples being deeply involved and often leading the demarcation process in many cases. Part III of the book has explored how human rights law plays an important role in the recognition of indigenous peoples as actors guiding their own future by deciding and participating in the elaboration of rules concerning the use and ownership of their traditional territories. This evolution is certainly one of the most promising developments, and human rights law acts as a very positive force in supporting the establishment of a dialogue between indigenous peoples and States. As Robinson stated:

> how crucial to the concept of rights is the concept of participation. People should not be just docile subjects of rights: rights are never 'given' to people. Rights must be asserted, and they must be asserted on one's own behalf of all other human beings, without distinction. [This] has produced an understanding of participation which allows people to become agents of their own change.[3]

This dialogue is crucial, as ultimately it means that indigenous peoples are recognized as guardians of their own future, and that they are to be regarded as partners not as peoples that have to be forcibly integrated and assimilated within the main society, as has been the case for centuries.

The Need for a Specific Legal Regime?

It was noted in the introduction that a central issue to consider is whether indigenous peoples' land rights can be addressed within the existing international legal framework or if they require the development of a new category of

2 On this issue, *see* Sandra Fredman, *Discrimination, in* The Oxford Handbook of Legal Studies 223 (Peter Cane & Mark Tushnet eds., 2003).

3 Mary Robinson, *quoted in* Christopher McCrudden, *Mainstreaming Equality in the Governance of Northern Ireland*, 22 Ford. Int'l L.J. 1697, at 1771 (1999).

sui generis rights. This issue is related to the more general debate on whether the general human rights discourse is sufficient to address indigenous peoples' claims or if there is a need for a specific branch of indigenous peoples' rights. Corntassel and Primeau suggested that the existing body of human rights law is adequate to address indigenous peoples' claims.[4] Brownlie has pushed the issue further by stating that: "[T]he heavy reliance on the still relatively controversial category of 'indigenous peoples' is difficult to understand and, frankly, it smacks of nominalism and a sort of snobbery."[5] On the other side of the spectrum, Berman has argued that indigenous peoples' rights constitute a *sui generis* category of rights that arise outside of the positive law system. They are "pre-existing rights in the sense that they are not developed from the legal system of surrounding states but [they] arise *sui generis* from the historical condition of indigenous peoples as distinctive societies with the aspiration to survive as such."[6] Kingsbury has pointed out that indigenous peoples' claims under international law come from five main different directions: non-discrimination, minority rights, self-determination, historical sovereignty and *sui generis* claims.[7] As it has been highlighted throughout the book, land rights concern all of these five categories.

The specific legal framework dedicated to indigenous peoples is in itself quite restricted. To date, the ILO 169 is still the only specifically dedicated binding treaty on the rights of indigenous peoples. As examined throughout the book, whilst the ILO 169 is a very comprehensive treaty encompassing many of the essential elements to protect and support indigenous peoples' land rights, there are nonetheless some limitations to the treaty. In terms of the content, it was highlighted that it does not include self-determination and also provides a restricted approach to rights over natural resources. But probably the main limitation of the treaty relates to the fact that so far only 22 States have ratified the treaty, including only one State from Africa and very few from Asia. From this perspective, the adoption of the UNDRIP is extremely significant as it offers a much more universal statement on indigenous peoples' rights. Moreover as highlighted throughout the book, the Declaration offers a very comprehensive and holistic approach to land rights. In this case, the limitation relates

4 Jeff J. Corntassel & Thomas H. Primeau, *Indigenous 'Sovereignty' and International Law: Revised Strategies for Pursuing 'Self-Determination,'* 17 Hum. Rts. Q. 342 (1995).

5 Ian Brownlie, Treaties and Indigenous Peoples 63 (1992).

6 Howard Berman, *Are Indigenous Populations Entitled to International Juridical Personality?* 79 Am. Soc'y Int'l L. Proc. 189, at 193 (1989).

7 Benedict Kingsbury, *Reconciling Five Competing Conceptual Structures of Indigenous Peoples' Claims in International and Comparative Law, in* Peoples' Rights 109 (Philip Alston ed., 2001).

more to its nature, as it is a declaration rather than a binding treaty. However, as it was highlighted, the Declaration has already had a significant impact in the jurisprudence of international, regional and national institutions, and does represents to some extent customary international norms. Nonetheless, the UNDRIP is not strictly speaking a binding legal treaty. However as examined it would be wrong to focus on land rights only though the lens of these two instruments. Indeed what is coming out strongly is the fact that the more general international treaties, and especially human rights treaties, can offer a relevant space for indigenous peoples' land rights. Thus, on the one hand, there is a need for a specific approach to indigenous peoples' land claims, but, on the other hand, it is suggested that the human rights discourse is moving towards the recognition of indigenous peoples' specific attachment to their territories. This comes mainly from the evolution of the findings of the CESCR, HRC and CERD, which in recent years have illustrated that the general human rights instruments have some capacity to address indigenous peoples' specific land claims. As Part III of the book argued, in exploring the content of the human rights discourse on indigenous peoples' land rights, one of the best methods to evaluate it is to examine the extent to which such a discourse provides indigenous peoples with a right to control their own future. After centuries of paternalism the key demand from most indigenous peoples is to have the right to decide and participate in decisions that are affecting their lands. The existing discourse should be seen as a basis to shape the future of indigenous peoples. It is suggested that indigenous peoples, through their land claims, have managed to influence the international system in two profound ways.

First, indigenous peoples have managed to question States' absolute sovereignty by entering into negotiations on territorial issues. By questioning the legality of States' territorial assertion over their traditional territories, indigenous peoples have succeeded in gaining recognition of their unique status as actors that have to be consulted in decisions affecting their lands. Indigenous claims to collective rights of control over lands and resources challenge the primacy of the State more fundamentally than the assertion of classical human rights. As Anaya puts it, "in pressing their demands internationally, indigenous peoples have undermined the premise of the state as the highest and most liberating form of human association."[8] As highlighted in Chapter 5, indigenous peoples have succeeded in modifying international law's traditional approach to self-determination. This development points towards the evolution of a specific indigenous approach to self-determination based on

8 James Anaya, *Indigenous Peoples and International Law Issues*, 92 Am. Soc'y Int'l L. Proc. 96, at 97 (1998).

a relational approach between States and indigenous peoples. Control over lands and natural resources constitute a central element of this new approach to self-determination. The recent practice of the international human rights treaty monitoring bodies indicates an evolution towards the recognition that self-determination encapsulates a right for indigenous peoples to participate in the decisions affecting their territories. In this regard, there is a clear evolution towards the recognition of self-determination as an important right for indigenous peoples to control their lands and territories. More generally, the maturing of the right to self-determination towards a right for indigenous peoples to consent, participate and manage the use of their lands and natural resources places itself in the broader development of international law which supports the right of indigenous peoples to be direct actors rather than passive subjects of protection. The main assumption of the book is that indigenous peoples and States have entered into an age of negotiations. In Part III, it has been observed that such negotiations take place in relation to issues such as autonomous arrangements, post-conflict settlements and land use agreements. As land rights for indigenous peoples are gradually being recognized as fundamental human rights, this development leads to some interesting advances in the relationship between State territorial integrity and indigenous peoples' land rights. This is the conclusion that this book has led to, i.e., that human rights law is playing an ever increasingly positive role in the development towards a right for indigenous peoples to enter into negotiations over the use and ownership of their territories. Overall, regarding indigenous peoples' land rights, probably the most forward looking outcome relates to the strong language of international law on the need to foster dialogue, the main principle being the idea of consent and, as a consequence, dialogue and consultation between States, indigenous peoples and private actors.

Second, indigenous peoples have managed, in a fairly short period of time, to shape the human rights discourse on cultural diversity. It has been pointed out that the existence of indigenous peoples' rights under international law can be traced to the early writings on international law from Vitoria, Las Casas, Vattel, Grotius and Pufendorf. However, as highlighted, the rejection of the idea of cultural superiority/inferiority and the recognition of diversity as a value are, from the point of view of history, very recent phenomena. Indigenous peoples' land claims and the recognition of indigenous specific cultural approach to lands and territories have opened the door towards the recognition and integration of "other" systems of laws within States' national systems, giving more space for legal pluralism. The gradual recognition of indigenous peoples' collective forms of land ownership and custodianship is pushing towards legal pluralism, with the recognition of both individual and indigenous collective ownership within the same system of law. The development of indigenous peoples' land rights has successfully shown the possibility of integrating indigenous customary laws within the national systems, an evolution which supports the development of more encompassing legal systems open to customary indigenous rights.[9]

On a less positive side, two major limitations seem to appear from the international legal approach to land rights. First, one of the dangers of the protection of indigenous peoples' land rights under property (Chapter 3) and cultural rights (Chapter 4) is that such protection compartmentalizes the various aspects of indigenous peoples' attachment to their lands. As noted by Coombe: "The West has created categories of property – intellectual property, cultural property, and real property – that divides peoples and things according to the same colonizing discourses of possessive individualism that historically disentitled and disfranchised Native peoples."[10] As examined in this book, the legal regime covering land rights for indigenous peoples is scattered and compartmentalized in a multitude of specialised different legal regimes. International law creates different legal regimes to address issues of land property, cultural heritage, and management of natural resources. All these issues are fundamentally entrenched and embedded in the similar attachment to a land for indigenous peoples. Hence there is an inherent danger of compartmentalization in the international legal framework which does not reflect indigenous peoples' holistic approach to lands and natural resources. While the book as pointed that there is some important and significant evolution to avoid such compartmentalization, notably though the emergence of legal concept such as the right to cultural integrity and the more encompassing approach to natural resources developed under the banner of self-determination, it is important to bear in mind such danger.

The second important limitation of the current legal regime relates to its inability to properly address the place and the role of private actors, especially corporations. As noted in Chapter 6, the main legal approach rely predominately on a voluntary approach by corporations. This approach is fundamentally driven by the dominant neo-liberal agenda of the principal international financial and developmental agencies, as well as the financial interest of corporations. In the word of Corntassel, under such approach there is still a

9 See: Brendan Tobin, Indigenous Peoples, Customary Law and Human Rights – Why Living Law Matters (2014).

10 Rosemary Coombe, *The Properties of Culture and the Politics of Possessing Identity, in* Explorations in Difference: Law, Culture and Politics 252 (Jonathan Hart & Richard Bauman eds., 1996).

fundamental "market" based vision of the relationship between a people and its environment.[11] While the agenda on business and human rights is still very much in development, the heavy reliance on this voluntary market orientated approach is a worrying development. The fact that indigenous peoples' land rights are so essential and fundamental gets diluted into other financial considerations. International law has not yet managed to ensure the priority to fundamental rights, such as land rights, over other considerations. As captured by Stavenhagen after his official visit as UN Special Rapporteur to the Philippines: "[T]he idea of prior right being granted to a mining or other business company rather than to a community that has held and cared for the land over generations must be stopped, as it brings the whole system of protection of human rights of indigenous peoples into disrepute."[12] Until a better, fairer and more respectful legal systems is put in pace to ensure that indigenous peoples' land rights get properly respected by the private sector, the whole international legal edifice will remain ineffective.

To return to the question of whether there is a need for a specific indigenous peoples' rights regime as opposed to simply accommodating their claims within the existing international legal framework, the answer is certainly not a choice of one over the other. The book has attempted to adopt a middle ground position, by seeking to demonstrate that both approaches are needed and that they already co-exist. Indigenous peoples' land claims appeal both to general norms, such as non-discrimination and economic, social and cultural rights, but also to specific rights, such as the right to collective custodianship, the right to consultation, and the right to FPIC. This latter aspect, especially the rights to consultation and FPIC, probably requires the establishment of a specific regime to support the monitoring of the negotiations and their implementation. Apart from the references to the need of consultation to be followed in good faith and to ensure equitable benefit sharing, international law remains relatively weak in terms of offering institutions to support and monitor these processes of consent and benefit-sharing. Regarding modern treaties and other forms of agreements between States, indigenous peoples and corporations it has been highlighted that the role of international law remains extremely limited. Even though international human rights treaty monitoring bodies have increasingly examined the interrelationship between these

11 Jeff Corntassel, "Toward sustainable self-determination: Rethinking the contemporary Indigenous-rights discourse", Alternatives: Global, Local, Political 33.1 (2008): 105–132.

12 *Report of the Special Rapporteur on the Situation of Human Rights and Fundamental Freedoms of Indigenous People, Mr. Rodolfo Stavenhagen, Mission to the Philippines,* U.N. Doc. E/CN.4/2003/90/Add.3, at 2.

agreements and human rights obligations, so far there has been a very limited contribution from international law. With the development of agreements between States, indigenous peoples, and corporations there is a need to ensure that independent institutions are in place to ensure that the processes are fair and impartial.

The main weakness of the international legal discourse on land rights does not seem to be the content of the rights, but rather the lack of proper independent and reliable place to get remedies. As the heavy reliance of the book on the jurisprudence of the Inter-American Court of Human Rights indicates, the Court has become a central battleground for the development of indigenous peoples' land rights. However, this is limited to Central and Latin America and despite the significant decision of the Court, these decisions usually suffer form a lack of implementation at the national levels. As noted, the African Commission on Human and Peoples' Rights has started to play a very active and significant role in Africa, but also suffers from a similar issue of non-implementation. As noted, the European Court of Human Rights has not yet made any well-defined impact on indigenous peoples' land rights. In 2015, The Caribbean Court of Justice has made a positive ruling to support indigenous peoples' land rights in Belize, but there is not certainty that this will be of relevance to other indigenous communities in the region. For the rest of the world indigenous peoples, in Asia, the Middle East, Oceania, or elsewhere, there are no regional courts to be reached. At the international level, the International Court of Justice is not directly opened to indigenous peoples, as only States can bring cases. This leaves indigenous peoples with very few options to receive any forms of international, independent and impartial access to remedies.

The call for an international and independent place for adjudication on land rights claims is not new. For instance, in 1896, the International Arbitration and Peace Association argued for the establishment of a Permanent International Commission for Africa, stating that indigenous populations were "especially exposed to acts of injustice and wrongful deprivation of their lands by ambitious and reckless agents or adventurers."[13] The Association recommended the creation of a Permanent Commission to regulate these problems and to refer territorial disputes between settlers and natives to the *Bureau International Permanent de la Paix*. More recently, in 2000, Daes has pointed out that the Permanent Forum on Indigenous Issues should consider:

- The creation of a fact-finding body, with a mandate to make site visits and to prepare reports concerning particular indigenous land and resources issues;

13 Hodgson Pratt & J.F. Green, *A Permanent International Commission for Africa*, at para. 7 (International Arbitration and Peace Association, 1896).

- The creation of an indigenous land and resources ombudsman or office which could provide response, mediation and reconciliation services;
- The creation of a complaint mechanism or procedure for human rights violations that pertain to indigenous land and resources situations;
- The creation of a body with 'peace-seeking' powers to investigate, recommend solutions, conciliate, mediate and otherwise assist in preventing or ending violence in situations regarding indigenous land rights;
- The creation of a procedure whereby countries would be called upon to make periodic reports with regard to their progress in protecting the land and resources rights of indigenous peoples.[14]

The UN Permanent Forum on Indigenous Issues, in its second report, recommended the establishment of a specific international instance in charge of land rights.[15] Indigenous peoples' representatives have made similar call for the development of a specific international forum. Les Malezer from Australia invited the former WGIP to "take up the challenge to pursue the establishment of a mechanism for Indigenous Peoples to register disputes with States over land."[16] Such an international dispute resolution mechanism is needed because, as pointed out, in most situations, the State is one of the parties in the dispute. It cannot be allowed to act as a judge and a party at the same time. Indigenous peoples' experience with treaty making during the colonial era highlights the need for such international supervision, as these treaties were usually disregarded and unilaterally abrogated by States. Based on such experience, a high degree of international monitoring is needed.

In the current climate of distrust regarding international law, it is hard to envisage that an international institution to monitor and adjudicate issues relating to land rights for indigenous peoples will be established. Likewise, the call for an international treaty to follow on the UNDRIP is also hard to envisage. However, a few years ago it was also hard to envisage that a Declaration would ever be adopted. The strength of the indigenous movement is its unprecedented ability to present the indigenous cause as a global one. Despite representing the most cultural and ethnic diversity of the world, indigenous peoples have approached international lawmakers and presented their cause for the protection and recognition of their fundamental rights to lands and territories from a unified position. Even though it might take some time, for such an approach

14 U.N. Doc. E/CN.4/Sub.2/2000/25, at 39–40, para. 152.

15 U.N. Doc. E/2003/43.

16 Les Malezer, *Foundation for Aboriginal and Islander Research Action*, 21st Sess. WGIP, Agenda item 4(a), July 22, 2003 (on file with the author).

is based on the principle of dialogue and consent, as stated by the International Indian Treaty Council: "[I]n truth, no one has ever said that acceptance by States of Indigenous human rights and fundamental freedoms would be an easy or timely process. It will take time. We should not panic or despair if the process takes longer than we would hope."[17]

17 International Indian Treaty Council, *Another Perspective on the Process Towards Adoption of the Declaration for the Rights of Indigenous Peoples* (Mar. 25, 2003), *at* www.treatycouncil.org/PDFs/Support_for_the_Declaration_paper.pdf.

Selected Bibliography

Aikio, P. & M. Scheinin, eds., Operationalizing the Right of Indigenous Peoples to Self-Determination (2001).

Alfredsson, G. & M. Stavroupoulo, eds., Justice Pending: Indigenous Peoples and Other Good Causes, Essays in Honour of Erica-Irene A. Daes (2002).

Allen, S. & A. Xanthaki, eds., Reflections on the UN Declaration on the Rights of Indigenous Peoples (2011).

Alston, P., Peoples' Rights (2001).

Amry, R.P., *Indigenous Peoples, Customary Law and the Peace-Process in Guatemala*, 10 L. & Anthropology 52 (1998).

Anaya, J., Indigenous Peoples in International Law (2d ed. 2005).

Anaya, J., Indigenous Peoples' Participatory Rights in Decisions about Natural Resources Extraction: The More Fundamental Issue of What Rights Indigenous Peoples have in Lands and Resources, 22 Ariz. J. Int'l & Comp. L. 7 (2005).

Anaya, J, ed., International Human Rights and Indigenous Peoples (2011).

Anaya, J. & R.A. Williams, *The Protection of Indigenous Peoples' Rights over Lands and Natural Resources Under the Inter-American Human Rights System*, 14 Harv. Hum. Rts. J. 33 (2001).

Arens, R., ed., Genocide in Paraguay (1976).

Asch, M., ed., Aboriginal and Treaty Rights in Canada (1997).

Assembly of the First Nations, *The Amicus Curiae Brief of the Assembly of First Nations*, 22 Hum. Rts. Q. 580 (2000).

Assies, W., G. van der Haar & A.J. Hoekema, eds., The Challenge of Diversity: Indigenous Peoples and Reform of the States in Latin America (1998).

Barelli, M, *The interplay between global and regional human rights systems in the construction of the indigenous rights regime*, Human Rights Quarterly 32.4 (2010): 951–79.

Barelli, M., Seeking Justice in International Law: The Significance and Implications of the UN Declaration on the Rights of Indigenous Peoples (2016).

Barnard, A. & J. Kenrick, eds., Africa's Indigenous Peoples: 'First Peoples' or 'Marginalized Minorities'? (2001).

Barsh, R.L., *Indigenous Peoples in the 1990s: From Object to Subject of International Law?*, 7 Harv. Hum. Rts. J. 33 (1994).

Barsh, R. & J. Youngblood Henderson, The *Supreme Court's Van der Peet Trilogy: Naive Imperialism and Ropes of Sand*, 42 McGill L.J. 993 (1997).

Bartlett, R., *Native Title: From Pragmatism to Equality Before the Law*, 20 Melbourne U.L. Rev. 284 (1995).

Barume, A, Land Rights of Indigenous Peoples in Africa (2014).

Bauer, J.R. & D.A. Bell, eds., The East Asian Challenge for Human Rights (1999).

Bedjaoui, M., Terra Nullius, 'droits' historiques et autodetermination (La Haye: Exposés oraux prononcés devanr la Cour Internationale de Justice en l'affaire du Sahara Occidental, 1975).

Bell, D.G, *Forum on R. Marshall: Was Amerindian Dispossession Lawful? The Response of 19th Century Maritime Intellectuals*, 23 Dalhousie L.J. 168 (2000).

Bennett, G., Aboriginal Rights in International Law (London: Royal Anthropological Institute of Great Britain and Ireland and Survival International, Occasional Paper No. 37, 1978).

Bennett, T.W. & C.H. Powell, *Aboriginal Title in South Africa Revisited*, 15 S. Afr. J. Hum. Rts. 449 (1999).

Berger, T.R., Village Journey: The Report of the Alaska Native Review Commission (1985).

Bhaumik, S et al., eds., Living on the Edge: Essays on the Chittagong Hill Tracts (1997).

Bhengra, R., C.R. Bijoy & S. Luithui, The Adivasis of India (1998).

Birks, P.B.H., *The Roman Law Concept of Dominium and the Idea of Absolute Ownership*, Acta Juridica 1 (1985).

Borrows, J., *Frozen Rights in Canada: Constitutional Interpretation and the Trickster*, 22 Am. Indian L. Rev. 37 (1997).

Borrows, J., *Listening for a Change: The Courts and Oral Tradition*, 39 Osgoode Hall L.J. 1 (2001).

Borrows, J., *Domesticating Doctrine: Aboriginal Peoples after the Royal Commission*, 46 McGill L.J. 615 (2001).

Bothe, M., T. Kurzidem & C. Schmidt, Legal Aspects of the Preservation of the Environment and Development in Last Open Spaces (1993).

Bourassa, S. & A.L. Strong, *Restitution of Land to New Zealand Maori: The Role of Social Structure*, 75(2) Pac. Aff. 227 (2002).

Bradly, B., *Property as Ontology: On Aboriginal and English Understandings of Ownership*, 13 Can. J.L. & Juris. 3 (2002).

Bravo, K., *Balancing Indigenous Rights to Land and the Demand of Economic Development: Lessons from the United States and Australia*, 30 Colum. J.L. & Soc. Probs. 529 (1997)

Brilmayer, L., *Secession and Self-determination: A Territorial Interpretation*, 16 Yale J. Int'l L. 177 (1991).

Brody, H., The Other Side of Eden, Hunters Farmers and the Shaping of the World (2002).

Brownlie, I., Treaties and Indigenous Peoples (1992).

Bulan, R., *Native Title as a Proprietary Right Under the Constitution of Peninsula Malaysia: A Step in the Right Direction?*, 9 Asia Pac. L. Rev. 1 (2001).

Bull, H., B. Kingsbury & A. Roberts, Hugo Grotius and International Relations (1990).

Burguete Cal Y Mayor, A., ed., Indigenous Autonomy in Mexico (IWGIA Doc. No. 94, 2000).

Carozza, P.G., *From Conquest to Constitutions: Retrieving a Latin American Tradition of the Idea of Human Rights*, 25 Hum. Rts. Q. 281 (2003).

Cassese, A., Self-Determination of Peoples, A Legal Reappraisal (1995).

Castellino, J. & S. Allen, Title to Territory in International Law (2003).

Castellino, J. & N. Walsh, eds., International Law and Indigenous Peoples (2005).

Challaye, F., *La Société des Nations et les Indigènes*, 5 Les Cahiers des Droits de L'homme (1928).

Charters, C. & A. Erueti, *Report from the Inside: The CERD Committee's Review of the Foreshore and Seabed Act 2004*, 36 Vict. U. Wellington L. Rev. 257 (2005).

Charters, C & R. Stavenhagen (eds) Making the Declaration Work: The United Nations Declaration on the Rights of Indigenous Peoples (IWGIA, 2009).

Cheney Hyde, C., *Conquest Today*, 30(3) Am. J. Int'l L. 471 (1936).

Christakis, T., Le droit a l'autodetermination en dehors des situations de decolonisation (1999).

Churchill, W., Perversion of Justice, Indigenous Peoples and Anglo-American Law (2003).

Clark, D. & R. Williamson, eds., Self-Determination: International Perspectives (1996).

Clinton, R.N., *Isolated in Their Own Country: A Defense of Federal Protection of Indian Autonomy and Self-Government*, 33 Stan. L. Rev. 979 (1981).

Cohen, F.S., *The Spanish Origin of Indian Rights in the Law of the United States*, 31 Geo. L.J. (1942).

Corntassel, J. & T. Hopkins Primeau, *Indigenous 'Sovereignty' and International Law*, 17 Hum. Rts. Q. 343 (1995).

Cowan, J.K., M.B. Dembour & R.A. Wilson, eds., Culture and Rights, Anthropological Perspectives (2001).

Craufurd-Lewis, M., *Treaties with Aboriginal Minorities*, 15(1) Can. J. Native Stud. 1 (1995).

Curtin, P.D., ed., Imperialism (1971).

Daes, E-I., *Equality of Indigenous Peoples under the Auspices of the United Nations: Draft Declaration on the Rights of Indigenous Peoples*, 7 St. Thomas L. Rev. (Summer 1995).

Dahl, J., J. Hicks & P. Jull, eds., Nunavut—Inuit Regain Control of the Lands and Their Lives (IWGIA, 2000).

Das, J.K., Human Rights and Indigenous Peoples (2001).

Davidson, J.S., *The Rights of Indigenous Peoples in Early International Law*, 5 Canterbury L. Rev. 391 (1994).

de Las Casas, B., The Defence of the Most Reverend Lord, Don Fray Baryolomé de Las Casas of the Order of the Preachers, Late Bishop of Chiapa, Against the Persecutors and Slanderers of the Peoples of the New World Discovered Across the Seas (1552, trans. and ed. 1974).

Deloria, V., Behind the Trail of Broken Treaties (1974).

Devasih, R., *The Discordant Accord: Challenges Towards the Implementation of the Chittagong Hill Tracts Accord of 1997*, 100 J. Soc. Stud. (2003).

Dick, D., *Comprehending 'the genius of the common law'—Native Title in Australia and Canada compared post-Delgamuukw*, 5 Australian J. Hum. Rts. 1 (1999).

Dinstein, Y., ed., Models of Autonomy (1981).

Dufraimont, L., *Continuity and Modification of Aboriginal Rights in the Nisga'a Treaty*, 35 U.B.C.L. Rev. 455 (2002).

Doyle, C., Indigenous Peoples, Title to Territory, Rights and Resources: The Transformative Role of Free Prior and Informed Consent (2015).

Ederington, L.B., *Property as a Natural Institution: The Separation of Property from Sovereignty in International Law*, 13 Am. U. Int'l L. Rev. 263 (1997).

Eide, A., *Legal and Normative Bases for Saami Claims to Land in the Nordic Countries*, 8 Int'l J. Minority & Group Rts. 127 (2001).

Eide, A., C. Krausse & A. Rosas, Economic, Social and Cultural Rights—A Textbook (1995).

Elias, T.O., *The Doctrine of Intertemporal Law*, 74 Am. J. Int'l L. 285 (1980).

Faulkner, R.K., The Jurisprudence of John Marshall (1968).

Ferch, M.L., *Indian Land Rights: An International Approach to Just Compensation*, 2 Transnat'l L. & Contemp. Probs. 302 (1992).

Ferguson, R.B. & N.L. Whitehead, eds., War in the Tribal Zone: Expanding States and Indigenous Warfare (1992).

Ferro, M., Histoire des Colonisations (1994).

Flanagan, T., *The Agricultural Argument and Original Appropriation: Indian Lands and Political Philosophy*, 22 Can. J. Pol. Sci. 589 (1989).

Foster, C.E., *Articulating Self-Determination in the Draft Declaration on the Rights of Indigenous Peoples*, 12 Eur. J. Int'l L. 141 (2001).

Fox Bourne, H.R., Expeditions de Represailles en Afrique (Mémoire présenté au Onzième Congrès Universel de la Paix, Monaco, Aboriginies Protection Society, 1902).

Franck, T., *The Emerging Right to Democratic Governance*, 86 Am. J. Int'l L. 46 (1992).

Franck, T.M., *Clan and Superclan: Loyalty, Identity and Community in Law and Practice*, 90 Am. J. Int'l L. 359 (1996).

Frickey, P., *Domesticating Federal Indian Law*, 81 Minn. L. Rev. 31 (1996).

Gaer, F.D., *UN-Anonymous: Reflections on Human Rights in Peace Negotiations*, 19 Hum. Rts. Q. 1 (1997).

Geer, M., *Foreigners in their Own Land: Cultural Land and Transnational Corporations—Emergent International Rights and Wrongs*, 38 Va. J. Int'l L. 331 (1998).

Gesell, J.N., *Customary Indigenous Law in the Mexican Juridicial System*, 26 Ga. J. Int'l & Comp. L. 643 (1997).

Ghanea, N. & A. Xanthaki, eds., Minorities, Peoples and Self-Determination: Essays in Honour of Patrick Thornberry (2005).

Gonzalez de Pazos, M., The Chiapas Uprising and the Negotiating Process, 7 St. Thomas L. Rev. 685 (1995).

Gouttenoire de Toury, F., *Les Revendications des Indigènes*, 6 Les Cahiers des Droits de L'homme (1926).

Griffiths, J., *What Is Legal Pluralism?*, 24 J. Legal Pluralism 1 (1986).

Grotius, H., The Law of War and Peace (Humphrey Milford, Classic of International Law, 1925).

Gutto, S.B.O., Property & Land Reform: Constitutional and Jurisprudential Perspectives (1995).

Hamilton, A.C., Canada and Aboriginal Peoples: A New Partnership, Report of Hon. A.C. Hamilton, Fact-Finder for Minister of Indian Affairs and Northern Development (1995).

Hanke, L., The Spanish Struggle for Justice in the Conquest of America (1949).

Hannum, H., Autonomy, Sovereignty, and Self-Determination: The Accommodation of Conflicting Rights (1990).

Hannum, H., ed., Guide to International Human Rights Practice (1992).

Hannum, H., ed., Documents on Autonomy and Minority Rights (1993).

Harding, G., *The Tragedy of the Commons*, 162 Sci. 1243 (1968).

Hart, J. & R. Bauman, eds., Explorations in Difference: Law, Culture and Politics (1996).

Havemann, P., ed., Indigenous Peoples' Rights in Australia, Canada and New Zealand (1999).

Hawkes, D.C., *Indigenous Peoples: Self-Government and Intergovernmental Relations*, 167 Int'l Soc. Sci. J. 153 (2001).

Hill, R.P., *Blackfellas and Whitefellas: Aboriginal Land Rights, The Mabo Decision, and the Meaning of Land*, 17(2) Hum. Rts. Q. 303 (1995).

Howitt, R., J. Connell & P. Hirsch, Resources, Nations and Indigenous Peoples: Case Studies from Australasia, Melanesia and Southeast Asia (1996).

International Work Group for Indigenous Affairs, Self-Determination (Indigenous Affairs, No. 3, 2001).

International Work Group for Indigenous Affairs, The Indigenous World 2002 (IWGIA, 2002).

International Work Group for Indigenous Affairs, The Indigenous World 2003 (IWGIA, 2003).

International Work Group for Indigenous Affairs, The Indigenous World 2004 (IWGIA, 2004).

Jaichand, V, Restitution of Land Rights: A Workbook (1997).

Jennings, R.Y., The Acquisition of Territory in International Law (1963).

Jennings, R.Y. & A. Watts, Openheim's International Law (1996).

Karpe, P., *Droit Colonial, Droit d'outre mer, Droit des Collectivités Autochtones*, 55(2) Revue Juridique et politique Independence et Cooperation 236 (2001).

Keal, P., *'Just Backward Children' International Law and the Conquest on non-Europeans Peoples*, 49(2) Australian J. Int'l Aff. 191 (1995).

Kemf, E., ed., Indigenous Peoples and Protected Areas: The Law of Mother Earth (1993).

Keon-Cohen, B., ed., Native Title in the Millenium (2001).

Kersey, A., *The Nunavut Agreement: A Model for Preserving Indigenous Rights*, 11 Ariz. J. Int'l & Comp. L. 429 (1994).

Kicher, I.A., The Kanaks of New Caledonia (MRG Report 71, 1986).

Kilcullen, J., The Origin of Property: Ockham, Grotius, Pufendorf, and Some Others (1995).

Kingsbury, B., *Claims by Non-State Groups in International Law*, 25 Cornell Int'l L.J. 481 (1992).

Kingsbury, B., *Competing Conceptual Approaches to Indigenous Group Issues in New Zealand Law*, 52 U. Toronto L.J. 101 (2002).

Kirgis, F.L., *The Degrees of Self-Determination in the United Nations Era*, 88 Am. J. Int'l L. 304 (1994).

Kirkby, D. & C. Coleborne, Law, History, Colonialism, The Reach of Empire (2001).

Korman, S., The Right of Conquest (1996).

Koskenniemi, M., *National Self-determination Today: Problems of Legal Theory and Practice*, 43 Int'l Comp. L.Q. 241 (1994).

Kreimer, O., *Indigenous Peoples' Rights to Land, Territories, and Natural Resources: A Technical Meeting of the OAS Working Group*, 10(2) Hum. Rts. Brief 13 (2003).

Kuper, A., Culture: The Anthropologists' Account (2000).

Kuprecht, K., Indigenous Peoples' Cultural Property Claims: Repatriation and Beyond (2013).

Kymlicka, W., Multicultural Citizenship, A Liberal Theory of Minority Rights (2001).

Kymlicka, W., Politics in the Vernacular: Nationalism, Multiculturalism, and Citizenship (2001).

Lâm, M., *Making Room for Peoples at the United Nations: Thoughts Provoked by Indigenous Claims to Self-Determination,* 25 Cornell Int'l L.J. 609 (1992).

Lâm, M., At the Edge of the State: Indigenous Peoples and Self-Determination (2000).

Levin, D., Terre des Hommes du Grand Ocean: De la Coutume au Droit International (1999).

Lijphart, A., *The Puzzle of Indian Democracy: A Consociational Interpretation*, 90 Am. Pol. Sci. Rev. 258 (1996).

Lindley, M.F., The Acquisition and Government of Backward Territory in International Law (Longmans, Green and Co., 1926, *reprinted in* Negro Universities Press, 1969).

MacKay, F., A Guide to Indigenous Peoples' Rights in the Inter-American Human Rights System (IWGIA, 2002).

MacKay, F., Addressing Past Wrongs, Indigenous Peoples and Protected Areas: The Right to Restitution of Land and Resources (Forest Peoples Programme, 2002).

MacKay, F., *Universal rights or a universe unto itself? Indigenous peoples' human rights and the World Bank's draft operational policy 4.10 on indigenous peoples*, 17(3) Am. U. Int'l L. Rev. 227 (2002).

Macklem, P., *Indigenous Rights and Multinational Corporations at International Law*, 24 Hastings Int'l & Comp. L. Rev. 475 (2001).

Makkonen, T., Identity, Difference and Otherness, The Concepts of 'Peoples,' 'Indigenous People' and 'Minority' in International Law (2000).

Matiation, S., *Impact Benefits Agreements Between Mining Companies and Aboriginal Communities in Canada: A Model for Natural Resource Developments Affecting Indigenous Peoples in Latin America?*, 7 Great Plains Nat. Res. J. 204 (2002).

McCaskill, D. & K. Kampe, eds., Development or Domestication?: Indigenous Peoples of Southeast Asia (1997).

McHugh, P.G. Aboriginal Societies and the Common Law (2004).

McHugh, P.G. Aboriginal Title: The Modern Jurisprudence of Tribal Land Rights (2011).

McNeil, K., Common Law Aboriginal Title (1989).

McNeil, K., *Aboriginal Title and the Division of Powers: Rethinking Federal and Provincial Jurisdictions*, 61 Sask. L. Rev. 431 (1998).

McNeil, K., *Extinguishment of Aboriginal Title in Canada: Treaties, Legislation, and Judicial Discretion*, 33 Ottawa L. Rev. 301 (2001).

McNeil, K., *The Vulnerability of Indigenous Land Rights in Australia and Canada*, 42 Osgoode Hall L.J. 271 (2004).

McSloy, S.P., *'Because the Bible Tells Me So': Manifest Destiny and American Indians*, 9 St. Thomas L. Rev. 37 (1996).

Meek, C.K., *Land Law and Customs in the Colonies* (1946).

Meijknecht, A., Towards International Personality: The Position of Minorities and Indigenous Peoples in International Law (2001).

Miller, M., *An Australian Nunavut? A Comparison of Inuit and Aboriginal Rights Movements in Canada and Australia*, 12 Emory Int'l L. Rev. 1175 (1998).

Minority Rights Group, ed., Polar Peoples: Self-Determination & Development (1994).

Mirow, M.C., *Latin American Legal History: Some Essential Spanish Terms*, 12 La Raza L.J. 43 (2001).

Moody, R., Indigenous Peoples, A Global Quest for Justice (Report for the Independent Commission on International Humanitarian Issues, 1987).

Morel, C., *Defending Human Rights in Africa: The Case for Minority and Indigenous Rights*, 1 Essex Hum. Rts. Rev. 54 (2004).

Morin, M., L'ursupation de la Souverainte Autochtone (1997).

Morsink, J., *Cultural Genocide, the Universal Declaration, and Minority Rights*, 21 Hum. Rts. Q. 1009 (1999).

Morsink, J., The Universal Declaration on Human Rights, Origins, Drafting and Intent (1999).

Newton, N.J., *Compensation, Reparations, & Restitution: Indian Property Claims in the United States*, 28 Ga. L. Rev. 453 (1994).

Ngugi, J., *The Decolonization-Modernization Interface and the Plight of Indigenous Peoples in Post-Colonial Development Discourse in Africa*, 20 Wis. Int'l L.J. 297 (2002).

Nowak, M., U.N. Covenant on Civil and Political Rights: CCPR Commentary (1993).

Nowlan-Card, L., *Public Government and Regulatory Participation in Nunavut: Effective Self-Government for the Inuit*, 5 Dalhousie J. Legal Stud. 31 (1996).

Nussbaum, A., A Concise History of the Law of Nations (1954).

O'Faircheallaigh, C. *Aboriginal-mining company contractual agreements in Australia and Canada: Implications for political autonomy and community development* Canadian Journal of Development Studies/Revue Canadienne D'études Du Développement 30.1-2 (2010): 69–86.

O'Faircheallaigh, C., Negotiations in the Indigenous World: Aboriginal Peoples and Extractive Industry in Australia and Canada (2016).

Orlin, T. & M. Scheinin, eds., The Jurisprudence of Human Rights: A Comparative Interpretive Approach (2000).

Osherenko, G., *Indigenous Rights in Russia: Is Title to Land Essential for Cultural Survival?*, 13 Geo. Int'l Envt'l L. Rev. 695 (2001).

O'Sullivan, M., *'Past Violations' under International Human Rights Law: The Indigenous 'Stolen Generation' in Australia*, 23(2) Neth. Q. Hum. Rts. 243 (2005).

Ouguerzgouz, F., The African Charter on Human and People's Rights: A Comprehensive Agenda for Human Dignity and Sustainable Development in Africa (2003).

Paquerot, S., Le statut des ressources vitales en droit international, Essai sur le concept de patrimoine commun de l'humanite (2002).

Pearce, R. & J. Mee, Land Law (2000).

Peirson, A. & X. Bothwell, *We Live on the Land: Implications of Long-Ago Takings of Native American Indian Property*, 6 Ann. Surv. Int'l & Comp. L. 175 (2000).

Pentland, D., ed., Papers of the Twenty-Eighth Algonquian Conference (1997).

Plant, R., *Land Rights in Human Rights and Development, Introducing a New ICJ Initiative*, 51 Int'l Comm. Jurists Rev. 17 (1993).

Pratt, H. & J.F. Green, *A Permanent International Commission for Africa*, Int'l Arb. & Peace Ass'n (1896).

Price Cohen, C., ed., The Human Rights of Indigenous Peoples (1998).

Pritchard, S., ed., Indigenous Peoples, The United Nations, and Human Rights (1998).

Psacharapoulos, G. & H. Patrinos, eds., Indigenous Peoples and Poverty in Latin America: An Empirical Analysis (1994).

Ramcharan, B., The Right to Life in International Law (1985).

Ramutsindela, M.F., *The Perfect Way to Ending a Painful Past? Makuleke Land Deal in South Africa*, 33 Geoforum 15 (2002).

Ratner, S., *Drawing a Better Line: Uti Possidetis & the Borders of New States*, 90 Am. J. Int'l L. 590 (1996).

Resiman, M., *Protecting Indigenous Rights in International Adjudication*, 89(2) Am. J. Int'l L. 350 (1995).

Reynolds, H., Aboriginal Sovereignty (1996).

Richard, W., Human Rights, Culture and Context: Anthropological Perspectives (1997).

Rose, C., *Property as the Keystone Right*, 71 Notre Dame L. Rev. 329 (1996).

Rosenthal, G., *The Peace Process in Guatemala and the Role of Third Parties*, 8 Int'l J. Minority & Group Rts. 55 (2001).

Rouland, N., S. Pierre-Caps & J. Poumarede, Droit des Minorites et des peuples autochtones (1996).

Rousseau, J.J., Discours sur l'origine de l'inegalite (1963).

Royal Commission on Aboriginal Peoples, Report of the Royal Commission on Aboriginal Peoples, Vol. ii, Part ii; "Restructuring the Relationship" (Minister of Supply and Services Canada, 1996).

Russell, L., ed., Colonial Frontiers, Indigenous-European Encounters in Settler Societies (2001).

Sager, L., *Rediscovering America: Recognizing the Sovereignty of Native American Indian Nations*, 76 U. Det. Mercy L. Rev. 745 (1999).

Sanders, D., *The Re-emergence of Indigenous Questions in International Law*, 3 Can. Hum. Rts. Y.B. 3 (1983).

Schabas, W., Genocide in International Law (2000).

Schrijver, N., Sovereignty over Natural Resources, Balancing Rights and Duties (1997).

Schulte-Tenckhoff, I., La Question des Peuples Autochtones (1997).

Schulte-Tenckhoff, I., *Reassessing the Paradigm of Domestication*, 4(2) Rev. Constitutional Stud. 239 (1998).

Schwarzenberger, G., *Title to Territory: Response to a Challenge*, 51 Am. J. Int'l L. 316 (1957).

Scott, C., *Indigenous Self-Determination and Decolonization of the International Imagination: A Plea*, 18 Hum. Rts. Q. 814 (1996).

Seokwoo, L., *Continuing Relevance of Traditional Modes of Territorial Acquisition in International Law and Modest Proposal*, 16 Conn. J. Int'l L. 1 (2000).

Sermet, L., The European Convention on Human Rights and Property Rights (1990).

Shaw, M., *The Heritage of States: The Principle of Uti Possidetis Juris Today*, 67 Brit. Y.B. Int'l L. 67 (1996).

Sheleff, L., The Future of Tradition: Customary Law Common Law and Legal Pluralism (1999).

Shelton, D., Remedies in International Human Rights Law (1999).

Shelton, D., *Decision Regarding Communication 155/96 (Social and Economic Rights Action Center/Center for Economic and Social Rights v. Nigeria). Case No. ACHPR/COMM/A044/1*, 96 Am. J. Int'l L. 937 (2002).

Sinha, S.P., *Is Self-Determination Passe?*, 12 Colum. J. Transnat'l L. 260 (1973).

Speed, S. & J.F. Collier, *Limiting Indigenous Autonomy in Chiapas: The State Government's Use of Human Rights*, 22 Hum. Rts. Q. 877 (2000).

Stavenhagen, R., Derecho Indigena y derecho Humanos en America Latina (1988).

Steiner, H., *Political Participation as a Human Right*, 1 Harv. Y.B. Int'l L. 77 (1988).

Sureda, R., The Evolution of the Right to Self-Determination: A Study of the United Nations Practice (1973).

Suski, M., ed., Autonomy: Applications and Implications (1998).

Swepston, L. & R. Plant, *International Standards and the Protection of the Land Rights of Indigenous and Tribal Populations*, 124 Int'l Lab. Rev. 91 (1985).

Tennant, C., *Indigenous Peoples, International Institutions, and the International Legal Literature, 1945–1993*, 16 Hum. Rts. Q. 1 (1994).

Tennant, C.C. & E. Turpel, *A Case Study of Indigenous Peoples: Genocide, Ethnocide and Self-determination*, 59–60 Nordic J. Int'l L. 287 (1990–91).

Thornberry, P., *Self-determination, Minorities, Human Rights: A Review of International Instruments*, 38 Int'l Comp. L.Q. 872 (1989).

Thornberry, P., Indigenous Peoples and Human Rights (2002).

Thornberry, P. & M. Amor Martín Estébanez, Minority Rights in Europe (2002).

Tie, W., Legal Pluralism: Towards A Multicultural Conception of Law (1999).

Timm, R.W., The Adivasis of Bangladesh (MRG, Report No. 92/1, 1992).

Tobin, B., Indigenous Peoples, Customary Law and Human Rights – Why Living Law Matters (2014).

Tomei, M. & L. Swepston, Indigenous and Tribal Peoples: A Guide to ILO Convention No. 169 (ILO, 1996).

Tomuschat, C., ed., The Modern Law of Self-Determination (1993).

Tsosie, R., *Land, Culture, and Community: Reflections on Native Sovereignty and Property in America*, 34 Ind. L. Rev. 1291 (2001).

Tulchin, J.S. & A.D. Selee, (eds.), Mexico's Politics and Society in Transition (2002).

Tully, J., Strange Multiplicity (1995).

Turpel, M.E., *Indigenous Peoples' Rights of Political Participation and Self-Determination: Recent International Legal Developments and the Continuing Struggle for Recognition*, 25 Cornell Int'l L.J. 579 (1992).

Udombana, N., *The Third World and the Rights to Development: Agenda for the Next Millennium*, 22(3) Hum. Rts. Q. 753 (2000).

Udombana, N., *How Should We Then Live? Globalisation and the New Partnership for Africa's Development*, 20 B.U. Int'l L.J. 1 (2002).

Ülgen, Ö., *Aboriginal Title in Canada: Recognition and Reconciliation*, 42(2) Neth. Int'l L. Rev. 147 (2000).

Ülgen, Ö., *Developing the Doctrine of Aboriginal Title in South Africa: Source and Content*, 46(2) J. Afr. L. 137 (2002).

Ulrich, G. & L. Krabbe Boserup, eds., Reparations: Redressing Past Wrongs (2003).

Unruh, J.D., *Land Tenure and Legal Pluralism in the Peace Process*, 28(3) Peace & Change 352 (2003).

van Harten, G., *Guatemala's Peace Accords in a Free Trade Area of the Americas*, 3 Yale Hum. Rts. & Dev. L.J. 113 (2000).

van Walt, M. & O. Seroo, eds., The Implementation of the Rights of Self-Determination as a Contribution to Conflict Prevention (1999).

Vásárhelyi, I., Restitution in International Law (1964).

Venne, S.H., Our Elders Understand our Rights: Evolving International Law Regarding Indigenous Peoples (1997).

Waldron, J., *Superseding Historic Injustice*, 103 Ethics 4 (1992).

Watson, I., Aboriginal Peoples, Colonialism and International Law: Raw Law (2015).

Weinberg, B., Homage to Chiapas: The New Indigenous Struggles in Mexico (2002).

Weiner, M., ed., Japan's Minorities, The Illusion of Homogeneity (1997).

Westra, L., Environmental Justice and the Rights of Indigenous Peoples: International and Domestic Legal Perspectives (2012).

Wiessner, S., *American Indian Treaties and Modern International Law*, 7 St. Thomas L. Rev. 567 (1995).

Wiessner, S., *Rights and Status of Indigenous Peoples: A Global Comparative and International Legal Analysis*, 12 Harv. Hum. Rts. J. 57 (1999).

Wilkins, D., *Bridging Theory and Practice: Quit-Claiming the Doctrine of Discovery: A Treaty Based Reapprisal*, 23 Okla. City U. L. Rev. 277 (1998).

Wilkinson, C.F. & J.M. Volkman, *Judicial Review of Indian Treaty Abrogation: "As Long as Water Flows, or Grass Grows Upon the Earth"—How Long Time Is That?*, 63 Cal. L. Rev. 601 (1975).

Williams, R.A., *The Medieval and Renaissance Origins of the Status of the American Indians in Western Legal Though*, 57 S. Cal. L Rev. 1 (1983).

Williams, R.A., The American Indian in Western Legal Though (1990).

Williams, R.A., *Colombus's Legacy: Law as an Instrument of Racial Discrimination Against Indigenous Peoples' Rights of Self-Determination*, 8 Ariz. J. Int'l & Comp. L. 51 (1991).

Wilmer, F., The Indigenous Voice in World Politics Since Time Immemorial (1993).

Woodman, G.R. & A.O. Obilade, African Law and Legal Theory (1995).

Wulf, S., *The Legal Bases for the Inughuit Claim to their Homeland*, 11 Int'l J. Minority & Group Rts. 63 (2005).

Wynberg, R., Doris Schroeder, & Roger Chennells, Indigenous Peoples, Consent and Benefit Sharing: Lessons from the San-Hoodia Case (2009).

Xanthaki, A., *Indigenous Rights in the Russian Federation: The Case of Numerically Small Peoples of the Russian North, Siberia, and Far East*, 26 Hum. Rts. Q. 74 (2004).

Xanthaki, A. Indigenous rights and United Nations standards: self-determination, culture and land. Cambridge University Press; 2007.

Xanthaki, A. *Indigenous Rights in International Law over the Last 10 Years and Future Developments*, 10 Melb. J. Int'l L. 27 (2009).

Yakemtchouk, R., *Les Frontières Africaines*, 74 R.G.D.I.P. 27 (1970).

Zirker, O.L., *This Land Is My Land: The Evolution of Property Rights and Land Reform in South Africa*, 18 Conn. J. Int'l L. 621 (2003).

Index